# PROGRESSIVE Skills in English

## Level 3 Teacher's Book

Terry Phillips and Anna Phillips

Garnet
EDUCATION

**Published by**
Garnet Publishing Ltd.
8 Southern Court
South Street
Reading RG1 4QS, UK

Copyright © 2011 Garnet Publishing Ltd.

The right of Terry Phillips and Anna Phillips to be identified as the authors of this work has been asserted by them in accordance with the Copyright, Designs and Patents Act 1988.

All rights reserved.
No part of this publication may be reproduced, stored in a retrieval system, or transmitted in any form or by any means, electronic, mechanical, photocopying, recording or otherwise, without the prior permission of the Publisher. Any person who does any unauthorized act in relation to this publication may be liable to criminal prosecution and civil claims for damages.

First edition 2011

ISBN: 978-1-85964-684-7

British Library Cataloguing-in-Publication Data
A catalogue record for this book is available from the British Library.

**Production**
Project managers:   Richard Peacock, Nicky Platt
Editorial team:     Emily Clarke, Sarah Mellowes,
                    Richard Peacock, Nicky Platt, Rod Webb
Research:           Lucy Phillips
Design:             Ed Du Bois, Mike Hinks
Typesetting:        Sarah Church, Bob House
Photography:        Clipart, Corbis, Digital Vision, Getty
                    Images, Image Source, Photodisc,
                    Istockphoto, Shutterstock
Audio and DVD:      EFS Television Production Ltd.

Every effort has been made to trace the copyright holders and we apologize in advance for any unintentional omissions. We will be happy to insert the appropriate acknowledgements in any subsequent editions.

**Printed and bound**
in Lebanon by International Press: interpress@int-press.com

# PROGRESSIVE Skills in English

## Contents

| | | |
|---|---|---:|
| Book maps | | 4 |
| Introduction | | 7 |
| **Theme 1** | Remembering and forgetting | 23 |
| **Theme 2** | Friends and family | 75 |
| **Theme 3** | Managing to be successful | 119 |
| **Theme 4** | Natural cycles | 167 |
| **Theme 5** | Customs: origins and effects | 217 |
| Word list | | 272 |

## Topics

| Listening | Speaking | Reading | Writing | Knowledge area |
|---|---|---|---|---|
| 1 Memory | Learner styles | Improving your memory | Rehearsal and prompts | Remembering and forgetting |
| 2 Making and keeping friends | Apologizing | Parents, Adults and Children | Decisions in families | Friends and family |
| 3 Managing time and self | The time thieves | Decisions, decisions, decisions | For and against | Managing to be successful |
| 4 Greening the desert | Oxygen and carbon | Chains, webs and pyramids | Energy and the oceans | Natural cycles |
| 5 Cultural diversity | Wedding customs | The price of happiness | Cultural change | Customs: origins and effects |

## Skills

| Listening | Speaking | Reading | Writing |
|---|---|---|---|
| 1 *lecture with sources*<br>• note-taking: recording sources | *talk about types of learner*<br>• preparing for a talk<br>• giving a talk clearly | *article with graph*<br>• recognizing sentence function<br>• reading line graphs | *Argument essay*<br>• writing thesis statements |
| 2 *lecture with several main points*<br>• note-taking: recognizing the main points | *talking about research*<br>• starting a turn<br>• ending a turn<br>• reporting problems | *article with diagram*<br>• distinguishing between fact and theory | *research report*<br>• topic sentences |
| 3 *lecture with contrast*<br>• recognizing lecture structure: signpost words and phrases | *tutorial about a problem*<br>• reacting to contributors: agreeing / disagreeing | *article with table*<br>• understanding non-text markers | *For and against essay*<br>• comparing with adjectives and nouns |
| 4 *lecture with numbers*<br>• note-taking: numbers and units of measurement | *talk about a process*<br>• intonation: rising to a comma; falling to a full stop | *encyclopedia entries*<br>• using cross referencing | *Description essay*<br>• describing graphics |
| 5 *lecture with mixed information types*<br>• common adjective endings<br>• note-taking: choosing type of notes | *tutorial about customs*<br>• checking; explaining; asking to wait | *newspaper article*<br>• recognizing the writer's point of view or bias | *Discussion essay*<br>• recognizing the thesis |

# Book maps

## Grammar

| Listening | Speaking | Reading | Writing |
|---|---|---|---|
| 1 • indirect questions<br>• verb patterns (1): *forget, remember, learn, remind* | • *should / could*<br>• *so / because* | • the complex noun phrase | • SVO and SVC (revision)<br>• adding information to basic SVO/C |
| 2 • verb patterns (2): transitive and intransitive verbs | • uses of *that* | • leading prepositional phrases | • permission and obligation with infinitive<br>• passives with *allow, expect*<br>• *be* + adjective |
| 3 • verb patterns (3): verb + (object) + *to do* | • tense agreement in short responses | • identifying missing subjects and verbs after co-ordinator | • describing trends with present continuous and present perfect<br>• present perfect *vs* past simple |
| 4 • replacement subject *it*: to indicate certainty; to indicate stance | • omitting items in repeated structures | • finding key information after *which / that* | • compound sentences: event and result, *as / when / if* |
| 5 • extra information after *who, which, where* | • *used to / didn't use to* | • conditionals: zero and first (revision); second conditional | • long subject noun phrases<br>• *also* with mixed tenses |

## Phonology, Everyday English and Portfolio work

| Listening | Speaking | Everyday English | Portfolio |
|---|---|---|---|
| 1 • guessing the spelling of proper nouns | • vowel sounds (revision) | • making friends | Memories |
| 2 • recognizing negative prefixes on adjectives | • normal stress in two-syllable words: nouns, adjectives, verbs | • apologizing | Relationships |
| 3 • recognizing adjective suffixes | • stress in multi-syllable words | • dealing with interruptions | Self-management |
| 4 • recognizing numbers | • unstressed syllables<br>• common intonation patterns | • making arrangements | The rock cycle |
| 5 • recognizing adjectives from endings | • same letters, different sounds; different letters, same sound<br>• consonant clusters | • suggesting and responding to suggestions | Cultures |

# Introduction Contents

| | |
|---|---|
| The series | 8 |
| Routes through the course | 8 |
| The themes | 8 |
| The sections | 8 |
| The lessons | 8 |
| Additional pages | 8 |
|   Everyday English | 8 |
|   Knowledge quiz | 8 |
|   Portfolio | 9 |
| Approach | 9 |
|   Aims | 9 |
|   Moving from teaching general to academic English | 9 |
|   Discrete skills or integrated? | 10 |
|   Receptive skills – listening and reading | 10 |
|     Top-down processes | |
|     Bottom-up processes | |
|   Productive skills – speaking and writing | 11 |
|   Syntactic grammar for EAP | 11 |
|   Syntactic grammar in this course | 12 |
|   Exercise naming | 12 |
|   Exercise types | 12 |
|   Vocabulary lists | 13 |
|   Skills Checks | 13 |
|   Pronunciation Checks | 14 |
| Recurrent activities | 14 |
|   Activating (background) knowledge / ideas | 14 |
|   Understanding words in context | 14 |
|   Transferring information (to the real world) / Using new skills in a real-world task | 14 |
|   Reviewing key words | 14 |
|   Identifying a new skill | 14 |
|   Predicting content | 14 |
|   Previewing vocabulary | 15 |
|   Hearing / Understanding / Studying a model / discourse structure | 15 |
|   Practising a model | 15 |
|   Producing a model | 15 |
|   Producing key patterns | 15 |
|   Showing comprehension | 15 |
|   Researching information | 15 |
|   Developing vocabulary | 15 |
|   Developing independent learning | 15 |
|   Developing critical thinking | 15 |
|   Remembering real-world knowledge | 15 |
|   Using / Applying a key skill | 15 |
|   Making and checking hypotheses | 15 |
| Methodology | 15 |
|   Everyday English | 15 |
|   Knowledge quiz | 16 |
|   Portfolio | 16 |
|   Feedback on oral presentations | 17 |
|   Dealing with writing | 17 |
|   Giving feedback on writing | 18 |
|   Listening | 18 |
|   Further speaking practice / drilling | 18 |
|   Setting up tasks | 19 |
|   Use of visuals | 19 |
|   Pronunciation | 19 |
|   Comparing answers in pairs | 19 |
|   Monitoring | 19 |
|   Feedback | 19 |
|   Confirmation and correction | 20 |
|   Highlighting grammar | 20 |
|   Self-checking | 20 |
|   Gap fill | 20 |
|   Two-column activities | 20 |
|   Ordering | 21 |
|   Tables and charts | 21 |
|   Error correction | 21 |
| Routes through the course | 21 |
|   The 25-hour course | 21 |
|   The 40-hour course | 21 |
|   The 60-hour course | 21 |
|   The 80-hour course | 21 |
|   The 100-hour course | 22 |
|   The 120-hour course | 22 |

# Introduction

## The series

This course is part of the multi-level *Progressive Skills in English* series. The series as a whole prepares students to study wholly or partly in English medium at tertiary level, or to join the world of academic English, on the Internet and in print.

## Routes through the course

*Progressive Skills in English* is an extremely flexible course. There are logical routes through the Course Book, from 25 hours to 120 hours. By adding the Workbook to the package, the course can provide all the input required on a complete academic year of 180 hours.

Some of the possible routes through the book are given at the end of this Introduction. For others, particularly with regard to the use of the extra pages – **Everyday English, Knowledge quiz** and **Portfolio** – see below.

## The themes

In each level of *Progressive Skills in English* there are five themes, covering a wide range of areas of human knowledge.

### Level 3
Theme 1: Remembering and forgetting
Theme 2: Friends and family
Theme 3: Managing to be successful
Theme 4: Natural cycles
Theme 5: Customs: origins and effects

## The sections

Within each theme there are four main sections, each dealing with a discrete skill: listening, speaking, reading or writing. A number of related topics are explored within each theme. For example, in Theme 5 the following areas are explored:
**Listening**: cultural diversity
**Speaking**: wedding customs
**Reading**: the price of happiness
**Writing**: cultural change

The focus in each section is on **one** specific skill. The Methodology notes in the lessons stress the discrete skills focus and caution against spending too much time on, for example, speaking in a listening section. This is not because the writers dislike integrated skills. Indeed, each theme ends with a section called Portfolio, which provides detailed guidance on integrated skills activities following the completion of a particular theme. The insistence on the target skill is because the writers believe that both the teacher and the students should focus on improvement in a specific skill in a particular lesson, rather than moving constantly between different skills. However, the key word here is *focus*. More than one skill will, of course, be involved in any particular lesson. For example, in listening lessons there is almost always a speaking output, and in writing lessons there is almost always a reading input.

The commonality of theme across the four skill sections means that, by the end of a theme, students have a much deeper knowledge of both the information and vocabulary that it comprises, than is normally achieved in ELT course books.

## The lessons

Each skill section contains five lessons, and each lesson has a clear focus and purpose, as shown in the following table. (See top of page opposite.)

## Additional pages

Every theme contains three additional pages:

### Everyday English
This page is in the speaking section and builds skills in survival language and social English. In Theme 1, for example, this page covers *Making friends* and in Theme 3, *Dealing with interruptions*. See the **Methodology** section for more guidance.

### Knowledge quiz
This page is in the reading section and tests students on their acquisition of common core knowledge and thematic vocabulary from the theme. In Theme 4, for example, this page ask students to remember information about *Natural cycles and processes,* including desertification and greening, the changing states of water, and food chains. See the **Methodology** section for more guidance.

| Lesson | Focus | Purpose and methodology points |
|---|---|---|
| X.1<br>X.6<br>X.11<br>X.16 | Vocabulary for the skill | To ensure that students understand and can recognize some basic vocabulary needed for the theme. This lesson also contains all the target words from the section, printed down the outer margin. The positioning is deliberate. You and the students should be able to flick back and find a thematic set easily. Note that only about half of the words in this list will be pre-taught in the first lesson. The remainder will be met in context during the rest of the section. Teachers might like to test students on the list before starting the lesson, and then again at the end of the section or the theme. |
| X.2<br>X.7<br>X.12<br>X.17 | Real-time practice | To practise a skill with the students' available linguistic resources. This lesson can be seen as an informal test of current knowledge and ability in a particular area. The text type encountered in this lesson is met again in the *Applying skills* lesson, so students get a second chance to understand or produce the text type after they have seen and practised relevant sub-skills and grammar. |
| X.3<br>X.8<br>X.13<br>X.18 | Learning skills | To highlight specific sub-skills which are required to complete the task(s) in the second and fifth lessons of the section. Note that the skills taught here are all transferable rather than simple exhortations to 'Listen carefully' or 'Read quickly'. |
| X.4<br>X.9<br>X.14<br>X.19 | Grammar for the skill | To highlight specific grammar points which are related to the text type in the Real-time practice lesson. In many cases, these are syntactic points – see **Syntactic grammar in EAP** below. The content of these lessons is directly related to the skill for that section, as the writers have discovered that there are significant differences between the grammar you need for each skill. |
| X.5<br>X.10<br>X.15<br>X.20 | Applying skills | To apply the skills learnt in the third and fourth lessons of the section to a new text. The text for reception or the target output for production contains the same linguistic features as that in the second lesson of the section. |

## Portfolio

This section – usually three pages – comes at the very end of each theme and provides an opportunity to integrate skills learnt during the course. Students are provided with tasks and research information in additional listening and reading texts, and asked to produce talks and/or written texts. In Theme 3, for example, students are asked to research and talk about *Self-management*. See the **Methodology** section for more guidance.

## Approach

### Aims

In *Progressive Skills in English,* students learn to understand the main types of academic spoken language, lectures and tutorials, and the main types of academic written language, journal articles and encyclopedia entries. They also learn to produce the main kinds of student academic language, oral presentations, contributions to a tutorial and written assignments.

### Moving from teaching general to academic English

Many of the teaching techniques and approaches used in general English teaching can be transferred to the teaching of academic English. The differences are more to do with the syllabus and course content. Some of the key differences we have noted include:

### Grammar

Most general English courses are driven by tense grammar. Since 80 per cent of academic English is in a present tense, the focus needs to move from tenses to syntactic grammar. For more details on this point, see **Syntactic Grammar in EAP** below.

### Skills

A general English course will focus mainly on oral communication. Listening will be extremely varied, from conversations and anecdotes to radio programmes. Reading is often relegated to third place and Writing to a very distant fourth. For the academic learner, reading and writing are at least as important as the other skills. For more details, see **Discrete skills or integrated?** below.

### Content

In EAP, listening to lectures will be more relevant than listening to anecdotes and stories. Academic students need to learn to 'grab' relevant information from a lecture after one listening only. Similarly with reading, required content will mostly be fact or theory or a mixture, rather than fiction and anecdote. Students need to be able to decide quickly which texts, or parts of texts, are relevant to the task and extract the information. Listening and reading texts in general will be much longer in EAP than in a general English course.

### Vocabulary
Students need a wide range of formal language. Academic texts about a single subject tend to use a lot of synonyms for key nouns and verbs, so students need to deepen and broaden their lexical range all the time.

### Topics and themes
Sometimes you find very familiar 'EFL' topics in *Progressive Skills in English*, but then you will see that the approach to that topic is different. For example, in a section on friends and family, students are not asked to describe these people but to explore relationship theories and analyze social data.

### Critical thinking
Students are encouraged to ask *why* and *how* throughout the course, and to relate information from a particular text to their own selves or their own country/area. They are shown the importance of evaluating information and looking for stance or bias on the part of the speaker or writer.

## Discrete skills or integrated?
In terms of presentation, *Progressive Skills in English* is very definitely a discrete skills course. Research has shown that students need to have a clear focus with measurable objectives in order to make real progress, and this is only really possible if the skills are initially separated out. However, integration is the norm in the real world and, since the course aims to mimic real-world skills usage, integration is automatic once one moves from presentation. For example, in the receptive skills lessons, as in the real world, students have to make notes from reading and listening and then discuss their findings, thus bringing in writing and speaking to listening and reading lessons. In the productive skills lessons, as in the real world, students have to research before producing, thus bringing in reading and listening skills.

## Receptive skills – listening and reading
Research strongly suggests that listening and reading are based on a continuous interaction between top-down and bottom-up processes. Top-down processes prepare the listener or reader to understand the information in the text. Bottom-up processes ensure than the listener or reader can decode information in real-time, i.e., as it is actually being heard or read.

### Top-down processes
Before we can understand information, we need to recognize the context. We expect to hear different things in a restaurant, for example, from a lecture room, or to read different things in a novel and a religious text. We use context and co-text clues (pictures, newspaper headlines, diagrams) to **activate schemata** – pictures, we could say, of familiar situations. In the process, the brain makes available to us vocabulary, discourse structures and **background knowledge** of the real world, which help with bottom-up decoding. We start to develop **hypotheses** about the contents of the text, and we continually **predict** the next word, the next phrase, the next discourse point or the next communicative value as we are listening or reading. In *Progressive Skills in English*, students are taught to bring top-down processing to bear on new listening and reading texts. The course works to build schemata and background knowledge which will help students to predict content, in general and in particular. In the academic world, listening and reading normally have a productive by-product – detailed notes. Throughout *Progressive Skills in English*, students are taught to take notes and to use these notes in later activities to prove comprehension of the text.

### Bottom-up processes
Top-down processes enable listeners and readers to get a good general idea of what will be heard or read in a text. However, to get a detailed and accurate understanding, the text must be broken down into meaningful units. In the case of spoken English, this means being able to turn the stream of speech into actual words, which in turn means knowing the phonological code of English. With written English, it is slightly easier, if your first language has a similar orthography to English but will continue to pose problems for students whose L1 is Chinese or Arabic, for example. Research has shown that we use syntax to achieve this breaking into meaningful units (see below on **syntactic grammar**). In *Progressive Skills in English*, students are taught to recognize all the phonemes of English in context and to identify multi-syllable words from the stressed syllable in the stream of speech. They also learn to identify written words from the first two or three letters, a key skill which enables native speakers to understand written text at high speed. Students are also exposed to common syntactic patterns and practise breaking up incoming language into **subject**, **verb**, **object / complement** and **adverbial**.

## Productive skills – speaking and writing

Production in speech and writing in the normal EFL classroom is often more or less spontaneous and personal. Students are asked to speak or write about themselves, their lives, families, opinions, etc., with very little preparation. This mimics real-life conversation and, to some extent, real-life informal letter and email writing. This type of production is rare in *Progressive Skills in English* because it is not the model for production in the academic world.

Production in academia begins with an **assignment** which requires **research**. The research almost always leads to **note-taking**. From these notes, an oral presentation, tutorial contribution or written assignment is produced. There are normally three stages to this production: **drafting**, **editing** and **rewriting**. In *Progressive Skills in English,* we teach the idea of the TOWER of writing – **t**hinking, **o**rganizing, **w**riting (for the writer), **e**diting, **r**ewriting (for the reader / listener).

## Syntactic grammar for EAP

Grammar in ELT has traditionally been seen as largely a question of verb tense, and that certain tenses are 'easy' and others are 'hard'. Progression through levels conventionally equates to the ability to manipulate different tenses, from present simple of the verb *be* at Beginners to present perfect continuous passive modal at Advanced. Most best-selling courses follow a structural syllabus which is, largely, a verb tense syllabus. However, English is a *syntactic* language where meaning is carried by word order rather than paradigmatic form. We cannot recover the meaning of a word or its role without a sentence or text context, because English words are not marked in most instances for part of speech or case. Many words can be nouns or verbs depending on context; *like,* to take an extreme example, can be a noun, a verb, a preposition or an adjective. Any noun can be the subject or object of a verb; only pronouns are marked for case, e.g., *He told him*.

Research has shown that native speakers use their knowledge of English syntax, together with their vocabulary, to decode sentences, in speech and in writing. They do this in real time. In other words, native speakers are constantly constructing tree diagrams of incoming data which help them to predict the next item and its role in the ongoing sentence.

It is somewhat strange that this key fact seems to have gone unnoticed for so long by ELT practitioners. The reason is probably that most ELT classwork, for many decades, has been based on spoken interaction, often of informal conversation, rather than the individual interacting with and decoding in real time a formal spoken or written text. Corpus research now shows us that conversation in English has an average phrase length of just over one word, and very short sentences, such as *I went there, She likes him, He's working in a bank*. In short sentences like this, the most salient area of difficulty is the verb form which must be dropped between the subject and the object, complement or adverbial. However, in academic or formal discourse, the average phrase length jumps to eight words. Analysis of this genre shows that noun phrases are particularly long, with pre- and post-modification of the head noun, and subject noun phrases are often preceded themselves by long adverbial phrases, so that a sentence may have a large number of words before the subject and more words before the main verb. For example:

> According to research at the University of Reading into the problems experienced by children growing up with a single parent, children from one-parent families in deprived areas have a much greater chance of developing personality disorders.

The native speaker has little problem with this sentence, either in speech or writing, because he/she knows that the phrase *According to* is not the subject and the subject will come along in a while, and that *children* can be post-modified so he/she must wait for this noun phrase to end before encountering the verb, etc. The non-native speaker, trained in decoding simple short utterances, will have considerable difficulty.

Complex tenses are in fact not at all common in academic/formal English. Research shows that the majority of sentences in this genre are in the present simple, including its passive forms, for the obvious reason that most formal English presents facts, theories or states of being, which are rendered in English by this tense. The next most common tense is the past simple, because the genre often contains historical background to current facts, theories or states of being, which in turn is normally rendered in past simple. In one particular corpus study, only one example of the present perfect continuous was found in the whole academic/formal corpus. A student equipped with facility in these two tenses will understand the tense information in around 90 per cent of academic/formal sentences. However, they may not understand the noun phrases and adverbial phrases which surround these 'simple' tenses.

There is a final key issue which applies in general to long texts in the EFL classroom. In the main, when students are exposed to longer texts with a formal structure, they are allowed, even encouraged, to engage in multiple listenings or multiple readings before being asked to complete an after-doing comprehension task such as multiple choice or true/false. This type of activity has no correlate in the real world, where listening has to be real-time – there is no opportunity for a second or subsequent hearing – and reading should be real-time if it is to be efficient. Comprehension occurs as the sentence is being received. However, real-time comprehension is only possible if the receiver understands the syntactic structures possible in the language and identifies, in real time, the structure being used at a particular time. The listener or reader is then ready for the required components of that structure and predicts their appearance and even the actual words. For example, once a native speaker hears the verb *give*, they will anticipate that a person and a thing will complete the utterance. Even if the 'person' noun phrase contains many words, the receiver will be waiting. For example: *The state gives unemployed people with a large number of children under the age of 18 still in full-time education ...* The native-speaker listener or reader is thinking, 'What? What does it give?' Conversely, the construction of extended formal text in speech and writing also requires a deep understanding of syntax, otherwise it is not possible to construct sentences of the complexity required by the genre.

While writing the syllabus for *Skills in English*, first published by Garnet Education in 2003, we were struck by the points above and began work on the implications for classroom practice. In *Progressive Skills in English*, we feel we have gone some way to presenting a coherent syllabus of relevant practice to build the skills required for real-time comprehension.

### Syntactic grammar in this course
If students have completed the A1/A2 course in this series, *New Starting Skills in English*, they will be fully familiar with parts of speech and with the most common syntactic patterns (see tables 1 and 2 below) by the time they start *Progressive Skills in English* Level 1. Since we cannot assume this familiarity, however, these points are quickly revised in the first few sections of the course. Thereafter, students are exposed mainly to basic S V O/C/A patterns, with co-ordination. Gradually, the length of the object noun phrase or complement is extended and co-ordination is introduced but with no ellipsis of subject or verb. This should ensure that students begin to get a natural feel for these patterns, can recognize them in real time in listening and reading, and produce them in speech and writing.

*Table 1: Sentence roles and parts of speech*

| Roles in sentences | Possible parts of speech | Notes |
|---|---|---|
| Subject | noun, pronoun | extended noun phrase can contain other parts of speech, e.g., *a very large* piece *of* research |
| Object | noun, pronoun | |
| Complement | noun, adjective, adverb | an object becomes a complement when it has the same reference as the subject, such as in sentences with *be* and related verbs, e.g., *She is a doctor. He was late. They seem tired.* |
| Verb | verb | extended verb phrase can contain adverbs, e.g., *They are still waiting.* |
| Adverbial | adverb, prepositional phrase | note that this role in a sentence can be filled by a prepositional phrase as well as by an adverb, e.g., *He works hard. She works in a bank.* |

*Table 2: Main sentence patterns in English*

| We left. | S V |
|---|---|
| She is a doctor. | S V C |
| I am cold. | S V C |
| They were late. | S V A |
| We have been to the back. | S V A |
| I gave her the book. | S V O O |
| They made him president. | S V O C |
| I told her to leave. | S V O V |
| We saw them later. | S V O A |
| Accept responsibility. | V O |

### Exercise naming
Many ELT course books give general names to groups of exercises, such as *Presentation* or *Pronunciation*. *Progressive Skills in English* goes much further and names the target activity for each exercise in its heading, e.g., *Activating ideas* or *Predicting the next word*. By this simple means, both teacher and students are informed of the purpose of an exercise. Make sure that your students understand the heading of each exercise so they can see clearly the point which is being presented or practised.

### Exercise types
As is probably clear already, *Progressive Skills in English* contains many original features, but teachers

and course leaders need not be concerned that a wholly new methodology is required to teach the course. On the one hand, exercise naming means that the purpose of new types of exercise is immediately clear. On the other, many traditional types of ELT exercises are used in the course, with only slight changes. The most significant of these changes are shown in table 3 below.

*Table 3: Adaptations to traditional exercise types*

| Traditional exercise | *Progressive Skills* version |
|---|---|
| grammar tables | - Parts of sentence are clearly shown with subject, verb, object/complement/adverbial columns.<br>- Parts of speech are clearly shown with colour-coding.<br>purple = noun<br>red = verb<br>blue = pronoun<br>orange = adjective<br>green = preposition<br>brown = adverb |
| gap fill | In some cases, one part of speech is removed so students can see the various contexts in which, e.g., a pronoun can appear. In other cases, one role in the sentence is removed, e.g., the subject, so students can see the different words which can make up this role. |
| sentence anagrams | Words are jumbled in a number of sentences in the traditional way, but when students have unscrambled them, all the sentences have the same syntactic structure, e.g., S V O A.<br>Words in a particular phrase are kept together during the jumbling, e.g., *in the UK*, rather than all being split; this helps students to think in terms of syntactic blocks rather than individual words. |
| transformation | Traditional transformation, e.g., positive to negative, appears regularly, but in addition, active to passive is introduced early on in the course, because of the relatively high frequency of passives in academic English. |
| joining sentences | Sentences are joined by co-ordinators from the beginning of *Progressive Skills in English*, but the second half of the sentence retains all its features, e.g., subject, verb, negation, for most of Level 1. This is because co-ordinated sentences with ellipses hide the kernel syntactic structure with which we want students to become familiar, e.g., *Some people do not know about the problem **or** care*. The second half of this sentence is originally: *Some people do not care about the problem* but with the ellipsis, the subject, the negation and the object disappear. |

## Vocabulary lists

Vocabulary is a key part of language learning of any kind but it is even more important for the student of academic English. Students need a huge vocabulary in order to understand or produce the lexical cohesion common to this genre. Each skill section in every theme begins with a vocabulary list of about 40 items in the right-hand column of the first lesson. This list contains items from the skill section which are linked to the theme. The part of speech is given in every case for single items. In addition, there is sometimes information on the precise meaning in the context of the theme, e.g., *area (n) [= location]* (as opposed to field of study, for example). There is space at the bottom of each list for students to add three or four more words which they wish to learn.

Most of the items in each list are probably new to the majority of the students in any class. A few of the items are likely to be known, but are so central to the theme that they are included for revision.

Normally, about 40 per cent of the words in the list are presented in the Vocabulary lesson, with some reference made to perhaps another 10 per cent. The remaining words will be encountered in other lessons and either specifically taught or understood in context.

You can use the lists in a number of ways:
- ask students to look at the list before the start of the skill section and tick the words they 'know'; do not test the students this time but encourage them to be honest
- ask students to repeat this activity at the end of the skill section, and again one week and one month later; on these occasions, test the students' knowledge, particularly in the relevant skill, e.g., to check that students can spell the words from a Writing section, or pronounce the words correctly from a Speaking section
- get students to mark the stress on each word as they encounter it
- get students to underline or highlight in some way unusual spelling and pronunciation points
- put students into pairs or groups to test each other
- allow students to write a translation beside some or all of the words

Please note: flashcards and detailed notes on using them can be found on the *Progressive Skills in English* website, www.skillsinenglish.com.

## Skills Checks

In every theme, there is at least one Skills Check. The naming of this feature is significant. It is assumed that many if not all students will have heard about the skills points in these boxes, i.e., they are skills *checks* not skills *presentations*. It is the writers' experience that many students who have gone through a modern ELT course have *heard of* the majority of skills points but cannot make practical use of them. If you feel, in a particular case, that the students have no idea about the point in question, spend considerably longer on a full presentation.

In most cases, the students are given an activity to do before looking at the Skills Check, thus a test-teach-test approach is used. This is quite deliberate. With this approach, there is a good chance that the students will be sensitised to the particular point before being asked to understand it intellectually. This is likely to be more effective than talking about the point and then asking the student to try to apply it. The positioning of the Skills Checks means that the information relevant to an activity or set of activities is available for consultation by the student at any time. Because some students have an inductive learning style (working from example to rule) and some have a deductive style (working from rule to example), the Skills Checks have rules *and* examples.

You can use the Skills Checks in a number of ways:
- ask students to read out the rules and the examples
- get students to give you more examples of each point
- ask students to read the Skills Check and then cover it; read it out with mistakes or with wrong examples of the point being presented
- at the end of the lesson, ask students to tell you the new skill(s) they have encountered, without looking at their Course Books

## Pronunciation Checks

In the Speaking section, and occasionally in the Listening section, there are Pronunciation Checks. In Level 1, these focus on phoneme discrimination. For example, in Theme 2 Listening, one Pronunciation Check deals with hearing the two phonemes /æ/ and /ɑː/, while in Theme 2 Speaking, another deals with the actual production of the two phonemes. The examples in these checks are recorded, so you can give students good models of the target point and then drill the items (see **Further speaking practice / drilling** below). Sometimes there is additional practice material to be completed after working through the check.

## Recurrent activities

As mentioned above, all exercises are named. Many of these names appear regularly throughout the course, sometimes with slight changes. This is because these activities are particularly valuable in language learning.

### Activating (background) knowledge / ideas
In line with basic communication theory, the lessons always try to move from the known to the unknown. This activity at the start of a lesson allows students to show that they have knowledge or ideas about the real world before learning new information. It also enables the teacher to gauge what is already known, and build on it if necessary, before moving further into the lesson.

While students are talking about a particular area, they are in effect activating schemata, which means they are more ready for further information in the same area.

### Understanding words in context
Research shows that it is possible to work out the meaning of a small proportion (perhaps ten per cent) of words in a text, if the remaining words and structures are well known. This activity guides students, perhaps through multiple matching, to show understanding of new items.

### Transferring information (to the real world) / Using new skills in a real-world task
It is essential that information is transferable outside of the classroom. This activity tries to make the bridge between information learnt in class and applications in the real world.

### Reviewing key words
Students are often given the opportunity to recall words from the previous lesson(s) of a skill section. This helps students to move information into long-term memory.

### Identifying a new skill
The methodology of *Progressive Skills in English*, as detailed above, is that students are presented with a text in the Real-time lesson which contains some recycled skills points and one or more new skills points. The students are not directed formally to the new point(s) but may notice while they are doing the real-time activity. Then in the next lesson, they are formally directed to the point(s). This is in line with the principle of noticing before learning.

### Predicting content
Listening and reading are real-time skills. The listener must be ahead of the speaker; the reader must be ahead of the text. Activities in this type of exercise help students to get ahead.

### Previewing vocabulary
This is a pre-teaching activity. Sometimes key vocabulary is required in order to complete a task later in a lesson. This key vocabulary is presented and needs to be practised thoroughly so it is fully available to students during the coming lesson.

### Hearing / Understanding / Studying a model / discourse structure
*Progressive Skills in English* follows the principle that students must see or hear what they are later asked to produce in speech or writing. In this exercise, they work with a model in order to recognize key features, such as discourse structure.

### Practising a model
Clearly, once students have seen key points about a model, they should be given the opportunity to produce the text.

### Producing a model
This is the third stage, after 'understanding' and 'practising'. Students are given a task which requires the production of a parallel text.

### Producing key patterns
This is related to producing a model, but is at the sentence level.

### Showing comprehension
Comprehension in the real world is a real-time activity and is something which happens in the brain: it is not directly observable. However, it is essential that both teachers and students see that comprehension has taken place. But remember, this sort of activity is a test of comprehension not a sub-skill in comprehension.

### Researching information
*Progressive Skills in English* is not convergent. Students are only sent back to their pre-existing ideas of knowledge at the beginning of lessons, in *Activating knowledge / ideas*. *Progressive Skills* is divergent. Students are sent off to research and bring back information, in order to give a talk, take part in a tutorial or produce a written text.

### Developing vocabulary
Students of academic English need constantly to develop their vocabulary knowledge. This exercise extends their existing vocabulary.

### Developing independent learning
Clearly, the ultimate aim of teaching a language is that students become independent learners who do not need a teacher to acquire new linguistic knowledge. This activity gives students a particular sub-skill to aid this process.

### Developing critical thinking
We must take students beyond the 'what' and the 'when' of information. We must get them to react to information, and to ask why something happened or why it is important.

### Remembering real-world knowledge
*Progressive Skills in English* is based on the theory that people need a framework of knowledge in order to understand new information as they read or hear it. Therefore, they need to remember real-world knowledge from lessons, not just vocabulary, skills and grammar.

### Using / Applying a key skill
Skills are learnt, then they need to be applied. This activity always connects directly to *Identifying a new skill* in an earlier lesson in the skill section.

### Making and checking hypotheses
Real-time listening and reading is about making and checking hypotheses. This is what makes it a real-time activity. Students need to learn a wide range of points about discourse, vocabulary and syntax which helps with making hypotheses. They then need to be given the opportunity to check these hypotheses.

## Methodology

### Everyday English
These additional lessons are designed to give university students some survival English for university life. The language and topics are freestanding so the lessons can be done at any time during the skill section or theme, or can be missed out completely should you so wish. The page could last a whole lesson or you could spend a shorter time and only work on two or three of the conversations. The format of all the Everyday English lessons is similar, with between four and six mini-dialogues on a similar topic or with a similar function.

Here are some ways of exploiting each stage of the lesson:

You may wish to highlight the grammar of some of the forms used in the conversations, but in general they can be learnt as phrases without going into too much explanation. Indeed, many of the forms that we often spend a lot of time on in class could probably be better learnt as fixed phrases, since their usage in everyday life is so limited, e.g., *How long have you been learning English?*

Ask students if they think the conversations take place in a formal or informal context. If conversations are formal, it is always important to remind students to use polite intonation.

Once any tasks set in the Course Book have been completed, and you have checked students understand the conversations, you can use the conversations for intensive pronunciation practice. Use one or more of the following activities:
- Play the CD, pausing after each line for students to listen and repeat, chorally and individually.
- Drill some of the phrases from the conversations, chorally then individually.
- Students practise the conversations in pairs, from the full transcript or from prompts.
- Students practise the conversations again, but substituting their own information, words or phrases where appropriate.
- Students extend the conversation by adding further lines of dialogue.
- Students invent a completely new conversation for the situation, function or photograph.
- Add some drama to the conversations by asking students to act out the conversations with different contexts, relationships or emotions (e.g., one student should act angry and the other student bored).

Monitor and give feedback after paired practice. You may want to focus on:
- intonation of closed and open questions
- stressed words in short answers, e.g., *Yes, it is. Yes, it does.*
- accurate use of auxiliary *do* in present simple questions

## Knowledge quiz
Although this is an optional part of each theme, the idea behind it is central to the approach of *Progressive Skills in English*. We have found from our work with universities around the world that students often fail to understand a text *not* because the English grammar is above their level, but because they do not have the framework of real-world knowledge or the breadth of topic-specific vocabulary in order to comprehend. This page makes these items central, but revises and tests them in a variety of enjoyable ways. There are several ways in which this page can be used. The Methodology notes for each theme suggest a particular way or ways on each occasion, but broadly the page can be done as:
- a quiz for individuals, pairs or groups where it appears, i.e., at the end of the Reading section
- a quiz, but *later* in the course, when students have had a chance to forget some of the knowledge and/or vocabulary
- a quiz, but *before* the students do the theme; keep the answers and see how much they have learnt after doing the theme
- a self-study test; students write their answers and hand them in, or self-mark in a later lesson in class
- a phase of a lesson – the teacher sets the task(s) in the normal way and feeds back orally

## Portfolio
The main features of the Portfolio lessons are:
- **versatility**
  It is possible to spend anything from part of a single lesson to four lessons on the activities; in addition, some, all or none of the work can be done in class.
- **integrated skills**
  All four skills are included in this lesson, though the focus will shift depending on the activity.
- **academic skills**
  The focus is on researching, digesting and exchanging information, and presenting information orally or in writing.
- **learner independence**
  At all stages from research through to oral or written presentations, the teacher should be in the roles of monitor, guide and, if necessary, manager, and should try to avoid being the 'knower' and 'controller'!

Here are some ways of exploiting each stage of the lesson:

### Activating ideas
Use the photographs in the book or show your own. Make sure students have the key vocabulary for all the activities.

### Gathering information
The course provides listening and reading texts. You can suggest extra Internet research if you wish. The information is often presented as an information gap, with groups listening to different texts then regrouping in order to exchange information. At first, you may need to suggest the best way to take notes, e.g., in a table with relevant headings. Later, however, you should encourage students to design their own note-taking tables and headings. At all stages, encourage students to help each other with comprehension or any problems, only calling on you as a last resort. The research stages can be done in class or for homework. However, check the research has been done effectively and reasonably thoroughly before moving on to the presentation stages.

### Oral presentations
To start with, these should be no more than a few sentences long. The organization of the presentations

is crucial and will depend on how much time you have and the number of students in your class.

- **Formal and teacher-centred**
  Set another activity for the class, or ask another teacher to do something with your class. Remove one student at a time (or one group, if the presentation is a collaboration) to another room so that you can listen to the presentation.
- **Student-centred to some extent**
  Students give presentations to other groups of students in the class. You may have between two and four presentations going on at the same time. Monitor as many as you possibly can. Make a note of students you have listened to and make sure you listen to different students next time round.
- **Student-centred and informal approach, requiring a mature class**
  Students give presentations to their groups as above. However, the 'listening' students give feedback after the talk, rather than you.

It is important that if you have students listening to talks, they are not simply 'passive' listeners. They will switch off and get bored. Wherever possible, therefore, assign tasks. This is relatively easy if students are listening to new information: they can complete notes or write answers to questions. However, if they are listening to talks similar to their own, give the 'listening' students feedback or comment sheets to complete (see below).

*Table 4: Example feedback form for group tasks*

| Did the speaker ... | always | sometimes | never |
|---|---|---|---|
| look up from notes? | | | |
| make eye contact? | | | |
| speak loudly enough? | | | |
| talk at correct speed? | | | |
| use good intonation patterns? | | | |
| use good visuals / PowerPoint slides? | | | |
| give all the important points? | | | |
| introduce the talk? | | | |
| conclude the talk? | | | |

Please note: many of the above suggestions for oral presentations in the Portfolio lesson, including the feedback form, are also relevant for lessons in the Speaking sections.

### Feedback on oral presentations

You can choose between giving formal, written feedback to individual students, and more informal oral feedback to each group or the whole class. Formal written feedback could be based on a checklist of speaking sub-skills such as those provided by IELTS or Cambridge ESOL for the FCE. Alternatively, you may prefer to devise your own checklist with broader headings, e.g.,

- accuracy
- fluency
- pronunciation
- grammar
- vocabulary, etc.

Informal feedback should include some positive and encouraging statements, as well as showing students what they need to work on. With the scaffolding in *Progressive Skills in English*, students should not make a large number of mistakes in producing spoken or written work, so it should be easier than otherwise to focus on a small number of areas for improvement. Make a note of grammar or vocabulary mistakes you hear while monitoring the class. Write the incorrect language on the board. Elicit from the class what the mistake is and how to correct it. Drill the correct sentence. Practise any words, phrases, sentences or questions that you noted were poorly pronounced.

Whichever method of feedback you choose, give the class one or two targets to work on for the next oral presentation, e.g., 'Look up from notes more often.' Even better, ask students to each set themselves a target for next time. Suggest ideas, which can be discrete (such as about the pronunciation of a particular sound) or much broader (such as about making clearer notes). Students should make a note of their target for next time and you can check it if you wish.

### Dealing with writing

In the Portfolio, you can adapt the final activity as you wish. You may like to give further practice of writing a full assignment-type essay, but there are other writing activities that are worth doing:

- notes only, possibly in a table
- PowerPoint slides
- a poster or wall presentation, particularly if you can display these publicly
- a one-paragraph summary
- a complete project on the topic, containing several different articles with accompanying visuals; this can be worked on individually or produced together in a group

Giving feedback on writing
*For work set for completion in class:*
Monitor and give some help to individuals. Make a note of common errors, i.e., mistakes that two or more students make. Then give feedback to the whole class. You can use the technique described above for feedback on oral errors; write the incorrect sentences the students have produced on the board and elicit the correct version.

*For work that you collect in:*
It is important not to get bogged down in detailed corrections and/or piles of written work waiting to be marked. For this reason, do not set too much written work as home assignments! You could, of course, ask students to comment on each other's writing in a phase in a later lesson, but this only works with relatively mature classes. Always set the length of the task, using these teaching notes as a guide.

Establish a marking key with the class early on in the course. For example, *sp* = spelling, *p* = punctuation, *gr* = grammar, and, if you feel it is necessary, provide this as a handout. A marking key means you are able to highlight the problem areas but leave students to make the corrections.

Focus on only two or three key areas each time you mark. Initially, these may simply be presentation and layout, e.g., using paragraphs, but later could include using more complex noun phrases or more formal language. Later you can focus on sub-skills such as organization and discourse, cohesion, longer sentences, etc.

We have tried to provide model answers wherever possible, even for open-ended activities like the writing and speaking assignments. Always show these to the class and discuss possible variations, in order to avoid the models being too prescriptive. If you have students with good writing skills, ask their permission to show their written work to the class as example answers.

Listening
'How many times should I play the DVD or CD of lectures?' This is a question we are often asked by teachers. On the one hand, we need to train our students to deal with the real-life lecture situation, in which students will only have the opportunity to hear the information once. On the other hand, students may simply not understand the lecture on the DVD after only one playing. So what is the solution?
- Firstly, it is important to make sure all the pre-listening activities are carried out effectively so that students can begin to predict the lecture content.
- Next, play the first section of the lecture once only for completion of the exercise or activity; this is a kind of 'test' to find out how well students would perform in the 'real-life' situation. It also trains students to listen for as much information as they can on the first hearing. Check how well students have completed the task and elicit the correct answers.
- Once you have confirmed the correct answers, move on to the next section of the lecture and corresponding exercise. Repeat the above procedure.
- When students have heard all the sections of the lecture, replay the complete lecture, with or without the transcript. This is where learning takes place, because students have the opportunity to see why they missed information or did not fully understand during the first playing.
- Finally, as a follow-up, students should be encouraged to listen to the complete lecture several times on their own at home, both with and without the transcript.

*What other strategies can the teacher use?*
- Remember that the key to comprehension in a foreign language is prediction, so students must have time to assimilate what they have just heard and predict what is coming next. You can pause the lecture any number of times during the first listening if you think your class needs this extra time. But, of course, pause at logical points – certainly the end of sentences and preferably the end of topic points.

*What other strategies can the students use?*
- Nowadays, most lecturers in the real world provide pre-lecture reading lists and notes, PowerPoint slides and visuals, and handouts. Summaries are also often available on the university's portal. There are Pourpoints available for all the lectures on the *Progressive Skills in English* website. Students should be made aware of all of these resources and encouraged to use them.

Further speaking practice / drilling
In the notes for individual Speaking lessons, we often say 'practise the sentences with the class'. You can use one or more of the example drilling techniques below. There are many other techniques, but we have just given a sample below. (The examples are all based on Level 1, Theme 1 Speaking.)

- **Simple repetition, chorally and individually**
  Highlight the pronunciation area you want to focus on when you model the sentence or question, e.g., showing the intonation pattern with your hand, or using an intonation arrow on the board.

- **Question and answer**
  *When do you take national exams in your country?*
  *We take them at 16 and 18.*
  (Do not simply accept *16 and 18* in a controlled practice phase – encourage a full sentence.)
  Alternatively, you can practise short answers. Tell students if you require *yes* answers or *no* answers:
  *Is a nursery school for young children?*
  *Yes, it is.*
  *Does primary mean 'first'?*
  *Yes, it does.*
  *Do most children leave school at 18?*
  *Yes, they do.*

- **Transformation**
  These examples focus on forms of the present simple tense.
  *Many children begin school at seven.*
  *Sorry, but they don't begin school at seven.* OR
  *Actually, they begin school at five.*

- **Substitution**
  Say a phrase or sentence and ask the class to repeat it. Then give prompts that can be substituted as follows:
  *History is a very important subject at school.*
  useful
  *History is a very useful subject at school.*
  isn't
  *History isn't a very useful subject at school.*
  university
  *History isn't a very useful subject at university.*
  Drama
  *Drama isn't a very useful subject at university.*

- **Prompts**
  These can be given orally or they can be written on the board. They are particularly good for practising question forms:
  *Nursery / young children?*
  *Is a nursery school for young children?*
  *When / take / A levels?*
  *When do you take A levels?*

## Setting up tasks
The teaching notes for many activities begin with the word *Set …* This single word covers a number of vital functions for the teacher, as follows:
- Refer students to the rubric, or instructions.
- Check that they understand **what** to do: get one or two students to explain the task in their own words.
- Tell the students **how** they are to do the task, if this is not clear in the rubric (as individual work, pairwork, or group work).
- Go through the example, if there is one. If not, make it clear what the **target output** is: full sentences, short answers, notes, etc. Many activities fail in the classroom because students do not know what they are expected to produce.
- Go through one or two of the actual prompts, working with an able student to elicit the required output.

## Use of visuals
There is a large amount of visual material in the book. This should be exploited in a number of ways:
- **before** an activity, to orientate the students; to get them thinking about the situation or the activity and to provide an opportunity for a small amount of pre-teaching of vocabulary
- **during** the activity, to remind students of important language
- **after** the activity, to help with related work or to revise the target language

## Pronunciation
Only the Speaking section of each theme directly focuses on oral production. In this section, you must ensure that all the students in your group have reasonable pronunciation of all target items. Elsewhere, in the other skill sections, it is important that you do not spend too long on oral production. However, do not let students get away with poor production of basic words, even if the focus of the lesson is not speaking.

## Comparing answers in pairs
This activity is suggested on almost every occasion when the students have completed an activity individually. This provides all students with a chance to give and to explain their answers, which is not possible if the teacher immediately goes through the answers with the whole class.

## Monitoring
Pairwork and group work activities are, of course, an opportunity for the students to produce spoken language. This is clearly important in the Speaking section but elsewhere, these interactional patterns provide an opportunity for the teacher to check three points:
- that the students are performing the correct task, in the correct way
- that the students understand the language of the task they are performing
- the elements which need to be covered again for the benefit of the whole class, and which points need to be dealt with on an individual basis with particular students

## Feedback
At the end of every activity there should be a feedback stage, during which the correct answers (or a model

answer, in the case of freer activities) is given, alternative correct answers (if any) are accepted, and wrong answers are discussed.

Feedback can be:
- high-speed, whole class, oral – this method is suitable for cases where short answers with no possible variations are required
- individual, oral – this method is suitable where answers are longer and/or where variations are possible
- individual, onto the board – this method is suitable when the teacher will want to look closely at the correct answers to highlight points of interest or confusion.

Remember, learning does not take place, generally speaking, when a student gets something right. Learning usually takes place after a student has got something wrong, and begins to understand why it is wrong.

### Confirmation and correction
Many activities benefit from a learning tension, i.e., a period of time when students are not sure whether something is right or wrong. The advantages of this tension are:
- a chance for all students to become involved in an activity before the correct answers are given
- a higher level of concentration from students – tension is quite enjoyable!
- a greater focus on the item as students wait for the correct answer
- a greater involvement in the process – students become committed to their answers and want to know if they are right and if not, why not

In cases where learning tension of this type is desirable, the detailed teaching notes say *Do not confirm or correct (at this point)*.

### Highlighting grammar
This course has specific grammar lessons but, in addition, in other lessons the expression *Highlight the grammar* is used in the teaching notes. This expression means:
- Focus the students' attention on the grammar point, e.g., *Look at the verb in the first sentence.*
- Write an example of the target grammar on the board.
- Ask a student to read out the sentence/phrase.
- Demonstrate the grammar point in an appropriate way (see below).
- Refer to the board throughout the activity if students are making mistakes.

Ways of dealing with different grammar points:
- for **word order**, show the order of items in the sentence by numbering them, e.g.,
  
  1    2      3    4
  *They often have a special party.*

- for **paradigms**, show the changes with different persons of the verb, e.g.,
  
  *I   go*
  *He  goes*

### Self-checking
On a few occasions during the course, the teaching notes encourage you to ask the students to check their own work. This can be done by referring students to the full transcript at the end of the course. This is an excellent way to develop the students' recognition and correction of error. Listening, in particular, obviously happens inside someone's head, and in the end each student has to understand his/her own error or misunderstanding.

### Gap fill
Filling in missing words or phrases in a sentence or text, or labelling a map or diagram, indicates comprehension of both the missing items and the context in which they correctly fit. It is generally better to provide the missing items to ensure that all the required items are available to all the students. In addition, the teacher can vary the approach to gap fills by sometimes going through the activity with the whole class, orally, pens down, then setting the same task individually. Gap fills or labelling activities can be photocopied and set as revision at the end of the unit or later, with or without the missing items box.

In *Progressive Skills in English*, gaps often contain the same kind of word (e.g., nouns) or the same role in a sentence (e.g., the subject) in order to reinforce word class and syntax.

### Two-column activities
This type of activity is generally better than a list of open-ended questions or gap fill with no box of missing items, as it ensures that all the target language is available to the students. However, the activity is only fully effective if the two columns are dealt with in the following way. Ask students to:
- **guess** the way to complete the phrase, sentence or pair
- **match** the two parts from each column
- cover column 2 and **remember** these parts from the items in column 1
- cover column 1 and **remember** these parts from the items in column 2

Additional activities are:
- students test each other in pairs
- you read out column 1 – students complete with items from column 2, books closed
- students write as many of the items as they can remember – Course Books closed

## Ordering

Several different kinds of linguistic elements can be given out of order for students to arrange correctly. The ability to put things in the correct order strongly indicates comprehension of the items. In addition, it reinforces syntactic structure, particularly if:
- you present a number of jumbled sentences together with the same underlying syntax
- you keep elements of each phrase together, e.g., *in the UK* rather than breaking everything down to word level

This type of activity is sometimes given before students listen or read; the first listening or reading task is then to check the order. To make the exercise more enjoyable, and slightly easier, it is a good idea to photocopy the items and cut them into strips or single words. Students can then physically move the items and try different ordering. The teacher can even make a whiteboard set of sentences and encourage students to arrange or direct the arrangement of the items on the board.

## Tables and charts

Students are often asked to transfer information into a table. This activity is a good way of testing comprehension, as it does not require much linguistic output from the students at a time when they should be concentrating on comprehension. Once the table has been completed, it can form the basis of:
- a checking activity – students compare their tables, note and discuss differences
- a reconstruction activity – students give the information in the table in full, in speech or writing

The second method should be used with caution, bearing in mind the focus on the receptive skill in the course rather than on written or spoken production.

## Error correction

It was once thought that showing students error reinforced the error, that students would be even more likely to make that error in the future. We now know that recognizing errors is a vital part of language learning. Rather than reinforcing the error, showing it can serve to highlight the problem much better than any number of explanatory words. Students must be able to recognize errors, principally in their own work, and correct them. For this reason, error recognition and correction activities are occasionally used.

## Routes through the course

### The 25-hour course

Firstly, each skill section contains 25 lessons which stand alone from the other skill sections. In other words, students do not need to have studied the Listening section of a theme, for example, in order to use the Speaking section effectively. However, there is a thematic link between all the skill sections in one theme, so if students *do* study more than one skill, they will broaden and deepen their ability to understand and/or produce text about the theme. Course leaders can, of course, choose more than one skill – for example, Listening and Speaking, or Listening and Reading, to match the exact needs of their students.

### The 40-hour course

Each skill section has two core lessons, the second and third lessons in the section. The first core lesson is called *Real-time*, e.g., *Real-time listening*, and includes a particular kind of text which contains new sub-skills and new grammar points. The second core lesson is called *Learning new skills*, e.g., *Learning new listening skills*. In this lesson, the new sub-skills are highlighted and practised. Ideally, the first core lesson should be prefaced by the vocabulary lesson, and the second core lesson should be followed by the grammar skills lesson, but it is possible to set the first for homework preparation *before* and the second for homework consolidation *after* the core lessons. In this case, all the themes can be covered in 40 hours.

### The 60-hour course

Each skill section contains a lesson which focuses on a grammar point related to the skill. Although there is quite a large amount of common core grammar in the genre of EAP, there are many points which are directly related to specific skills. For example, it is easy to *see* negation in English because the word *not* is clearly evident in negative sentences. However, it is very hard (often impossible) to *hear* negation, so understanding that spoken sentences are negative requires different skills. The 60-hour course is the 40-hour course plus the grammar lesson in each skill.

### The 80-hour course

Each skill section begins with a vocabulary lesson. Research has shown how important vocabulary is in the acquisition of language, and this is particularly true of academic English, which uses a very large number of synonyms in order to achieve lexical cohesion in a text. The 80-hour course is the 40-hour course plus the vocabulary lesson and grammar lesson in each skill.

### The 100-hour course

A key feature of the *Progressive Skills* approach is the use of parallel texts. In all Listening and Reading sections and in nearly all Speaking and Writing sections, the fifth lesson contains the same text type as that in the second lesson, requiring understanding and use of the same sub-skills and grammar points. The fifth lesson, *Applying new skills*, therefore gives students the immediate opportunity to prove that they have understood and can apply the new points presented. The fifth lesson in each section adds another 20 hours to the course.

### The 120-hour course

This involves using all the material in the Course Book, including the three extra pages in each theme.

*Table 5: Possible routes through the course*

| | | | |
|---|---|---|---|
| Listening | Vocabulary | D | can be set for self-study preparation |
| | Real-time | A | core material |
| | Learning new skills | A | core material |
| | Grammar | B | can be set for self-study |
| | Applying new skills | C | can be omitted |
| Speaking | Vocabulary | D | can be set for self-study preparation |
| | Real-time | A | core material |
| | Learning new skills | A | core material |
| | Grammar | B | can be set for self-study |
| | Applying new skills | C | can be omitted |
| Reading | Vocabulary | D | can be set for self-study preparation |
| | Real-time | A | core material |
| | Learning new skills | A | core material |
| | Grammar | B | can be set for self-study |
| | Applying new skills | C | can be omitted |
| Writing | Vocabulary | D | can be set for self-study preparation |
| | Real-time | A | core material |
| | Learning new skills | A | core material |
| | Grammar | B | can be set for self-study |
| | Applying new skills | C | can be omitted |
| Extra pages | Everyday English | E | can be omitted |
| | Knowledge quiz | E | can be omitted |
| | Portfolio | E | can be omitted |
| Key | Route 1 = A | 40 hours | |
| | Route 2 = A + B | 60 hours | |
| | Route 3 = A + B + D | 80 hours | |
| | Route 4 = A + B + C + D | 100 hours | |
| | Route 5 = A + B + C + D + E | 120 hours | |

# Theme 1

## Remembering and forgetting

- **Memory**
- **Learner styles**
- **Improving your memory**
- **Rehearsal and prompts**

# Listening: Memory

### 1.1 Vocabulary for listening: Types of memory

**Objectives**

By the end of the lesson, students should be able to:
- demonstrate understanding of information about short-term and long-term memory;
- demonstrate recognition of target vocabulary for the Listening section, both in isolation and in context.

**Methodology note**

The following words were taught for this skill and theme at Level 1 of *Progressive Skills in English*. If your students studied this theme and skill at Level 1, you might want to review this vocabulary, particularly for spoken recognition.

| | |
|---|---|
| academic (*adj*) | lecture (*n*) |
| access (*n* and *v*) | lecturer (*n*) |
| accommodation (*n*) | librarian (*n*) |
| article (*n*) | look up (*v*) |
| assignment (*n*) | participation (*n*) |
| bursar (*n*) | professor (*n*) |
| campus (*n*) | projector (*n*) |
| contribute (*v*) | research (*n*) |
| deadline (*n*) | resource centre |
| dean (*n*) | responsible [for] (*adj*) |
| degree (*n*) | schedule (*n*) |
| faculty (*n*) | semester (*n*) |
| fee (*n*) | socialize (*v*) |
| field trip | staff (*n*) |
| fresher (*n*) | students' union |
| graduate (*n* and *v*) | subject (*n*) |
| hall of residence (*n*) | tutorial (*n*) |
| head (of) (*n*) | undergraduate (*n*) |
| in charge of (*adj*) | vice chancellor (*n*) |

**Introduction**

Write the following questions on the board for students to discuss in pairs or small groups:
*What's your earliest memory?*
*How old were you?*
*Who were you with?*
*Where were you?*

You can also ask some supplementary questions (depending on the level of your class), such as:
*Do you associate any particular smells or feelings with your earliest memory?*
*What about sounds or music?*

**A** Activating knowledge

Students discuss the question in pairs. Elicit ideas.

Answers

Answers depend on the students, but these are some possibilities:
- lists
- 'post-it' notes
- notes stuck on fridge
- calendars
- diaries
- various computer programs
- mobile phones, MP3 players, etc., can be used as reminders
- ask people to remind you
- making notes
- repeating things to yourself
- asking a friend to 'test' you
- reading and rereading
- underlining key words in a text

**B** Understanding vocabulary in context

Say each word aloud for the students to hear so that they can recognize it in context later; however, do not explain the words' meanings at this stage.
In pairs, students can briefly discuss which words they think they already know the meanings of. Do not confirm or correct ideas at this stage.
Now set the task. Play 1.1 as far as the first example and check students understand the task. Play the rest of the CD; students number the remaining words. If you like, you can pause the recording at the end of each sentence containing the target words. Students compare their answers in pairs. Replay the CD if students found the activity difficult.
Elicit answers and replay any sentences students had difficulty with.
Ask the following questions:
*How many types of memory are there?* (two: short-term and long-term)

*How many types of long-term memory are there?* (three)

### Optional activity

Give students copies of the transcript as a gap-fill exercise (with the target words deleted). Students try to predict the answers, then listen to 🔊 1.1 to check their ideas.

Answers

| 10 | encoded |
| 6 | long-term |
| 3 | memorize |
| 1 | memory |
| 7 | perform |
| 8 | autobiographical |
| 9 | recall |
| 2 | remembering |
| 12 | retrieved |
| 4 | rote learning |
| 5 | short-term |
| 11 | stored |

Transcript

🔊 1.1

Presenter: 1.1. Theme 1: Remembering and forgetting
Lesson 1.1 Vocabulary for listening: Types of memory
Exercise B. Listen to a text. Number the words and phrases below in the order you hear them.

Lecturer: Have you got a good memory? Some people are good at remembering names. Other people have a good memory for faces, or telephone numbers or events from their own lives. Some people seem to be able to memorize facts easily, for example the date of a battle, or the capital of a country. For centuries, teachers used rote learning, or 'learning by heart', for information such as the times tables; for example, 7 times 8 is 56.

According to some researchers, there are two main kinds of memory. First, there is short-term memory. This helps us remember a telephone number, for example, just long enough to write it down. Secondly, there is long-term memory. In theory, we can remember things in long-term memory for ever.

Psychologists say there are three main kinds of long-term memory:

Firstly, we remember how to do things. This means we can perform skills, such as driving or playing a sport.

Secondly, we remember facts. We remember the dates of famous battles, for example, the name of the first President of the United States, or the population of our country.

Finally, we remember autobiographical events. In other words, we can recall personal experiences and recognize familiar faces, for example. We remember going to interesting places when we were younger.

Neuroscientists point out that memory has three stages. Firstly, the information must be encoded or taken in. Secondly, the information must be stored. Thirdly, the information must be correctly retrieved. Memory can fail in any of the three stages. In other words, we can forget the information if we don't regularly remind ourselves about it.

### Methodology note

1. If you did not replay 🔊 1.1 for Exercise B, you may need to let students listen to the recording all the way through once more before eliciting the answers to Exercise C.

2. The three kinds of long-term memory are in fact called by psychologists *procedural*, *propositional* and *recollective*.

   We have avoided the use of these terms for simplicity, but with a more able class you may wish to teach them.

### C  Using new vocabulary

Ask students to read the rubrics, then check understanding. Students complete the diagram in pairs. Elicit answers, preferably using an electronic projection.

Ask a few further questions to check understanding of the text, e.g., you could ask students to give you examples of each kind of long-term memory.

Answers

Long-term memory

| You can remember *skills* | You can remember *facts* | You can remember *autobiographical events* |

### Methodology note

Exercise D discriminates between some commonly confused words in the lexical set for this lesson. It is important that students understand why their answers are wrong. You may need to give further revision or practice in the following lessons, depending on whether students have ingrained errors with these words.

**D** Understanding vocabulary patterns
Set the task. Students can discuss each sentence in pairs. Elicit answers.

Answers

1. Have you got a good *memory* for names? (refers to area of brain; *reminder* = spoken or written item)
2. I need to *learn* how to drive. (*memorize* is only for facts, not a skill)
3. Please *remind* me to complete that form. (grammatical; *remind* + someone + to do something)
4. I've *left* my book at home. (grammatical; *leave* + something + somewhere; *forgotten* + something)
5. Can you *remember* her name? (register / collocation – *retrieve* is too formal / scientific)
6. Do you *recognize* this person? (*remind* = wrong meaning)
7. I've *learned* my bank account number by heart. (collocation; *learn by heart*)

**Closure**
Give out copies of the transcript from Exercise B if you have not already done so. Play 🎧 1.1 again with students following the transcript.

### 1.2 Real-time listening: Memory models

**Objectives**

By the end of this lesson, students should be able to:
- attempt to understand a lecture about memory and learning;
- have a better understanding of the meaning of target vocabulary for the Listening section;
- relate spoken vocabulary to its written forms.

**Introduction**
This suggestion can be used before setting Exercise B or you can do the revision as your introduction to the lesson.

Revise the information students learnt in the previous lesson about memory. Basically, they learnt that some researchers say there are two types of memory: short-term and long-term. However, there are three types of long-term memory; build up the following diagram on the board.

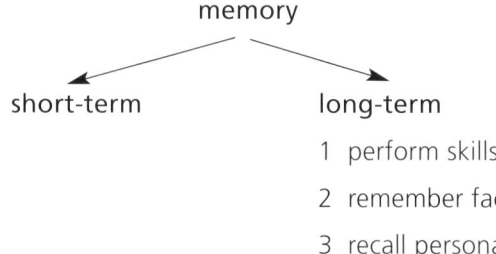

1 perform skills
2 remember facts
3 recall personal experiences

Leave this on the board, or have it available on an electronic projection, to show when studying Exercise D at the end of the lesson.

In this lesson, students will learn that some researchers say there are three types of memory. Do any students know what the third type is? (Sensory memory – but do not confirm or correct at this stage.)

**A** Activating ideas

Students discuss the questions in pairs. If students are not sure of the meaning of *senses*, you might need to give them *sight* as an example. Elicit answers. Point out that we have specific noun forms for *sight*, *taste* and *smell*. However, for the other words we say *hearing*, *feeling*. Some people say *touch* instead of *feeling*. It is also possible to say *seeing* instead of *sight*.

**Optional activity**

Some people say we have a 'sixth sense'. Ask students:

*What is it? Do you agree with this idea?* (It is a special feeling that warns us about danger, for example.)

Answers

1. Sight / seeing, hearing, feeling / touch, taste, smell.
2. Answers depend on students.

## B Predicting the content of a lecture

Students discuss the questions in pairs. Elicit ideas. Elicit the meanings of the words in the title:

*multi* = 'many'
*store* = 'place where you keep something'
*model* = 'description'

The words *store* and *model* can have different meanings in different contexts and can be nouns or verbs.

### Answers

1. Memory, in particular the Multi-store memory model. In other words, the lecture is going to be about another theory about memory and learning.
2. Three types of memory.
3. Answers depend on students. They can check their ideas in Exercise C.

### Methodology notes

1. In the Introduction to this Teacher's Book, there are some suggestions for exploiting the use of DVDs. For example, you can first play the DVD without the sound on. This can be particularly useful in this lesson because the lecturer uses a lot of gesture to emphasize each point.
2. We recommend that you only play the DVD once for the main activity (Exercise C1) as in real life students will only have the opportunity to listen to a lecture once. However, as this is the beginning of the course, and if your students find listening difficult, you may want to replay the DVD, or at least sections of it. You can gradually wean students off doing this as you go through the course.

## C Understanding key information

Check students understand the task. Students discuss in pairs. Elicit ideas but do not confirm or correct at this stage. Students may not understand the phrase *pay attention*; if possible, leave explanation of this as they should be able to work out the meaning in context when they watch the lecture.

1. Set the task. Play DVD 1.A. Elicit answers and find out if students can remember any other information. For example, for Sentence 1 students might have understood that it is an important process, and that there is more than one model for the process. Try not to pre-empt the next exercise when you do this, perhaps by not confirming or correcting ideas. (If students cannot remember any more information, it does not matter at this stage. Students may not understand the phrase *pay attention*; if possible, leave explanation of this as they should be able to work out the meaning in context when they watch the lecture.)
2. Try to get students to attempt the activity without watching the DVD again. Once you have elicited as many answers as possible, you can then replay the DVD – or sections of it – so that students can fill in any gaps in their answers. Check understanding of key points and vocabulary, for example, *pay attention, rehearsal, hold something in your memory*, the verb *last*, etc.

### Answers

1. Answers depend on students.
2.

| a. Who proposed the Multi-store memory model? | b | 1968 |
| --- | --- | --- |
| b. When did they do this? | e | 1–3 seconds |
| c. Who conducted research into short-term memory? | f | 15–30 seconds |
| d. When did he do this? | j | we need to **rehearse** it |
| e. How long does sensory memory last? | g | forever |
| f. How long does short-term memory last? | d | 1956 |
| g. How long does long-term memory last? | h | we must pay **attention** to it |
| h. How can we move information in sensory memory into short-term memory? | i | 7 |
| i. How many pieces of information can short-term memory hold? | c | Miller |
| j. How can we move information from short-term into long-term memory? | a | Atkinson and Shiffrin |

## Transcript

1.2 DVD 1.A

**Presenter:** 1.2. Lesson 1.1. Real-time listening: Memory models

**Lecturer:** In this lecture, we are going to look at a very important process. It is the process of getting new information into long-term memory. There are several memory models from different researchers. But we are only going to look at one model today. It is the Multi-store memory model. Firstly, we'll look at the components of the model. Then we'll see how information moves through the different parts of the brain, according to the model.

So first, let's look at the components of the Multi-store memory model. It was proposed by two researchers called Atkinson and Shiffrin. They wrote an article in 1968. It was entitled 'The psychology of learning and motivation'. In the article, Atkinson and Shiffrin say that there are three parts to memory. Firstly, there is sensory memory. The word *sensory* is the adjective from *sense*. It means 'related to sight, hearing' and so on. Sensory memory lasts from one to three seconds. The second part of the Multi-store model is short-term memory. Short-term memory lasts from 15 to 30 seconds. Finally, we have long-term memory. Long-term memory can last for a lifetime.

Now let's consider how information moves through the three parts of the memory. Firstly, sensory memory. All five senses can lead to memories. For example, we use sight for recognizing people. We use hearing for recognizing a piece of music. Atkinson and Shiffrin say that we must pay attention to a piece of sensory information to move it into short-term memory. For example, our eyes see a telephone number. But we only put it into short-term memory when we actually look at it.

So the first stage of memory is paying attention. When we pay attention, we move information. It goes from sensory memory to short-term memory. But short-term memory does not last for long. We must do something with the information in short-term memory. If we don't, new information from sensory memory pushes out old information. The best-known research in this area was conducted by Miller. In 1956, he wrote an article. It was called 'The Magical Number Seven, Plus or Minus Two'. In the article, Miller says that short-term memory can only hold about seven pieces of meaningless information. For example, it can hold a telephone number. When an eighth piece comes along, one of the seven pieces is pushed out.

Long-term memory is the final stage in this model. According to Atkinson and Shiffrin, we need rehearsal to move information from short-term memory. In other words, we need to repeat information in our heads. We need to say it again and again. Then it will be moved from short-term to long-term memory.

So that's the Multi-store model. In the next lecture, we'll look at the idea of rehearsal in more detail. Is it just repetition, or is there more involved? That's next time.

### D  Transferring information to the real world

1. Refer students back to the table on the board about memory (from the introduction). Elicit answers to the question or get students to discuss it in pairs.

2. Check students can remember what Miller's theory is. Students discuss the question in pairs. If you wish, the students could actually try to conduct the experiment in class.

3. Students discuss the question in pairs. Elicit ideas.

### Answers

1. Basically, the first model students looked at in Lesson 1.1 says there are two types of memory: short-term and long-term. On the other hand, the Multi-store memory model suggests there are three types of memory.

2. Students could design an experiment where the participant is shown seven random numbers, or simple shapes, for example. These are then removed. After 15 seconds the participant is asked to remember them. More numbers or shapes would then be added, and again the participant would be asked to remember them after 15–30 seconds.

3. This research is very important for learning. As learners, it tells us we must pay attention to, and rehearse, information if we want to learn it. As teachers, it means that we must get students' attention, and also review and revise information as much as possible, especially when it is new.

### Closure

Do one of the following if you have not already done so:

- Play the DVD with students following the transcript.
- Do an experiment with the class based on Miller's theory (see Exercise D2).

## 1.3 Learning new listening skills: Recording sources

### Objectives

By the end of this lesson, students should be able to:

- listen and make notes of the topic, the researcher's name and date of sources;
- recognize a target word from its stressed syllable.

**Introduction**

Revise the information from the two previous lessons on memory and learning. If you have not already done so, you could replay [DVD] 1.A from Lesson 1.2 with the students following the transcript.

> **Methodology note**
>
> If your students did not study Level 1 of *Progressive Skills in English*, you may need to explain the rationale behind Exercise A (see Introduction, page 14).

**A** Predicting the next information

Check students understand the task and go over the example. Give students a minute or two to read through the sentence endings. Play 1.3. Students complete the answers individually and compare their answers in pairs. Replay the CD if necessary. Elicit answers.

Answers

| 6  | the adjective from *sense*. |
| 9  | short-term memory. |
| 5  | there is sensory memory. |
| 8  | from one to three seconds. |
| 2  | 1968. |
| 10 | long-term memory. |
| 7  | related to sight, hearing and so on. |
| 3  | 'The psychology of learning and motivation'. |
| 4  | Atkinson and Shiffrin say that there are three parts to memory. |
| 1  | Atkinson and Shiffrin. |

Transcript

1.3

Presenter: 1.3. Lesson 1.3. Learning new listening skills: Recording sources. Exercise A. Listen to part of the lecture from Lesson 1.2. Number the sentence endings in the correct order.
Lecturer: The model was proposed by …
They wrote an article in …
It was entitled …
In the article, …
Firstly, …
Sensory is …
Sensory means …
Sensory memory lasts …
The second part of the Multi-store model is …
Finally, we have …

**B** Identifying a new skill

Check students understand the phrase *recording sources*. Explain that, in this context, *record* is a verb. It means *to make a note of* or *write something down*. Elicit different kinds of sources: books, articles, journals, research, websites, documents, etc.

Students read the Skills Check box and discuss questions B1 and B2. Elicit answers.

Play the example lecture extracts on 1.6, making sure students are studying the notes at the same time. Ask students to notice how the dates are written (in brackets). Elicit why the date is important (the researchers have probably written more than one book or article).

Answers

1. The topic, the name of the researcher(s) and the date of the research.
2. The exact name of the research, book or article.

> **Methodology notes**
>
> 1. Many lecturers will give out the names of researchers and other sources on their Powerpoint slides or in handouts for the lecture. However, it is important for students to be able to use the skill (of listening and making their own notes) in the cases where lecturers do not give out the information, and also as confirmation or checking that they have the correct source for a piece of research.
>
> 2. Students may find this activity quite difficult to start with; reassure them they will get better with practice. There will be revision activities throughout this course.

**C** Practising a new skill

Check students understand the task and emphasize they should have a go at spelling the names mentioned in the lecture, even if they are not quite sure how to spell them. Remind students to write the general topic or subject of the research but tell them they do not have to write the exact name. Play the extracts from 1.4. Students complete the task individually, then compare their answers in pairs. Elicit answers, preferably using an electronic projection. Explain that the phrase *et al.* stands for 'more than one author'.

Give out copies of the transcript, if you wish, and play the extracts one more time.

### Optional activity

Show the line graph of Peterson and Peterson's research (Course Book page 26). Discuss what it shows. (The vertical line shows the percentage of information that the participants could remember; the horizontal line shows the number of seconds.)

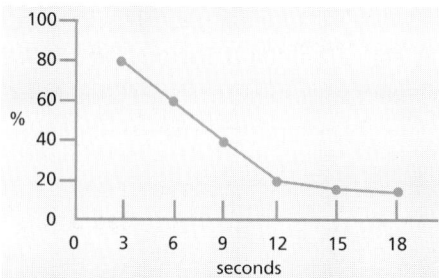

Fig. 1: *% of three-letter combinations remembered*

### Answers

Extract 1 = primary memory / Joseph Jacobs (1887)

Extract 2 = encoding sensory information / Conrad (1964) / Shulman (1970)

Extract 3 = short-term memory length / Peterson and Peterson (1959)

Extract 4 = long-term memory length / Bahrick et al. (1975)

Extract 5 = ST memory model / Baddeley and Hitch (1975)

### Transcript

🔊 1.4

**Presenter:** 1.4. Exercise C. Listen to some extracts from a lecture on memory.

**Presenter:** One.
**Lecturer:** Short-term memory was originally called *primary memory*. The first real investigation of primary memory was in 1887. That's 1887, not 1987, so well over one hundred years ago. A man called Joseph Jacobs conducted an experiment. He gave people sets of numbers to remember. The sets got longer and longer. Jacobs found the average is around six or seven.

**Presenter:** Two.
**Lecturer:** Let's see how we encode sensory information. A man called Conrad did some experiments in 1964. In an article entitled 'Acoustic confusions in immediate memory', Conrad said that we encode sensory information as sound. But only six years later, in 1970, another researcher called Shulman did some more experiments. He reported his findings in the *Journal of Verbal Learning & Verbal Behavior*. Shulman found that some information is encoded for meaning, not sound.

**Presenter:** Three.
**Lecturer:** Peterson and Peterson published a study in 1959. It was called *Short-term retention of individual verbal items*. They looked at the length of short-term memory if there was no rehearsal. Peterson and Peterson found people can remember meaningless shapes without rehearsal for about three seconds. But after 18 seconds, nearly everything is forgotten. Did I say the date? It was 1959.

**Presenter:** Four.
**Lecturer:** A group of researchers looked at long-term memory in 1975, I think it was. Let me check my notes. Yes, 1975. Bahrick *et al* wanted to test the length of long-term memory. They showed people photographs of school classmates and asked them to recognize the people. Bahrick and his team found that long-term memory declines over long periods of time.

**Presenter:** Five.
**Lecturer:** Another model of memory is called the Working memory model. This was proposed by Baddeley and Hitch in 1975. So that's the same year as Bahrick *et al*'s research. Baddeley and Hitch looked mostly at short-term memory. There is one main difference between this model and the Multi-store model. The Working memory model suggests that short-term memory has several different parts, and each part has its own function.

### D  Identifying words from the stressed syllable

Remind students about the importance of stressed syllables in multi-syllable words, e.g., 'pro-cess, pro-'pose. They must learn to recognize a word in context from the stressed syllable.

Briefly revise the meanings of some of the words in the table.

Play 🔊 1.5. Students complete the task individually, then compare their answers in pairs. Elicit answers.

### Transcripts and Answers

🔊 1.5

**Presenter:** 1.5. Exercise D. Listen to the stressed syllable of some words from this theme. Number the correct word in each case.

**Voice:**
1. [in]volve
2. mem[ory]
3. [con]sid[er]
4. rec[ognize]
5. [at]ten[tion]
6. [re]search
7. in[formation]
8. [repe]ti[tion]
9. [per]form
10. [en]code
11. [re]trieve
12. [re]call

🔊 1.6

**Presenter:** 1.6. Exercise D. Skills Check. Listen to extracts from the lecture in 1.1 again.

One.

Lecturer: So, first, let's look at the components of the Multi-store memory model. It was proposed by two researchers called Atkinson and Shiffrin. They wrote an article in 1968. It was entitled 'The psychology of learning and motivation'.

Presenter: Two.

Lecturer: We must do something with the information in short-term memory. The best-known research in this area was conducted by Miller. In 1956, he wrote an article. It was called 'The Magical Number Seven, Plus or Minus Two.'

## Closure

If you have not already done so, play the extracts from Exercise C with students following the transcript. Spend a few minutes discussing each piece of research from Exercise C.

- *Which piece of research is most interesting?*
- *Which piece of information is most useful for learners of English?*
- *Are there any similarities (or differences) between the Multi-store memory model and Miller's research on short-term memory?*
- *Which piece of research is most useful if you have an assignment about ...*
  *... short-term memory?*
  *... long-term memory?*
  *... sensory memory?*

### 1.4 Grammar for listening: Indirect questions; verb patterns

**Objectives**

By the end of this lesson, students should be able to:
- use indirect questions to make headings for notes;
- discriminate between the verb patterns for *forget, learn, remember, remind*.

## Introduction

Write some questions on the board, for example:
- *Who proposed the Multi-store memory model?*
- *When did they publish this theory?*
- *How long does sensory memory last?*
- *What relevance is there for education?*

Tell students these are called **direct** questions.

Write the following indirect questions on the board:
- *Can you tell me who proposed the Multi-store memory model?*
- *The lecturer told us when they published this theory.*
- *I'll explain how long sensory memory lasts.*
- *I'm not sure what relevance there is for education.*

Explain that these are examples of **indirect** questions. Elicit some of the differences between the original direct questions and the indirect questions, e.g., word order, auxiliaries, etc.

Tell students that this lesson will explain indirect questions in more detail.

### Grammar box 1

Ask students to study the table for a couple of minutes. Ask different students to read out a sentence each from the table. Check understanding of vocabulary, e.g., *rehearsal, proposed, components*, etc.

**Methodology note**

During feedback time for Exercise A, remind students that when using the present simple or past simple in direct questions, the auxiliary normally has to go back in (except with *be*) – e.g., question 4. However question 2, which is in the past simple, does not need the auxiliary *did* because it is a question about the subject.

**A** Direct questions

Check students understand the task and go over the example. Students should use their notebooks to write the answers. Students compare their answers in pairs. Elicit answers. Elicit what tense each question is in.

Answers

| | |
|---|---|
| 1. Is rehearsal just repetition? | rehearsal = repetition? |
| 2. Who proposed this model? | who? |
| 3. What are the components of the model? | components? |
| 4. How does the process work? | how / work? |
| 5. Why is this important? | why / important? |

## B  Indirect questions

Check students understand the task and go over the example. Play 🔘 **1.7**. Students complete the activity individually, then compare their answers in pairs. Elicit answers, preferably using an electronic projection.

### Answers

| 1. I'm going to discuss how we encode sensory information. | how / encode sens. inf.? |
|---|---|
| 2. We'll see what the researchers discovered. | what / res. discover? |
| 3. I'm going to explain why this research is important. | why res. imp.? |
| 4. Let's consider how this happens. | how / happens? |
| 5. We'll find out who the famous people are in this area. | people in area? |
| 6. Let's consider how many pieces of information we can remember in short-term memory. | how many pieces inf. in sh-t. mem.? |
| 7. I'll explain why this research is important for learners. | why imp. for learners |
| 8. We'll look at how information moves through the brain. | how inf. moves through brain |

### Transcript

🔘 1.7

Presenter: 1.7. Lesson 1.4. Grammar for listening: Indirect questions; verb patterns. Exercise B. Listen to some more indirect questions. Make a heading for the notes in each case.

Voice:
1. I'm going to discuss how we encode sensory information.
2. We'll see what the researchers discovered.
3. I'm going to explain why this research is important.
4. Let's consider how this happens.
5. We'll find out who the famous people are in this area.
6. Let's consider how many pieces of information we can remember in short-term memory.
7. I'll explain why this research is important for learners.
8. We'll look at how information moves through the brain.

### Methodology note

Tell students the verbs in Grammar box 2 are often confused in English. Remind students of Exercise D in Lesson 1.1 Vocabulary for listening, which practised some of these verbs for meaning. If you wish you could even repeat it here, perhaps doing it on the board this time with the students' books closed. In this activity, students will study the grammar of this vocabulary in more detail.

### Grammar box 2

Set the task, then elicit answers. Ask students to cover the first four columns of the tables, leaving just the last column with the end of the sentence. Elicit the complete sentence for each ending.

#### Answers
- remembered
- reminded
- learnt
- forgot

## C  Predicting sentence endings

Set the task. Play 🔘 **1.8**. Students number the endings in the correct order and compare their answers in pairs. Elicit answers. Replay the CD if you wish.

Now say the introductory phrase and elicit different possible ways to complete each sentence:

T: *I remember …*
S1: *… names very easily.*
S2: *… seeing her in the canteen.*

### Answers

| 3 | getting my first bicycle. |
|---|---|
| 6 | seminar dates. |
| 4 | to cook. |
| 1 | the countries of the region. |
| 5 | my mother. |
| 2 | to hand in the assignment on time. |

## Transcript

🔊 1.8

**Presenter:** 1.8. Exercise C. Listen to the beginning of some sentences. Choose the best way to complete each sentence.
1. At school, we learnt about …
2. Don't forget …
3. I remember …
4. I'd like to learn how …
5. My tutor is very nice. She reminds me of …
6. My tutor usually reminds me about …

## Closure

Summarize the introductory phrases for the indirect questions from Grammar box 1 and Exercise B:
- I'm going to discuss / explain …
- We'll see / look at / discover …
- I'll identify / explain / show …
- X explained / showed / discovered …
- Let's consider / look at / discuss …

Elicit ideas for how each phrase could be continued by the lecturer.

### 1.5 Applying new listening skills: Moving information into long-term memory

#### Objectives

By the end of this lesson, students should be able to:
- demonstrate understanding of a lecture about learning and memory;
- make notes of sources when following a lecture.

## Introduction

Use Exercise A as the introduction.

#### Methodology notes

1. The sentence for the mnemonic does not really make much sense. However, syntactically it is correct so the pattern helps us to remember the order of the planets. This mnemonic is particularly helpful because it contains the phrase 'nine planets' so it reminds us about the number as well as the names of the planets.

2. A controversial point is that some astronomers say that Pluto is too small to be a planet. Many now call it a *planetoid* or 'dwarf planet'.

3. Mnemonics can be sentences or short poems. They help us to remember information or scientific rules, for example. The word comes from ancient Greek, hence the strange spelling in English.

### A   Activating ideas

1. Exploit the visual and teach or elicit the words *Solar System* and *planets*. Explain it is not really important to understand the meaning of the sentence. Students discuss the question in pairs. Elicit ideas.

2. Say the word *mnemonic* /nəˈmɒnɪk/ for the class, making sure students realize the first *m* is not pronounced.

3. Students discuss the lecture question in pairs. Elicit feedback.

#### Answers

1. The first letter of each word in the sentence helps us remember – in the correct order – the names of the planets shown in the picture:
   *My* = Mercury
   *Very* = Venus
   *Efficient* = Earth
   *Memory* = Mars
   *Just* = Jupiter
   *Stores* = Saturn
   *Up* = Uranus
   *Nine* = Neptune
   *Planets* = Pluto

2. A mnemonic is a sentence that helps us remember a piece of information.

3. Answers depend on students.

#### Methodology note

In this context the meaning of the word *rehearsal* is similar to *repetition* or *practice*. *Rehearsal* in general English usually refers to the practice that actors do before the performance of a play.

**B** Understanding an introduction

Revise what students learnt in Lesson 1.2 Real-time listening about the Multi-store memory model.

Set the task. Play the introduction of the lecture in DVD 1.B. Students discuss answers to the questions in pairs. Elicit answers. Check understanding of the word *rehearsal*.

Ask students, *Which researchers say that rehearsal is just repetition?* (Atkinson and Shiffrin)

Students should be able to remember the names of the researchers from Lesson 1.2 Real-time listening.

Answers

1. Researchers disagree about the meaning of *rehearsal*.
2. They agree that rehearsal is necessary.

## Transcript

🔊 1.9  DVD 1.B

Presenter: 1.9. Lesson 1.5. Applying new listening skills: Moving information into long-term memory

Lecturer: In the last lecture, I described how the Multi-store memory model works. We saw what the components are, and I explained how memory is moved through the system. At the end, I mentioned repetition. According to Atkinson and Shiffrin, you need rehearsal to move the information into long-term memory. Atkinson and Shiffrin said that rehearsal is simply repetition. But other researchers disagree. In this lecture, we're going to look at how you can rehearse information. In other words, we'll consider what you can do to move information into long-term memory. We'll also consider how teachers can help students with this process.

**Methodology note**

As this is Theme 1, you may need to explain to students who did not study Level 1 of *Progressive Skills in English* that they will only watch the DVD once in order to complete the task in Exercise C. This is because in real life they will only have one chance to take in information from a lecture. However, they will have another opportunity to watch the DVD for follow-up work and to analyze why they made mistakes.

**C** Following a lecture

Remind students of the work they did in Lesson 1.3 Learning new listening skills about recording sources. Go over the example notes:
*What is the topic?* (variety)
*Who was the researcher?* (Thurgood)
*When did he/she do the research?* (1989)
*What is the title of the research?* (We do not know; remind students this is not important as we can look that up after the lecture.)

Play DVD 1.C as far as the example in order to further check students' understanding of the task.

Play the rest of the DVD. Students complete the task individually, then compare their answers in pairs. Elicit answers, preferably using an electronic projection. Replay any sections of the DVD that students had difficulty with.

Answers

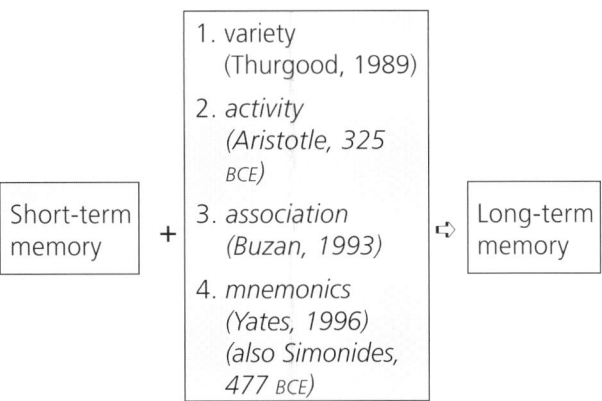

## Transcript

🔊 1.10  DVD 1.C

Lecturer: Firstly, rehearsal involves frequency. Repetition of new information ensures frequency. So, for example, when you hear a new word, you can say it to yourself ten times. But other researchers say repetition is not enough to move information into long-term memory. You need variety as well. A man called Thurgood wrote an article about learning in 1989. I think that's correct – yes, 1989. It is entitled 'The Integrated Memory and the Integrated Syllabus'. Thurgood agreed that you need frequency. But he said you also need variety. For example, you need to read a new word in several different situations. Then you need to hear it in some more situations. Then, perhaps, you need to use it yourself. So, first, rehearsal involves frequency, but second, according to Thurgood and others, it also involves variety. It involves doing different things with new information.

The third idea is activity. More than 2,000 years ago, Aristotle wrote a book in around 325 BCE. It is called *Ethics*. Aristotle said in this book that we learn by doing. So he believed in activity. In fact, he believed it is the only way to learn. So Aristotle was writing about memory and learning in 325 BCE. I find that incredible.

Association is the fourth idea. A little more recently than Aristotle, less than 20 years ago in fact, a man called Tony Buzan wrote a well-known book in 1993. It is called *The Mind Map Book*. In this book, Buzan says that it is very important to make associations between pieces of information. His main method is the mind map. A mind map looks like a spidergram. In a mind map, you draw lines to link information. Buzan says this will help you remember new information. Since 1993, Buzan has written several other books on this subject. Finally, we have the idea of mnemonics. A mnemonic is a clever way of remembering something. For example, perhaps you want to remember the names of the nine planets in our Solar System. There is a well-known mnemonic for this in English: My Very Efficient Memory Just Stores Up Nine Planets.

Frances Yates wrote a book in 1966. It is called *The Art of Memory*. In the book, Yates says that mnemonics were first proposed by a Greek man. This was before Aristotle's time, in around 487 BCE. Sorry, that should be 477 BCE. He was called Simonides. So we can thank Simonides for this useful way of remembering information.

So, according to different researchers in this field, there are at least five ways to rehearse information. They are: frequency, activity, variety, association and mnemonics. You should try all of these methods during your course. See which ones work for you.

## Closure

Choose one of the following activities:

- Discuss with the class which of the activities from the discussion in Exercise D3 they would find most useful.
- Give students copies of the transcript if you have not already done so. You could also play the DVD one more time.
- Check some of the vocabulary in the transcript, e.g., *process*, *involve*, etc.

## D Checking understanding

1. Check students understand the task. Put them in pairs to describe the process to one another.
2. In the same pairs, students answer the questions.
3. Put the pairs together into small groups to discuss this question. Elicit ideas onto the board.

### Answers

1. Students' own answers.
2. a. Aristotle
   b. Tony Buzan
   c. Frances Yates; Simonides
   d. Thurgood
3. Answers depend on students, but they could suggest teachers do the following:
   *variety* = Ask students to read the same word in many different contexts.
   *frequency* = Set repetition, revision activities.
   *activity* = Ask students to use new language in spoken and written sentences, write on the board or do jigsaw activities; encourage students to use new language outside the classroom.
   *association* = Link new language to language students already know; encourage mind maps, spidergrams, to use pictures, put vocabulary into word groups, etc.
   *mnemonics* = Suggest some either in English or in students' own language; encourage students to make up their own.

# Speaking: Learner styles

## 1.6 Vocabulary for speaking: Types of learner

### Objectives

By the end of this lesson, students should be able to:

- show understanding of, and pronounce, target vocabulary from the Speaking section;
- show understanding of different learning types;
- use pauses in appropriate places in spoken sentences.

### Introduction

Choose one of the following activities:

- Use Exercise A as the introduction.
- Revise some of the information about short-term and long-term memory from the Listening section.
- Revise some of the vocabulary from the Listening section.

### A  Activating ideas

Set the task for discussion in pairs. Students should discuss if they agree or disagree with the proverb. Elicit ideas.

### Answers

Answers depend on students.

### Methodology note

Many dictionaries give the pronunciation of the word *aural* as the same as the word *oral*: /ˈɔːrəl/. However, many language teachers and other professionals tend to pronounce the word with the initial vowel sound /aʊ/ in order not to confuse the two words. Here we pronounce the word *aural* as /ˈaʊrəl/. You might wish to point out the two pronunciations of the word and also to explain the difference in meaning between *aural* = 'of the ears' and *oral* = 'of the mouth'.

### B  Understanding new vocabulary

1. Make sure students have covered the text. Give students a minute to study Figure 1. Elicit or explain that the figure shows different types of learner. Play 🔊 1.11. Tell students to listen for the pronunciation of the words and their meanings.

2. Elicit the pronunciation of each word. Practise pronunciation, especially for:
   *visual* /ˈvɪʒʊəl/
   *kinaesthetic* /kɪnəˈθetɪk/
   *aural* /ˈaʊrəl/

   Check understanding of the meaning of each word.

3. Students discuss the figure in pairs. Elicit ideas.

### Answers

2. Answers depend on students.
3. The figure shows that learners are often a mixture of types.

### Transcript

🔊 1.11

**Presenter:** 1.11. Lesson 1.6. Vocabulary for speaking: Types of learner. Exercise B1. Cover the text at the bottom of the page. Look at Figure 1. Listen.

**Lecturer:** How do you learn? If you like pictures, graphs and charts, you are probably a visual learner. *Visual* means 'of the eyes'.

If you like talking about new information with your friends, you are probably an aural learner. *Aural* means 'of the ears'.

If you like using the library and the Internet to find new information, you are probably a read/write learner. In other words, you need to read things or write them to remember them.

If you like to move around when you are studying, you are probably a kinaesthetic learner. *Kinaesthetic* means 'of feeling and movement'.

Finally, if you like to do two or more of these things, you are probably a multi-mode learner. *Mode* means 'method or way or doing something', and *multi* means 'many'. Sixty to seventy per cent of learners are multi-mode.

> **Methodology note**
>
> Exercise C helps students focus on using pauses when they speak. We give a few examples here of when a native speaker would naturally pause in speech. There are several others. However, the most important thing is for students to develop a natural 'feel' for when to pause. This is normally after a 'sense group' of words. For example, the following sentence is marked for sense groups:
> *If you like talking about new information / with your friends, / you are probably an aural learner. //*
>
> However, if you paused as marked in the following sentence, you would probably be almost unintelligible to your listener:
> *If you like / talking about new / information with your / friends, you are / probably an aural learner. //*
>
> Another point worth bearing in mind is that less fluent speakers may need more pauses than more fluent ones:
> *If you like talking about / new information / with your friends, / you are probably / an aural learner. //*
>
> You can also encourage students to keep their intonation raised when they pause, except when they come to a full stop. In this case, the intonation should fall.
>
> Finally, you can mention to students that as well as helping the listener to follow what you are saying, pauses give the speaker time to think about what he/she is going to say next.

### C Producing clear speech

1. Set the task. Tell students to study the Skills Check and elicit answers.
2. Play the first paragraph from 🔊 **1.12**. Discuss where the pauses are:
   *longer pause – after a full stop; before joining words*
   *shorter pause – at commas*
   Write these 'pause rules' on the board.
3. Drill the phrases from the paragraph and check students are using the correct intonation (see Methodology note above). Let students practise in pairs. Monitor.
4. Check students understand the task. Students can discuss and mark up the text in pairs. Play 🔊 **1.11** from the previous exercise again so that students can check their ideas. Discuss and practise with students any phrases they found difficult. Students should have noticed that there is a pause after the word *finally*. Add the rule to the ones already on the board:
   *longer pause – after signpost words, e.g., 'finally'*

   In pairs or small groups, students practise saying the paragraphs. Each student takes a turn to say a paragraph. The others listen and say if the pauses are in the correct place.

### Answers

3/4.

How do you learn? // If you like pictures, / graphs / and charts, / you are probably a visual learner. // *Visual* means 'of the eyes'. //

If you like talking about / new information / with your friends, // you are probably an aural learner. // *Aural* means 'of the ears'. //

If you like using the library / and the Internet / to find new information, // you are probably a read/write learner. // In other words, // you need to read things / or write them / to remember them. //

If you like to move around / when you are studying, / you are probably a kinaesthetic learner. // *Kinaesthetic* means 'of feeling and movement'. //

Finally, // if you like to do two or more / of these things, // you are probably a multi-mode learner. // *Mode* means 'method / or way of doing something', // and *multi* means 'many'. // Sixty to seventy per cent of learners / are multi-mode. //

### Transcript

🔊 1.12

**Presenter:** 1.12. Exercise C2. Listen again to the first paragraph.
**Lecturer:** How do you learn? If you like pictures, graphs and charts, you are probably a visual learner. *Visual* means 'of the eyes'.

### D Using new vocabulary

Divide the class into pairs for the quiz. Students ask each other the questions and make a note of the answers. Check students understand how the scoring works. Students read the text to find out what their score is and what kind of learner they are.

Theme 1: Speaking    37

Redivide the class into groups of four by getting each pair to work with another pair close to them. Students report their results to the other pair and say if they agree or disagree with the analysis.

Finally, ask one person in each group to report on what kind of learner each person in their group is.

Check some of the target vocabulary in the quiz, for example, *recommendation*, *preference*, etc.

Answers
Answers depend on students.

**Closure**

Have a brief discussion on the quiz and the results:
*Can you think of a better question for any of the learner types?*
*How many students are multi-mode learners?*
*How many students disagreed with their results?*

## 1.7 Real-time speaking: The visual learner

### Objectives

By the end of this lesson, students should:
- be familiar with a model of a lecture using explanation and recommendation;
- have attempted to give extracts from a lecture;
- have learnt some common core knowledge about the needs of visual learners.

### Methodology note

In this lesson we have used a 'test-teach-test' methodology in which students 'have a go' at giving an extract from a lecture. This gives you an opportunity to assess the students' spoken ability during this first theme of the course. Students should also be encouraged to assess their own performance as well, of course.

Towards the end of the lesson, students can compare their performance with a model on the DVD.

However, if you prefer, there is no reason why you cannot take a more traditional approach and start with the DVD model first. Follow this up with some controlled practice before asking students to reproduce the complete talk, or sections from it.

**Introduction**

Write the following verbs on the board and elicit the nouns. Check the meanings. Elicit the stressed syllable in each word. Practise the pronunciation of each noun.

| verb | noun |
| --- | --- |
| pre'fer | 'preference |
| recom'mend | recommen'dation |

### A  Activating ideas

Ask students to study the mind map. This explains the preferences of visual learners. Ask students:
- *Are there any visual learners in the class?* (Students should know if they are visual learners because of the quiz they did in Lesson 1.6 Vocabulary for speaking.)
- *Do you find anything surprising about the activities that the visual learners prefer?*
- *Do you agree or disagree with the recommendations?*

Ask students to study the assignment information in the box on the right. Ask students some questions to check understanding:
- *Which faculty has set the assignment?* (Education)
- *Who says there are seven types of learning style?* (the Institute of Learning Styles Research)
- *How many learning styles can you name?* (In Lesson 1.6, students learnt a little about five learning styles: *visual*, *aural*, *read/write*, *kinaesthetic* and *multi-mode*.)
- *What should the lecture be about?* (one learning style)
- *What information should the lecture include?* (learning preferences and recommendations)

Set the task, making sure students understand they are looking for:
(1) the learning preferences of visual learners;
(2) recommendations for visual learners.

Students discuss in pairs. Elicit answers.

Answers

The sections closest to the central title of the mind map give the learning preferences, e.g., *they don't like noise*.

The sections further along each line give the recommendations.

### Methodology note

In Exercise B3, students create three more paragraphs from the talk. We do not expect them to produce the introduction or the summary at this stage.

The talk extract of four paragraphs can be done in a variety of ways. For example:
- In pairs – students can give alternate paragraphs. Alternatively, the first student can give the first two paragraphs, and then the second can give the last two paragraphs.
- In groups of four – each student gives one paragraph of the talk in turn. Alternatively, each student takes it in turn to give the complete talk.

The method you choose will depend on the level of your class and if they are familiar with giving talks in English or not. Pairwork or group work will help students gradually to build up their confidence towards finally being able to give a talk to the whole class later in the course.

### B  Preparing to give a talk

1. Tell the class that the extract explains the 'green line' of information in the mind map. Read the extract aloud with the students following. Elicit which section explains the learning preference. Then elicit the two recommendations.

    Highlight the language used in the extract, preferably using an electronic projection:
    for explaining preferences – 'need' + to do
    for recommendations – 'should' / 'could' + do

    However, do not spend too long on this now as students will practise *should* and *could* in Lesson 1.9 Grammar for speaking.

2. Practise the sentences in the extract with the class, making sure students pause briefly at the end of each sense group. More explanation of sense groups is given in Lesson 1.9.

Remind students of:
- the pronunciation of *visual* /ˈvɪʒʊəl/
- consonant clusters in, for example, *should make* in which the final *d* of *should* is not usually pronounced /ʃʊmaːk/

Divide the class into pairs. Encourage them to practise the extract again, preferably using only prompts rather than reading the whole sentences aloud. Monitor and give feedback.

3. Divide the class into pairs. Students make notes or write out further recommendations for visual learners based on the information in the mind map.

    Finally, students give the four paragraphs as a complete talk (see Methodology note above).

    Monitor and give feedback, reminding students they will have further opportunities to practise problem areas in the follow-up lessons.

    **More able classes:** You may also be able to explain and practise with more able students the intonation patterns for sense groups. The intonation usually stays quite high at the end of the sense group if it is NOT at the end of the sentence. Intonation usually falls at a full stop. More practice will be given in this area in later themes.

Answers

1. Learning preference – they need to see written text; recommendations – make notes, draw diagrams and make flow charts.
2/3. Answers depend on students.

### C  Studying a model

Tell students they are now going to watch a student giving the same talk about visual learners. Students should watch and compare this performance with their own.

Give students time to read through the four questions in the Course Book. Play [DVD] 1.D. Elicit answers. Spend two or three minutes discussing the student's performance on the DVD.

### Optional activities

At this point in the lesson, you have several alternatives:
- Students can watch the DVD again, following the transcript.
- Students give the complete talk, using the transcript or prompts based on the transcript.

- Drill or practise key sentences from the talk.

Answers

1. There are three sections: introduction, main body, conclusion
2. Introduction – what information, order of information
   Main body – learning preferences and recommendations
   Conclusion – reminder of the information
3. *firstly, secondly, thirdly, finally*
4. looks at audience
   looks at cards
   speaks clearly, slowly
   pauses

Transcript

1.13 DVD 1.D

Presenter: 1.13. Lesson 1.7. Learning new speaking skills: The visual learner

Student: According to the Institute for Learning Styles Research, there are seven types of learning style. Today, I'm going talk about one of the seven types, the visual learner. How does the visual learner prefer to learn? How can the visual learner improve learning efficiency? I'll mention some learning preferences and make some recommendations in each case.

Firstly, visual learners need to see written text, so they should make notes of lectures. They could draw diagrams and make flow charts from the notes.

Secondly, they remember visual information. Therefore they should make flashcards of words. They could test themselves or put the flashcards on the walls of their bedroom.

Thirdly, visual learners like colour so therefore, they should use colour for their notes. They could use colour pens during the lecture or they could mark the text later, with circles, underlining and highlighting.

Finally, visual learners don't like noise. Therefore, they should not listen to music while they are studying. They should work in a quiet place.

So, to sum up, I have explained some of the learning preferences of visual learners, and I have also made you some recommendations to improve learning efficiency. If you are a visual learner, try some of the ideas which I have suggested.

### D Developing critical thinking

Students discuss one or both of the questions in small groups. Monitor for the correct pronunciation of target vocabulary. Elicit ideas.

Answers

Answers depend on students.

**Closure**

Practise the pronunciation of any target words students had difficulty with during the lesson.

### Everyday English: Making friends

### Objectives

By the end of this lesson, students should be able to:
- use appropriate language to socialize with other new students.

**Introduction**

Hold a brief class discussion about the students' experiences of arriving at their present university or institution. Who were the first people they met?

### A Activating ideas

1. Elicit one or two ideas, and then put students into pairs to discuss the question.

   Give feedback orally. Accept all reasonable suggestions.

2. Elicit ideas for Picture 1. Set the task for pairwork or small group discussion.

   Give feedback orally, eliciting what is happening in each picture. Accept all reasonable answers. Make sure you cover the following words, which appear later in the lesson: *course, halls (of residence), seminar, tutorial*.

Answers

1. Answers depend on students.
2. Answers depend on students, but here are some suggestions:
   Picture 1 – lectures, lessons
   Picture 2 – around the town, the local area, the campus
   Picture 3 – arriving, travel
   Picture 4 – courses
   Picture 5 – study bedrooms, studying
   Picture 6 – meeting tutors

## B Studying models

1. Cover the conversations. Go through the six questions with the class. Clarify any problems. Set the task for pairwork. Elicit ideas.
2. Set the task for individual work and pairwork checking.
Play 🔘 1.14. Give feedback orally.

### Optional activity

Review or work on the language in the conversations.

**present perfect forms**

*Have you been into town yet?*

*Have you met your tutor?*

*How long have you been here?*

**present continuous for future reference**

*I'm going today.*

**be + like**

*What's she like?*

**useful phrases**

*full time; on campus; as well; know (one's) way around*

### Answers

1. What course are you doing?
2. Are you staying on campus?
3. Have you been into town yet?
4. Have you met your tutor?
5. How long have you been here?
6. When are your lectures?

## Transcript

🔘 1.14

Presenter: 1.14. Everyday English: Making friends. Exercise B2. Listen and complete the conversations.

    One.
Student A: What course are you doing?
Student B: Environmental Science.
Student A: Is that a BSc?
Student B: Yes. It's three years, full time.

Presenter: Two.
Student A: Are you staying on campus?
Student B: Yes. I'm in the halls of residence. It's really good.
Student A: Are the rooms shared or single?
Student B: They're all single study bedrooms.

Presenter: Three.
Student A: Have you been into town yet?
Student B: No, not yet. Have you?
Student A: I'm going today. I've got a map here.
Student B: Oh great. Can I come with you?

Presenter: Four.
Student A: Have you met your tutor?
Student B: Yes, I went to her office yesterday.
Student A: What's her name?
Student B: I've forgotten. But she seems really nice.

Presenter: Five.
Student A: How long have you been here?
Student B: I arrived on Sunday by train. You?
Student A: I've been here for a week.
Student B: So you know your way around then?

Presenter: Six.
Student A: When are your lectures?
Student B: I've got five hours a week, on three days.
Student A: My lectures are on Monday and Friday.
Student B: Oh, that means no long weekends for you then?
Student A: Yes, it's a bit annoying.

## C Practising the model

1. Set the task for pairwork. Monitor and assist with students' pronunciation. Note any common pronunciation errors. Play 🔘 1.14 again if you wish.
2. Demonstrate the task with one of the students. Continue the conversation for a short time, but keep it on the original topic.

Set the task for pairwork. Do a further example if you wish. Monitor and assist. Again, make a note of common problems and errors.

As feedback, ask volunteers to perform one of their role plays.

## Closure

1. Go over any errors that you picked up during your monitoring.
2. Ask students to cover the texts in the Course Book and look at the pictures. They must try to remember the conversation.

### 1.8 Learning new speaking skills: Giving a short talk

### Objectives

By the end of this lesson, students should be able to:

- discriminate between words with similar vowel sounds;
- practise target sub-skills by giving a talk about themselves.

**Note:** You will need to bring sets of file cards (also known as library cards) to the lesson. Failing this, you can use any squares of card or pieces of paper. This is for students to make notes on for giving a talk. You can also suggest students buy their own sets of cards as they are very useful for vocabulary, revision notes, etc.

### Introduction
Use Exercise A as the introduction.

### A Reviewing vowel sounds

1. Use an electronic projection to show the phonemic script (only) for each word in the Pronunciation Check box. See if students can work out the correct word. Then practise the pronunciation. Reassure students they do not need to learn the phonemic script, but by referring to a phonemic chart and a dictionary, they can work out the pronunciation of new words. Play 1.15 to confirm correct pronunciation, if you wish.

2. Divide the class into small groups of three or four. Students discuss the meaning and pronunciation of each word. If nobody in the group knows the word, they can look up the meaning and pronunciation in a dictionary.

   Still in groups, students take it in turns to pronounce one word in each pair. The others identify the correct word.

   Monitor while students are working. Practise the pronunciation of any pairs of words students are having difficulty with.

### Transcript

 1.15

Presenter: 1.15. Lesson 1.8. Learning new speaking skills: Giving a short talk. Pronunciation Check.
Voice: pat, part; pet, pert; pit, Pete; pot, port; putt, put; pout, pate

### Answers
1. There are 12 vowel sounds in the examples.
2. Answers depend on students.

### B Identifying a key skill

Students discuss the questions in pairs. Elicit ideas but do not confirm or correct any at this stage.

Students read the Skills Check. Check students understand the information. Refer students back to the talk on the DVD they watched in Lesson 1.7 Real-time speaking and ask if the student followed all the advice in the Skills Check.

> **Methodology note**
>
> Since we are still near the beginning of a new course, Exercise C is a good opportunity for students to get to know each other a little better. On this occasion students do not have to research information, but they do need to organize and express it clearly.

### C Rehearsing a model

1. Elicit ideas and possible sentences for the talk. Make a list of suggestions on the board. You can suggest other related topics for students to talk about – for example, why they are on this course and why they chose this university. They could also talk about their nationality or which town/country they come from.

   Remind students about tenses, for example, they can use the past simple to talk about previous schools, etc.

   Drill some of the most useful sentences or phrases.

   Students should make notes on file cards or pieces of paper. Monitor and give help where necessary.

2. Monitor while students give their talks. If necessary, stop the class and remind them about the skills they should be using, looking at the audience, for example.

   Give feedback, focusing on what students did well, as well as what they need to work on.

### D Evaluation

Students discuss the questions in their groups. Monitor and find out who was the 'best' student in each group. If you think it is appropriate, you could ask two or three of the 'best' students to give their talks to the whole class.

### Closure
Use flashcards of the words in Exercise A and/or the words from the Pronunciation Check.

### 1.9 Grammar for speaking: should / could; so / because

#### Objectives

By the end of this lesson, students should be able to:
- pronounce and form sentences with *should* and *could* for recommendations and possibilities;
- produce sentences with *so* and *because*.

### Introduction

Ask students if they can remember the recommendations for visual learners. If you wish, play [DVD] 1.D from Lesson 1.7 Real-time speaking again.

#### Methodology note

Native speakers would not normally pronounce the final *d* sound in *should* or *could* when followed by another consonant. For example:
*should make* /ʃʊmeɪk/
*could draw* /kʊdrɔː/

However, current thinking in EFL suggests that non-native speakers should not be expected to pronounce *should* and *could* in this way. As long as students do not pronounce the final *d* with an exploded plosive sound, it will not impede comprehensibility. Students must be aware of this pronunciation area so that they can recognize the modals when listening.

### Grammar box 3

Ask students to read the information and study the table for a minute or two. Check understanding:

- *When do we use* should? (for strong recommendations)
- *When do we use* could? (for suggestions, ideas, alternatives)

Drill the words *should* and *could* to check students are using the correct vowel sounds. Then drill the sentences in the tables. Play 1.16, if you wish.

### Transcript

🎧 1.16

Presenter: 1.16. Lesson 1.9. Grammar for speaking: *should / could; so / because*. Grammar box 3.
Voice: Visual learners should make notes of all lectures.
They could draw diagrams.
They could make flow charts.

#### A Talking about recommendations

Ask students to look at the *should* situations. Make sure students understand the situations.

Students discuss possible recommendations in pairs. Monitor. Elicit ideas. Drill some of the recommendations that students suggest.

Ask students to write a few of the answers for consolidation.

#### Answers

Answers depend on the students, but here are some possibilities:
1. You should explain the reason to your tutor.
2. You should leave immediately by the fire exit.
3. You should refuse the offer.
4. You should go to bed early.
5. You should ask the bank for a loan.

#### B Talking about suggestions

Ask students to look at the *could* situations. Make sure students understand the situations and that they see there is more than one possibility for each situation.

Students discuss possible suggestions in pairs. Monitor. Elicit ideas. Drill some of the suggestions.

Ask students to write a few of the answers for consolidation.

#### Answers

Answers depend on the students, but here are some possibilities:
1. You could ask another student for help. / You could ask the tutor to explain it to you.
2. You could go to the accommodation office.
3. You could relax. / You could go away.
4. You could make a housework rota. / You could spend the whole weekend tidying and cleaning!
5. You could find some recipes on the Internet. / You could get a takeaway!

**Grammar box 4**

Check students understand the information in the tables. Drill the sentences, making sure students pause in the appropriate places as the sentences are quite long. Play 1.17, if you wish.

Transcript

1.17

Presenter: 1.17. Grammar box 4.

Voice: Visual learners need to see written text so they should make notes of lectures.
Because visual learners need to see written text, they should make notes of lectures.
Visual learners should make notes of lectures because they need to see written text.

**C  Giving reasons**

The task – giving a reason for the recommendations in Exercise A – is quite difficult, so you will need to set it carefully. Elicit several examples, or give prompts for answers before students continue in pairs. Give feedback and choose the best reason in each case.

Answers

Answers depend on the students, but here are some possibilities based on the sentences in Exercise A:
1. You should explain the reason to your tutor because then he/she will still mark it.
2. You should leave immediately because it might be dangerous. / It might be a real fire so you should leave immediately.
3. You should refuse the offer because it is dishonest. / It is dishonest so you should refuse the offer. / Because it is dishonest, you should refuse the offer.
4. You should go to bed early because you need to be fresh for the test. / You need to be fresh so you should go to bed early. / Because the test is important, you need to go to bed early the night before.
5. You should ask the bank for a loan because you must pay your rent on time.

**Closure**

Ask students to make some recommendations for a new student at their university or institution.

## 1.10 Applying new speaking skills: The aural learner

**Objectives**

By the end of this lesson, students should be able to:
- give a talk with recommendations using target language and sub-skills from the theme;
- show understanding of common core knowledge regarding aural and kinaesthetic learners.

**Introduction**

Show the mind map from Lesson 1.7 Real-time speaking on the board, using an electronic projection. Use the mind map to revise information and recommendations for visual learners.

**Methodology note**

Exercise A previews some of the sentence patterns and vocabulary that students will need for their talk. It is therefore a good idea to spend a few minutes drilling the sentences when you have elicited the correct answers.

**A  Previewing vocabulary**

Set the task. Students complete the activity individually, then compare answers in pairs. Elicit answers. Remind students about sense groups (see Lesson 1.6 Vocabulary for speaking). If there is time, students can mark the sentences for sense groups. Drill the sentences, focusing on the following:
- pausing for sense groups
- pronunciation of *should* and *could*
- pronunciation of *visual*, *recommendations*, *preferences*, etc.

Answers
1. According *to* the Institute for Learning Styles Research, there are seven types of learning style.
2. Today, I'm going to talk *about* one of the seven types, the visual learner.
3. How *does* the visual learner prefer to learn?
4. How *can* the visual learner improve learning efficiency?

5. I'll mention some learning preferences and make recommendations in each case.
6. Visual learners *should* make notes of lectures.
7. They *could* draw diagrams or make flow charts from the notes.
8. *Because* visual learners like colour, they should use colour for their notes.
9. I *have* explained some of the learning preferences of visual learners.
10. *If* you are a visual learner, try some of the ideas that I have suggested.

### B Activating ideas

Divide the class into:

- Group A – aural learners
- Group B – kinaesthetic learners

If you have a large class, you may need to have two or three groups for each learning style.

Students discuss the questions to see if they can predict any of the information for their learning type. Monitor and assist where necessary.

Answers
Answers depend on students.

### C Researching information

Briefly discuss which method students prefer (notes, mind map or spidergram) and perhaps the advantages or disadvantages of each one.

Make sure each group is looking at the correct text. Monitor while students make notes.

Answers
Answers depend on students.

**Methodology note**

See the Introduction in the Teacher's Book (page 19) for detailed notes on how to monitor and give feedback on these freer speaking activities.

Students can either work in pairs for Exercise D2 or in groups of four or six, with half the students from each original group. Larger groups will give students practice in speaking in front of an audience. If there is not time for every student to give their talk in a larger group, make sure you make a note of which students have missed out and give them the opportunity another time.

### D Using a key skill

1. Go through each of the points and elicit examples where possible as you go along. Alternatively, you could have the mind map and/or transcript from the talk in Lesson 1.7 Real-time speaking on an electronic projection and refer to those for each point.

   If they wish, students can write out the talk in full. However, they should not give the talk from full sentences, but from notes.

   Students should help each other to practise sentences from the talk. Monitor and give feedback.

2. Encourage students to stand up when giving their talks. 'Listening' students should make notes on the information given in the talk. Listening students can also give feedback on whether the talk was clear, spoken at the right speed and if there was eye contact with the speaker. Monitor and give feedback on common errors noted.

Answers
Model talks:

<u>The aural learner</u>

According to the Institute for Learning Styles Research, there are seven types of learning style. Today, I'm going to talk about one of the seven types, the aural learner. How does the aural learner learn? How can aural learners improve their learning efficiency?

Firstly, aural learners like to *hear* new information so they should read all their notes aloud. They could record them and listen to them later.

Secondly, they need to talk about new information. They should discuss lectures and reading assignments with other students. They could form a discussion group, or they could talk to another student on the phone.

Finally, aural learners need aural reminders. Therefore, they should make mnemonics of key information, like lists. They could say the mnemonics in their heads to help them remember.

So to sum up. I have explained some of the learning preferences of aural learners, and I have also made some recommendations to improve their learning efficiency. If you are an aural learner, try some of the ideas that I have suggested.

<u>The kinaesthetic learner</u>

According to the Institute for Learning Styles Research, there are seven types of learning style. Today, I'm going to talk about one of the seven types, the kinaesthetic learner. How does the kinaesthetic learner prefer to learn? How can kinaesthetic learners improve their learning efficiency?

Firstly, kinaesthetic learners learn better by doing something. So they should make learning into a physical activity. They could write new information on cards. Then they could lay out the cards on a table and arrange the cards in different ways.

Secondly, kinaesthetic learners do not like to sit still, so they should walk around while they are studying. They could record information and listen to it while they are jogging.

Finally, because kinaesthetic learners use a lot of energy in learning, they should take a lot of breaks during study.

So to sum up. I have explained some of the learning preferences of kinaesthetic learners, and I have also made some recommendations to improve their learning efficiency. If you are a kinaesthetic learner, try some of the ideas that I have suggested.

**Closure**

Give out copies of the model talks for students to compare with their own versions.

If you think it is appropriate, you can ask some of the more able students to give their talks to the whole class.

# Reading: Improving your memory

**Methodology note**

The following words were taught for this skill and theme at Level 1 of *Progressive Skills in English*. If your students studied this theme and skill at Level 1, you may wish to revise or teach some of them.

| | |
|---|---|
| accurate (*adj*) | plagiarize (*v*) |
| analyze (*v*) | portal (*n*) |
| attachment (*n*) | primary (*adj*) |
| cut (*v*) | program (*n*) |
| data (*n*) | record (*n* and *v*) |
| domain (*n*) | relax (*v*) |
| efficiently (*adv*) | remind (*v*) |
| extracurricular (*adj*) | respect (*v*) |
| heading (*n*) | search engine |
| (the) Internet (*n*) | secondary (*adj*) |
| link (*n*) | sensibly (*adj*) |
| manage (*v*) | source (*n*) |
| mark (*n* and *v*) | subheading (*n*) |
| opinion (*n*) | topic (*n*) |
| out (*adj*) | virus (*n*) |
| password (*n*) | webpage (*n*) |
| paste (*v*) | website (*n*) |
| permission (*n*) | wireless (*adj*) |
| plagiarism (*n*) | |

## 1.11 Vocabulary for reading: Internal and external factors

**Objectives**

By the end of this lesson, students should be able to:

- recognize and understand target vocabulary from the Reading section;
- show understanding of information about internal and external factors.

**Introduction**

Use Exercise A as the introduction.

**Methodology note**

Exercise A revises some of the words about memory and remembering from the Listening section, which will also be useful for this section. If your students are not very confident with these words, you can go back and repeat them. For example, you can use Exercise D in Lesson 1.1 Vocabulary for listening and Exercise C in Lesson 1.4 Grammar for listening, and the related grammar tables.

### A Reviewing words

Check students understand the task. Remind students to use the correct tense (all the answers are verbs). Students complete the table individually, then compare their answers in pairs. Elicit answers.

Discuss some of the problem areas, for example, *remember* vs *recall*: *recall* is only used when we are trying to remember something deliberately or consciously; *remember* can be used for both conscious and unconscious remembering.

**Less able classes:** Put all the answers (verbs) in the infinitive on the board, in the wrong order. Students write the verbs in the correct tense in the correct places.

### Answers

The other day I noticed a new *research* assistant in the laboratory. We were at school together. I *recognized* his face but I couldn't *recall* his name. I suddenly *remembered* it a few days later. I was *revising* some notes about memory on my computer. I saw the name *Miller*. That *reminded* me of my friend's name – Adam Miller. So that's a real-life example of how we *retrieve* information from the brain.

### B Understanding new words in context

Exploit the visuals. Encourage students to produce sentences such as *He looks bored*, *The room is noisy*, etc.

Students read the rubrics. Check understanding of the meanings of *internal* and *external factors*, and *concentrate* (or you can leave students to infer their meanings from context during the activity). Set the task and go over the example. Point out the adjective *bored* and

Theme 1: Reading 47

show how we need the noun form *boredom* in the sentence.

Students complete the task individually. Elicit answers pointing out that as long as students have grouped the internal and external factors correctly, it does not matter which order the nouns come in.

Ask students if they can think of any other internal or external factors that can stop you concentrating, for example:
*feeling unwell*
*interruptions (from people, the phone, etc.)*
*disturbances*
*problems with equipment*

Ask students to make a sentence with each noun. Alternatively, they can use the following sentences as a basis for a completion or prompt activity:
*One of the main causes of traffic accidents is tiredness.*
*Problems with teenagers are often caused by boredom.*
*Thirst and hunger are serious problems in developing countries.*
*Noise is becoming as serious as other types of pollution.*
*Some badly designed office chairs can cause serious discomfort.*

### Answers

**Note:** As already pointed out, the words can also come in other orders, as long as students have not confused internal and external factors.

I investigated the internal and external factors which affect *concentration*. There were ten participants from the university. All of them said that the main problem was *boredom*. Other internal factors were also important. Four of them talked about *tiredness*, and three mentioned *hunger* and *thirst*. Two people referred to external factors. One complained about *discomfort* and one mentioned *noise* in her study area.

### C Understanding new phrases in context

Elicit ideas to complete each sentence, with students' pens down. Check understanding of each phrase. Students complete each sentence individually; they can either use some of the ideas from the elicitation stage or they can write their own ideas. Monitor and give help where necessary. Make a note of which students have produced particularly good or interesting sentences, and ask some of them to read out one or two sentences at the end. Give feedback on any common errors.

### Answers

Answers depend on students.

### Closure

1. Students' books closed. Write the first word from each of the phrases in Exercise C on the board. Ask students to copy the word and complete the phrase.

2. Ask students to tick the words from the word list that they have covered in this lesson. Ask students to give you the meanings of any of the remaining words that they know.

## 1.12 Real-time reading: Remembering learnt information

### Objectives

By the end of this lesson, students should be able to:
- use context to complete missing information in a text;
- show understanding of a text describing revision schedules for students;
- show understanding of target vocabulary in context.

### Introduction

Use Exercise A as the introduction.

### A Activating ideas

Set the task for students to discuss in pairs. If students have not done an academic test recently, or prefer to discuss other types of test (such as driving tests or training qualifications), that is also acceptable.

Briefly give feedback to the class. Elicit the fact that practice and/or revision of key information was almost certainly key in the students' success – or the lack of it – in tests.

### Answers

Answers depend on students.

### B  Predicting content

Make sure that students understand the word *forever* (note that the spelling *for ever* is also possible).

1. Tell students to cover the text, leaving only the title visible. Set the discussion for small groups. Give feedback orally. Encourage students to give reasons for their opinions. Accept all reasoned ideas.

2. Go through the sentences and the example, clarifying any vocabulary problems. Point out that students do not need to know the answers, but must use their knowledge and opinions to decide whether the statements are true or false. Set the task for individual work; then students in pairs or small groups can compare their ideas.

   As feedback, elicit ideas but do not confirm or correct at this stage (students will look for the real answers in Exercise C). Again, ensure that students support their ideas with reasons.

### Answers

1. Answers depend on students.
2. See Answers for Exercise D.

---

**Methodology note**

Exercise C is a type of task that students have not come across before in this course. However, they will meet it in many public examinations, e.g., the Cambridge First Certificate in English (FCE) Reading exam. To do the task successfully, students must learn to follow a certain procedure:
– read through all the sentences;
– read the text without completing the gaps;
– complete the sentences that they are sure of;
– complete the rest of the sentences.

---

### C  Understanding the paragraph structure

Set the task. Point out that students will need to refer to the graph as well as to the body of the text. Ask them to follow the procedure described in the Methodology note above. In the first stage, help students with any vocabulary problems in the sentences in the table.

Give feedback, using an electronic projection of the text.

### Answers

<u>Can you remember things forever?</u>

Do you remember everything that you learnt at school? Everybody knows that the human brain cannot remember everything. (4) *However, science has not discovered the exact reason for this.* We do not have a complete picture of human memory.

Forgetting is a natural process. In Figure 1, the red line on the graph shows that, within 24 hours of learning, you have forgotten nearly 80 per cent of the new information. (2) *After a month, only about ten per cent remains.* In Education, we need to consider how to mitigate this loss of information.

Research shows that revision is the key. You must take the information out of your memory, use it, and store it again, several times. Then it will become fixed, and it will stay in your memory for years. (1) *The need to repeat this process many times was first described in the 1930s by Cecil Mace.* Mace's theory was later used to design a novel system of flashcards for learning languages (Leitner, 2003).

In everyday life, we repeat this cycle of retrieval–use–storage without thinking. (5) *Take, for example, how to ride a bicycle, a very happy event in your life, or the way to your home.* You have retrieved that information hundreds of times so you have not forgotten it. In the field of academic study, the repetition comes from recall. In other words, the student purposely finds the information in their memory, brings it out and reviews it. Then he/she stores it again. (8) *We call this 'revision'.*

(7) *You must continue to retrieve information if you want to remember it forever.* Each retrieval should happen at a longer interval, according to the idea of 'spaced repetition' (Mace, 1932). The first review is very important and should be after only ten minutes. As the blue line on the graph shows, this review actually boosts memory to 100 per cent. However, if you do not look at the information again, you still forget nearly everything. (3) *Note that the same line is at a level of only 20 per cent after six months.* Review the information again after, say, one day, one month and then six months (see the green line on the graph). You will then remember the information forever.

Since the 1960s, new research has indicated that information is connected in our memory.

The connections have two important features. Firstly, we can retrieve groups of connected ideas more readily than single ideas. (6) *So make connections with other pieces of knowledge when you review information.* Secondly, if you retrieve and store information often, the connections become stronger. So it is better to spend a short time on retrieval every few weeks rather than a long time on retrieval every few months.

### D  Understanding the text

Set the task for pairwork or small group discussion, without allowing students to reread the text. If you wish, you can allow the group to reread the text to check their answers.

Give feedback orally. Elicit which piece(s) of information in the text the students have based their answers on.

#### Answers

a. Modern scientists understand how human memory works.
   False – *Everybody knows that the human brain cannot remember everything. However, science has not discovered the exact reason for this. We do not have a complete picture of human memory.*

b. Reviewing information helps you remember it.
   True – *In Education, we need to consider how to mitigate this loss of information. Research shows that revision is the key.*

c. We review information about our lives without thinking.
   True – *In everyday life, we repeat this cycle of retrieval–use–storage without thinking. Take, for example, …*

d. A student needs to review the same information every day.
   False – *Each retrieval should happen at a longer interval, according to the idea of 'spaced repetition' …*

e. Without review, you will forget about 90 per cent of the information in a month.
   True – *After a month, only about ten per cent remains.*

f. It is not possible to remember 100 per cent of information for six months.
   False – *According to the green line on the graph, 100 per cent of the information can be remembered for six months.*

g. You should pay attention to connections between ideas when you study.
   True – *… we can retrieve groups of connected ideas more readily than single ideas.*

#### Methodology note

The skill practised in Exercise E will be worked on explicitly in Lesson 1.15 Applying new reading skills, so there is no need to spend too much time on it here.

### E  Working with vocabulary

1. Elicit ideas for the part of speech of the first highlighted word, *mitigate*. Set the task for pairwork. Give feedback orally, using an electronic projection of the text. Elicit from students what features of the text tell them the part of speech – even if they think they know the meaning of the word.

2. Students may have met some of the words before. However, in this case they should base their definition on the context. Do not allow the use of dictionaries at this stage.

   Set the task for individual work. Students compare their ideas in pairs.

   Give feedback orally. Encourage students to give reasons for their definitions, and praise all reasonable efforts. The task here is to use the context sensibly rather than to arrive at the exact dictionary definition.

3. Set the task for individual work and pairwork checking. Monitor and assist as necessary. Again, do not insist that students find synonyms or near-synonyms for the words. The point of the task is that they use the context to help them think of a word with a similar kind of meaning.

   Give feedback orally. Allow students to look up the words in their dictionary to check their ideas.

#### Answers
1. • *mitigate* – verb. It comes after the subject and a modal verb, and before the object *this loss*.
   • *novel* – adjective. It comes between an article and a noun.
   • *storage* – noun. It comes in a phrase with two other nouns. It looks like the word *store*, but *store* is used as a verb elsewhere in the text, so *storage* is probably a noun. Similarly, *retrieval* must

be a noun form, as the verb *retrieve* is used later. The word *use* can be either a noun or a verb, but the context of this phrase tells us it must be the noun here.
- *purposely* – adverb. It ends with *~ly* and comes between the subject and the verb.
- *interval* – noun. It comes after an article + adjective.
- *boosts* – verb. It comes between two nouns, a subject and an object; it ends in *~s*.
- *readily* – adverb.

2. Definitions depend on the students. Real definitions of the highlighted words might be:
   - *mitigate* – make less the negative effect of something
   - *novel* – different from anything that has gone before
   - *storage* – a system or place for keeping something
   - *purposely* – with intention; for a reason
   - *interval* – a space of time
   - *boosts* – pushes up; makes bigger
   - *readily* – without a lot of effort

3. Again, these depend on the students, but some suggestions are:
   - *mitigate* – reduce
   - *novel* – original, new, innovative
   - *storage* – putting back, putting away, keeping
   - *purposely* – deliberately, on purpose
   - *interval* – gap, space, period
   - *boosts* – increases
   - *readily* – easily

## Closure
Exploit the text further, as follows:
- Write or show the first sentence from each paragraph on the board. Read phrases/sentences from the text at random. Each time, students must say which paragraph they come from, then check by quickly finding the phrase/sentence in the text.
- Give information from the text but make mistakes. Students must correct you.
- Read the text and pause at key points. Students must supply the next word.
- Ask students to use the information in the text to give advice to new students, using *should*.

Example:
*You should review information four or five times. You shouldn't wait until the next day to start reviewing.*

### 1.13 Learning new reading skills: Dealing with research texts

**Objectives**

By the end of this lesson, students should be able to:
- recognize target vocabulary from the theme using the first few letters;
- distinguish between fact and prediction and advice in a written text;
- read a simple line graph.

**Methodology note**

In Level 1 of *Progressive Skills in English*, text-attack skills are developed carefully. For Level 2, it is assumed that students will have some of these crucial skills in place. The introduction to this lesson contains three tasks, focusing on *before* reading, *while* reading and *after* reading. It is much longer than the introduction tasks in the rest of the themes and may take up a large part of the lesson, but as text-attack skills are central to reading skills development, you should not skip these exercises. You will need to prepare worksheets or visual media.

The same text-attack skills will be practised in Lesson 1.15 Applying new reading skills.

## Introduction

1. Elicit from students the fact that before they read a new text they can predict a lot of its content. Ask them how they can do this.

   Put the following on the board and ask students, in pairs, to decide on the best order for doing these things so that they can predict the content of a text.
   a. *use the introduction/first paragraph*
   b. *use any illustrations*
   c. *use the title/heading*
   d. *use the topic sentences of the other paragraphs*

   Write feedback on the board or use visual media to show the answers.

2. Elicit the fact that new words are one of the main problems while reading a new text. Display the flow chart in Answers below. Ask students to decide whether the following statements are true or false. They must correct the false statements.

   a. *When you meet a new word in a text, you should immediately look it up in a dictionary.*

b. *You should never look up a new word while you are reading.*
   c. *You should decide the part of speech before looking up a word in the dictionary.*

   Set the task for small group discussion.

   Give feedback to the class as a whole using the flow chart.

3. Elicit things that students can do after reading a text to help them remember the content. Accept all reasonable answers.

   Display or give out the following gapped text for completion. They should complete it using the words in the box. Set the task for individual work and pairwork checking.

   Give feedback using an electronic projection.

   | highlight | notes | illustration | reaction |
   |---|---|---|---|
   |  | summary | vocabulary |  |

   After reading a text you can:
   - Write a _____ of the information in one or two sentences.
   - Draw an _____ or a graph of the information.
   - _____ important points in the text.
   - Make _____ of the information.
   - Add new words to your _____ lists.
   - Think about your personal _____ to the text:
     a. Do you think it is true in general, or for you in particular?
     b. Will the information change your behaviour in any way?

   ### Answers
   1. The correct order is:
      - use the title/heading (c)
      - use any illustrations (b)
      - use the introduction/first paragraph (a)
      - use the topic sentences of the other paragraphs (d)
   2. a. False – you should try to understand the sentence without the word first. Then you should try to understand it from context.
      b. False – it is correct to look up a word after you have tried ignoring it and guessing its meaning.
      c. True – this will guide you to the correct part of the dictionary entry for the word.

New word?
↓
Underline it.
↓
Can I understand the sentence without the word?

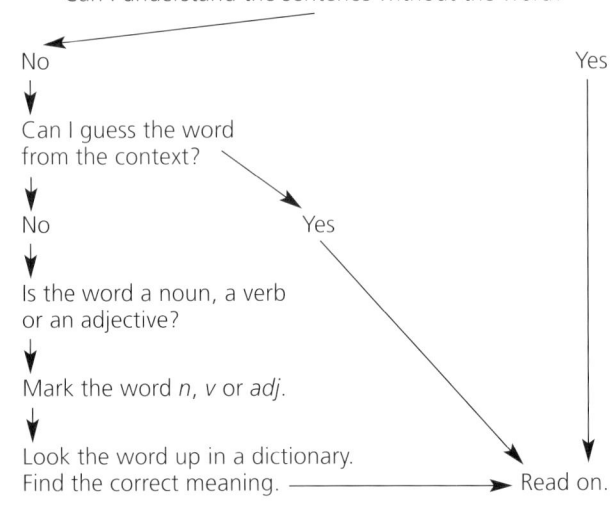

No ←                         Yes
↓
Can I guess the word from the context?
↓
No           Yes
↓
Is the word a noun, a verb or an adjective?
↓
Mark the word *n*, *v* or *adj*.
↓
Look the word up in a dictionary. Find the correct meaning. ⟶ Read on.

3. Target words are in *italics*.

   After reading a text you can:
   - Write a *summary* of the information in one or two sentences.
   - Draw an *illustration* or a graph of the information.
   - *Highlight* important points in the text.
   - Make *notes* of the information.
   - Add new words to your *vocabulary* lists.
   - Think about your personal *reaction* to the text:
     a. Do you think it is true in general, or for you in particular?
     b. Will the information change your behaviour in any way?

### A   Reviewing vocabulary

Refer the students to the Course Book.

Go over the example and make sure that students understand what they have to do. Do another example if you wish.

Set the task for individual work and pairwork checking.

Give feedback using an electronic projection.

### Answers
1. se*ver*al
2. int*erv*al
3. ret*rieval*
4. rem*ember*
5. for*getting* / for*gotten*
6. rep*etition* / rep*eat*
7. l*oss*

**52**    Theme 1: Reading

8. fixed
9. store / storage
10. reviews / revise

### B  Identifying a new skill (1)

1. Give students time to read through Skills Check 1. Clarify any problems. Then tell them to cover the Skills Check. Elicit the three functions mentioned and the type of language which can indicate each one. With a more able class, ask the students to try to remember the example sentences, which are all from the text in the previous lesson.

2. Go over the example. Set the task for individual work and pairwork checking. Give feedback using a copy of the sentences on the board.

3. Refer students to the text in the previous lesson. Give them time to find at least one example of each function in the text. Monitor and assist as necessary.

   Give feedback to the class as a whole, ideally using an electronic projection.

### Answers

1. general facts = present simple
   past facts = past simple
   predictions = *will / may / might*
   advice = *must / imperative*

2. a. The solution will become clear. P
   b. You should do exercise once a week. A
   c. The first king of a united England was Athelstan (899–1016 CE). PF
   d. This is a new area of research. GF
   e. Always carry a book in your bag. A
   f. The company will expect you to meet customers. P
   g. You must do all your tasks on time. A
   h. You will probably lose contact with friends from early childhood. P
   i. Average temperature falls as you move away from the Equator. GF
   j. The research was conducted by Atkinson and Shiffrin. PF

3. Answers depend on the students, but some examples are:

   **general facts**
   *We do not have a complete picture of human memory.*

   **past facts**
   *The need to repeat this process many times was first described in the 1930s by Cecil Mace.*

   **predictions**
   *Then it will become fixed, and it will stay in your memory for years.*
   *You will then remember the information forever.*

   **advice**
   *Each retrieval should happen at a longer interval.*
   *Make connections with other pieces of knowledge when you review information.*

> **Methodology note**
>
> Before doing Exercise C, you may wish to review verbs and expressions for describing graphs, but do so briefly. Remember that this is a reading lesson, so do not expect students to describe graphs here, either orally or in writing.

### C  Identifying a new skill (2)

Refer students to the line graph at the bottom of the page, which in fact refers to Peterson and Peterson's research (1959) studied in the Listening section of this theme. Get students to identify the elements:
horizontal axis = time in seconds
vertical axis = percentage of information remembered
the line = shows that the percentage remembered falls steeply with time

1. Go through Skills Check 2 with the class. Clarify any vocabulary problems. Again, tell students to cover the Skills Check and elicit the four expressions used to refer to graphs.

   **Note:** These phrases are fairly fixed and can be learnt as such. However, you may also wish to point out that the tense used to describe graphs (and other illustrations) is usually the present simple, and not the present continuous.

2. Give students time to study the graphs on page 177 of the Course Book. Ask them to discuss briefly, in small groups, what the graphs show (they do not need to guess exactly what processes are represented).

   Set the task for individual work and pairwork checking. Monitor and assist as necessary. Give feedback orally.

Answers

a. As the yellow line shows, the temperature rises quickly. *Graph 4*

b. Fig. 1 shows the initial results. *Graph 1*

c. … (see the red line in Figure 6). *Graph 2*

d. Note the change in speed at 30m. *Graph 3*

e. Note the pressure at 12 seconds (black line). *Graph 1*

f. The blue and orange lines in the graph are very similar. *Graph 2*

**Closure**

1. Do some further vocabulary review: write the first two or three letters of words from the theme on the board. Students must say the word.

2. Give some more statements about the graphs as further practice. If you have a more able class, ask volunteers to give the statements themselves. The other students must say which of the graphs is being described.

### 1.14 Grammar for reading: The complex noun phrase

**Objectives**

By the end of this lesson, students should be able to:
- show understanding of the basic SVO / C sentence structure;
- identify extra information about the subject and the object.

**Introduction**

Elicit the basic elements of a sentence: subject, verb, object and complement, and the meaning of these terms.

**A** Identifying SVO structure

Give students time to read **Grammar box 5**. Then, with the first table covered, elicit the three example sentences and ask students to tell you which part is the subject, the verb and the object in each case. Elicit answers and give feedback.

Go over the example in Exercise A with the class. Point out that the sentence comes from the text in Lesson 1.12 Real-time reading on page 25 of the Course Book. Do a further example with the class if you wish. Set the task for individual work and pairwork checking. Point out that students should mark a single word for the subject and object where possible – they should ignore articles.

Monitor and assist as necessary.

Give feedback using an electronic projection of the answers.

Get students to cover the page and ask them to try to expand the basic SVO. They can do this by using information from the original sentences or from their own ideas.

Note: The sentences in this exercise and in Exercise B are taken – with slight changes – from the reading lessons in Level 1 of *Progressive Skills in English*.

Answers

|   | S | V | O |
|---|---|---|---|
| 1. | You | have retrieved | that information |
| 2. | You | need | a degree |
| 3. | People | eat | snacks |
| 4. | China | has | (a) coastline |
| 5. | The Internet | is changing | the relationship |
| 6. | The Black Death | killed | people |
| 7. | A magazine | attracts | a group |
| 8. | Students | will have | a talk |

**B** Identifying extra information

Once more, give students time to read the second table. Clarify any problems. Again, with the table covered, elicit the example sentences. Ask students to tell you what the extra information is in each example, and whether it refers to the subject or to the object.

Do the first sentence in Exercise B with the class as a demonstration. Set the task for individual work and pairwork discussion. Monitor and assist with the vocabulary. Analyze a further sentence if you think the students need it.

Give feedback using an electronic projection of the sentences.

Answers

1. American (scientists) at Cape Canaveral in the USA launched the first (Space Shuttle).
2. The human (body) needs more than 40 different (nutrients).
3. (The Himalayas), a mountain range in Asia, contains the highest (peaks) on earth.
4. (Archaeologists) have discovered an early (form) of draughts.
5. Young (men) from ten of the teams take part in each (race) which lasts only 90 seconds.
6. College and university Media Studies (courses) look at (communication) in the mass media.
7. Some modern teen (magazines) reflect the readers' self (image).
8. (Websites) for students do not always have complete or correct (information).

## Closure

Ask students to choose five sentences from the text in Lesson 1.12 Real-time reading. Tell them to analyze them for S, V, O/C and for extra information about the S and O/C.

### 1.15 Applying new reading skills: Studying for a test

**Objectives**

By the end of this lesson, students should have:
- applied appropriate strategies for attacking a new text;
- identified the components of complex sentences;
- extracted information from a graph.

## Introduction

Elicit some of the information from the text in Lesson 1.12 Real-time reading.

### A  Reviewing vocabulary

The target words in this activity are from the text in Lesson 1.12 Real-time reading.

Go over the example with the class. Set the task. Students work individually, then compare their answers in pairs. Elicit answers. Give further explanations of each word if necessary.

Answers

1. We need to understand more about the *store* / *storage* of information in the brain.
2. You often remember very little if you are *tired* / *tiredness*. Your brain is not *efficiency* / *efficient* at those times.
3. You must *repetition* / *repeat* your review of information at regular intervals.
4. *Forgetting* / *forget* information is natural, but it can be avoided.
5. The key to effective learning is *revise* / *revision* at spaced intervals.
6. A lot of factors can *affect* / *effect* your concentration negatively.

### B  Activating ideas

Exploit the two photographs. Elicit who the people are, what they are doing and how they are feeling.

Remind students that they studied text-attack skills in Lesson 1.13 Learning new reading skills on page 26 of the Course Book. Elicit one or two ideas; then set the task for small group discussion.

Give feedback orally to the class as a whole. Build up a list of points on the board. Refer students back to Lesson 1.13 to check their answers.

Answers

*Before you read the text:*

Look at illustrations; look at the title; look at the introduction/first paragraph; highlight the topic sentences of the other paragraphs; try to predict the content from the illustrations (e.g., pictures, diagrams, graphs); try to predict the content from the title/heading; try to predict

Theme 1: Reading   55

the content of each paragraph; try to predict the order of information in the text.

*When you meet new vocabulary:*
Try to understand the sentence without the word; try to understand the word from the context; work out the part of speech; mark the word *n, v, adv* or *adj*; look up the word in a dictionary.

*After reading the text:*
Write a summary in one or two sentences; draw an illustration of the information; highlight important points in the text; make notes on the information; add new words to your vocabulary lists; think about your personal reaction to the information.

### C Understanding a text

1. Remind students of the grammar taught in Lesson 1.14 Grammar for reading. Use one or two of the sentences from that lesson to elicit the S, V and O, as well as extra information about the S and the O.
   
   Set the task for individual work. Tell students to do only one or two of the 'after-reading' tasks, and monitor and assist as they do this.
   
   With a particularly able group, you may wish students to do all three tasks before giving them feedback. Alternatively, you can offer feedback after each one of the three steps.
   
   During feedback time, elicit from students:
   - what they were able to predict from each element of the text before they read it;
   - which words they were able to guess as they read;
   - what they wrote in the after-reading stage – you could ask pairs or small groups to compare what they wrote.

2. Go over the example with the class.
   
   Set the task for individual work and pairwork checking. Monitor and assist as necessary.
   
   Give feedback using an electronic projection.
   
   **Extra activity:** You may wish to ask students to highlight the verb and object in each sentence. This will help less able groups in particular, and prepare them for the next task.

3. Again, go over the example with the students. Set the task for individual work and pairwork checking. Monitor and assist as necessary.
   
   Give feedback using an electronic projection.

### Answers

2.
1. For successful revision, *we* need to understand brain processes during a period of study.
2. However, in the test, *you* will often remember better the things that you revised at 9.30 or 10.00 than the things you revised at 1.00 or 1.30.
3. During a very long session, internal *factors* start to affect your memory.
4. In the example of the five-hour revision period above, *you* should take a ten-minute break every hour.
5. In each new session, the green *line* goes up again, because the tiredness, discomfort, hunger or boredom have gone.
6. Sometimes *people* remember more if they write notes.

3.
a. You probably do not notice any *difference* <u>in your level of understanding</u> during the revision period.
b. There is a *difference* <u>between understanding and memory</u>.
c. You should also vary the *activity* <u>that you do during the breaks</u>.
d. As the green line shows, you will remember <u>about 75 per cent of</u> the *information* <u>from the beginning of each session</u>.
e. There are also personal *factors* <u>that define good revision</u>.
f. Note the *level* <u>of the red line in Figure 2</u> after five hours.

### D Understanding a graph

Set the task for individual work and then for pair or small group discussion.

### Answers

1. The graph is from the Education Research Council data.
2. Red line = regular breaks; green line = no breaks.
3. The eighth green square tells us that with regular breaks, after three-and-a-half hours, we will remember about 70 per cent of the information we have studied.
   
   The sixth red triangle tells us that with no breaks, after two-and-a-half hours, we will remember 55 per cent of the information.
4. The graph is similar to Figure 1 in Lesson 1.12 in that both graphs show: (a) the

percentage of information remembered against time; (b) a way of remembering more information; (c) that we forget quickly if we do not take special steps to remember the information we study.

### E  Critical thinking

Set the tasks for pair or small group discussion. Monitor and assist as necessary.

As feedback, hold a brief class discussion. Encourage all contributions and insist that students give reasons to support their ideas.

Answers

1. Answers depend on students.
2. In Western academic texts, it is a requirement that writers always credit ideas and opinions to their authors. At the same time, where opinions are the author's own, he/she must state this clearly.

## Closure

1. Exploit the text in Lesson 1.12 Real-time reading for further work on SVO:
   - Ask students to find the subject and verb of sentences in the text.
   - Ask them to identify extra information about the object of sentences from the text.

2. Ask students questions about the graph in Lesson 1.12 Real-time reading.

   Example:
   T: *What does the fourth red dot mean?*
   Ss: *It shows that if you don't review, you forget 90 per cent of the information after a week.*

3. Review some of the grammatical features of both texts on pages 25 and 29 of the Course Book – imperatives, time phrases, frequency adverbs, comparatives, superlatives, phrases at the beginning of sentences with a preposition, noun–verb pairs, zero conditionals, possessive adjectives, pronouns.

## Knowledge quiz: How much can you remember … about memory?

### Objectives

By the end of this lesson, students will have:
- reviewed core knowledge from Theme 1;
- recycled the vocabulary from Theme 1.

### Introduction

Point out that you are going to do a game based on the vocabulary in Theme 1. Choose some of the words from below. Write each letter on the board in turn until students recognize the word, e.g., r – e – c – a – l – l. Allow students to shout out guesses. Point out that some letters can form more than one word, e.g., *memory / memorable*. Elicit answers and continue adding letters until they get the word you have in mind.

| recall | memory | theory |
| recognize | memorable | visualize |
| remember | forget | boredom |
| retrieve | efficiency | concentrate |
| store | consider | gradually |
| perform | preference | internal |
| propose | recommendation | decrease |

Ask students to choose some of the words and make sentences from them. Set for pairwork. Monitor and assist as necessary. Get students with the best sentences to read them out loud to the rest of the class.

### Figures 1, 2 and 3

If you have plenty of time for this revision quiz, set each figure in turn for discussion. Monitor and assist, then give feedback.

If you have less time, put students into three groups to study one figure each, then give feedback to the class as a whole. As you can see from the answers, the first figure is much more complicated than the other two, so set that one for the most able group in your class.

Less able classes: Set the vocabulary exercise for each figure. Then read the model description in Answers below, pausing for students to complete the information, or making mistakes for students to correct.

Answers

Figure 1

Vocabulary

|  | **se*nsory* memory** |  | **sh*ort-term* memory** |  | **lo*ng-term* memory** |
|---|---|---|---|---|---|
|  | 1–3 secs | → | 15–30 secs | → | 1 sec – lifetime |
| *information* e.g., *sight* *hearing* *touch* |  | *attention* |  | *rehearsal = frequency activity variety association mnemonics* |  |

*skills* ← *facts* ← *autobiographical* events

## Model description

Some researchers believe that there are three parts to memory. Firstly, there is sensory memory which lasts from one second to three seconds. Information comes into sensory memory all the time from the senses, for example, sight, hearing and touch. But most of the information does not stay in memory. We must pay attention to something. Then we keep it in short-term memory for 15 to 30 seconds. If we don't do anything with the information, we forget it. If we rehearse the information, we can move it into long-term memory. Rehearsal can involve a number of components. For example, there is frequency, which involves using the information many times. There is also activity, which means doing something with the information. Variety means doing different things, and association involves connecting new information with old information. Finally, we can use mnemonics to help us remember information such as lists. There are three main types of long-term memory. Firstly, we have memories for skills, like driving a car. Secondly, there are memories for facts, like the rulers of our country. Finally, there are autobiographical memories, like holidays when we were young.

Figure 2

Vocabulary

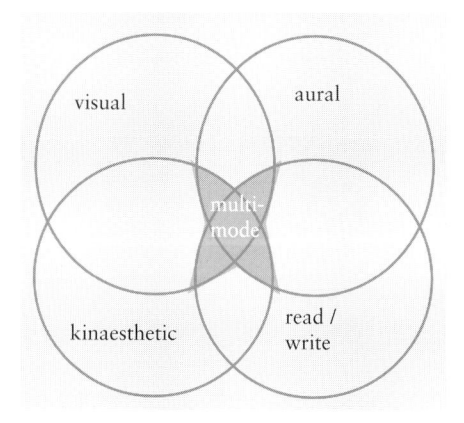

visual — aural — multi-mode — kinaesthetic — read / write

## Model description

There are four main types of learners. Firstly, there are visual learners. They like to see new information. Secondly, we have aural learners. They prefer to hear new information. Thirdly, kinaesthetic learners need to do something active with new information. Finally, read/write learners need to read information and write it down. There is a fifth type, the multi-mode learner. This type of learner uses a combination of learning styles. The majority of people are multi-mode learners.

Figure 3
Vocabulary

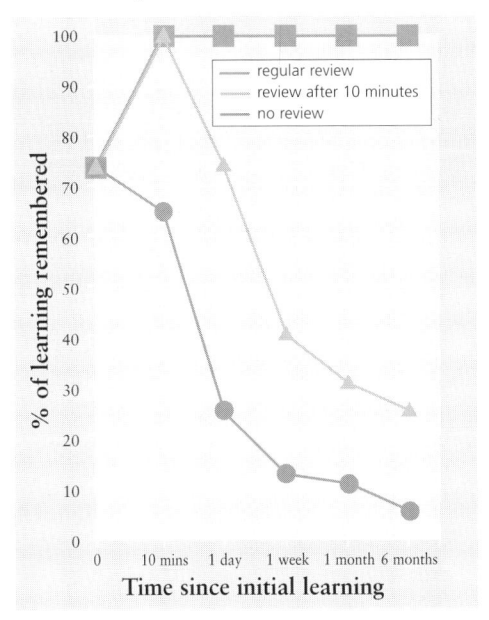

## Model description

We must review information regularly or we will forget it. If we do not review new information, we forget 95 per cent of it in six months. If we review the information regularly, we can keep it in long-term memory. The first review after ten minutes actually increases our memory. We should then review new information after one day, one week, one month and six months. Then we will remember the information forever.

# Writing: Rehearsal and prompts

## 1.16 Vocabulary for writing: Storage and retrieval

### Objectives

By the end of the lesson, students should be able to:
- demonstrate understanding of some of the target vocabulary for the theme;
- learn common core knowledge that underlies the model and the output texts in this theme;
- produce written sentences using target vocabulary.

### Introduction

Write the two words from the title on the board, *rehearsal* and *prompts*. Ask students what they mean in acting / the theatre. Elicit answers – *going over scenes again and again until you can do them perfectly* and *giving an actor a word or two words during a scene if they forget their lines*. Point out that in the Writing section, students are going to learn about the value of rehearsal and prompting both in language learning and language testing.

### A Reviewing vocabulary

Students complete the spelling activity individually, then compare their answers in pairs. Write the correct spellings on the board so that students can check their own answers.

Check the meanings of some of the words. Elicit the part of speech of each word.

Set the sentence-writing task. Students complete the task individually. Monitor and give help where necessary. Ask some of the students to read out their sentences.

### Answers

1. component
2. memory
3. theory
4. *in*terval
5. repet*i*tion
6. effic*i*ent
7. variety
8. encode

### B Understanding and using new words

Exploit the visuals. Make sure students realize that they show a flashcard with three consonants on it, and a photograph of classmates at school.

Put the students into two groups.

1. Ask students to try to complete their text alone, then check their answers with the other people in their group. Tell them to especially check the form of the word, as this is a writing lesson. Monitor and assist.

2. Ask students to work out the important information so that they can put it into the one-sentence summary. Elicit answers – *date, name of researchers, conclusion of experiment*. Get students to have a go at this individually, then ask them to compare their answers with the other students in their group and agree on the best summary. Do not confirm or correct answers at this stage.

### Answers

1.

Text 1

In 1959, two researchers conducted an experiment into memory *storage*. The experiment *demonstrated* the value of rehearsal in storing new information. The researchers were called Lloyd and Margaret Peterson. They showed participants three-letter combinations, like BGH, for a few seconds. The combinations did not make words. Then they asked the participants to count backwards from 100 in threes, e.g., *100, 97, 94*, etc. This *ensured* that the participants did not have the *opportunity* to rehearse the letters. Finally, they asked the participants to say the letters. Most participants could not recall the new information. This shows that new information does not stay in short-term memory *without* rehearsal.

Text 2

In 1975, a group of researchers conducted an experiment into memory *retrieval*. The experiment demonstrated the value of *prompts* in remembering old information. The researchers were led by Dr Harold Bahrick. They asked adult participants to give the names of their classmates at school. They did not show them photographs. Many people over 60 could not remember the names *without* any prompts.

Then the researchers showed the participants photographs. Most participants could *name* the majority of their classmates. This shows the difference between *storage*, which is keeping information in memory, and *retrieval*, which is getting information out of memory. People *store* information in memory but they often cannot recall it without a prompt.

2. See Answers for Exercise C.

> **Methodology note**
>
> In Level 1 of *Progressive Skills in English*, students are trained in a technique called the TOWER of writing. You might want to remind students of this here, or you can introduce the idea to students who did not study Level 1.
>
> – **T**hinking about what you're going to write
>
> – **O**rganizing your ideas – perhaps into a table, a spidergram, a mind map
>
> – **W**riting a first draft – writing for the writer, you convey the message
>
> – **E**diting the first draft – for spelling, grammar and punctuation, but most of all for coherence (a logical flow of ideas)
>
> – **R**ewriting in order to produce a second draft – writing for the reader, you make sure the reader understands the message

**C** Editing and rewriting

Put students in pairs – with one student from Group 1 and the other from Group 2 in each pair. If you have an odd number, put two students from Group 1 with one student from Group 2.

1. Set for individual work. Tell students to ask each other questions if they do not understand the summary. They should also mark the work for mistakes in spelling (S), grammar (G) and punctuation (P).

2. Get students to return the summary for rewriting.

   Elicit the summaries and decide on the best ones. Put the best summaries on the board for all students to see.

**Answers**

Model answers:

1. In 1959, Peterson and Peterson demonstrated that new information does not stay in short-term memory without rehearsal.

2. In 1975, Bahrick et al.* demonstrated that people sometimes cannot retrieve stored information without prompting / prompts.

\**et al.* = 'and others' (teach this at this point if necessary)

**Closure**

Get students to do the first experiment by Peterson and Peterson from Exercise B.

Students make one set of three-letter combinations, A or B, into flashcards with large letters.

| A |
|---|
| BGH |
| ZQR |
| FDM |
| YPL |
| JTC |
| WKV |

| B |
|---|
| QRT |
| PDN |
| HKW |
| BVM |
| LSZ |
| GCH |

Students work in pairs. They show a flashcard to a participant for five seconds.

Then the participant is asked to count backwards from 100 in threes, e.g., *100, 97, 94, 91 ...*

Ask the participant to recall the trigram. Vary the amount of time before the recall as follows: 3, 6, 9, 12, 15, 18 seconds.

Record the results and make a graph.

Here are the actual results of the Peterson and Peterson experiment:

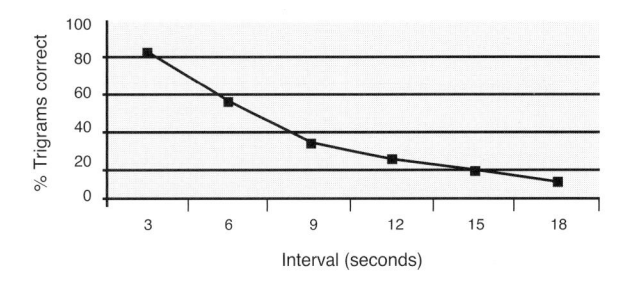

### 1.17 Real-time writing: Learning new vocabulary

#### Objectives

By the end of the lesson, students should be able to:
- show understanding of the discourse structure of an Argument essay;
- use notes and target vocabulary to produce sentences for a guided writing activity;
- show understanding of knowledge about rehearsal and learning vocabulary.

#### Introduction

Dictate some sentences based on the experiments of the previous lesson for students to write, as follows:
*In 1959, / two researchers / conducted an experiment / into memory storage.*
*The experiment / showed the value of rehearsal / in storing new information.*
*In 1975, / a group of researchers / carried out an experiment / into memory retrieval.*
*They demonstrated the value of prompts / in remembering old information.*

#### Methodology note

In this activity, which uses a 'deep-end strategy', students attempt a piece of writing with very little input from the teacher. This is an opportunity for you to monitor the students' written ability, and can be used to help you decide which activities during the next few lessons you should spend more time on.

### A  Activating ideas

Students discuss the question in pairs. Encourage students to think of example activities for each of the aspects of 'knowing' a word, for example: *meaning – ask a teacher, look it up in a dictionary*, etc. Tell students to make notes, if you wish. Elicit answers.

Students should try to write about five sentences about 'knowing' a word. Set a time limit of no more than five minutes for the activity. Monitor and give help where necessary. Make a note of common errors. Give feedback but do not spend too long on this. Tell students that in this lesson, they are going to learn how to write a more detailed essay about learning vocabulary.

#### Optional activities

1. Students exchange and read each other's sentences. They should tell each other if the sentences are clear but should not correct mistakes.
2. Ask one or two students to read out their sentences, or – if possible – use an electronic projection to show the sentences on the board for students to discuss.

#### Answers

1. Knowing a word means: *meaning, grammar, pronunciation* and *spelling*.
2. Answers depend on students.

### B  Gathering information

1. Check students understand the assignment question. Check understanding of what *discuss with reference* means and remind students that they need to show they have read the relevant research.

   Students discuss the question in pairs. Elicit answers. Make sure students realize this is not the everyday meaning of *argument*; in this context, it means to give an opinion backed up by research.

2. Set the task. Elicit one or two ideas. Then students continue in pairs.

#### Answers

1. This should be an Argument essay.
2. Answers depend on the students but they could suggest, for example, that teachers ensure new vocabulary items are remembered by:
   - revising grammar, vocabulary, spelling, etc.
   - asking students to repeat words, sentences, etc.
   - giving students different types of exercises, etc.
   - making students copy information from the board
   - giving homework

> **Methodology note**
>
> Exercise C makes the discourse of the model text more explicit to the students. It is very important students become aware of the way that text is organized in English, which may be very different from their own language.
>
> If you prefer, Exercise D (completing notes) can be done first before moving on to this exercise.

### C  Noticing the discourse structure

1. Ask students to look at the essay title. Remind students what they learnt in the Listening section about the importance of rehearsal in moving information into long-term memory. Set the task: students read the first paragraph and then compare ideas in pairs. If students find it difficult, put the first few words of the answer on the board so that students can complete the sentence: *Teachers should ensure that ...*

   Remind students of how to refer to authors or researchers: *name + (date)*.

2. Check students understand the meaning of the word *term* in this context. Set the task. When students finish reading the second paragraph, they should discuss the questions in pairs. Elicit answers.

3. Remind students that it is important to vary your language when you are giving a list, like in the text's third paragraph, for example. The writer uses different ways to introduce each component. Elicit the first way. Set for individual work and pairwork checking.

4. Set the task. Students read the final paragraph, then compare their answers in pairs. Elicit answers. Explain that we use the present perfect tense in a conclusion like this because it is talking about a point made earlier in the essay. However, the reader has not finished reading the essay yet, so we need the present perfect rather than past simple. The present prefect tense always links the past and the present in some way.

### Answers

1. Teachers should ensure that all new vocabulary is rehearsed. (This previews the idea of the 'thesis statement' which is covered in the next lesson.)

2. The writer defines *rehearsal, knowing a word*; the writer uses *means* and *is about* to define each term.

3. Underlined elements (see below) vary the way of introducing / explaining each component. Notice that you do not need constantly to repeat *component of knowing a word*.

   <u>The first component of knowing a word is</u> meaning, <u>which is</u> the dictionary definition of the word. It is also the connections between a word and other words.

   <u>Secondly, we have</u> pronunciation. Pronunciation of words <u>involves</u> the sound of individual letters.

   <u>Thirdly</u>, spelling.

   <u>Finally, there is</u> usage, <u>which means</u> the way the word is used in a sentence.

4. Present perfect simple.

### D  Writing notes

Check students understand the notes and the way the information is organized. Show how one or two points in the notes relate to the essay, and discuss which words have been added to the notes to form complete sentences. For example:

*value of rehearsal = demonstrated the value of rehearsal*

Students complete the notes individually, then compare their answers in pairs. Elicit answers, preferably using an electronic projection.

### Answers

See notes on next page.

> **Methodology note**
>
> There are several ways you can approach Exercise E. Here are just a few suggestions:
>
> - Set the task as it is and see how well students can write the essay with the minimum of help (good for more able classes).
>
> - Write the topic sentence on the board for each paragraph; students copy and complete.
>
> - Retype the model answer with gaps for either verbs or key words in each sentence. Students complete the sentences (good for less able classes).

## Rehearsal in vocabulary learning

- **terms**
  - **rehearsal** = going over things, e.g., repetition
- **research**
  - Peterson & Peterson (1959) = value of rehearsal
- **vocabulary learning**
  1. meaning = definitions / opposites / synonyms
  2. pronunciation = sounds / stress
  3. spelling = spelling rules complicated
  4. usage = use in a sentence
- **thesis**
  - rehearsal is important
  - ts. should ensure rehearsal
- **rehearsal**
  - e.g., match word / meaning
  - e.g., drill
  - e.g., write 10x
  - e.g., write sentences

---

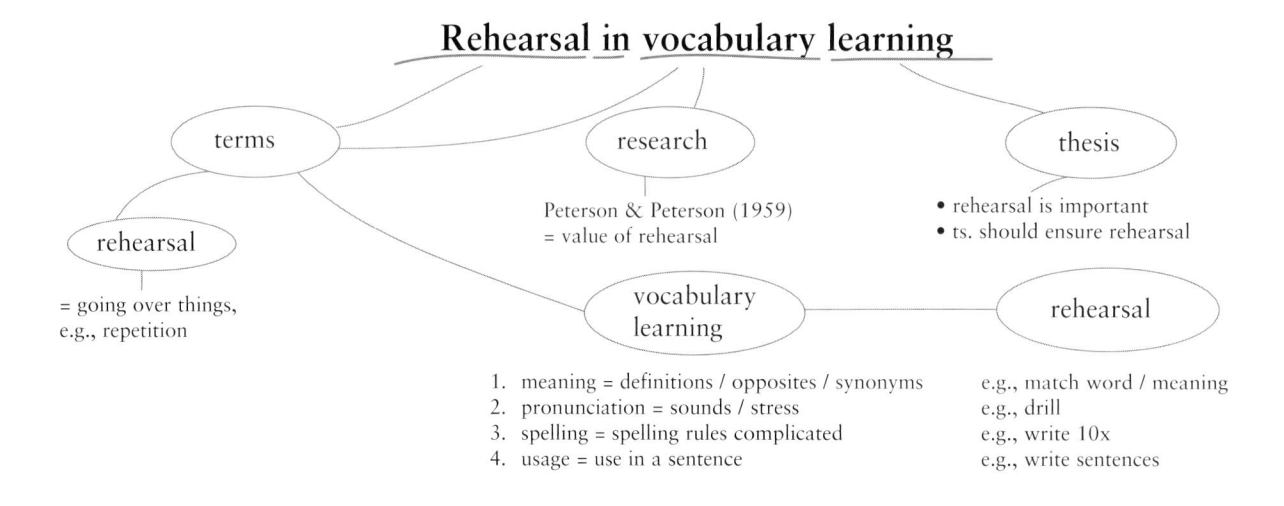

• Give students two or three minutes (depending on the length of the text) to study each paragraph. Students write the paragraph. Give feedback before moving on to the next paragraph.

Students do not have to write the essay in exactly the same way as the model answer.

### E Writing the essay

Check students understand the task (see Methodology note above). Monitor and give help where necessary. Make a note of common errors. Make sure there is enough time left at the end of the lesson for you to give feedback on common errors.

### Closure

You can use the feedback on Exercise E for Closure and/or focus on any other language points from the text, for example:
*could* for suggestions
*mean* + *~ing*
signpost words

## 1.18 Learning new writing skills: The Argument essay

### Objectives

By the end of this lesson, students should be able to:
- show understanding of the organization of an Argument essay;
- produce simple thesis statements.

### Introduction

Use Exercise A as the introduction.

### A Reviewing vocabulary

Set the task. Students complete the activity individually, then compare their answers in pairs. Write the correct spellings on the board so that students can correct their own work. Highlight some of the spelling patterns. For example:

- double letters in *opportunity* and *recommend*
- words with two consecutive vowels – *research*, *language*, *individual*

Check students' understanding of some of the words' meanings.

### Answers

1. information
2. definition
3. research
4. language
5. ensure

6. opportunity
7. component
8. importance
9. recommend
10. individual

> **Methodology note**
>
> In Level 2 of *Progressive Skills in English*, we taught students the essay type that they must write; in this theme, students focus on the Argument essay. In the next level, students will have to identify the essay type for themselves. However, students can begin to notice the direction verbs in the essay titles. In this lesson, the direction verb is *discuss*. Other direction verbs for the Argument essay include *consider* and *evaluate*, *to what extent*, *how far*.
>
> In an Argument essay, students are expected to give a set of reasons to show something is true, correct or a good idea.

**B** Identifying a key skill (1)

1. Ask students to read Skills Check 1. Remind students of the meaning of *argument* in this context (see notes for Lesson 1.17 Real-time writing and the Methodology note above). Reassure them that they do not need to understand all the information in the writing plan at this point – this will become clearer in the next activity.

   Elicit answers. Ask a follow-up question:
   *Which word in the essay title tells you this is an Argument essay? (discuss)*

2. Show students how to write each part next to the correct section of the essay. Set for individual work and pairwork checking. Give feedback, ideally using an electronic projection.

Answers

1. Four
2. See table below.

| introduction | Research has shown that new information does not stay in short-term memory very long. If new information is not rehearsed, it is forgotten very quickly. For example, Peterson and Peterson (1959) demonstrated the value of rehearsal. Rehearsal of new words is extremely important in language learning. |
| --- | --- |
| thesis statement | Teachers should provide opportunities for the rehearsal of new vocabulary items. |
| defining terms 1 | *Rehearsal* means going over something several times. Rehearsal could involve repetition or other activities. |
| defining terms 2 | Vocabulary learning is about knowing words. There are four main components of knowing a word in a foreign language: meaning, pronunciation, spelling and usage. |
| point 1 | The first component of knowing a word is meaning |
| explanation 1 | which is the dictionary definition of the word. It is also the connections between a word and other words. |
| example 1 | Teachers could ask students to match words with their dictionary definitions. Students could also match words with their opposites or with synonyms. |
| point 2 | Secondly, we have pronunciation. |
| explanation 2 | Pronunciation of words involves the sound of individual letters. It also involves the stress in multi-syllable words. |
| example 2 | Teachers could drill new words, on their own and in sentences. |
| point 3 | Thirdly, spelling. |
| explanation 3 | Spelling rules in English are complicated. |
| example 3 | Students could write out a new word ten times to rehearse the spelling, or correct misspelt words. |
| point 4 | Finally, there is usage |
| explanation 4 | which means the way the word is used in a sentence. |
| example 4 | Students could complete sentences with new words correctly or write their own sentences with new words. |
| summary | In this essay, I have explained the importance of rehearsal in vocabulary learning. I have also described the four components of knowing a word. Finally, I have recommended some activities to rehearse each component. |

### C Identifying a key skill (2)

1. Give students time to study the information in Skills Check 2. Ask questions to check understanding:
*What should Argument essays contain?* (a thesis statement)
*How long is this statement?* (one sentence)
*What is the statement?* (your opinion about the essay topic)
*What will a good essay do?* (it will support the statement)
*What does 'support' mean in this context?* (show that something is correct)

Ask students to cover the thesis statement and rewrite it from memory. If necessary, write the first two or three words on the board for students to copy and complete. When most of the students have finished writing, they can check their own work with the sentence in the Course Book.

2. Set the task. Students discuss each statement in pairs. Elicit answers. Discuss why the correct answer is a good thesis statement (see Answers below).

Discuss why the rest of the statements are not acceptable:

   - a. *Students must learn new vocabulary items* – this is about students, the question is about teachers.

   - b. *Teachers should ensure that new vocabulary items are remembered* – this just repeats the question and does not explain how items can be remembered.

   - d. *Vocabulary is hard to learn* – this is only a statement of fact and does not answer the question.

3. Students discuss the questions in pairs. Elicit some of their ideas. Now ask students to write a thesis statement for each of the essay questions. Monitor and give help where necessary. When most of the students have finished writing, ask some of them to read out their statements (or ask them to write them on the board). Point out to them that they do not have to agree with the idea that is suggested in an Argument essay title, e.g., *How important = very important*. However, if they disagree, their argument probably has to be stronger!

### Answers

1. See thesis statement in Skills Check 2 in the Course Book.

2. c. *Teachers should test students regularly on new vocabulary items* – it's a logical way for teachers to ensure new vocabulary items are remembered.

3. Answers depend on the students, but here are some ideas:
   a. *Homework is an essential part of language learning.*
   *Homework does not help in any way in language learning.*
   *Homework is useful for some parts of language learning but not others.*
   b. *Teachers should set formal tests regularly to inform learning.*
   *Formal tests are not a useful part of language learning.*
   *Formal tests are useful for reading and writing but not for speaking.*
   c. *Rote learning is an essential first stage with vocabulary items.*
   *There is no benefit to rote learning with vocabulary items.*
   *Rote learning is extremely valuable for words such as 'book', 'table' but not for words such as 'honesty', 'truth'.*

### Closure

Use some of the students' thesis statements from Exercise C3 as a basis for discussion.

## 1.19 Grammar for writing: SVC and SVO; adding to basic sentence patterns

### Objectives

By the end of the lesson, students should be able to:

- show understanding of basic SVC and SVO sentence patterns;
- add extra information to basic SVC and SVO sentences.

### Introduction

Revise some of the grammar from the previous sections in this theme.

**Grammar box 6**

Ask students to study Table 1. Remind them that any word following the verb *be* is called the *complement* and not the *object*.

Students then study Table 2. Explain these are two of the basic sentence patterns in English. They are simple to understand but do not give the reader much information. When writing an academic essay, students would need to add more information to the sentences.

Students read Table 3. Make sure students understand these are the same sentences from Table 1 but with extra information added. Elicit the extra pieces of information, for example: *of new words, extremely, in vocabulary learning*.

Emphasize that:
- the basic SVC pattern is still the same for both sentences
- the word order cannot be changed (except for the phrases *in vocabulary learning* and *in English* which could also go at the beginning of the sentences).

Repeat the procedure with Table 4.

### A  Adding extra information to SVC sentences

Check students understand the task and go over the example with them. Students should work individually. Ask them to write the sentences out in full in a notebook or on a piece of paper. Students compare their answers in pairs. Monitor and give help where necessary. Elicit answers, preferably using an electronic projection.

Answers

See Table A.

### B  Adding extra information to SVO sentences

Repeat the procedure for Exercise A.

Answers

See Table B.

**Closure**

Write some SVO and SVC basic sentences on the board (or dictate them). Ask students to add extra information to each sentence. For example:

- *Learners should use pens.*
  Students could write: *Visual learners should always use coloured pens.*

Table A

| | | |
|---|---|---|
| 1. | There are components. <br> four / of knowing a word / in a foreign language / main | There are four main components of knowing a word in a foreign language. |
| 2. | The component is meaning. <br> first / a word / of knowing | The first component of knowing a word is meaning. |
| 3. | Pronunciation involves the stress. <br> also / of / words / multi-syllable | Pronunciation also involves the stress of multi-syllable words. |
| 4. | There are models. <br> from / researchers / of memory / several / different | There are several models of memory from different researchers. |
| 5. | The model is famous. <br> by Atkinson and Shiffrin / the most / in this area / Multi-store memory | The Multi-store memory model by Atkinson and Shiffrin is the most famous in this area. |
| 6. | Memory is the stage. <br> final / of this model / long-term | Long-term memory is the final stage of this model. |

Table B

| | | |
|---|---|---|
| 1. | Pronunciation involves the sounds. <br> of words / of / letters / individual | Pronunciation of words involves the sounds of individual letters. |
| 2. | I have described the components. <br> four / a word / of knowing | I have described the four components of knowing a word. |
| 3. | Information pushes out information. <br> new / from short-term / old / memory | New information pushes out old information from short-term memory. |
| 4. | Miller conducted research. <br> the researcher / the best-known / in this area | The researcher Miller conducted the best-known research in this area. |
| 5. | Memory can hold information. <br> seven pieces / short-term / of / meaningless / about | Short-term memory can hold about seven pieces of meaningless information. |
| 6. | Researchers looked at memory. <br> a group of / Bahrick / and / long-term | Bahrick and a group of researchers looked at long-term memory. |

- *Teachers set tests.*
  Students could write: *Effective teachers should set formal tests regularly.*

- *Homework is important.*
  Students could write: *Written homework is not important for language learning.*

### 1.20 Applying new writing skills: Long-term memory and testing

#### Objectives

By the end of the lesson, students should be able to:
- produce an Argument essay from given notes on an educational topic;
- use target vocabulary, grammar and sub-skills from the theme in an Argument essay;
- use the TOWER process to produce a final written draft.

**Introduction**

Revise the information from Lesson 1.16 Vocabulary for writing about rehearsal and prompts. This will help students with writing their essays in this lesson.

**A  Reviewing vocabulary and grammar**

Check students understand the task and go over the example. Students complete the activity individually, then compare their answers in pairs. Elicit answers and give feedback, preferably using an electronic projection.

#### Optional activities

1. If you are short of time, divide the class into pairs. Student 1 completes all the odd-numbered sentences, while Student 2 completes all the even-numbered sentences. When they have finished, students exchange information so that they have a complete set of sentences.

2. Ask students to identify the basic SVO or SVC pattern in each sentence (see Lesson 1.19 Grammar for writing).

**Answers**

1. Research *has* shown that new information does not stay in short-term memory very *long*.
2. For example, Peterson and Peterson (1959) *demonstrated* the value of ~~the~~ rehearsal.
3. Teachers should *ensure* that new vocabulary *is* rehearsed.
4. They could ~~to~~ provide opportunities in class or for ~~the~~ homework.
5. Rehearsal means *going* over something several ~~of~~ times.
6. *There* are four main components of *knowing* a word in a foreign language.
7. *The* first component is meaning which *involves* dictionary definition.
8. *Pronunciation* of words involves *the* sound of individual letters.
9. In this essay, I *have* explained the importance of *rehearsal* in vocabulary learning.
10. I have *also* described *the* four components of knowing a word.*

* Note: without *the* = acceptable sentence but different meaning = there are more than four components.

**B  Thinking and organizing**

Remind students about the TOWER approach to writing that was taught in Level 1 of *Progressive Skills in English*:
- **T**hinking about what you're going to write
- **O**rganizing your ideas
- **W**riting a first draft
- **E**diting the first draft
- **R**ewriting in order to produce a second draft

1. When students have finished reading the assignment instructions, elicit answers to the question in the rubrics (it is an Argument essay). Ask students:
*How do you know this is an Argument essay?* (because of the word *discuss*)

2. Remind students of the meaning of *prompts* from Lesson 1.16 Vocabulary for writing. Elicit suggestions for possible prompts in testing, e.g., multiple choice questions, comprehension questions, etc. In pairs, students discuss the assignment question.

Students work individually to write a thesis statement. Monitor and give help where necessary. Ask some of the more able students to write their thesis statements on the board (or ask them to read them out).

Answers

1. It is an Argument essay.
2. Answers depend on the students but some possibilities are:
*Prompts are an essential part of language testing (for grammar and vocabulary / writing, speaking, etc.).*
*Prompts are useful for some components, such as grammar and vocabulary, but not for other components, like essay writing.*
*Free essays are better tests of language learning than prompted answers.*

### C Writing about testing

Ask students to study the notes for a few minutes. Ask a few questions to check understanding. Go through the main points to remember; how much detail you choose to go into will depend on the level of your class. Refer students back to the lessons where all these points have been covered (Lesson 1.18 Learning new writing skills and Lesson 1.19 Grammar for writing, on pages 34–35 of the Course Book).

If necessary, start the essay off on the board with the first one or two sentences from the model answer below (see Answers for Exercise D).

Monitor while students are writing their first draft and make a note of common errors. Give feedback on some of the common errors before moving on to the next exercise.

Answers

See Answers for Exercise D.

### D Editing and rewriting

1. Remind students of things to check for: *spelling*, *correct tenses*, etc. Monitor and give help where necessary.
2. The final version can be written in class or set for homework. If done in class, monitor and make a note of common errors. Give feedback on students' common writing errors to the whole class.

Answer

Model answer:

<u>The importance of prompts in testing of language learning</u>

Research has shown that memories can last a very long time. However, there is a difference between memory storage and memory retrieval. Bahrick et al. (1975) demonstrated the importance of prompts in memory retrieval. Tests of language learning should provide prompts to ensure that students recall learnt information.

Prompts are words or pictures which help you remember something. There are three main kinds of language test. They are true/false statements, multiple choice questions and gap fills.

Firstly, we have true/false statements. In this kind of test, all the information is given. The student only has to decide if it is true or false. For example, the past tense of *give* is *gave*. True or false?

Secondly, there are multiple choice questions. The students are given choices, with one correct answer, e.g., the past tense of *give* is (a) gave; (b) given; (c) gives; or (d) give.

Finally, gap fill. In gap fills, students have to complete a sentence with one or more items. For example, *Yesterday, the teacher ... us a test*.

In this essay, I have explained the importance of prompts in remembering learnt information. I have described some types of prompts that are useful in language testing.

Analysis

See table on following page.

**Closure**

Give feedback on the written work produced so far in this lesson.

If students completed their essays in class, you can now give out copies of the model answer and go through it with them. Use an electronic projection to highlight the discourse structure of the text on the board (see 'Analysis' above).

Theme 1: Writing 69

| introduction | Research has shown that memories can last a very long time. However, there is a difference between memory storage and memory retrieval. Bahrick et al. (1975) demonstrated the importance of prompts in memory retrieval. |
|---|---|
| thesis statement | Tests of language learning should provide prompts to ensure that students recall learnt information. |
| defining terms 1 | Prompts are words or pictures which help you remember something. |
| defining terms 2 | There are three main kinds of language test. They are true/false statements, multiple choice questions and gap fills. |
| point 1 | Firstly, we have true/false statements. |
| explanation 1 | In this kind of test, all the information is given. The student only has to decide if it is true or false. |
| example 1 | For example, the past tense of *give* is *gave*. True or false? |
| point 2 | Secondly, there are multiple choice questions. |
| explanation 2 | The students are given choices, with one correct answer. |
| example 2 | e.g., the past tense of *give* is (a) gave; (b) given; (c) gives; or (d) give. |
| point 3 | Finally, gap fill. |
| explanation 3 | In gap fills, students have to complete a sentence with one or more items. |
| example 3 | For example, *Yesterday, the teacher ... us a test.* |
| summary | In this essay, I have explained the importance of prompts in remembering learnt information. I have described some types of prompts that are useful in language testing. |

## Portfolio: Memories

### Objectives

By the end of the lesson(s), students should have:
- revised target vocabulary from the theme;
- used integrated skills to practise language and revise knowledge from the theme;
- practised questions to check information;
- used integrated skills to talk and write about memory;
- learnt more common core knowledge about memory.

**Introduction**

Ask students to tell you about the memory experiments from this theme. Alternatively, do a quick quiz on key information about the memory experiments from this theme.

**A** Activating ideas

Refer students to the visuals. Ask students to discuss the photographs in pairs. Elicit ideas. Make sure students notice the topic of the final photograph in the bottom right corner – the death of Kennedy. Ask students if they know anything about it. Whether they do or not, point out that it was as shocking an event at the time as 9/11 was for this generation.

Answers

Students may mention some of the following:
1. People have thousands of memories of their earlier years.
2. Songs bring back memories – we associate particular songs with particular memories.
3. Many people take photographs to remind them of happy events.
4. We write lists to help us remember.
5. People send postcards of holidays and sometimes collect postcards as reminders.
6. We remember toys we used to play with.
7. We remember older relatives – and the food they cooked!
8. We remember people at funerals.
9. We remember terrible events in our lifetimes, like the assassination of President Kennedy in 1963.

## B  Gathering and recording information (1)

1. Work through the questions. Elicit the kind of information they will hear to answer each question (see Answers below).

   Check/pre-teach some key vocabulary from the listening text, e.g.,
   *ethnic group*
   *culturally determined*
   *flashbulb*

   It would also be useful to teach *minor details*.

   Play 🎧 1.18. Pause if necessary to give time to students to make a few notes for each question. Do not give feedback at this stage.

2. Put students into small groups. Monitor and assist groups as necessary. Give feedback by putting a model answer on the board.

3. Set for individual work.

### Answers

1. Possible expected answers:
   When = date
   What = a kind of memory
   Who = names
   Why = hypothesis
   How = questionnaire
   What / discover = results
   What / conclude = implications

2. Notes should be much shorter than this in most cases – given in full here to avoid confusion.

   See table opposite.

3. Possible summary:

   *In 1977, Brown and Kulik demonstrated that people remember very clearly shocking events which are important to them.*

### Transcript

🎧 1.18

**Presenter:** 1.18. Portfolio: Memories. Exercise B1. Listen to information about some research into memory.

**Lecturer:** In 1977, two researchers conducted an experiment into memory. They were interested in memories of shocking events, like 9/11, but, of course, this was many years before that event. The researchers were called Roger Brown and James Kulik.

They wanted to see if memory is culturally determined – in other words: Do people remember important events differently, depending on their ethnic group?

Brown and Kulik asked 40 black Americans and 40 white Americans to fill out a questionnaire. The questionnaire contained a list of ten national events, including the death of President Kennedy 14 years earlier. Participants were asked to recall the circumstances surrounding the event.

| When was the research conducted? | *1977* |
|---|---|
| What was the research about? | *memories of shocking events, like 9/11* |
| Who did the research? | *Brown and Kulik* |
| Why did they do it? | *memory = culturally determined?*<br>*e.g., people remember important events differently, depending on ethnic group* |
| How did they do it? | *40 black and 40 white Americans*<br>*questionnaire with events from previous 14 years inc. death of Kennedy*<br>*Do you recall these events?* |
| What did they discover? | *white Americans – remembered events involving white people;*<br>*black Ams = black people*<br>*remembered where, what doing, what others doing, who told them and the effect of the news*<br>*But could not remember events day before / after.* |
| What did they conclude? | *Brown and Kulik concluded that flashbulb memories are different from other memories, even minor details are recorded. They also concluded that people have flashbulb memories for things that are personally important to them, e.g., white Americans remember events with white people.* |

Brown and Kulik found that white Americans had better recall for events involving white people whereas black Americans had better recall for events involving black people. They also found that people remembered many facts about important events. They remembered where they were, what they were doing, what other people were doing, who told them about the event, and the effect the news had on them and on other people. But, and this is the important point, they could not remember events on the day before or the day after.

Brown and Kulik concluded that there is a special kind of memory. They called it *flashbulb memory*. The name comes from the flash on a camera. The researchers thought that some memories are like photographs. They also concluded that people have flashbulb memories for things that are personally important to them, hence white Americans remembering events with white people.

## C  Gathering and recording information (2)

1. Divide the class into pairs. Give each student in each pair a number, 1 or 2. Allocate the texts as follows:

   S1– should read *How do we remember stories?* on page 38

Theme 1: Writing   71

S2 – should read *How do we remember events?* on page 39

Set task for individual work. Remind students that the questions in Exercise B are a good basis for making notes with this kind of information. With a less able class, allow students to work for a short time in groups – all student 1s or all student 2s to make notes. Monitor and assist each group/student. During this stage, refer students back to the text if they have missed any key points. Use the model notes (see below) and check them against the notes that are emerging from each group.

2. Set for pairwork. Monitor and assist. Give feedback, using an electronic projection of the model notes.
3. Set for individual work. Give feedback, showing some of the model summaries on the board.

Answers

Model notes:

1.

| When? | 1932 | 1974 |
|---|---|---|
| What about? | remembering stories | remembering events |
| Who? | Frederick Bartlett | Loftus and Palmer |
| Why? | believed culture affects memory | do leading questions affect memory |
| How? | – gave people stories from different cultures, e.g., 'War of Ghosts' from Native American culture to non-Native Americans<br>– asked them to recall several times<br>– recorded what they said each time | – 45 participants in 5 groups<br>– same question except one = How fast going when hit / smashed into / collided with / bumped into / hit |
| What discover? | – remembered diff. parts of stories<br>– changed parts to fit cultural expect. e.g., canoe to boat | – diff. estimates with diff. speeds. e.g., smashed = ave 41 mph; contacted = 32 mph |
| What conclude? | – brain = changes memories to make them easier to remember<br>– uses schema = how the world works to reconstruct memory | – words used = affect answers<br>– serious for eye-witness test |

2/3. Answers depend on students.

**Methodology note**

The original story 'The War of the Ghosts' is reproduced at the end of these notes (opposite). You might like to repeat Bartlett's experiment with the students and see if you get the same results as he did.

**D** Giving a talk about memory

Make sure students notice the point *refer to research in the area*. They should introduce their talk with a brief summary of the relevant research, e.g.,

- *I'm going to talk about a world event which happened in my lifetime. Brown and Kulik demonstrated in 1977 that people have flashbulb memories for events which are important to them. They remember all the details about the event, although they cannot remember events the day before, for example, or the day after.*

  *The world event that I remember well is …*

- *I'm going to talk about a traditional story from my culture. Bartlett demonstrated in 1932 that people remember stories from their own culture. They cannot remember well stories from other cultures. One of the best-known stories from my culture is …*

# The War of the Ghosts

One night two young men from Egulac went down to the river to hunt seals, and while they were there it became foggy and calm. Then they heard war-cries, and they thought: 'Maybe this is a war-party.' They escaped to the shore, and hid behind a log. Now canoes came up, and they heard the noise of paddles, and saw one canoe coming up to them. There were five men in the canoe, and they said:

'What do you think? We wish to take you along. We are going up the river to make war on the people.'

One of the young men said, 'I have no arrows.'

'Arrows are in the canoe,' they said.

'I will not go along. I might be killed. My relatives do not know where I have gone. But you,' he said, turning to the other, 'may go with them.'

So one of the young men went, but the other returned home.

And the warriors went on up the river to a town on the other side of Kalama. The people came down to the water and they began to fight, and many were killed. But presently the young man heard one of the warriors say, 'Quick, let us go home: that Indian has been hit.' Now he thought: 'Oh, they are ghosts.' He did not feel sick, but they said he had been shot.

So the canoes went back to Egulac and the young man went ashore to his house and made a fire. And he told everybody and said: 'Behold I accompanied the ghosts, and we went to fight. Many of our fellows were killed, and many of those who attacked us were killed. They said I was hit, and I did not feel sick.'

He told it all, and then he became quiet. When the sun rose, he fell down. Something black came out of his mouth. His face became contorted. The people jumped up and cried.

He was dead.

Adapted from
http://penta.ufrgs.br/edu/telelab/2/war-of-t.htm.

# Theme 2

## Friends and family

- **Making and keeping friends**
- **Apologizing**
- **Parents, Adults and Children**
- **Decisions in families**

# Listening: Making and keeping friends

### Methodology note

The following words were taught in this theme and skill at Level 1 of *Progressive Skills in English*. You may wish to revise or check/teach some of them.

| | |
|---|---|
| act (v) | link (n) |
| aim (n) | medicine (n) |
| alone (adj) | memory (n) |
| ancient (adj) | mind (n) |
| behave (v) | modern (adj) |
| belong (v) | neighbourhood (n) |
| brain (n) | pattern (n) |
| century (n) | philosopher (n) |
| club (n) | poor (adj) |
| cognitive (adj) | primary (adj) [main] |
| colleague (n) | psychologist (n) |
| control (v) | psychology (n) |
| different (adj) [from] | relationship (n) |
| family (n) | religion (n) |
| form (v) | rich (adj) |
| friend (n) | rights (n) |
| friendship (n) | rule (n) |
| group (n) | separate (adj) |
| human (n and adj) | social (adj) |
| human race | sociologist (n) |
| identity (n) | sociology (n) |
| important (adj) | term (n) [name] |
| individual (n) | the same as |
| key (adj) | |

## Introduction

Choose some of these adjectives for describing people (from Level 1 of *Progressive Skills in English*) and spend a few minutes revising them:

| | |
|---|---|
| polite | sensible |
| efficient | responsible |
| confident | careful |
| shy | employable |
| miserable | friendly |
| helpful | punctual |
| practical | violent |
| introvert | sociable |
| extrovert | |

You could ask students to find in the list:
- *pairs of 'opposites'*
- *positive and negative adjectives*
- *spelling patterns, e.g., ending in ~ent, ~ble, ~ful, ~al*

Ask students what we mean if we say a person is ...
- *impossible*
- *impressive*
- *warm*
- *cold*
- *creative*

Students could add some of these words to the vocabulary list on the right-hand side of their Course Book.

### 2.1 Vocabulary for listening: Describing personality

### Objectives

By the end of the lesson, students should be able to:
- relate spoken vocabulary on the topic of the theme to their written forms;
- show understanding of meanings and use of target vocabulary from the theme.

### A  Activating ideas

Exploit the visuals of the social network sites. Ask students:
- *Do you use any of them?*
- *How long do you spend on them each day?*
- *What does* reunite *mean?*

Go over the example. Divide the students into pairs or small groups. Play each statement from ⏵ 2.1, and pause to allow students to discuss each one. Check some of the vocabulary:
- *waste of time*
- *silly*
- *marvellous*
- *bring people together*
- *replace*
- *meet someone face to face*

When all the statements have been played, ask students to report back on whether they agreed or disagreed with each one.

Answers

Answers depend on students.

## Transcript

🎵 2.1

Presenter: 2.1. Theme 2: Friends and family
Lesson 2.1 Vocabulary for listening: Describing personality
Exercise A. Listen to some statements about the Internet. Do you agree or disagree with each one?

Voices:
1. Websites like Facebook waste a lot of time.
2. Twitter is just silly. Why do you want to know about every second of another person's life?
3. Friends Reunited is a marvellous site. It brings people back together, sometimes after years and years.
4. Social networking sites are dangerous. They have replaced real communication between people.
5. You cannot be friends with someone you have only met on a website. You must meet them face to face.

### B Understanding vocabulary in context

1. Check students understand the task. Students complete the activity individually, then compare their answers in pairs. Elicit answers. Say each adjective so that students can hear the correct pronunciation. Some explanation of meaning may be necessary at this stage but try not to go into too much detail as the target vocabulary is explained during the rest of this exercise.

2. Check students understand the task and go over the example. Play 🎵 2.2. Students compare their answers in pairs. Elicit answers. Elicit where the stressed syllable is in each adjective.

3. Do an example with the class using the adjective *independent* (see Answers below). Play 🎵 2.3. Pause after each extract to give students time to make notes. Elicit answers, preferably using an electronic projection.

### Answers

1. Adjectives describing people from the word list are:
*available, communicative, complex, considerate, critical, honest* (given as the adverb *honestly* in the word list), *independent, negative, positive, reliable, supportive*

2–3. See table opposite.

|   | adjective | meaning |
|---|-----------|---------|
| 1 | inde'pendent | lives own life; doesn't ask for help all the time |
| 2 | 'positive | optimistic, even when things are bad |
| 3 | re'liable | does things as promised |
| 4 | con'siderate | asks how people are feeling, if they need any help |
| 5 | su'pportive | there for you, doesn't criticize |
| 6 | 'honest | tells the truth, all the time |
| 7 | a'vailable | there when you need someone |
| 8 | co'mmunicative | gives information about themselves, listens |

## Transcripts

🎵 2.2

Presenter: 2.2. Exercise B2. Listen to some people. Each person is talking about his/her best friend. Number the adjectives in the order you hear them.

Voices:
1. I love her because she is so independent. She just lives her own life. She doesn't ask you for help all the time.
2. He's a very positive guy. I mean, he is always optimistic about situations, even when they are very bad. He makes me feel positive when I am with him.
3. She's totally reliable. If she promises to do something, she does it. Every time. I really like that.
4. He's extremely considerate. You know, he always asks me how I am feeling. He asks me if I need any help with anything. I believe he thinks about other people more than he thinks about himself.
5. She's very supportive. I have had a lot of problems, but she is always there for me. She doesn't criticize.
6. She always tells you the truth, even if you don't really want to hear it. She is too honest at times, but I admire that, really.
7. He's available. That's what I like about him. Do you know what I mean? He's always there when you need someone.
8. She's very communicative. You know, some people don't give you any information, about themselves, their work, their feelings. But he tells me everything – and he listens, too.

🎵 2.3

Presenter: 2.3. Exercise B3. Listen again and make a note of the meaning of each adjective.
[REPEAT OF SCRIPT FROM 🎵 2.2].

### Methodology note

*so* + adjective – Make sure students realize this is a different use of the word *so* – it is being used as an adverb here, not a conjunction.

*totally* – This can be collocated with *reliable* and *honest*, but not usually with the other adjectives in this set. However, a lot depends on context and intonation.

Theme 2: Listening  77

### C  Using new vocabulary

Play ⊙ 2.2 from Exercise B again if necessary, or using the transcript, focus on how adjectives are made stronger. For example:

Extract 1: *she's **so** independent*

Extract 4: *he's **extremely** considerate*

Go over the patterns in the tables.

Suggest or elicit other vocabulary and collocations. For example, we often say *totally* or *extremely reliable* instead of *very reliable*.

Set the task. Monitor and give help where necessary. Students should report back on what their partner said about his/her friends. This is in order to make sure students listened to each other's descriptions.

### Answers

Answers depend on students.

### Methodology note

A prefix added to adjectives often gives them a negative connotation. An exception to this is the word *independent* which has a positive connotation, whereas the word *dependent* can sometimes have a negative connotation. Discuss the meaning of *dependent* and elicit examples of people who are very dependent, e.g., babies and very young children, elderly people, people who are sick or disabled, etc. Compare the meaning with this sentence: *He's 40 years old but he's still very dependent on his mother.*

### D  Word-building

Set the task. Students complete the activity individually, then compare their answers in pairs. Elicit answers.

### Answers

|  | un | in | im | dis |
|---|---|---|---|---|
| friendly | ✓ | | | |
| considerate | | ✓ | | |
| honest | | | | ✓ |
| communicative | ✓ | | | |
| reliable | ✓ | | | |
| confident | ✓ | | | |
| polite | | | ✓ | |

### Closure

Discuss the difference in meaning (if any) between these pairs of sentences:
- *She's too independent. / She's very independent.*
- *He's quite interesting. / He's boring.*
- *That lecturer is extremely communicative. / That lecturer is very communicative.*
- *My boss is really inconsiderate. / My boss is quite considerate.*
- *I like him because he's so positive. / I like him because he's very positive.*

## 2.2 Real-time listening: Making friends

### Objectives

By the end of the lesson, students should be able to:
- attempt to understand a lecture about the psychology of friendship;
- use previously learnt sub-skills about making a note of the research source;
- have a better understanding of the meaning of target vocabulary for the Listening section.

### Introduction

Revise some of the adjectives for describing people from the previous lesson. Focus on the following:
- using prefixes to make 'opposites', for example, *(dis)honest, (un)reliable*, etc.
- stressed syllables
- using adjectives with intensifiers, for example, *very, so, really*, etc.

Ask students to complete the sentences below using adjectives:

*Many politicians are ... communicative, dishonest,* etc.
*Most film stars are ...*
*Nurses are usually ...*
*Teachers should be ...*
*Mothers are always ...*
*Teenagers are sometimes ...*
*Some footballers are ...*

Exploit the visuals on page 45 of the Course Book. Ask:
*Who can you see in each picture?*
*Where are the people?*

*What is the relationship between the people?*
*What are they doing?*
*How does each person feel?*

Push students to be specific about the people, the locations and their actions.

Say: *The pictures could show different aspects of friendship.*

Match the pictures to the statements below. Read the statements and ask students to discuss, and then tell you, the correct number in each case.

Note that some statements could match with more than one picture.

| He doesn't feel part of the group anymore. | 3 |
| It's fun to tell stories about other people, even if they used to be your friends. | 7 |
| She has so many friends. She sometimes doesn't even know I'm here. | 9 |
| Sometimes you really need a friend. | 6 |
| They are best friends at primary school. | 1 |
| They argue all the time but it is just in fun. | 5 |
| They don't talk very much but they enjoy being in each other's company. | 8 |
| They tell each other everything. | 4 |
| These girls change their friendships regularly. | 2 |

### A  Activating ideas

Check students understand the vocabulary in the text by the Sociology Department:
*in sociological terms* = in this particular situation, i.e., not in everyday conversation
*uncertainty*
*classical* = e.g., Greek
*views*

Students discuss the three questions in pairs or small groups. Elicit ideas.

### Answers

Answers depend on students.

### B  Understanding an introduction

1. Set the task. Remind students how to make a note of research sources – this was covered in Lesson 1.3 Learning new listening skills in Theme 1 (page 14 of the Course Book). Remind students not to worry about spelling at this stage. Play DVD 2.A. Elicit answers, preferably using an electronic projection. Show the spelling of *Ueno* which can be pronounced /weɪnəʊ/ or /uːweɪnəʊ/. (This is a Japanese name, so exact equivalents are difficult to express in phonemic script.)

2. Explain that the lecturer is going to tell the students exactly what points will be covered in the rest of the lecture. Having listened to the first part of the introduction, students should be able to predict which points will be covered.

   Check the meaning of *acquaintance* and elicit the meaning of the first point *(how an acquaintance can become a friend)*. Ask students to discuss the six points and decide on any that are irrelevant. Elicit ideas but do not confirm or correct at this stage.

   Now set the task. Students should watch DVD 2.B and number the relevant points in order. Play the DVD. Elicit answers.

### Answers

1. *Friendship in adolescents*
   Ueno (2004)
2. 

| 2 | acquaintance → friend |
| 3 | characteristics of people with many friends |
| 4 | personal survey on friendship |
|   | difference between friends / family members |
| 1 | difference between friends / acquaintances |
|   | problems with friends |

### Transcripts

🔊 2.4   DVD 2.A

Presenter: 2.4. Lesson 2.2. Real-time listening: Making friends.
Lecturer: Today, I'm going to talk about a basic idea which links psychology and sociology. Psychology, as you know, is about the individual. Sociology is about people in groups. One part of everyday life links individuals and makes them into groups. It is friendship. Research has shown that people with a number of close friends are generally healthier, in mind and body, than people without. For example, there is research from 2004. It is by Koji Ueno from Florida State University. Ueno studied adolescents – that is, teenagers. He questioned over 11,000 teenagers, and found that the people with more friends were happier.

🔊 2.5   DVD 2.B

Lecturer: Today, I'm going to talk about friendship. First, I will discuss two words which are often used together – friends and acquaintances. I will identify the key difference between the two words. After that, I'm going to talk about how an acquaintance can become a friend. Next, I will list the characteristics of people with a lot of friends. We'll see the view of psychologists. Finally, you're going to do a personal survey. You'll find out if you can make a lot of friends.

Theme 2: Listening   79

### Methodology note

The statement in Exercise C, question 5 is possibly the most difficult one to understand. It uses the structure *make someone do something*. The usual meaning of this pattern is often explained as 'to force, compel or oblige someone to do something', e.g., *My mother made me stay at home yesterday evening*. The meaning here is not really one of force, but more one of making something happen as in *That song makes me want to dance*.

**C** Understanding a lecture

Give students time to read through the statements. Play DVD 2.C. Students discuss the statements in pairs. Elicit answers. Ask students, with books closed, to summarize the main points of the lecture. This can be done orally or in writing, for example:
*Everyone has many acquaintances.*
*However, friends and acquaintances are not the same.*
*Acquaintances only become friends if we like them.*
*Family members can be friends.*
*People like you because you make them like you.*

### Answers

1. Some people do not have many acquaintances. *F*
2. Friends and acquaintances are very similar. *F*
3. Acquaintances only become friends if we like them. *T*
4. Family members can never be true friends. *F*
5. People like you because you make them like you. *T*

### Transcript

2.6 DVD 2.C

Lecturer: So, first, let's try to understand the difference between friends and acquaintances. Everyone has many acquaintances. Acquaintances are simply people that we know. We know them from the social clubs that we go to, from the places that we work in or from our local neighbourhood. We know them from university. We see them around the campus at university and we say hello to them. Some acquaintances are also relatives. We meet them on family occasions.

But there is a big difference between an acquaintance and a friend. What is the key difference? It is simply this. A friend always starts out as an acquaintance. But something draws the acquaintances together, and they become friends. It is obvious but the point is ... we must like acquaintances for them to become friends. Perhaps we don't like everything about them, but we feel positive about most of their characteristics. Incidentally, relatives can also be friends. I know that we talk about friends and family, or relatives and friends, which suggests that they must be different people. But mothers and fathers can be friends with their sons and daughters. In fact, some of the closest friendships can be inside a family.

Now let's consider what makes us like an acquaintance. What makes us like someone so much that he or she becomes a friend? Psychologists say if you want to make friends, you must think about yourself. What I'm saying is ... you must make people like you. It is possible to change your behaviour or your attitude, to become more likable. But what should you change? Again, psychology has the answer. Ask yourself what you like about other people. Ask yourself what you dislike. Then ask yourself if you would like to be your friend.

So, to sum up ... firstly, we must like acquaintances for them to become friends. We've heard that likeable people make friends easily. So the point is, you must make yourself likeable. Finally, as we have seen, psychologists say there are certain characteristics that make people likeable.

OK. Let's finish with a bit of fun! Are you a likeable person? I've prepared a handout. Can you take one and pass the rest on? Work through the statements on the handout and find out whether you are likeable. Psychologists suggest that likeable people can answer yes – honestly – to most or all of these statements. Check your answers with someone who knows you well.

### Methodology note

We have deliberately avoided the use of *quite* as an intensifier in this section. The rules of use are very complex and the meaning can change depending on the intonation of the speaker. It does not collocate with some adjectives unless the correct intonation pattern is used. However, if your students already 'know' the word and produce sentences such as *I am quite independent*, etc., then you can accept them without going into too much explanation.

**D** Applying information to the real world

Check students understand the task. Students read the handout. If necessary, check the meanings of the adjectives. Practise some of the target sentences with the class and elicit some possible variations. Highlight the word order on the board:
*I am very / extremely / really / totally independent.*
*I am not very independent. / Sometimes I am independent.*
*I am not (very) independent at all. / I am never independent.*

Students complete the 'handout' in pairs. Monitor. Ask students to report on their friend's results. Give feedback.

**Closure**

Ask students if they think any other adjectives should be in the questions on the 'handout', for example, *friendly*, *happy*, *polite*, *sociable*, etc.

### 2.3 Learning new listening skills: The main idea

**Objectives**

By the end of this lesson, students should be able to:
- recognize the language used to introduce the main points in a lecture;
- predict nouns in some common fixed phrases.

**Introduction**

Do further revision work on adjectives for describing people, for example:
*Write five sentences describing yourself.*

Encourage students to use phrases such as *very, really, not ... at all*, etc.

Ask some of the students to read out their sentences.

**Methodology note**

There are many fixed phrases in English for which there are no rules. Students simply have to learn them as words that 'go together'. If students hear the start of the phrase, they should be able to predict the end of the phrase. In the cases shown here, the words can often be in a different order, for example: *old and young, children and adults*.

**A** Recognizing fixed phrases

Check students understand the task. Play 2.7. Do not elicit answers until you have played every phrase. When you have reached the last phrase, rewind to the beginning again. Replay each phrase and elicit answers.

Finally, ask students to close their books or cover the exercise. Say the beginning of each phrase and ask students to complete it.

**Transcript and Answers**

2.7

Presenter: 2.7. Lesson 2.3. Learning new listening skills: The main idea. Exercise A. Listen and number the next noun in each case.
1. friends and…
2. family and…
3. mothers and …
4. sons and …
5. brothers and
6. men and
7. adults

**B** Identifying a new skill

Revise the meaning of the adjective *main* (taught in Theme 5 in Level 1) in this context. Explain that this Skills Check is about understanding the main – or most important – point(s) in a lecture.

Students read the information. Ask the class: *What phrases do speakers use to introduce the main idea? (The point is …, The thing is …, etc.) What phrases do speakers use at the end of a lecture? (To sum up …, As we have seen …, etc.) What should you do when you hear these phrases?* (write the main idea, underline the main idea in your notes)

Set the task. This can be done in a number of ways:
- Students can complete the task from memory, either individually or in pairs.
- You can give the class prompts to help them remember each point.
- Elicit each point.
- Give out copies of the transcript of the DVD extracts from Lesson 2.2 Real-time listening, if you have not already done so.
- Play the DVD extracts of the lecture in Lesson 2.2 one more time.

**Answers**

Model answers (other wordings are possible):
1. we must like acquaintances then they may become friends
2. likeable people make friends easily
3. you must make yourself likeable
4. psychologists say certain characteristics make you likeable

> **Methodology note**
>
> Try to play the CD only once for the main activity, Exercise C. However, you can replay it for follow-up activities and/or analysis of the language used.

### C  Practising a new skill

Explain that the main point is not always at the end of the extract. Play the first extract from ♪ 2.8 and check students understand the task. Play the rest of the extracts.

Students complete the notes individually, then compare their answers in pairs. Elicit answers, preferably using an electronic projection of the notes. Give out copies of the transcript if you wish.

### Answers

1. Psych = ind. ; Soc. = group
2. people w. friends = healthy – body + mind
3. give prompt in lang. tests
4. will forget if not rehearsed
5. must pay att. – move to short-term memory

### Transcript

♪ 2.8

Presenter: 2.8. Exercise C. Listen to some extracts from lectures and tutorials. Make a note of the main idea in each case.

Lecturer 1: We've heard a lot of information about psychology and sociology in today's lecture. I've mentioned some of the definitions of the fields of study, and I've pointed out some areas where the two disciplines overlap. But the key difference is, psychology is about the individual and sociology is about groups.

Lecturer 2: So to sum up. Most people want to have friends. Life is better with friends. It is more fun. But research suggests that friends are not just for fun. They are very important in everyday life. As we have heard today, Ueno conducted research into this in 2004. The point is … people with friends are more healthy, in their bodies and in their minds.

Lecturer 3: There are many kinds of language test. There are true/false tests, multiple choice tests, gap fills. They all give the students prompts. The most important thing is, give a prompt in a language test. Unfortunately, a lot of teachers don't really think about this when they write tests.

Lecturer 4: You meet a lot of new words in every lesson. You hear new words from the teacher, and maybe from other students. You read new words in texts and in exercises. But the thing to remember is, you will forget all of them if you don't rehearse them. It's nothing to do with intelligence, or how many hours you study. It just the way that the brain works.

Lecturer 5: The human brain receives information all the time from the outside world. The information comes through the eyes, through the ears, through the nose. It goes into the sensory memory. Most of it, 99.9% of it probably, goes straight out of sensory memory within three seconds. The point is … we must pay attention to the information. Then we move it into short-term memory.

### Closure

If you have not already done so, give out copies of the transcript from Exercise C. Elicit and revise the vocabulary in the extracts.

## 2.4 Grammar for listening: Transitive and intransitive verbs

> **Objectives**
>
> By the end of the lesson, students should be able to:
>
> - predict content when listening to the start of sentences with transitive and intransitive verbs;
> - demonstrate understanding of the difference between transitive and intransitive verbs.

### Introduction

Revise the meanings of the following pairs of words:

- *teenagers* and *adolescents*
- *psychology* and *sociology*
- *friends* and *acquaintances*
- *friends* and *colleagues*
- *considerate* and *careful*
- *several* and *many*

All these words are used in the lesson, with the exception of *careful* and *many*.

### Grammar box 7

Students' books closed. Write the first half of each sentence (subject and verb) from Table 1 on the board and elicit different possible ways to complete each sentence. For example:
*We go …*
*to a restaurant on Sundays.*
*to the cinema occasionally.*
*to Italy for our holidays.*

Now ask students to study the information and the table in their books. Check students understand all the information.

Repeat this procedure for Table 2.

## A  Predicting the type of information

Set the task, making sure students understand they should predict the type of information (e.g., location, job, etc.) as well as the possible words.

Divide the class into small groups of three or four. Play 2.9, pausing after each sentence. Allow students to discuss different possibilities. Elicit possible answers. Give out copies of the transcript, or display it on the board using an electronic projection.

### Answers

1. location? e.g., *at / for the university of Florida*; job? e.g., *as a Psychology professor*
2. manner, e.g., *quickly*
3. manner, e.g., *steeply*; time, e.g., *yesterday*
4. manner, e.g., *well*
5. location, e.g., *with a friend; in a tent*
6. time, e.g., *in the summer*; frequency, e.g., *every two years*
7. reason, e.g., *because people have different personalities*
8. location, e.g., *in central Africa*

### Transcript

2.9

Presenter: 2.9. Grammar for listening: Transitive and intransitive verbs. Exercise A. Listen to the start of some sentences with intransitive verbs. What kind of information do you expect to come next?

Voices:
1. At the time of his most famous research, Ueno worked …
2. She was very late so she walked …
3. The price of oil fell …
4. The plant in the first pot grew …
5. He was very poor and he lived …
6. The biggest cultural event of the year happens …
7. Many problems in families occur…
8. Thousands of years ago, many tribes existed …

## B  Predicting the object

Check students understand the task and go over the example. Remind students about transitive verbs and if necessary refer them back to Table 2 again.

Give students time to read all the phrases for completion. Play 2.10. Students complete the task individually, then compare their answers in pairs.

Do not elicit answers. Play 2.11, which has the full sentences, so that students can check their ideas. Finally, go over any sentences that students had difficulty with.

### Answers

| 1. Ueno questioned … | 5 | considerate people. |
|---|---|---|
| 2. I want to talk about … | 6 | a handout. |
| 3. Let's discuss … | 1 | over 11,000 teenagers. |
| 4. Everybody has … | 8 | several colleagues. |
| 5. I like … | 4 | a lot of acquaintances. |
| 6. I've prepared … | 7 | acquaintances in many different places. |
| 7. We meet … | 2 | friendship. |
| 8. Bahrick worked with … | 3 | the differences between friends and acquaintances. |

### Transcripts

2.10

Presenter: 2.10. Exercise B1. Listen to the start of some sentences with transitive verbs. Find and number a suitable object in each case.

Voices:
1. Ueno questioned …
2. I want to talk about …
3. Let's discuss …
4. Everybody has …
5. I like …
6. I've prepared …
7. We meet …
8. Bahrick worked with …

2.11

Presenter: 2.11. Exercise B1. Listen to the start of some sentences with transitive verbs. Find and number a suitable object in each case.

Voices:
1. Ueno questioned over 11,000 teenagers.
2. I want to talk about friendship.
3. Let's discuss the differences between friends and acquaintances.
4. Everybody has a lot of acquaintances.
5. I like considerate people.
6. I've prepared a handout.
7. We meet acquaintances in many different places.
8. Bahrick worked with several colleagues.

### Methodology note

An alternative procedure to the one given below is that you simply play each sentence, pause the CD and elicit possible completions. This is a more teacher-paced activity rather than the student-centred one given below.

## C  Predicting the next word or phrase

Divide the class into pairs. Play 2.12 and pause after each sentence. In each pair, each student should suggest a possible ending to their partner. They should then decide which is the 'best' suggestion. You can either elicit ideas after each sentence or you can wait until all the sentences have been discussed.

## Transcript and Answers

🔊 2.12

Presenter: 2.12. Exercise C. Listen to the start of some more sentences with transitive verbs. Complete each sentence with something logical.

Voices:
1. Short-term memory stores …
2. At school, we had to memorize …
3. I'm sorry. I can't remember …
4. Last year, I went …
5. In a vocabulary lesson, you must rehearse …
6. New information in short-term memory pushes out …
7. The train arrived …
8. I need to improve …
9. What do you think of …
10. The child was crying …
11. Do you prefer …
12. I always find it difficult to concentrate on …
13. Teachers should vary …
14. During the summer, she worked …
15. I'm going to demonstrate …
16. I always misspell …

## Closure

Remind students that dictionaries will tell them if a verb is transitive or intransitive. You could spend a few minutes asking students to look up some verbs (write a list on the board) to find this information out:

*trust* (t)
*allow* (it)
*make* (t)
*support* (t)
*promise* (it)
*demonstrate* (t)

Warn students, though, that some verbs can be both! This depends on the different meanings some verbs can have. For example:

*The teacher could communicate the meanings of new words very well.* (Transitive – meaning = explain, express)

*He's deaf so he uses sign language to communicate with other people.* (Intransitive – meaning = give information)

*Criticize* is another example of a verb (also in this section) which can be either transitive or intransitive.

However, do not spend too much time on this language point. It is enough that students are simply aware of the concept at this stage.

## 2.5 Applying new listening skills: Keeping friends

### Objectives

By the end of the lesson, students should be able to:
- make notes of the main points from a Psychology lecture;
- show understanding of facts about the psychology of friendship.

### Introduction

*Keep* can have many different meanings. Ask students to use their dictionaries for two minutes to only find out some different meanings, for example:
- *keep a friend* (not lose)
- *keep someone's book, DVD, CD, pen, etc.* (not give back)
- *keep warm, dry, etc.*
- *keep something clean, tidy, etc.*
- *keep doing something*
- *keep something in a drawer, cupboard, etc.*
- *keep a secret, promise, etc.*
- *keep food*

There are also many colloquial expressions and phrasal verbs with *keep*.

Tell students that in this lesson they are going to learn about *keeping friends*. Elicit the opposite meaning of *keep* in this context (*losing friends*).

### A  Activating ideas

Students discuss in pairs. Elicit ideas.

**Answers**

Answers depend on students.

### B  Understanding an introduction

Check students understand the task. Remind them how make a note of the research source (topic, author and date).

Ask them to cover the student notes in the Course Book. Play the introduction of the lecture from DVD 2.D. Students complete the task individually, then compare their research source notes in pairs. Elicit answers, preferably using an electronic projection. Tell students not to worry about the meaning of *acceptance*, *approval* and *appreciation*. Students should listen for the definitions of these three words in the next part of the lecture.

### Answers
See Exercise C.

### Transcript

2.13  DVD  2.D

**Presenter:** 2.13. Lesson 2.5. Applying new listening skills: Keeping friends

**Lecturer:** In the last lecture, I looked at the importance of friendship, and the process of making friends. We saw that there are certain characteristics which make you likeable, like independence and honesty. They make you a good friend for most people. But what about keeping friends? According to many psychologists and sociologists, it is not enough just to be likeable yourself. You must actually like other people. Perhaps this sounds easy but, for many people, it is not. In this lecture, I'm going to look at barriers to friendship. Barriers are things which get in the way. The psychologist, Mary Milliken, says that there are three barriers, things that get in the way of liking another person. In her book *Understanding Human Behaviour*, which was published in 1981, Milliken calls them the three As – acceptance, approval, and appreciation. So let's look at each one in turn.

### C  Following a lecture

Remind students how to listen for the main points – if necessary, refer them back to the Skills Check box in Lesson 2.3 Learning new listening skills. Also, remind students that the main points will be repeated in a summary at the end of the lecture.

Play  DVD  2.E. Students complete their notes individually, then compare their answers in pairs. Elicit answers, preferably using an electronic projection.

Check students have understood the meanings of the three nouns *acceptance*, *approval*, *appreciation*.

### Answers
Model answers:

> <u>Barriers to friendship</u> –
> Milliken (1981)
> 1. <u>Acceptance</u>
>    Do not try to change your friends
> 2. <u>Approval</u>
>    Notice other people – appearance, actions, achievements
> 3. <u>Appreciation</u>
>    Don't just accept and approve. Show appreciation

### Transcript

2.14  DVD  2.E

**Lecturer:** Firstly, we have acceptance. Some people want to change other people. They cannot accept them the way they are. They don't allow other people to be themselves. In particular, people often cannot accept the other relationships of a close friend. Why is she friendly with her? But human needs are complex and you will never understand all the needs of other people, even your closest friends. The point is … you should not try to change your friends. Most people don't want to change, or can't change, so that is the first barrier to friendship.

Secondly, there is approval. Some people find it easier to criticize than to find the good things in a person. Have you ever failed to show approval when a friend has been successful? Sometimes we find it difficult to be happy for another person's success, even a close friend. You need to fight this feeling, which is really simply jealousy. Milliken says we should start by looking for something that you can approve of, something you can like, in another person. At first, it can be something small – like the way that they dress or the way they smile. But once you start to approve, you will find the number of things grow and become more important. This does not mean insincere compliments. What I'm saying is, you must notice other people – their appearance, their actions, and their achievements. People want to be approved of, so constant lack of approval is the second barrier to friendship.

Finally, appreciation. We have heard that you must accept a person for what they are. We have also heard that you must approve of your friends, their behaviour, their attitudes or their achievements. But you must go further if you want to keep friends. You must show that you accept and approve. Show that you value them. Thank them for any kind words or helpful actions. Show them that you appreciate them, that they are special to you. Many countries now have special days for appreciation of particular people – mothers, fathers, children, teachers. Some people say, 'This is just commercial. It's just an opportunity for shops to sell silly cards.' But a mother, or a father or a child or a teacher may feel hurt if you do not buy a card, to show your appreciation of the special day. So the thing to remember is … don't just accept and approve – show appreciation.

So, to sum up, you need to be likeable to make friends easily but you need to like other people to keep friends. You need to accept them. Do not try to change them. You need to approve of them. You need to notice their appearance, their actions and their achievement. Finally, you need to show appreciation. Don't just accept and approve.

### Methodology note
You could spend a few minutes discussing if the verbs in Exercise D are transitive or intransitive (see previous lesson) as this will help students understand the type of word that follows. In fact, all the verbs in this exercise are transitive except for:
Sentence 3 – *get*
Sentence 5 – *are* (be)

Theme 2: Listening  85

Also note that *criticize* can be transitive or intransitive depending on the meaning. Here it is used transitively.

### D  Checking understanding

Set the task. Students can work on each sentence in pairs. It does not matter at this stage if they cannot remember many of the words and phrases to complete each sentence. Ask students to focus on the type of word or information that should come next. Do not elicit answers. Play the DVD again from the previous exercise for students to check their answers. Elicit answers, preferably using an electronic projection. You could also give out copies of the transcript at this point.

#### Answers

Possible endings:

1. In the last lecture, I looked at *the importance of friendship*.
2. You must like *other people to make a lot of friends*.
3. There are many barriers which get *in the way of friendship*.
4. Milliken has written *a book about the barriers to friendship*.
5. The barriers are *acceptance, approval and appreciation*.
6. Some people cannot accept *people the way they are*.
7. They don't allow *people to be themselves*.
8. Some people criticize *other people all the time*.
9. Some people don't show *approval of other people*.
10. If you accept, approve and show appreciation, you will make *friends easily*.

### E  Transferring information

Display the table below on the board without the verbs. Ask students to copy and complete the table.

| verbs | nouns |
| --- | --- |
| accept | acceptance |
| approve | approval |
| appreciate | appreciation |

Students discuss ideas about acceptance, approval and appreciation in pairs or small groups.

#### Answers

Answers depend on students.

### Closure

Choose one of the following:

- Use Exercise E for Closure.
- Revise some of the vocabulary from the Listening section – especially adjectives, and prefixes to give 'opposite' adjectives, for describing people.
- Students discuss in pairs if they have ever lost a friend, the reasons for this happening and how it felt.

# Speaking: Apologizing

**2.6 Vocabulary for speaking:**
*Sorry is the hardest word*

### Objectives

By the end of the lesson, students should be able to:
- show understanding of, and pronounce, target vocabulary from the Speaking section;
- report sentences using *apologize for* + *~ing*.

| verb | adjective | noun |
|---|---|---|
| 1. con'sider | con'siderate | conside'ration |
| 2. re'ly | re'liable | relia'bility |
| 3. 'criticize | 'critical | 'criticism |
| 4. a'ppreciate | a'ppreciative | appreci'ation |
| 5. co'mmunicate | co'mmunicative | communi'cation |
| 6. su'pport | su'pportive | su'pport |
| 7. like | 'likeable | |
| 8. | 'honest | 'honesty |

## Introduction

Exploit the visuals. Discuss if it is acceptable to say sorry in writing rather than face to face (check/teach the expression). If so, when is it acceptable? What does the phrase *sorry is the hardest word* mean?

### A  Reviewing key vocabulary

Briefly revise some of the words in the table and check pronunciation and stress. In pairs, students discuss the answers for the missing words and also decide on the stressed syllable. Point out how the stress sometimes moves as the part of speech changes. Elicit answers and practise each word.

In pairs, students decide which word in each row they want to work on. Each student thinks of a good sentence to say for the chosen word. Students decide which is the 'best' sentence out of the two (this may be because it is longer or more interesting, or because it uses better vocabulary). Students practise saying the chosen sentence with good pronunciation. Students repeat this process with each row of words. Monitor and give help where necessary. Ask some of the students to say their sentences for the rest of the class to hear.

### Answers
1. See table opposite.
2. Answers depend on students.

### Methodology note

If you wish, you can highlight the verb forms when following another verb, e.g.,
*promise (not)* **to do**
*avoid* **doing**, etc.

However, these are dealt with in more detail in Theme 3 (as well as in later themes) so do not spend too long on them at this stage.

### B  Understanding new words in context

1. Elicit the meaning of *upset*. Elicit possible situations where students might have upset someone, for example:
   *forgetting to phone, text, meet*
   *saying something unkind about the other person*
   *not returning something they borrowed*
   *'stealing' someone's boy/girlfriend*

   In pairs, students discuss what they would do to try to put things right. Elicit ideas but do not confirm or correct at this stage.

2. Still in pairs, students discuss each possible solution. Students should try to work out the meanings of the target vocabulary from context:
   *ignore*
   *carry on*
   *avoid*
   *make an excuse*
   *emphasis*
   *promise not to do something*
   *apologize*
   *put things right*

If you wish, students can also use dictionaries. Monitor and give help if students really cannot work out the meaning of a particular word or phrase.

Find out if any of the students' solutions in Exercise B1 matched one of the solutions given here.

Check and practise the pronunciation of *emphasis* /ˈemfəsɪs/ and *avoid* /əˈvɔɪd/.

3. Check students understand the task. One way to do the activity is for students to listen and make notes next to each solution in the 'problem box' in the Course Book. Play DVD 2.F. Students compare their notes in pairs. Play the DVD again if necessary. Elicit answers.

Spend a few more minutes checking vocabulary and phrases from the transcript, e.g.,

*problems don't go away by themselves ...*
*... even between friends*
*even harder*
*deal with*
*common*
*sincere* vs *sincerity*
*emphasis* vs *emphasize* (note the change in the pronunciation of the verb's ending: /ˈemfəsaɪz/)
*combination*
*face to face*

4. The role play can be done using one of the following methods, depending on the level of your class:
   - *Students work from the transcript.*
   - *Give out a gapped version of the transcript.*
   - *Students do the role play using their notes/answers from Exercise B3.*

Whatever method you decide to use, it is a good idea to drill some of the key phrases and/or sentences before students do the role play.

Monitor and give feedback.

### Answers

1–2. Answers depend on students.
3. See table opposite.

| solutions | responses |
|---|---|
| a. Ignore it and carry on as if nothing has happened. | Problems don't go away by themselves. |
| b. Avoid your friend for a little while and hope he/she forgets about it. | It may be even harder to deal with the problem the longer you leave it. |
| c. Say sorry but make an excuse for your actions or words. | Your friend may think you are not sincere if you make too many excuses. |
| d. Meet your friend and apologize with emphasis – *I'm very, very sorry.* | Emphasis shows your sincerity. |
| e. Say sorry and promise not to do it again. | This is a good solution – apologies should be face to face. |
| f. Say sorry and ask the person to forgive you. | This is a good solution. |
| g. Apologize for behaving badly. | This is a good solution. |
| h. Offer to put things right. | This is a good solution. |

### Transcript

2.15 DVD 2.F

Presenter: 2.15. Lesson 2.6. Vocabulary for speaking: *Sorry is the hardest word*
Tutor: So, what do you think? Which is the best solution?
Student 1: I think you should ignore it and carry on as if nothing has happened.
Student 2: But people don't usually forget insults or bad behaviour. Problems don't usually go away by themselves, even between friends.
Student 3: I agree. That's not a good solution, although I do it myself sometimes!
Tutor: So, other ideas?
Student 3: I think you should avoid your friend for a little while.
Student 2: By that's the same as the first solution. In fact, it's worse. If you don't see your friend for a few days, it may be even harder to deal with the problem.
Tutor: Yes, I agree. It's a very bad solution, but of course, in some cultures, it is quite common.
Student 1: It certainly is in mine.
Student 3: I think you should say sorry but make an excuse for your actions or words.
Tutor: What do other people think? Marie – you haven't spoken yet.
Student 4: I think it is quite a good solution, but the person may think you are not sincere if you make too many excuses.
Student 1: So you could do the next one. Meet your friend and apologize with emphasis – I'm very, very sorry.
Student 4: OK. I suppose. I think that emphasis shows your sincerity.
Student 1: Actually, I've changed my mind. I think you should say sorry and promise not to do it again.
Student 2: Sometimes, in my culture, we do the next one. I mean, we ask for forgiveness.
Student 3: Yes, we do that, too. And we also offer to put things right.
Tutor: So, what about a combination of actions.
Student 1: Yes, you should apologize …
Student 2: Face to face …

88  Theme 2: Speaking

Student 1: Yes, you should emphasize your words and … what was the last one?
Student 4: You should offer to put things right.
Tutor: Great! Next problem …

### C  Understanding and reporting apologies

Check students understand the task and go over the example.

Highlight the grammar of the verb *apologize*: *apologize + for + ~ing*

Play 🔊 2.16. Pause after each line. Elicit the reported sentence. Drill the sentences.

### Answers

| 1. I'm sorry I lost your pen. | He/she apologized for losing my pen. |
|---|---|
| 2. I'm sorry. I forgot your book. | He/she apologized for forgetting my book. |
| 3. I'm really sorry. I left your CD at home. | He/she apologized for leaving my CD at home. |
| 4. I'm so sorry. I broke a glass. | He/she apologized for breaking a glass. |
| 5. I'm sorry I came late. | He/she apologized for coming late. |

### Transcript

🔊 2.16

Presenter: 2.16. Exercise C. Listen to some apologies. Report them.
Voices: 1. I'm sorry I lost your pen.
2. I'm sorry. I forgot your book.
3. I'm really sorry. I left your CD at home.
4. I'm so sorry. I broke a glass.
5. I'm sorry I came late.

### Closure

Do one of the following:

1. Use flashcards to practise the pronunciation of target vocabulary, especially for *apologize, apology, emphasize, emphasis, sincere, sincerity*, etc.

2. Ask students to make sentences with the following verbs:
*apologize*
*emphasize*
*avoid*
*carry on*
*put something right*
*ignore*
*go away*
*make an excuse*

## 2.7 Real-time speaking: Components of apologizing

### Objectives

By the end of the lesson, students should:
- be familiar with a model of an extended turn in a tutorial;
- have attempted to give an extended turn;
- have learnt some common core knowledge about a few of the sociocultural aspects of apologizing.

### Introduction

Use Exercise A as the introduction.

### Methodology note

*Do* and *make* are often confused by students as they can be the same verb in some languages. It is important to encourage students to learn the various expressions with each verb as they arise. They could make a special page in a vocabulary notebook or on file cards for expressions with each verb.

### A  Previewing vocabulary

Set the task and explain that some nouns can go with more than one verb. Students complete the activity individually, then compare their answers in pairs. Elicit answers.

Ask students to give some sentences using a few of the verb + noun combinations. Elicit sentences and drill them with the whole class.

### Answers

See table on following page.

### B  Activating ideas

1. Students discuss the question in pairs. Elicit ideas.

2. Set the task. Students discuss in pairs. Elicit answer. Ask some follow-up questions:
   - *Who were the authors of the research?* (Cohen and Olshtain)
   - *When did they write the research?* (1981)

Theme 2: Speaking   89

| verb | expression |
|---|---|
| 1. do | research |
| 2. make | a promise<br>a mistake<br>an excuse<br>an effort<br>an offer |
| 3. give | a promise<br>an excuse<br>a reason<br>an offer |
| 4. have | an excuse<br>a reason |
| 5. accept | an excuse<br>a reason<br>an offer |
| 6. reject | an offer |
| 7. apologize for | a mistake |

- *What was the name of the research?* ('Developing a measure of sociocultural competence: the case of apology')
- *Where was the research published?* (in a journal – Language and Learning)

### Answers
1. Answers depend on students.
2. It means 'different in different cultures'.

> **Methodology note**
>
> At some point during Exercise C, you may wish to remind students what they learnt on the subject of talking about research. In Level 1, students learnt phrases such as:
> *According to ...*
> *Apparently ...*
> *It seems that ...*
>
> You can also remind students about zero conditionals (taught in Theme 4 in Level 2). See the following extract for an example:
> *If you don't give a reason, people think that you don't care.*

**C** Understanding a model

1. Ask students to look at the table. Elicit the meaning of *component*. Set the task and go over the example. Play 🔊 2.17. Students discuss what the components are in pairs. Elicit answers, preferably using an electronic projection of the table.

2. Repeat the above procedure. Play 🔊 2.18. Then ask students what they think about the information. Did they find any of it surprising?

   Students may wish to make comparisons with their own culture, but try not to let any discussion go for too long as this will pre-empt the final activity.

### Answers
1. They researched the different components of apologizing in different cultures.
2. 

| component | British culture |
|---|---|
| excuses | ✓ so people think that you care |
| offers | ✓ but people often reject |
| promises | ? good – will make effort in future |
| eye contact | ✓ look person in eye |
| formality | ✓ big difference but use informal language for spoken apology |
| emphasis | ✓ make apology stronger |

### Transcripts

🔊 2.17

Presenter: 2.17. Lesson 2.7. Real-time speaking: Components of apologizing. Exercise C1. Listen to the first part of a tutorial. What did the students research?
Tutor: At the moment, we are looking at apologizing in different cultures. I asked you to research different aspects of apologizing in British culture. Let's hear what you found.

🔊 2.18

Presenter: 2.18. Exercise C2. Listen to each student. What did he or she discover about British culture?
Student 1: I looked at excuses. An excuse is a reason for your action. For example, you can say 'I'm sorry I'm late. The train didn't come on time.' According to my research, in some cultures, it is not polite to give an excuse. It means you are not really sorry for your action. You think that you had a good reason. But it seems that, in British culture, it is good to give a reason. If you don't give a reason, people may be angry. They may think that you don't care. And that's it, really.

Student 2: My topic was offers. Sometimes people offer to replace an item. For example, you can say 'I'm sorry I broke your glass. I'll buy you another one.' Apparently, in some cultures, it is rude to make an offer. The other person cannot accept it. But in British culture, offers are good. If you make an offer, people may not accept it, but they will be pleased. That's what I found.

Student 3: I researched promises. A promise talks about the future. For example, you can say 'I'm sorry I'm late. It won't happen again.' I couldn't find any information about this in other cultures. In British culture, I believe that

Student 4: I was asked to look at eye contact. This means looking at people while you are apologizing. According to my research, in some cultures, it is not polite to look at people. But in British culture, it is very important to look the person in the eye. It shows that you are sincere. I found a lot more information but that is the main point.

Student 5: I did some research on formality. This is the level of language that you use. For example, you can say 'I'm sorry that I got angry' in *speech*, but you might *write* 'I apologize for my anger.' One website said that all cultures have formal and informal speech but another one said it is not true. In British culture, there is a big difference between formal language and informal language. But informal language is fine for a spoken apology. That's what I found.

Student 6: I looked at emphasis. Emphasis means making something stronger. In some cultures, you can emphasize by repeating. For example, you can keep saying 'I'm sorry. I'm sorry. I'm sorry.' I found that, in British culture, you can emphasize an apology with *really* or *very*. For example, you can say, 'I'm really sorry' or 'I'm very sorry' to make it stronger. I think that's all.

### Methodology note

Remind students that both in this exercise and the next one, they should do their best to give their talks or 'have a go'. In this lesson, students will learn what they need to work on in order to produce a more successful talk.

Students should also revise the importance of body language, for example, eye contact with the audience. They should also speak loudly and clearly, and at the right speed (see the Speaking section of Theme 1 for more details).

Finally, two points about turn-taking. Firstly, students should understand that they should not interrupt another speaker during an extended turn in this context. The second point concerns intonation. Intonation tells the listener if the speaker is about to finish his/her turn or not. Therefore, when students use phrases for ending turns – such as *that's it really* – they should practise a falling intonation to emphasize completion.

### D Practising a model

1. Set the task. Students discuss in pairs. Elicit answers. Highlight and practise some of the language used. Elicit alternative language where possible, for example:
    - area of research: *I looked at … / I investigated …*
    - explanation: *An (excuse) is a … / Excuse means …*
    - example: *For example, …*
    - findings: *In British culture, it is … / Many British people … / In Britain they … / If you don't give a reason, …*

2. Remind students about sense groups and pauses (see Lesson 1.6 Vocabulary for speaking in Theme 1 on page 17 of the Course Book). Students discuss in pairs where the sense groups could be and mark up the text. Elicit answers; you could use an electronic projection for this or simply elicit the sense group and then drill it.

3. Drill the sense groups chorally and individually, unless you have already done so in Exercise D2 above.

4. Check students understand the task. Elicit some of the phrases from the class. Drill.

    Divide the class into pairs or small groups. Students practise giving the complete talk, or they can take it in turns to give sections of the talk. It is better if students give the talks using only a few notes, rather than having the talk written out in full. Monitor and give feedback.

### Answers

2.
*I looked at / excuses. An excuse / is a reason / for your action. // For example, / you can say / 'I'm sorry I'm late. // The train didn't come / on time.' // In some cultures, / it is not polite / to give an excuse. // It means / you are not really sorry / for your action – / you think / that you had a good reason. // In British culture, / it is good to give a reason. // If you don't give a reason, / people think / that you don't care. // And that's it, really. //*

### Methodology note

How you deal with this activity will partly depend on whether you have a multi-national or a mono-cultural group. Students from the same culture can work in pairs or small groups to make notes. Students from different cultural backgrounds can give their talks to each other. Do not be surprised, however, if students from the same culture disagree about the same information!

### E  Producing a model

1. Set the task and elicit one or two examples. Put students from the same culture into pairs to complete the notes together (see Methodology note above). Otherwise, students can complete the task individually. Monitor and give help where necessary.

2. In a multicultural class, students can work in groups to give their talks. For feedback, ask one or two students to report on the differences and similarities between the cultures represented in their group.

   In a mono-lingual group – in order to keep students focused while others are giving their talks – ask students to evaluate each talk for:
   - *eye contact*
   - *pauses in correct places*
   - *correct speed*
   - *loudness*
   
   Monitor and give feedback.

#### Answers
Answers depend on students.

### Closure
Use the feedback stage from Exercise E as Closure.

---

## Everyday English: Apologizing

### Objectives
By the end of the lesson, students should be able to:
- use appropriate language to apologize in different situations.

### Introduction
Remind students of the work they have already done in this theme on the idea of apologizing.

### A  Activating ideas

1. Elicit what can be seen, what has probably just happened and how the people feel.

2. Elicit one or two ideas. Then briefly put students into small groups to think of as many situations as they can.

   Give feedback orally. Accept all reasonable suggestions.

   **Note:** British English commonly uses *I'm sorry / I'm afraid* to make an unpleasant statement more polite – for example, in a shop: *I'm afraid we're closing now*; in a hotel: *I'm sorry, but the TV in my room doesn't work*. The speaker is apologizing for the possible inconvenience that he/she might be causing to the listener, not for any harm done.

3. Elicit the word *sorry*. Then put students to work in pairs. Ask them to think of other expressions for apologizing and for answering an apology. The expressions can include the word *sorry*.

   **Note:** The expressions *Pardon?* and *I beg your pardon?* are not used for apologies, but to show that you have not heard clearly what another person has said.

   Give feedback orally. Do not put the expressions on the board yet – wait until the end of the next exercise.

#### Answers
1. Answers depend on students.
2. Answers depend on students, but here are some suggestions.

   You probably apologize when you accidentally:
   - upset someone
   - physically hurt someone
   - arrive late
   - break something
   - go back on an agreement
   - forget to do something
   - decline an invitation
   - cancel an appointment
   - are using something that someone else was using
   - don't understand what someone said
   - cause a misunderstanding

3. Some possibilities are:

| apologies | responses |
|---|---|
| Sorry. | Don't worry. |
| I'm very sorry. | It's OK. |
| I'm really sorry. | Never mind. |
| Sorry about that. | It doesn't matter. |
| I want to apologize. | Forget it. |
| I'd like to apologize. | |
| I think I should apologize. | |
| I must apologize. | |

### B  Studying models

1. Cover the conversations. Go through the sentences with the class. Clarify any vocabulary problems.

   Elicit some ideas for the first sentence. Then set the question for pairwork discussion.

   As feedback, elicit ideas orally. Accept all reasonable suggestions, but do not confirm any of them at this stage.

2. Set the task for individual work and pairwork checking. Play 2.19. Elicit answers.

> **Optional activity**
>
> Review, or work on some of the language in the conversations, for example:
>
> **verb phrase:**
> *I don't think* + positive verb form
> *have time* + infinitive
> *forget* + infinitive
> *mean* + infinitive
>
> **prepositions:**
> verb + prep
> *sleep in / come in*
> *apologize to sb*
>
> **adj + prep:**
> *be rude to sb*
>
> **time:**
> *for Monday / for next week / on time*

### Transcript and Answers

 2.19

Presenter: 2.19. Everyday English: Apologizing. Exercise B2. Listen and complete the conversations.

One.
Voice A: Sorry I'm late. Can I come in?
Voice B: Of course. What happened?
Voice A: I slept in. I'm really sorry.
Voice B: OK. Have a seat. We're just starting.

Presenter: Two.
Voice A: Oh, I forgot to bring that book for you!
Voice B: Never mind. I'll get it tomorrow.
Voice A: Sorry about that. Do you need it for the lecture?
Voice B: No. Not today.

Presenter: Three.
Voice A: I'm very sorry. I don't think I can finish my assignment on time.
Voice B: What's the problem?
Voice A: I don't have time to do the research.
Voice B: Don't worry. Can you do it for Monday?

Presenter: Four.
Voice A: Excuse me, I was sitting there.
Voice B: Oh were you? Sorry. I didn't realize.
Voice A: That's OK.
Voice B: Let me move my things.

Presenter: Five.
Voice A: I don't think I've got your assignment.
Voice B: I'm sorry. I thought it was for next week.
Voice A: No. The deadline was this week.
Voice B: I'm sorry. I misunderstood.

Presenter: Six.
Voice A: What's wrong with her?
Voice B: She's upset because you were rude to her.
Voice A: But I didn't mean to be rude!
Voice B: Well, I think you should apologize to her.

### C  Practising the model

Put on the board, and review, all the expressions in the lesson for apologizing and responding to apologies.

1. Set the task for pairwork. Monitor and assist with students' pronunciation. Note any common pronunciation errors. Play 2.19 again if you wish.

2. Demonstrate the task with one of the students. Continue the conversation for a short time, but keep it on the original topic.

   Set the task for pairwork. Do a further example if you wish. Monitor and assist. Again, make a note of common problems and errors.

   As feedback, ask volunteers to perform one of their role plays.

### Closure

1. Go over any errors that you picked up during your monitoring.

2. Do further practice: refer students back to the situations they thought of in Exercise A, and ask them to do quick role plays based on them.

---

## 2.8 Learning new speaking skills: Starting and ending a turn

### Objectives

By the end of the lesson, students should be able to:

- pronounce the stress in two-syllable nouns, adjectives and verbs;
- practise target sub-skills by introducing and ending turns.

Theme 2: Speaking    93

**Introduction**

Use Exercise A as the introduction.

### A  Reviewing sounds

Set the task. Students discuss in pairs. Do not elicit answers. Students read the Pronunciation Check.

Elicit answers. Ask students to close their books or cover the Pronunciation Check box. Elicit the rules for stress in two-syllable words. Drill some of the example words and make sure students are using the correct stressed syllable. Play 🔊 2.21, if you wish.

### Answers

1. *ex'cuse* – the others are stressed on the first syllable
2. *a'loud* – the others are stressed on the first syllable
3. *'offer* – the others are stressed on the second syllable

### Transcript

🔊 2.21

**Presenter:** 2.21. Pronunciation Check. Examples:

Voice: reason, effort, action; excuse, support; honest, angry, tidy; afraid, polite; reject, accept, prepare; promise, offer.

---

**Methodology note**

Elicit/teach the meaning of *turn* in this context (it is the time when you should – or can – do something; in this case, speak). In the Reading section of Theme 4 in Level 2 of *Progressive Skills in English*, the word was used when describing the rules for board games. We also often use *turn* with the verb *take*, for example: *We take it in turns to do the cooking each evening.*

---

### B  Identifying a key skill

1. Drill the example phrases. Play 🔊 2.22, if you wish. When students have finished reading Skills Check 1, you can refer them back to the transcript for the tutorial on apologizing in different cultures (see Lesson 2.7 Real-time speaking on page 50 of the Course Book). Ask students to find examples of introducing and ending turns.

2. Drill the example phrases. Play 🔊 2.23, if you wish. As before, when students have finished reading Skills Check 2, you can refer them back to the transcript from Lesson 2.7. Ask them to find examples of reporting problems. Make sure students use a falling intonation (see Methodology note in Lesson 2.7).

### Transcripts

🔊 2.22

**Presenter:** 2.22. Skills Check 1. Examples:
Voice: I looked at excuses.
My topic was formality.
That's it, really.
That's what I found.

🔊 2.23

**Presenter:** 2.23. Skills Check 2. Examples:
Voice: I couldn't find any information about …
There wasn't much information …
One website said …
but another one said …

### C  Practising key skills

1. If students have copies of the transcript from Lesson 2.7, make sure they put them away now. Set the task and go over the example. Students complete the activity individually, then compare their answers in pairs.

2. Play 🔊 2.20. Students check their answers. Explain why the sentences in the exercise are wrong or, better still, ask the students to explain why. When you get to g), remind students of the work they did on phrases with *do* and *make* in Lesson 2.7.

3. Drill a few of the phrases, if you wish.

### Answers

a. My topic was *offers*.
b. In British culture, ~~the~~ offers are good.
c. That's what I found ~~it~~.
d. Sorry, I didn't get ~~many~~ much information.
e. I was asked *to* look at eye contact.
f. I ~~find~~ found a lot of information.
g. I ~~made~~ did some research on formality.
h. One website ~~it~~ said that all cultures have formal and informal speech.
i. … but *another* one said it is not true.

## Transcript

🔊 2.20

**Presenter:** 2.20. Lesson 2.8: Learning new speaking skills: Starting and ending a turn. Exercise C2. Listen and check your answers.

**Voices:**
a. My topic was offers.
b. In British culture, offers are good.
c. That's what I found.
d. Sorry, I didn't get much information.
e. I was asked to look at eye contact.
f. I found a lot of information.
g. … but that is the main point.
h. I did some research on formality.
i. One website said that all cultures have formal and informal speech.
j. … but another one said it is not true.

### D Rehearsing key skills

Set the task and go over the example. Practise the sentences in the example. Explain that students should vary the structures they use. Elicit different ways of varying the example text.

1. Divide the class into pairs. Refer students to the pieces of research as follows:
   Student A – should read the text on page 177
   Student B – should read the text on page 170
   Make sure students do not look at their partner's text. While students are reading, go around the class and give help if any students are having problems understanding the piece of research.
2. Monitor while students are working. Give feedback.

## Closure

Use the feedback stage from Exercise D for Closure.

---

### 2.9 Grammar for speaking: Uses of *that*

**Objectives**

By the end of the lesson, students should be able to:
- pronounce and form sentences with *that* for finishing a turn and introducing a sentence;
- produce sentences with *that* using the correct word order.

### Introduction

Play one more time the CD of the tutorial from Lesson 2.7 Real-time speaking (on page 50 of the Course Book) with students following the transcript. This will give students the opportunity to notice how this lesson's language is being used in context.

**Methodology note**

The last phrase in Table 2 is an example of indirect speech:
*One website said that …*

In the example given, you might expect the second verb to be in the past tense:
*One website said that all cultures **had** formal and informal speech.*

However, in this case, the student is reporting a present idea. It is rare in academic English to put present ideas into the past, even when reporting.

Indirect speech is dealt with in more detail later in the course, so do not go into too much detail at this stage.

### Grammar box 8
#### Table 1

Give students time to study the three points in the top of the box. If you did not do the suggested task in the introduction above, remind students about the tutorial in Lesson 2.7. Remind them also about the work they did on completing a turn in Lesson 2.8 Learning new speaking skills. Ask students to study Table 1. Drill the sentences, checking that students pronounce the word *that* correctly – with a full vowel.

If you wish, refer students to the transcript of 🔊 2.18 (in Lesson 2.7) and ask them to find and underline the expressions from Table 1.

#### Table 2

Ask students to study Table 2 and the sentences underneath. Drill some of the sentences, making sure students try to pronounce *that* correctly – with a schwa sound.

Ask students to 'mix and match' the sentences to produce alternatives, for example:
*I found (that) British people say sorry a lot.*
*One website said (that) British people often offer to pay for mistakes.*

Ask students to suggest some sentences about other topics – such as the Solar System, memory, etc. – where *that* is not used after an introduction. For example, they could say:
*One website said there are only eight planets in the Solar System.*
*Research suggests you should always give prompts in a language test.*

## Transcript

🔊 2.24

Presenter: 2.24. Lesson 2.9. Grammar for speaking: Uses of *that*. Grammar box 8.

Presenter: Table 1.
Voice: That's what I found.
And that's it, really.
That's the end.
I think that's all.
That's all I want to say.

Presenter: Table 2.
Voices: I think that British people say sorry a lot.
I believe that promises are good.
I found that you can emphasize an apology with *really* or *very*.
I understand that British people often offer to pay for mistakes.
Research suggests that British people usually give a reason.
It seems that it is good to give a reason.
One website said that all cultures have formal and informal speech.

### A Introducing sentences

1. Exploit the visuals. Set the task and go over the example. In pairs, students make each set of words into sentences.
2. Play 🔊 2.25 so that students can check their ideas and listen to the correct pronunciation. Briefly discuss with the class what information they have learnt from these sentences about apologizing in different cultures and their reaction to it.
3. Ask students to close their books. Drill the sentences – either from the CD, pausing after each sentence for repetition, or say the sentences yourself for students to repeat.

## Transcript

🔊 2.25

Presenter: 2.25. Exercise A2. Listen and check your answers.
Voices: a. I believe that Japanese people apologize a lot.
b. I understand that Americans apologize for lateness.
c. It seems that Americans do not apologize after an accident.
d. One website said that Chinese people apologize more to strangers than to friends.
e. I understand that Chinese people apologize if they make someone look silly.
f. Research suggests that Mexicans often ask for forgiveness for their actions.
g. I found that Americans are told not to apologize for legal reasons.
h. I understand that Japanese people do not make eye contact when they apologize.

### Closure

Ask students if they are familiar with any of the cultures mentioned in Exercise A and, if so, whether they agree with the points made.

Ask students to make their own sentences beginning with the introductory phrases.

## 2.10 Applying new speaking skills: Apologizing around the world

### Objectives

By the end of the lesson, students should be able to:

- introduce, end and take turns in a tutorial, using target language from the Speaking section;
- show understanding of information about apologizing in different cultures.

### Introduction

Revise what students have learnt about apologizing in the Speaking section so far.

### A Previewing vocabulary

1. Check the meaning and pronunciation of the word *component*. Practise the pronunciation of each verb in Figure 1. Set the task.
2. Play 🔊 2.26 and pause after each sentence for students to discuss answers in pairs. Elicit answers and correct students' pronunciation if necessary.
   Drill each phrase.

### Answers

2. See table on next page.

| a. I'm very, very sorry. | emphasizing |
| b. I missed the train. | explaining |
| c. It's my fault. | taking responsibility |
| d. I'll buy you another one. | offering |
| e. It won't happen again. | promising |

## Transcript

2.26

**Presenter:** 2.26. Lesson 2.10. Applying new speaking skills: Apologizing around the world. Exercise A2. Listen to some sentences. What is the speaker doing in each case?

**Voices:**
a. I'm very, very sorry.
b. I missed the train.
c. It's my fault.
d. I'll buy you another one.
e. It won't happen again.

### Methodology note

For Exercise C2, if your group of students does not divide into groups of four, you can do the following:
- Have one or two groups of five, and ask one of the students to be the tutor and ask supplementary questions, etc.
- Alternatively, you can ask one of the students to talk about their own culture.

It does not matter if most groups do not have a 'tutor'; students can simply take it in turns to speak.

### B Researching information

1. Students read the assignment and discuss the questions in pairs. Elicit answers. Ask more questions:
   *Who were the researchers?* (Bergman and Kasper)
   *What did they research?* (apologizing in different speech groups)
   *When did they do the research?* (1993)

2. Divide the class into groups as follows:
   Group 1 – should read the text on page 175
   Group 2 – should read the text on page 172
   Group 3 – should read the text on page 176
   Group 4 – should read the text on page 178

   Check students understand the task. In their groups, students should first discuss together the information they have read and then help each other with new vocabulary and so on. They can also help each other with completing the table. Monitor and give help where necessary.

### Answers

2. Model table:

### C Using a key skill

1. Go over each point in the list, referring students back to the relevant pages or exercises in the Course Book when necessary. Drill some of the phrases if you wish.

   Set the task for group work and ask students to help each other practise their turns. In particular, they can advise each other if:
   - *there is enough eye contact*
   - *it is loud enough*
   - *it is given at the correct speed*
   - *there are pauses in the correct places*

   Students should practise their turns from notes and *not* from reading the research text aloud. Monitor and give help where necessary.

2. Re-divide the class into groups so that there is one student from Groups 1, 2, 3 and 4. Each student has a turn and gives information about their speech group. The other students make notes. Monitor and give feedback on all the points listed in Exercise C1, as well as correcting the pronunciation of target vocabulary. Tell students if they are improving on:
   - *eye contact*
   - *loudness*
   - *speed of delivery*
   - *pauses / sense groups*

Table 1: *Components of apologizing for selected speech groups*

| speech group | actual words | emphasis | responsibility | explanation | offer | promise |
|---|---|---|---|---|---|---|
| Americans | nearly always | no information | always | sometimes | never | never |
| Russians | usually | no information | usually | occasionally | never | never |
| British | very often | sometimes | very often | very rarely | rarely | occasionally |
| Germans | usually | occasionally | very often | very rarely | rarely | rarely |
| own speech community | | | | | | |

Theme 2: Speaking  97

Use an electronic projection of the completed table so that students can check their answers.

**Closure**

Ask students if they know the cultures described in the preceding activities. Do they agree with the information given?

If they have not already done so, students complete the final section in Table 1 about their own speech group.

Finally, discuss how apologizing in other cultures differs from the students' own culture(s).

# Reading: Parents, Adults and Children

## 2.11 Vocabulary for reading: Stimulus and response

**Objectives**

By the end of the lesson, students should be able to:
- recognize and understand target vocabulary from the Reading section;
- show understanding of information about the analysis of verbal transactions.

### Introduction

Exploit the visuals. Explain that this section is all about the psychology of relationships. What relationships do the pictures show? Use this question to show that *relationship* can have more than one meaning – firstly, it determines whether it is a mother–daughter relationship, for example; and secondly, whether you have a good or bad relationship with another person.

### A  Reviewing vocabulary

Set the task. Students complete the activity individually, then compare their answers in pairs. Elicit answers, preferably using an electronic projection.

**Answers**

1. fri*end*
2. colle*ague*
3. nei*ghbour*
4. ac*quaintance*
5. rel*ative* / rel*ation*
6. ado*lescent*

### B  Identifying part of speech in context

Set the task. Students complete the activity individually, then compare their answers in pairs. Elicit answers.

Ask students what all the words in italics have in common (there is no change for the verb/noun forms).

Elicit examples of other verbs/nouns with the same form. Students can look back through the previous vocabulary lists for Themes 1 and 2 for ideas:

control    name     supply
decrease   point    support
increase   rent     view

There is also the word *rebel*, which students will learn in the next activity.

**Optional activity**

Either in class or for homework, students could write two sentences for five of the italicized words, using each word as a noun in one sentence and as a verb in the other.

**Answers**

1. noun
2. noun
3. verb
4. verb
5. verb
6. noun

### C  Understanding new words in context

Check students understand the task. Students complete the text individually, then compare their answers in pairs.

If students find the activity difficult, write the first letter of each word/answer on the board. Elicit answers.

Ask further questions to check understanding of both the vocabulary and the text:
- *What kind of relationship problems can people have?* (parents with children/teenagers; husbands and wives; workmates)
- *Why do we study people's conversations?* (to understand their problems)
- *What form do conversations have?* (stimulus–response)
- *What does an unexpected response show?* (a problem with the relationship)
- *What does Figure 1 show?* (an expected response and an unexpected response)

Finally, you can write the following on the board for students to discuss in pairs or small groups:

*Discuss these questions.*
1. What do adolescents often rebel about?
2. What do husbands and wives often argue about?
3. What do workmates often disagree about?

Theme 2: Reading   99

### Answers

Relationships with other people are never simple. *Parents* often have problems with their children. Young children usually *obey* their parents but adolescents often *rebel*. Husbands often say 'My *wife* doesn't understand me.' *Workmates* have problems with each other.

We can often understand the issues between two people by analyzing the verbal *transactions*. In other words, we study their conversations. A lot of conversations have the form of stimulus–*response*. In other words, one person says something – the *stimulus* – and the other person *responds*. Sometimes, the response is expected. We know the person will reply in that way. But sometimes, it is *unexpected*. An unexpected response may reveal a problem with the relationship.

### Closure

Ask students to act out the conversations in Figure 1. Students first discuss how the people in each conversation are feeling, and then what their relationship is to each other. Students should extend the conversations if possible.

---

### 2.12 Real-time reading: Games people play

### Objectives

By the end of the lesson, students should be able to:
- predict content from a figure and topic sentences;
- show understanding of a text about a psychological model for relationships;
- show understanding of target vocabulary in context.

### Introduction

Select from the following or use a mixture:
- Write the title of the lesson on the board, *Games people play*, and discuss the possible meanings.
- Revise the meanings of some of the lesson's target vocabulary, especially for Exercise B: *stimulus, response, transaction*.
- Revise the expected and unexpected responses from Figure 1 in the previous lesson.

### A Activating ideas

Set the task. Students discuss the questions in pairs. Elicit ideas.

### Answers
1. Parents are (nearly always) adults, so asking if you are a parent or an adult is strange.
2. Answers depend on students.

### B Using illustrations to predict content

Ask students to read through the statements. Check the meaning of *caption*. Set the task. Students complete the activity individually, then compare their answers in pairs. Elicit answers.

### Answers
1. F
2. T
3. T
4. T
5. F

### Methodology note

Remind students what a topic sentence is. Elicit why it is important to read one carefully (it will often summarize the whole text, enabling reading for gist and/or helping students to predict the content of the paragraph).

### C Using topic sentences to predict content

1. Ask students to read phrases a–e. Elicit who Berne probably is (a psychiatrist).

   Set the task with a time limit of two minutes. Students complete the activity individually, then compare their answers in pairs. Do not elicit answers at this stage.

2. Students check their ideas with the text. Elicit answers.

### Answers
a. 4
b. 3
c. 5
d. 2
e. 1

### D  Understanding the text

Ask students to read the incomplete sentences. As a fun activity, you could ask them to predict the sentences' endings – accept anything that is grammatically and cohesively correct, even though some suggestions may be slightly ridiculous.

Check understanding of *practise psychiatry* and *problems arise*.

Set the task. Students complete the activity individually, then compare their answers in pairs. Elicit answers.

#### Answers
1. Eric Berne was from *Montreal*.
2. He first practised psychiatry in *New York*.
3. Berne developed his ideas in *San Francisco*.
4. Berne believed that personal problems come from *people's relationships*.
5. Berne thought that you sometimes feel good because *you have made another person feel bad*.
6. Berne said that people can behave like a *Parent, an Adult or a Child*.
7. Berne believed that people can switch *between roles (without problems)*.
8. Berne said that problems arise if *both people want to play the same role*.

#### Methodology note

Academic students often have to mark up transcripts for various reasons, including for discourse features. Exercise E is a gentle introduction to this type of activity, as well as reinforcing information from the lesson.

You may also find it generates quite a lot of discussion; the answers to some of the transactions may depend on intonation and the manner in which the language is spoken.

### E  Transferring information to the real world

Check students understand the task and go over the example. Students discuss the transactions in pairs. Elicit answers.

#### Answers
1. P–C
2. A–A
3. C–P
4. A–P

### Closure

Choose one of the following:

- If your students are working towards the IELTS exam, you can ask them to write a summary for Figures 1 and/or 2, either in class or for homework (this type of activity is usually found in Part 1 of the IELTS writing paper). For example:
  *This figure shows a mixed transaction. One person wants to behave like an adult and the other wants to behave like a parent or a child. This can cause problems in a relationship.*

- Students act out and extend the conversations in Exercise E.

- Discuss the information students have learnt in the lesson. Does any of the information apply to couples they know?

## 2.13 Learning new reading skills: Recognizing theories

### Objectives

By the end of the lesson, students should be able to:
- identify factual and theoretical statements;
- identify some common introductory phrases.

### Introduction

Use Exercise A as the introduction or ask students to spend a few minutes re-reading 'Are you a Parent, an Adult or a Child?' from Lesson 2.12 Real-time reading.

### A  Reviewing vocabulary

Go over the example. Students discuss the remaining answers in pairs. Elicit answers. Ask students make sentences using some of the phrases.

#### Answers
See table on next page.

| 1. train   | 5 | a new idea       |
|------------|---|------------------|
| 2. practise| 7 | a role           |
| 3. obey    | 6 | a school         |
| 4. join    | 1 | as a psychiatrist|
| 5. develop | 8 | like an adult    |
| 6. found   | 2 | psychiatry       |
| 7. play    | 4 | the army         |
| 8. behave  | 3 | an order         |

| a. Berne founded a school of psychiatry. | ✓ |
| b. Berne moved to San Francisco. | ✓ |
| c. People always behave in one of three ways. | ? |
| d. Berne died in California in 1970. | ✓ |
| e. People often play games with their friends, family and workmates. | ? |
| f. People try to feel better by making other people feel worse. | ? |
| g. There was a strong demand for psychiatrists during the Second World War. | ✓ |

**Methodology note**

There is more information in the next lesson about introductory verbs such as *stated*, *said*, *explained*, etc. However, students may be surprised to see that the second verb in the fourth example sentence in the Skills Check is in the present tense:
*He said that people always **behave** in one of three ways.*

This is because the information is still correct, even though the person who said it is now dead.

**B**  Identifying a new skill

1. Discuss the difference between a *fact* and a *theory*. Explain that sometimes a theory is just an *opinion*. Theories can be disproved later. If they were facts, they would no longer be theories. Give students plenty of time to read and take in all the information in the Skills Check. Elicit the answer to the question.
2. Check students understand the task. Point out that ✓ shows the objective truth of a fact, whereas ? shows that this is a theory which could be disproved later. Students complete the activity individually, then compare their answers in pairs. Elicit answers.

Answers

1. There is often an introductory verb or phrase – but sometimes there is not. Then we must work it out from context.
2. See next table.

**Methodology note**

The students will learn the word *psychoanalyst* in this text. There may be some confusion over the three similar words they have now met on this topic:
- *psychiatrist* – a medical doctor trained in the treatment of mental illness
- *psychologist* – someone who studies human behaviour – how we think, learn, feel, etc.
- *psychoanalyst* – someone who follows a method for helping people with mental illness

However, there is quite a lot of overlapping, especially between the two latter words. As long as students understand the general meaning of these words, it will be sufficient for the purposes of this section.

**C**  Practising a new skill

Check students understand the task and go over the example.

Students read the text, then discuss the answers in pairs. Elicit answers.

Answers

Eric Berne wrote eight major books in his lifetime but the most famous is *Games People Play*, which he published in 1964. In this book, Berne said that people <u>behave in one of three ways in all transactions.</u> ?

Berne grew up in Canada although his family were from Eastern Europe. Berne's father was a doctor, and some people say that <u>Berne's mother encouraged Eric to study medicine.</u> ? He trained as a doctor and surgeon, then moved into the field of psychiatry. He applied to become a registered psychoanalyst in 1956 but his application was rejected. Many people believe that this rejection affected him deeply. ? As a result*, ? he started to develop his own theories of psychoanalysis.

*Note: We cannot be certain that rejection led to the theory.

## Closure

Check some of the vocabulary and phrases in the text from Exercise C, for example:
*affect deeply*
*reject, rejection*
*as a result*
*surgeon*
*registered*

### 2.14 Grammar for reading: Prepositional phrases; past and present

### Objectives

By the end of the lesson, students should be able to:
- identify the subject and verb in long sentences;
- decide if 'facts' are true or false.

## Introduction

Students' books closed. Ask students to draw Figures 1 and 2 of Berne's transactional theories from memory (see Lesson 2.12 Real-time reading on page 57 of the Course Book).

Spend two or three minutes revising some information about Berne's life. It is referred to in Exercise A.

## Grammar box 9

Students study the information and the examples in the table. Highlight some of the grammar of the introductory phrases:
*After + ~ing*
*By + ~ing*
*As + you can see*
*According + to*

### A  Finding subject and verb in long sentences

Check students understand the task and go over the example. Students complete the activity individually, then compare their answers in pairs. Elicit answers.

Answers

1. On 10th May 1910 <u>Eric Berne</u> *was born* in Montreal.
2. At the age of eighteen <u>Berne</u> *entered* McGill University.
3. During his time at university <u>he</u> *wrote* for several student newspapers.
4. After graduating from university <u>Berne</u> *started* to study Psychiatry at Yale.
5. At the university at that time <u>the professor</u> *was* Dr Paul Federn.
6. At the end of his training in 1938 <u>Berne</u> *became* an American citizen.
7. During Berne's training in psychiatry <u>the Second World War</u> *started*.
8. As a result of the mental problems of soldiers during the war <u>a large number of psychiatrists</u> *were needed* by the army at that time.
9. At the end of the war in 1945 <u>Berne</u> *went* to study in San Francisco.
10. At that time in the San Francisco Psychoanalytic Institute <u>Erik Erikson</u> *was* the director.

## Grammar box 10

As well as focusing on the verb in the statement, you may wish to point out that the verb in the introductory phrase also gives us useful information. A present tense verb, as in *Psychiatrists accept ...*, shows that the theory is still current. A past tense verb, as in *Most psychiatrists believed ...*, shows that modern psychiatrists do not believe the theory any more. In the last example, *Berne thought ...*, the past tense tells us that Berne is dead but that his theory may still be valid.

### B  Identifying present and past theories

Check students understand the task and go over the example.

Students discuss the remaining sentences in pairs. Elicit answers.

Answers
See table over.

Theme 2: Reading   103

| 1. People believed that the Earth was flat. | 'The Earth is flat.' = old / false |
| 2. Aristotle believed that earthquakes were caused by winds under the earth. | 'Earthquakes are caused by winds under the earth.' = old / false |
| 3. Aristotle thought that we learn by doing. | 'We learn by doing.' = true / possibly true |
| 4. Paiget said that children go through four stages. | 'Children go through four stages.' = true / possibly true |
| 5. Pavlov stated that you can make people behave in particular ways. | 'You can make people behave in particular ways.' = true / possibly true |
| 6. Al Gore says that man is the cause of global warming. | 'Man is the cause of global warming.' = true / possibly true |

**Closure**

Students' books closed. Write the introduction for each sentence in Exercise B on the board:
*People believed ...*
*Aristotle believed ...* etc.

Students copy and complete.

### 2.15 Applying new reading skills: I'm OK, you're OK

**Objectives**

By the end of the lesson, students should have:
- applied appropriate strategies for attacking a new text (revision);
- distinguished between fact and theory in order to understand a text;
- learnt information about the 'I'm OK, You're OK' model in psychology.

**Introduction**

Revise the verbs/nouns that do not change form from Exercise B in Lesson 2.11 Vocabulary for reading:
*promise*
*blame*
*support*
*point*
*excuse*
*store*

### A  Reviewing vocabulary

Explain to the class that this exercise is again about verbs and nouns that do not change form, and that the same words have different meanings. Go over the example. In pairs, students discuss the meanings of the other sentences.

Point out that we never actually have two forms of the same word in English; it does not 'sound right'. Ask students how each sentence could be improved, for example:
He learnt to be a train driver. / He went on a train-driving course.
She played Ophelia in Hamlet. / She was Ophelia in the play Hamlet.
He discovered the school that Berne founded.

This activity will check students understand the meaning of each sentence.

Answers

| 1. He **trained** to be a **train** driver. | studied | transport method |
| 2. She **played** Ophelia in the **play** Hamlet. | acted | kind of literature |
| 3. He **found** the school that Berne **founded**. | discovered | started |
| 4. Berne's **school** of psychiatry did not have a **school** building. | type | institution |
| 5. The lecturer **pointed** out several important **points**. | said | issues / ideas |
| 6. She **demanded** to know the **demand** for psychiatrists. | asked | how many are needed |
| 7. The **rebel** didn't like the government policies so he **rebelled**. | person against a government or government idea | acted against the government |
| 8. The judge didn't even **try** to **try** the men in a fair way. | attempt | deal with in court |

### B  Activating ideas

Exploit the visual:
- where are the people?
- what's happening?
- what's the problem?

Divide the class into groups of three to discuss the statements. After a few minutes, elicit which students agreed with each statement. Keep a tally on the board. Which statement has the most support in the class?

Answers

Answers depend on students.

### C Understanding a text

Elicit what students should look at in order to prepare for reading the article and writing a list on the board:
*title*
*illustrations*
*tables, graphs, figures, etc.*
*first paragraph*
*topic sentences*

Ask students to prepare to read the article by going through the list on the board with the text.

Discuss Figure 1 at the bottom of page 61 in the Course Book, and elicit what it means. The easiest way to do this, perhaps, is by relating it to the activity they have just done in Exercise B. For example, sentence 1 in Exercise B relates to relationship type 1 in the figure.

Ask a few more questions based on the first paragraph and topic sentences:
*Who wrote 'I'm OK, You're OK?* (Thomas Harris)
*Who was he?* (a psychiatrist)
*What is the healthiest relationship?* (type 1 – I'm OK, you're OK)

1. Remind students of the work they did on facts and theories in Lesson 2.13 Learning new reading skills. Go over the example. Students complete the task individually, then compare their answers in pairs. Elicit answers, preferably using an electronic projection.

2. Students complete the task individually, then compare their answers in pairs. Elicit answers.

Answers

See next table.

### D Transferring information to real-world situations

Set the task. Students work in pairs. Elicit ideas.

Answers

A = Relationship Type 1
B = Relationship Type 4
C = Relationship Type 3
D = Relationship Type 2

| | | |
|---|---|---|
| a. | Where did Harris train in psychiatry? | Washington D.C., i.e., the capital |
| b. | Where did he practise psychiatry? | in the (US) Navy |
| c. | What were the connections between Harris and Berne? | he worked with him, then took over as director of the Transactional Analysis Society |
| d. | What is the name of the model discussed in this article? | I'm OK, you're OK |
| e. | What did some people believe before Berne's theory? | that people were born with particular attitudes |
| f. | Which type of relationship do people have when they are young? | Type 1 |
| g. | What sometimes happens as people grow up? | they may change to other types of relationship |
| h. | Why is Relationship Type 1 healthy? | people are happy to work with other people, respect contribution of self and others |
| i. | How did Harris feel about the other types of relationship? | there are problems |
| j. | How can you move the other types to Type 1?: | |
| | • from Type 2 to Type 1? | find things to value in people |
| | • from Type 3 to Type 1? | make a list of good things about yourself |
| | • from Type 4 to Type 1? | find things to value in people including yourself |

### E Developing critical thinking

Set the question for discussion in pairs or small groups.

**Closure**

Choose from the following:

1. Ask students to compare the information in the two texts from this section (on pages 57 and 61 of the Course Book). What are the similarities and differences? For example, in both cases, the writers described relationships between people. Berne suggested that people change relationships with different people, whereas Harris suggested that people have one basic type of relationship with people.

2. Ask students to write a few sentences describing Figure 1 on page 61.

### Knowledge quiz: Relationships

### Objectives

By the end of this lesson, students will have:
- reviewed core knowledge from Theme 2;
- recycled the vocabulary from Theme 2.

**Introduction**

Tell students they are going to do a knowledge and vocabulary quiz on Theme 2 of the course. If you like, while you are waiting for everyone in the class to arrive, students can spend a few minutes looking back over the theme.

### Methodology note

See notes in the Introduction (page 16) for further ideas on how to do the quiz. As usual, the focus should be on the content rather than using the correct grammar.

**Closure**

Tell students to learn the information or vocabulary for any of the answers they got wrong in class.

Answers

See table.

| | | |
|---|---|---|
| 1. | What is an *acquaintance*? | a person you know from work, study, family |
| 2. | What is a *stranger*? | a person you don't know |
| 3. | What is a *relative*? | someone from your family |
| 4. | What is an *adolescent*? | a person between the ages of 13 and 19 – a teenager |
| 5. | What is a *barrier*? | something which stops you doing something |
| 6. | What is a *neighbourhood*? | the area that you live in |
| 7. | What is an *excuse*? | a reason for doing something bad |
| 8. | What is a *stimulus*? | something which makes you do something |
| 9. | What is *psychiatry*? | the treatment of problems in the mind |
| 10. | What is an *issue*? | a problem |
| 11. | When might you *forgive* a person? | when they have done something bad to you |
| 12. | When might you *apologize* to a person? | when you have done something bad to them |
| 13. | When might you *blame* someone? | when you think they have done something bad |
| 14. | When might you *avoid* someone? | when you think they are angry with you |
| 15. | When might you *bow* to someone? | when you meet a very important person |
| 16. | When might you *criticize* someone? | when you think they have done something wrong and you tell them |
| 17. | When might you *ignore* someone? | when you are angry with them or don't want to be friends with them |
| 18. | When might you take *responsibility* for something? | when you have done something wrong and you admit it |
| 19. | How might you *upset* someone? | by saying or doing something bad |
| 20. | How might you *emphasize* an apology? | with 'very, very', or 'terribly', or 'really' |
| 21. | How might you *support* someone? | with money, attention, interest |
| 22. | Why might you feel *inferior* to someone? | because you think they are better, much more intelligent or more beautiful than you |
| 23. | Why might you *rebel* about something? | because you do not think it is fair |
| 24. | Who wrote *Games People Play* in 1964? | Eric Berne |
| 25. | Who wrote *I'm OK, You're OK* in 1969? | Thomas Harris |

106    Theme 2: Reading

# Writing: Decisions in families

### 2.16 Vocabulary for writing: Parents and children

**Objectives**

By the end of this lesson, students should have:
- revised and practised spelling of target words from previous lessons;
- demonstrated understanding of target vocabulary for the Writing section;
- used target vocabulary in a brief text about children and physical activity.

**Introduction**

Write the following misspelt words on the board for students to correct:
1. independant
2. atitude
3. apreciation
4. forgivness
5. agriement
6. behaivour
7. approuve
8. apollogy
9. critisize
10. infearior

Students work individually, then compare their answers in pairs. Write the correct spellings on the board so that students can check their own answers.

Check the meanings of the words. Elicit the part of speech of each word.

**Answers**

1. independent (adj)
2. attitude (n)
3. appreciation (n)
4. forgiveness (n)
5. agreement (n)
6. behaviour (n)
7. approve (v)
8. apology (n)
9. criticize (v)
10. inferior (adj)

### A Activating ideas

Refer students to the pictures. Ask:

*What people can you see in the pictures?* (baby; girls / twins; schoolchildren / teenagers; teenagers / adolescents – 'punks' / 'goths')

*Who decided the clothes that the people are wearing?* (elicit possible answers, e.g., mother, mother, school)

Remind students of the word *self* for a person.

**Answers**

Answers depend on students.

### B Understanding new vocabulary in context

Spend a few minutes going over the bar chart with the students, eliciting the figure number, the source and the title. Ask them what the scale on the left shows (the percentage of decisions made by the parents).

Set the task for individual work. Monitor and assist as necessary.

Students can compare ideas. Give feedback orally.

**Answers**

The illustration in Fig. 1 is a *bar chart*. It is a type of graph which *displays* research data. In this case, it makes a *comparison* between four types of people. The *categories* are babies, children, teenagers and adults. The *participants* in the research were British. For each *category*, the graph shows the *percentage* of decisions which are made by the *parents*. For example, according to the research, parents make all the decisions on *behalf of* a baby, but only 80 per cent of decisions for a child. They make about half of the decisions which affect a teenager. An adult makes almost all decisions for *himself* or *herself*.

### C Building vocabulary

Ask students to find words in the vocabulary list which refer to quantity. They should find the following:

*a fifth, a third, almost all, approximately, exactly, fraction, just over / under, more / less than, per cent, percentage, roughly, two thirds*

Set the task for individual work and pairwork checking. Give feedback using an electronic projection. Go over any problems students had with new vocabulary.

**Note:** The tilde (~), pronounced /tɪldə/, meaning 'approximately', is often used in quick note-taking. The formal technical symbol is the double tilde, ≈.

Answers

| 1. 21%   | just over a fifth           |
|----------|-----------------------------|
| 2. 98%   | almost all                  |
| 3. 48%   | less than half              |
| 4. 66.6% | exactly two thirds          |
| 5. ~75%  | approximately three quarters |

### D  Using new vocabulary

1. Make sure all the students understand what to do. Elicit ideas for the first item, *work in government offices*, on to the board as a demonstration.

   Set the task for individual work. Monitor and assist as necessary.

   Place feedback on the board, preferably using an electronic projection.

2. Tell students to think about the people they know in the four age groups. They should write some more sentences about these groups. Emphasize that students do not need to give accurate numbers and percentages, but to use their own knowledge.

   When they are ready, students should compare their sentences.

Answers
Answers depend on students.

### Closure

1. Ask volunteers to read out some of their sentences from Exercise D. Ask the rest of the class to comment on these and say whether they agree or not.

2. Do more work on percentage expressions as in Exercise C.

## 2.17 Real-time writing: Making decisions in the family

### Objectives

By the end of the lesson, students should be able to:
- show understanding of the discourse structure of a 'research report' essay;
- interpret bar charts and use target vocabulary to complete a guided writing activity;
- show understanding of the use of topic sentences to begin paragraphs.

### Methodology note

The discourse type in this section is the research report. Students who have studied Level 2 of *Progressive Skills in English* did some work on this in Theme 3 of that level. However, the work in this lesson does not assume that students have done Level 2.

### Introduction

Dictate vocabulary items from the previous lesson, or ask students to dictate them to each other in pairs, in order to review spelling.

### A  Activating ideas

Students work in pairs. They should aim to put three or four items in each box, although more items are possible. Elicit answers.

Answers

| children | adolescents | young adults |
|----------|-------------|--------------|
| • food<br>• clothes<br>• school<br>• bed time | • friends<br>• *study time*<br>• *going out or not*<br>• *using the Internet* | • getting married<br>• job<br>• *university*<br>• *leaving home* |

### B  Gathering information

Refer students to the assignment. Make sure students understand *cultural issue* (i.e., depends on the culture; might be different from culture to culture). Remind them that they must always choose what type of essay to write for an assignment, because each essay type has its own discourse structure or ordering of information – see Exercise C. Check/teach the word *survey* – see note below.

Set the task for pairwork. Give feedback orally.

**Note:** A survey is designed to be given or sent to people in order to collect data about them. After filling in the form, the person returns the form to the researcher. The researcher then analyzes the data in order to find out something about the people. Surveys are done in person or via surface mail, e-mail or webpages.

### Answers

Research report – because you are asked to conduct a survey = get original research

### C  Choosing the discourse structure

Go through the assignment with the students. Clarify any problems.

Elicit ideas as to whether the first item, *Conclusions*, should be included. Do not confirm or correct ideas at this stage. Students continue in pairs. Elicit answers.

Point out that a research report will certainly also have an Appendix (where you put the raw data and, possibly, the graphed data). Tell students that the Appendix goes at the back of the report.

### Answers

| 4 | Conclusions |
|---|---|
|   | Participants |
|   | Opinions |
| 2 | Methods |
| 3 | Results |
| 1 | Introduction |
|   | Recommendations |

### D  Gathering data

1. Give the students time to read through the survey form. Check that they understand what it is. Elicit a few ideas. Students, in pairs, then discuss the questions. Elicit answers.
2. Refer students to Appendix 1 on page 65 of the Course Book. Allow time for them to read, discuss and comment on the data.

Clarify the word *other*. In this survey, most people have responded with either 'mother', 'father' or 'self', so the researcher has decided to record the answers into just three columns, with an additional column for 'other' answers, which he/she has noted by hand.

Go through the example. Set the writing task for individual work. Encourage students to use expressions of quantity from Lesson 2.16 Vocabulary for writing. Monitor and assist as necessary. Get students to read out some of the 'best' sentences.

### Answers

1. Answers depend on students, but presumably *mother*, *father*, etc.
2. Answers depend on students.

---

**Methodology note**

In the case of Appendix 2, the researcher has recorded the total number of answers in each category as a number. You could also spend some time explaining the system of tallying responses. This might be useful later in the section. To tally answers, a small vertical mark is made for each answer in a certain category. When there are four such marks, the fifth is made as a diagonal line across them. Then a new set of five marks is begun. This grouping into five makes the total quicker to count.

---

### E  Writing the essay

1–2. Students work individually, then compare their ideas in pairs. Elicit answers using an electronic projection of the text.

3. Get students to cover the bottom half of the page so they can only see Appendix 1. Set for individual work. Monitor and assist as necessary. Remember that students have still not learnt some of the key skills required here so make sure they notice all the main points. Be careful not to pre-empt the work coming up in Lesson 2.18 Learning new writing skills and Lesson 2.19 Grammar for writing.

### Answers

Note that at this stage, the essay does not include topic sentences. Notice also that there may be other correct ways to complete the information.

Theme 2: Writing  109

*Introduction*

This study identifies the key decision-makers in families. These decisions affect *children*, *teenagers* and *young adults*. It examines the decisions that people are allowed to make for themselves. It also looks at changes in the power to make decisions over time.

*Methods*

*Four* key decisions were selected for each *age group*. A total of *eighteen people* responded to the survey. There were ten females and *eight males* in the sample. The raw numbers of responses are shown in *Appendix 2*. The responses were converted into a series of bar charts (*Appendix 1*).

*Results*

For children in this culture, all key decisions are made by *their parents*, as Fig. 1 shows. Sometimes they let them *choose their clothes*. As far as adolescents are concerned, parents allow them to take more responsibility (*see Fig. 2*). Most of them are free *to choose their friends*. On average, about *one third* can decide on Internet usage. However, a father sometimes does not allow his son or daughter *to go out with friends*. Both parents make their children *study*. As we can see in Fig. 3, about *half of* young adults are expected to decide things for themselves. *Grandparents* are still consulted in cases such as *the choice of school or future husband/wife* (see Appendix 2).

*Conclusions*

In this culture, young children are not allowed to make many decisions. Adolescents are allowed to make more decisions. Some young adults make nearly all their own decisions but parents always have a lot of influence.

The data does not record the difference between male and female children in the family. In addition, the key decisions for each age group are different. This means that comparison between age groups is difficult.

**Closure**

1. Ask some further questions about the data in the bar charts, for example:
   *How many people said that the mother decides children's bed time?*
   *What percentage of people said that adolescents choose their friends themselves?*

2. Exploit the raw data in Appendix 2.
   Ask students to convert the numbers to tallies and percentages.

## 2.18 Learning new writing skills: The research report

### Objectives

By the end of the lesson, students should be able to:
- show understanding of the organization of a research report;
- produce appropriate topic sentences.

**Introduction**

Use Exercise A as the introduction.

**A** Reviewing vocabulary

Set the task. Students complete the activity individually, then compare their answers in pairs. Write the correct spellings on the board so that students can correct their own work. Highlight some of the spelling patterns, for example:
- double letters (*difference*, *appendix*)
- unusual spellings (*adolescent*)

Check the meanings of some of the words.

Answers

| a. | decision   | d. | investigate |
| b. | appendix   | e. | adolescent  |
| c. | difference | f. | sample      |
| d. | choice     | g. | conclusion  |

**B** Identifying a key skill (1)

Give students time to read through Skills Check 1. When they are ready, ask them to close their books and elicit answers.

**Note:** Students who have studied Level 2 of *Progressive Skills in English* saw a similar Skills Check in Theme 3 there. The present Skills Check serves both as a reminder to them and as a source of new information to students who have not done Level 2.

Answers
When designing a survey it is important to collect the information into categories, to give clear instructions, and to make sure you give enough space for people to write their answers.

### C Practising a key skill (1)
Elicit a couple of ideas, then set for pairwork. Give feedback, getting a good version on the board.

Answers
1. Answers depend on the students, but some of the categories could be:

   Decisions about:
   - children's *upbringing* (teach word); this category could also be broken down into, e.g., education, religion, out-of-school activities
   - meal times
   - food
   - housing – could be broken down into *location*, *décor*, etc.
   - holidays

2. Clear instructions could be:
   *For each decision area, write* husband, wife *or* both.

### D Identifying a key skill (2)
Go through Skills Check 2 with the class. Clarify any problems.

Ask students to close their books and do the two exercises in pairs.

Give feedback orally, then refer students to the Skills Check box again so that they can check their own answers.

Answers
In Skills Check 2.

### E Identifying a key skill (3)
Refer students to Skills Check 3. Make sure they understand *general idea* and *introduce*. Check the questions quickly.

Answers
In Skills Check 3.

**Methodology note**

Students have already come across the concept of 'topic sentence' in their reading. Exercise F is the first time, however, that they are specifically asked to write topic sentences. In fact, this skill is quite complex and students will not learn it from just one exercise. From now on, remind students in every essay writing exercise that they do about the need to write a topic sentence to introduce each paragraph.

### F Practising a key skill (3)
1. Set for individual work and pairwork checking. Do not give feedback at this point.
2. Set for individual work. Give feedback, ideally using an electronic projection of the text.

Answers
Text with topic sentences in *italics*:

#### Introduction
*This study aims to analyze the way decisions are made in the family*. This study identifies the key decision-makers in families. These decisions affect children, teenagers and young adults. It examines the decisions that people are allowed to make for themselves. It also looks at changes in the power to make decisions over time.

#### Methods
*A survey was conducted among families of the same culture*. Four key decisions were selected for each age group. A total of eighteen people responded to the survey. There were ten females and eight males in the sample. The raw numbers of responses are shown in Appendix 2. The responses were converted into a series of bar charts (Appendix 1).

#### Results
*The results show clear differences for the three groups*. For children in this culture, all key decisions are made by their parents, as Fig. 1 shows. Sometimes they let them choose their clothes. As far as adolescents are concerned, parents allow them to take more responsibility (see Fig. 2). Most of them are free to choose their friends. On average, about one third can decide on Internet usage. However, a father sometimes does not allow his son or daughter

to go out with friends. Both parents make their children study. As we can see in Fig. 3, about half of young adults are expected to decide things for themselves. Grandparents are still consulted in cases such as the choice of school or future husband/wife (see Appendix 2).

## Conclusions

*We can draw clear conclusions from this survey*. In this culture, young children are not allowed to make many decisions. Adolescents are allowed to make more decisions. Some young adults make nearly all their own decisions but parents always have a lot of influence. *There are some problems with the data*. The data does not record the difference between male and female children in the family. In addition, the key decisions for each age group are different. This means that comparison between age groups is difficult.

## Closure

1. Students' books closed. Ask students to tell you the information from each of the three Skills Check boxes.
2. Elicit a topic sentence for the Introduction of the survey in Exercise C.

---

### 2.19 Grammar for writing: Permission and obligation with infinitives

**Objectives**

By the end of the lesson, students should be able to:
- show understanding of a variety of verb structures expressing obligation and permission;
- use these verbs in active and passive sentence structures.

## Introduction

Revise some of the grammar from the previous sections in this theme.

---

**Methodology note**

Some teachers and students learn that the term *infinitive* refers to *to* + verb. For others, this form is called a *to-infinitive*. In this lesson, the terms *infinitive with to* and *infinitive without to* are used to avoid confusion.

### Grammar box 11

Ask students to study Tables 1 and 2. All the sentences are from the text in Lesson 2.17 Real-time writing on page 65 of the Course Book. Point out or elicit the fact that the verbs *let* and *allow* have similar meanings. Go over the different structures that follow each main verb.

**Note:** This lesson focuses on the form *prevent* + object + *from* + gerund. The form *prevent* + object + gerund is also possible, e.g., *Clear signs prevent visitors getting lost*.

### Grammar box 12

Repeat the above procedure for Tables 3 and 4. Point out the position of *not* in the negative.

**Methodology note**

You might also want to deal with the contrast between *can / could* and *be able* for permission. The main usage points are:

1. *can* is used for expressing permission in **general** terms
   Example: *I'm sorry, but children can't come in here.*

2. for permission in **future** situations, *be able to* is used in preference to *can*
   Example: *You will be able to decide that when you are older.*

3. in **past** situations, both are possible
   Example:
   *At one time, children weren't able to make any decisions for themselves.*
   *At one time, children couldn't make any decisions for themselves.*

### A  Active verb forms

Go through the first sentence with the class as an example. Students continue individually. Monitor and assist as necessary. When they are ready, pairs of students can compare ideas. Elicit answers using an electronic projection.

## Answers
1. Young children are not allowed to watch television late in the evening.
2. My company does not make us wear a uniform.
3. Open windows let warm air escape.
4. The law in Britain does not allow you to drive a car until you are 17.
5. Internet telephoning allows you to make very cheap phone calls.
6. Drinking a lot of water before a meal makes you eat less.

### Methodology note
Highlight the difference in register between the two texts in this exercise. In the poster, it is informal. The modals *can* and *must* are used. The passive verb structures in Tables 3 and 4 are used in the written text.

### B  Passive verb forms
Give students time to study the poster. Elicit or clarify the fact that the coffee in this case is not free, but that it is up to the drinker to make it and leave the appropriate money in a box provided.

Tell students to read through the text. Point out that it comes from the college prospectus and describes the same photography studio as the one in the poster. Elicit the answer to the first text gap. Students continue individually. Monitor and assist as necessary. When they are ready, pairs of students can compare their ideas. As before, elicit answers using an electronic projection.

### Answers
The studio has a relaxed atmosphere, but there are some rules. All students *are expected to take care of equipment*. It is very expensive. They *are free to wear casual* clothes and to drink coffee, but they *are not allowed to bring in* food. They *are expected to pay for their* coffee by putting the money in a box. Students *can bring one visitor* – he/she must sign the visitors' book. Finally, nobody *is allowed to use mobiles*, because this disturbs people who are working.

## Closure
Ask students to write a text for the prospectus in Exercise B, describing the rules for areas of their college or university.

## 2.20 Applying new writing skills: Individual decision-making

### Objectives
By the end of this lesson, students should be able to:
- design and conduct a survey on a sociological topic;
- produce a research report from the data they collect;
- use target vocabulary, grammar and sub-skills from the theme in a research report;
- use the TOWER process to produce a final written draft.

### Introduction
Revise the information from Lesson 2.17 Real-time writing about decision-making. This will help students with writing a report in this lesson.

### Methodology notes
1. This exercise type appears in many international examinations, including the Cambridge FCE (First Certificate in English) and CPE (Certificate of Proficiency in English). Point this out to your class, as they may have seen or taken – or be intending to take – these examinations.
2. Note that this type of exercise often throws up additional word order points, e.g., sentence 3 = position of a frequency adverb with passive constructions.

### A  Reviewing vocabulary and grammar
Make sure that students understand that they must use the word in brackets *as it is*. They must not change the form of the word. Do the first sentence as an example. Students continue individually. Monitor and assist as necessary. Refer students back to Lesson 2.19 Grammar for writing, if necessary. Elicit answers, using an electronic projection.

### Answers
1. Young people are often allowed by their parents to choose their husbands or wives. (let)

*Parents often let young people choose their husbands or wives.*

2. The total number of *yes* answers was 99 per cent. (all)
*Almost / Nearly all the answers were yes.*
3. Children cannot usually decide their school. (allowed)
*Children are not usually allowed to decide their school.*
4. Adolescents generally have to look after their own possessions. (take)
*Adolescents generally take responsibility for their possessions.*
5. We asked people about their phone use. (survey)
*A survey was conducted about phone use. / A survey about (of / into) phone use was conducted. / We conducted a survey about (of / into) phone use.*
6. The number of car drivers in the group (60 people) was 45. (per cent)
*Seventy-five per cent (three quarters) of the people in the group were car drivers.*
7. In some families the older members decide the important things. (made)
*In some families important decisions are made by the older members.*
8. The Appendix shows all the answers, before the analysis was done. (raw)
*The Appendix shows the raw data.*

> **Methodology note**
>
> The writing task in this exercise will require more time than usual, as students have to do three things: design their survey; carry out the survey; and write their report. Make sure you allow enough time in your lesson-planning for all of these stages. You may prefer to do these three things over more than one lesson. Monitor closely and make sure you give students all the help they need.

### B Thinking and organizing

Remind students again about the TOWER approach to writing:
- **T**hinking about what you're going to write
- **O**rganizing your ideas
- **W**riting a first draft
- **E**diting the first draft
- **R**ewriting in order to produce a second draft

Refer students to the assignment. Elicit how they know it is a research report task (because it asks for a survey to be conducted, and for a report with illustrations). Clarify the meaning of *illustrate*, as well as the meaning of the compound noun *decision-making*, if necessary.

1. Give students time to consider the options here. They can choose freely. Students can include as many categories as they wish in their survey. However, we suggest that they only choose two or three from the list. Give feedback.

   Elicit choices and encourage students to give reasons for them.

2. Again, to keep the scale of the survey and writing task reasonable, we suggest students add no more than two categories to those they have already chosen. This will give them a total of four or five.

   Give feedback as before.

3. Go through tasks a)–e) with the students.

   With a more able class, ask students to work individually. With less able groups, put them into pairs for this stage (they will write the report individually later). During these tasks, monitor closely and make sure students know what to do. Help with vocabulary, and refer students to Lesson 2.18 Learning new writing skills and the model survey and research report in Lesson 2.17 Real-time writing. Make sure students understand how to tally numbers (see Methodology note, page 109 above).

### C Writing a research report

Refer students to the list of sections. Elicit the kind of information that each one contains. A more able class might be able to remember some of the exact information from the research report in Lesson 2.17.

1. Start the students off by eliciting a topic sentence for the Introduction onto the board. Revise the purpose of topic sentences.

   Monitor and assist while students write topic sentences for their other sections. These will be the same for all students, as they do not depend on the categories in students' individual surveys.

2. Students complete their research reports individually. Monitor and assist as necessary. If you wish, students can prepare their illustrations on a computer outside class. Alternatively, they can draw the bar charts by hand. In either case, make sure the

writing of the first draft is done in class so that students can work in pairs to edit each other's work.

## D  Editing

Remind students of things to check for: spelling, correct tenses, etc. Monitor and help as necessary.

## E  Rewriting

The final version of the report can be written in class or set up for homework. If done in class, monitor and make a note of common errors.

### Answers

The reports will depend on each student's choice of categories. Use the text in Lesson 2.17 as a model when assessing and giving feedback on the students' work.

## Closure

Give feedback on the work done so far in this lesson – the survey design will probably be complete by now.

Also give feedback to the whole class on any common writing errors you noted while monitoring.

## Portfolio: Relationships

### Objectives

By the end of the lesson(s), students should have:
- revised target vocabulary from the theme;
- used integrated skills to practise language and revise knowledge from the theme;
- practised questions to check information;
- used integrated skills to talk and write about relationships;
- learnt more common core knowledge about relationships.

## Introduction

Revise adjectives for describing people from the theme, e.g., *optimistic*, *negative*, etc. or use the A–Z list below:

athletic; amusing
brave; bully
clever
dull
easy-going
friendly
good-looking
hard-working
intelligent
jealous
kind
loner
musical

noisy
open
pretty; proud
quiet; quick
reasonable; religious
sensible; stupid; silly
tidy
untidy; un~ (+ many things)
vain
willing; wise
youthful
zealous

## A  Activating ideas

Elicit one or two ideas for the first question and point out that we can have relationships with many people, not just relations. Students continue discussing the other two questions in pairs. Elicit ideas.

### Answers

1. Students may suggest: parents, other relatives, friends, brothers and sisters, acquaintances, teachers, neighbours.
2. Students may suggest some relationships are closer than others; they may even mention control over younger brothers and sisters, and respect or obedience to older members of the family.
3. Answers depend on students.

## B  Gathering and recording information: listening

1. Work through the questions. Elicit the kind of information students will hear to answer each question – see Answers.

   Check or pre-teach some key vocabulary from the recording, e.g.,
   *put someone down*
   *enthusiastic*

   Play 🎵 2.27. Pause if necessary to give time for students to make a few notes for each question. Do not feed back at this stage.

   Put students into pairs or small groups to check their ideas. Monitor and assist the groups of students as necessary. Give feedback to the class by placing the model answer on the board, preferably using an electronic projection.

2. Set for individual work.

   Discuss with the class how Melville-Ross's

ideas fit with other research they have studied about relationships, for example, Milliken's three As of acceptance, approval and appreciation.

## Transcript

2.27

Presenter: 2.27. Portfolio: Relationships. Exercise B1. Listen to a lecture about relationships.

Lecturer: So far in this course we've looked at making friends and also how to keep friends.

In this lecture, we're going to look at these ideas in more detail. Some people seem to make friends easily. They are popular and have few problems with relationships. On this occasion, we're not looking at the work of a psychologist or a piece of research. This is a theory from a management consultant called Tim Melville-Ross. The theory is based on his experiences in management from the 1990s. So let's look at what he said.

Melville-Ross divided people into two types: radiators and drains. In general English, a radiator is a device for giving out heat. A drain is a hole for taking away water. For example, there are drains in the street for rain water. There is a drain in your shower.

Melville-Ross said that, in his experience, radiators give out energy whereas drains take it away. Radiators are happy and enthusiastic. They listen to you and help you with your problems. They don't usually take their problems out on you. According to Melville-Ross, radiators don't try to put you down. Most importantly, they like everyone to be happy. So the point is, people who are radiators are usually popular and successful.

On the other hand, drains bring people down to make themselves feel better. They think their problems are the most important and like to be the centre of attention.

They complain a lot and are generally pessimistic and negative. Often people don't realize that they are drains. So the first step in changing is awareness.

So, to sum up, it is much better to be a radiator than a drain. Everyone loves radiators and radiators love other radiators. It is also better to be with a radiator. Look for the positive in everything and be enthusiastic and encouraging. It will help those around you improve the quality of their lives.

### Answers

1. Model notes: see table below.
2. Summary:
Melville-Ross said there are basically two types of people: radiators and drains. Radiators are positive and helpful but drains are negative and unhelpful.

### C Gathering and recording information: reading

1. Put the students into pairs, numbered 1 and 2. Refer the pairs of students to the texts as follows:

    S1 – should read *Are You useful, just for fun, or real?* on page 70

    S2 – should read *From physical interaction to autonomous interdependence* on page 71

    Set task for individual work. Remind students that the questions in Exercise B are a good basis for making notes with this kind of information. With a less able class, allow students to work for a short time in groups –

| What is the theory about? | what about? | different types of people in the world |
|---|---|---|
| Who made it? | who? | Tim Melville-Ross – management consultant |
| When did he make it? | when? | in the 1990s |
| How many kinds of people are there? | how many? | two main types |
| What does he call the different kinds? | call? | radiators and drains |
| What do the names mean? | mean? | In general English, a radiator is a device for giving out heat. A drain is a hole through which water or other liquid can run away. |
| What does each kind of person do? | do? | Ross said that radiators give out energy whereas drains take it away. Radiators are happy and enthusiastic. They listen to you and help you with your problems. They don't take their problems out on you. They don't try to put you down. They like everyone to be happy. |
|  |  | Drains, on the other hand, bring people down to make themselves feel better. They think their problems are the most important and like to be the centre of attention. |
|  |  | As Melville-Ross said, it is much better to be a radiator than a drain. Everyone loves radiators and radiators love other radiators. It is also better to be with a radiator. |
| Which kind of person is usually the most popular? | most popular? | radiators |

all student 1s or all student 2s to check their notes together. Monitor and assist each group/student. During this stage, refer students back to the text if they have missed any key points. Use the model notes (see below) and check them against the notes that are emerging from each group.

2. Set for pairwork. Monitor and assist as necessary. Give feedback to the class by placing the model notes on the board, preferably using an electronic projection.

3. Set for pairwork. Elicit ideas.

Answers

1–2. Model notes: see table below.
3. Answers depend on students.

> **Methodology note**
>
> An alternative method for Exercises D2 and D3 is to divide the class into five groups. Give each group a letter from A–E. Each group works together on the allocated text. Then re-divide the class into groups of five so that there is one student from each of the original groups, A–E. Students can now exchange information.

**D** Integrating skills

1. Give students time to read the extract, then elicit answers to the questions. Elicit further examples of *when* and *how* people control each other, for example: parents and children, teachers in the classroom, etc.

2. Divide the class into groups of five and allocate a letter from A to E, to each student. Set the task carefully, making sure students know which text they are supposed to be reading. If necessary, you can suggest an outline for the table of notes, as well as possible headings (see Model notes below). Monitor while students make notes and give help where necessary.

3/4. Still in their groups, students take it in turns to give information, as if they were taking part in a tutorial. Remind students about the language they learnt in the Speaking section for introducing and ending turns. Monitor and give feedback. Rearrange the groups or get students to discuss the questions in pairs.

5. Students discuss the questions in their groups. However, if you prefer, you can rearrange the groups or get students to discuss the questions in pairs.

Answers

1. a. *Manipulate* means to make people do what we want.
   b. Answers depend on students.

| who? | Aristotle | R.L. Selman |
|---|---|---|
| when? | 350 BCE | 1970s and 80s |
| what exactly? | types of friendship | stages of friendship |
| how many? | 3 | 5 |
| call / mean | • utility – I help you, you help me<br>• pleasure – I make you laugh, you make me laugh<br>• real – I accept you, you accept me | • momentary physical interaction – you are near me<br>• one-way assistance – you can help me<br>• fair-weather cooperation – we agree<br>• intimate and mutual sharing – we need each other<br>• autonomous interdependence – we help each other |
| do? | • utility – people are useful; when they are not, friendship ends; common at school, workplace and in the elderly<br>• pleasure – have fun together, not intimate, common in young<br>• real – perfect type; don't expect to gain directly or get pleasure but may do; like each other for what they are = v. rare | 0 play with people near you<br>1 help you play a game<br>2 have the same interests, opinions<br>3 become possessive, jealous of other friends<br>4 rely on each other, get strength from each other<br>(some people never get to 4) |

2–3.
Model notes: see table below.
4–5. Answers depend on students.

> **Methodology note**
>
> This can be a brief activity in which students just say a few sentences about their friends. Or it could be quite lengthy, with students taking more time to revise all the information they have learnt in the theme about relationships and friendships.

### E  Giving a talk

Set the task. Ask students to make notes about their closest friends. Students should then spend some time working in pairs and practising their talks.

Finally, put students into larger groups of four or five to give their final talk. Monitor and give feedback.

**Answers**
Answers depend on students.

## Closure

If there is time, ask one or two confident students to give their talks to the class.

| ways of manipulating | The Dictator | The Weakling | The Calculator | The Clinging Vine | The Bully |
|---|---|---|---|---|---|
| meaning | in charge, can do what he/she wants, nobody tells him/her what to do | no strength physically or mentally | machine for calculations, clever ways to achieve aims | climbing plant | pick on someone weaker |
| behaviour | believe they are right, have authority, order people to do things | passive | takes actions because of effect on others, plot and scheme | appear helpless emotionally | makes other people do things for fun |
| examples | rich people + family, workers | ask others to open bottles, lift heavy objects | tell one person one thing, another person the opposite | say 'you must help me, I need you', etc. | aggressive, shout, threaten people |

# Theme 3

## Managing to be successful

- **Managing time and self**
- **The time thieves**
- **Decisions, decisions, decisions**
- **For and against**

# Listening: Managing time and self  3

## 3.1 Vocabulary for listening: Important vs urgent

**Objectives**

By the end of the lesson, students should be able to:
- relate spoken vocabulary on the topic of the theme to their written forms;
- show understanding of meanings and use of target vocabulary from the theme.

**Introduction**

Write the following sentences on the board but without the word in brackets. Elicit what verb is missing in each space:
1. *He (managed) to lose ten kilos in weight.*
2. *I can't (manage) without my mobile phone.*
3. *He's lost his job so he's (managing) on very little money.*
4. *It's OK thanks. I can (manage).*
5. *She (manages) eleven restaurants in this area.*
6. *I'm hopeless at (managing) my money.*

Discuss the meaning of *manage* in each of the above sentences:
1. *do something difficult*
2. *deal with a problem*
3. *live without much money*
4. *not need help*
5. *direct or control a business*
6. *use money or time well*

Explain that, in this section, students will be looking at the meanings of sentences 5 and 6 for *manage*.

### A  Activating ideas

Exploit the visuals. Elicit vocabulary, for example:
*busy*
*stress/ stressed / stressful*
*(dis)organized*
*To Do list*
*post-it note*
*message*

Ask students to look at the notes in the To Do list. Elicit a full sentence for each note, for example:

*I must finish my Business Studies assignment by Friday.*
*I need to see my tutor about my project.*

Students discuss the question in pairs. Elicit ideas. Discuss why it is important to write a To Do list and elicit the verbs that collate with some of these words:
*If you don't write a list, you might ...*

| forget | an appointment |
| be late for | a deadline |
| miss | your lecture |
| not be ready / prepared for | a meeting |
| | a tutorial |

**Answers**

appointments
deadlines
lectures
meetings
tutorials
tasks
chores

### B  Understanding vocabulary in context

Check students understand the task and go over the example. Play ⓓ 3.1. Students complete the activity individually, then compare their answers in pairs. If necessary, play the CD again. Elicit answers. Check meanings of the target vocabulary, especially for the word *urgent* (something that needs immediate action). The difference in meaning between *important* and *urgent* will be dealt with in more detail in Exercise C.

**Answers**

| 6 | order. |
| 10 | important. |
| 7 | urgent. |
| 1 | time management. |
| 5 | prioritize. |
| 8 | faces. |
| 2 | the To Do list. |
| 9 | urgency. |
| 3 | stressed. |
| 4 | impossible. |

## Transcript

🌐 3.1

**Presenter:** 3.1. Theme 3: Managing to be successful
Lesson 3.1 Vocabulary for listening: Important *vs* urgent
Exercise B. Listen to part of a lecture on the management of To Do lists. Number the word or phrase to complete each sentence.

**Lecturer:** Have you ever said, 'I'm hopeless at managing my time'? Everyone has to deal with the issue of …
One of the most useful tools of time management is …
But To Do lists often get longer and longer and become a waste of time. In the end, the To Do list itself can make us feel …
You can't do everything at the same time – it's …
So, you have to …
In other words, you have to number the items on the list in …
This sounds easy but it's not. The problem is sometimes called important *versus* …
This is a problem which everybody …
The management consultant Althea DeBrule points out that other people often give us the …
They say to you, 'You must do this now.' But only you can say if something is ….

---

**Methodology note**

We have suggested answers for Exercise C2 but there could well be quite a lot of discussion about them. Some answers may depend on the circumstances, for example, if there is a serious problem with your work, then seeing your tutor may be urgent as well as important.

---

**C** Using new vocabulary

1. Give students time to study the table. Elicit ideas for activities that may be important but not urgent, and vice versa. Play 🌐 3.2. Students complete the table individually, then compare their answers in pairs. Elicit answers.

2. Check students understand the task. Students discuss the answers in pairs or small groups. There may be quite a lot of discussion and it does not really matter if students' answers are not the same as the ones given below. Give feedback.

### Answers
1. See next table.

Table 1: *Rating items on a To Do list*

| rating | important | urgent |
|--------|-----------|--------|
| A      | ✓         | ✓      |
| B      | ✓         | ✗      |
| C      | ✗         | ✓      |
| D      | ✗         | ✗      |

2. Possible answers:

| | TO DO |
|---|---|
| | Wed. 15th |
| A | finish Bus. Stud. assignment (by Fri) |
| B | see tutor re. project |
| C | call Jane re. weekend |
| A? | get food! |
| C | take books back to library – overdue! |
| B | revise for exams – only 28 days left |
| A | prepare for 3.30 lecture today |
| B | tidy desk |
| B | do the chores |

## Transcript

🌐 3.2

**Presenter:** 3.2. Exercise C1. Listen to some advice about using To Do lists.

**Tutor:** Go through your To Do list and mark each point A, B, C or D.
Give an A rating to things which are important and urgent and a B to things which are important but not urgent. C is for things which are urgent but not important while D, of course, is given to things which are not urgent and not important. In fact, D things should probably be crossed out.

**D** Word-building

1. Check students understand the task and go over the example. Set for pairwork. Do not confirm or correct answers at this stage.
2. Play 🌐 3.3. Students check their own answers.
3. Check the meanings of some of the words that may not have the meanings that students would expect, e.g., *hopeless*, *timeless*.

Answers

| noun | -ful | -less | notes |
|---|---|---|---|
| use | ✓ | ✓ | |
| stress | ✓ | – | |
| waste | ✓ | – | |
| hope | ✓ | ✓ | *hopeful* = believing something will happen<br>*hopeless* = no good at |
| truth | ✓ | – | = tells the truth all the time |
| care | ✓ | ✓ | |
| beauty | ✓ | – | opposite = *ugly* |
| harm | ✓ | ✓ | |
| time | – | ✓ | = lasting for all time |
| fear | ✓ | ✓ | *fearful* = afraid<br>*fearless* = completely without fear |

## Transcript

🔊 3.3

Presenter: 3.3. Exercise D2. Listen and check your answers.
Voice: useful, useless; stressful; wasteful; hopeful, hopeless; truthful; careful, careless; beautiful; harmful; timeless; fearful, fearless

## Closure

Students make sentences with the adjectives from Exercise D.

## 3.2 Real-time listening: Work *vs* time

### Objectives

By the end of this lesson, students should be able to:
- attempt to understand a lecture about the 'work = time available' equation;
- use previously learnt sub-skills about understanding an introduction;
- have a better understanding of the meaning of target vocabulary for the Listening section.

## Introduction

Revise the difference in meaning between *important* and *urgent* from the previous lesson.

### A  Activating ideas

Refer students to the photographs on page 77 of the Course Book. Elicit some vocabulary relating to each photo. Ask students in particular what the photographs show about time and work.

Set the activity for pairwork. Play 🔊 3.4 and pause after each sentence. Allow students enough time to discuss the possible photograph for each sentence. Do not confirm or correct answers at this stage. Give feedback, getting students to try to remember the sentence they heard for each photograph.

Answers

| 1. B | 2. D | 3. D | 4. F | 5. I |
| 6. H | 7. E | 8. A | 9. C | 10. G |

## Transcript

🔊 3.4

Presenter: 3.4. Lesson 3.2. Real-time listening: Work *vs* time. Exercise A. Listen to some sentences. Find the correct photograph on the opposite page for each sentence.
Voices:
a. How come they have time to have fun?
b. I always have so much work to do.
c. I am SO late. The lecturer is going to be furious.
d. I'm never going to finish all this tonight.
e. If only we had a bigger flat.
f. It's difficult. Every time I sit down to study somewhere, my friends turn up.
g. The lecture is boring but you still shouldn't fall asleep.
h. The tutorial started at 9.00. Where have you been?
i. We get a lot of work done together in our study group.

### Methodology note

From now on, students will have to work out the structure of the lecture from the introduction. Previously, the information was given to them. In this way, we are helping to encourage independent learning.

### B  Understanding an introduction

1. Set the task and remind students how to make a note of the research source (see Lesson 1. 3 Learning new listening skills,

Theme 1, on page 14 of the Course Book). Play [DVD] 3.A. Students work individually, then compare their answers in pairs. Elicit answers, preferably using an electronic projection.

2. Set the task. Play [DVD] 3.B. Elicit answers and check the meaning of the word *equation*.

### Answers

1. *Managing Time*, Melissa Raffoni (2006)
2. reasons (for managing time)
basic equation
balancing the equation

### Transcripts

🔊 3.5 [DVD] 3.A

Lecturer: I am going to talk to you today about a problem. It is a problem which all of us face at one time or another. It is a problem which starts when you are a student. If you don't solve it then, it will get worse and worse. When you leave university and get a job, the problem will follow you. The problem is managing time. It is so important that Harvard Business Press published a whole book on the subject in 2006. Melissa Raffoni wrote in the introduction, 'Managing your time is much more than making a to-do list …' Let's see what managing time is all about.

🔊 3.6 [DVD] 3.B

Lecturer: Firstly, I'm going to talk about the reason for managing time – Why do we have to manage our time? Then, I'm going to explain the basic equation of time management. You know equations from mathematics. One plus two equals three. Well, there is a basic equation in time management which is very useful. Finally, I'm going to look at ways of making the equation balance. As I'm sure you know from maths, equations must balance – both sides must be the same. How can you make the time management equation balance?

### C Understanding a lecture

Give students time to read through the sentence openers. Revise the following vocabulary:
*amount of*
*types of*
*increase*
*reduce*

Set the task. Play [DVD] 3.C, pausing briefly after each sentence to give students time to write. Students compare their answers in pairs. Elicit answers.

### Answers

1. There is a basic time management *equation*.
2. The equation is *work = time available*.
3. Both sides of the equation must *balance*.
4. Can you reduce the amount of *work*?
5. No, because you can't *refuse to do things*.
6. Can you increase the amount of *time available*?
7. No, because rest is as important *as work*.
8. There are basically two types of *work*.
9. There is current work and *previous work*.
10. Today's work is current work plus *previous work*.

### Transcript

🔊 3.7 [DVD] 3.C

Lecturer: So, first, why must we manage our time? The reason is simple. If we don't manage our time today, the problem will be worse tomorrow. Let me explain.

This is the basic equation of time management. On one side, we have *work*. On the other side, we have *time available*. Equations must balance. Both sides must be the same. Work must equal time available. In other words, we must have enough time to do the work we have to do. How can we ensure that work equals time available?

So how can you ensure that work equals time available? Let's start with the work side of the equation. You could try to reduce the amount of work that people give you to do. Some management books say you must prioritise. You must decide what is important. Other books tell you to say no to work. But that is very difficult when you are studying. Everything is important. Which things can you refuse to do? None. Tutors expect you to complete all assignments on time. They don't want you to miss lectures because you are behind in your written work.

Alternatively, you could try to increase the time available. You could get up an hour earlier, or go to bed later, or you could reduce the number of breaks during the day, but I'm not going to tell you to do that. Rest and relaxation is just as important as work, to my mind.

So we can't reduce the amount of work we are given and we shouldn't try to work every hour of the day and night. Are there any other alternatives?

Let's think about the type of work you have to do every day. Basically, there are two types of work. Firstly, there is *current work*. These are the things that managers or tutors want you to do today. There is usually enough time in the working day to complete all the current work. But there is another type of work as well. This is *previous work* – these are the things that you promised to do yesterday, or intended to do last week, or forgot to do last month.

All work begins as current work – your tutor asks you to do an assignment, for example. At that time, all your colleagues are doing the same assignment so you can get lots of help with current work. But if you don't do current work at the correct time, it becomes previous work. So today's work is always current work + previous work. The thing to remember is – do current work today! Don't leave it to become previous work.

To sum up … Work must balance with time available. You can't refuse to do work, and you shouldn't increase the time available because rest is as important as work. The key point is, always do your current work well and on time. Then you should find that you will have plenty of time available without getting up at 5.00 a.m. every day.

Theme 3: Listening 123

### D Summarizing a lecture

Check students understand the symbols and the information given in the slides. Elicit some possible sentences to describe the information. Divide the class into pairs. Each student takes it in turns to summarize the information. Monitor. Elicit two or three possible versions of the summary.

Show the model summary (see Answers) on the board, preferably using an electronic projection.

**Answers**

Answer depends on the students, but here is a possible model:

**Summary**

You must balance the work and time equation. You can't refuse to do work. You can't increase the amount of time you have because rest is also important. Therefore, you should do current work at the correct time. Don't let it become previous work.

### E Transferring information to the real world

1. Students work individually then, in pairs, show each other their lists. Elicit a few items from the students' To Do lists.
2. Students discuss in pairs. Elicit some of their ideas.

**Answers**

Answer depend on the students.

## Closure

Give feedback on Exercise E. Have a discussion with the class on how they are finding the work on their course. This might be an opportunity for you to find out if students are being given too much or too little work. Students can also advise each other on strategies for managing their time and work.

## 3.3 Learning new listening skills: Signpost words and phrases

**Objectives**

By the end of the lesson, students should be able to:
- recognize signpost words and phrases in a lecture;
- make notes of the organization of a lecture from the introduction.

**Introduction**

Use Exercise A as the introduction.

### A Reviewing vocabulary

Check students understand the task and do an example with them, perhaps *yesterday* and *tomorrow*. Students continue in pairs. Elicit answers.

**Answers**

| reduce | increase |
| current | previous |
| firstly | finally |
| yesterday | tomorrow |
| earlier | later |
| work | rest |

### B Identifying a new skill

1. Check students understand the task. Students discuss the question in pairs. Do not elicit answers.
2. Use the visual to explain the word *signpost* in its usual meaning. Tell students we often use signposts when we are speaking. Students read the Skills Check. Now go back and elicit the answers to Exercise B1. As well as discussing other signpost words, you can elicit the functions that will follow.

Ask students:
*Why is it important to listen for signpost language?* (It tells us the organization and sometimes the content of the lecture.)

## Answers

| 1st signpost | other signposts | function |
|---|---|---|
| a. Firstly, I'm … | Secondly / Then, etc. | lists of points |
| b. On one side … | On the other side … | two elements |
| c. Some management books say … | Other management books say … | two or more elements |
| d. There are two types of work … | The first type / the second type … | lists of points |
| e. You could get up … | Or / Alternatively you could try … | possibilities – note that the use of *could* here implies that there are other alternatives. If there was only one possibility, the speaker would probably use *can*. |

> **Methodology note**
>
> The word *some* is stressed in this situation, whereas in other cases it is normally unstressed. Similarly, the modal *could* is often stressed in this situation, whereas – like *some* – it is normally unstressed in other cases.

### C  Recognizing stress patterns

Do the first sentence as an example with the class, showing that the stressed word helps you to predict what is coming next, i.e., *Firstly* = there will be at least a *Secondly*. Set the task for individual work. Play 3.8. Give feedback, getting students to stress the phrases correctly. Drill the phrases.

## Transcript

🔊 3.8

**Presenter:** 3.8. Lesson 3.3. Learning new listening skills: Signpost words and phrases. Exercise C. Listen to extracts from the lecture in Lesson 3.2. Underline the stressed words in each signpost phrase.

**Lecturer:** Firstly, I'm going to talk about the reason for managing time.
On one side, we have work.
Some management books say you must prioritise.
There are two types of work. Firstly, there is current work. But there is another type of work as well. This is previous work.
You could get up an hour earlier, or go to bed later, or you could reduce the number of breaks during the day.

### D  Practising a new skill

Check students understand the task and go over the example. Set the task for individual work. Play 3.9, pausing briefly after each extract so that students have time to make notes. Students compare their answers in pairs. Elicit answers, using an electronic projection. If you wish, play the CD again with students following the transcript.

## Transcript

🔊 3.9

**Presenter:** 3.9. Exercise D. Listen to the introductions from some lectures. Make notes of the organization of each lecture.

One.

**Lecturer:** There are basically two types of work. On the one hand, we have work which other people give us. We could call that *external work*. On the other hand, we have work which we choose to do ourselves. We could call that *internal work*. Both types of work are very important, but of course, if you do not do external work, someone will be unhappy.

**Presenter:** Two.
**Lecturer:** There are three types of memory. There is sensory memory, which only lasts for a few seconds. There is short-term memory, which can last up to 30 seconds. Finally, there is long-term memory, which can last a lifetime.

**Presenter:** Three.
**Lecturer:** There are several ways of moving information into long-term memory. I'm going to talk about three of them today. Firstly, there is frequency, which means using new information a lot. Secondly, we have activity, which means doing something with new information. Finally, I'm going to discuss association, which is linking new information to existing information in our memories.

**Presenter:** Four.
**Lecturer:** Now let's consider global warming. Most people nowadays believe that the planet is getting warmer. But there are two ideas about this warming. On the one side, we have people who believe the warming is man-made. We are changing the average temperature of the planet with air travel, car exhaust and burning fossil fuels. On the other side, there are people who say the warming is natural. It is part of a cycle in nature.

**Presenter:** Five.
**Lecturer:** We're going to look at the Solar System today. Just before we start, I must tell you that there is one area of disagreement. It is quite a basic point. How many planets are there in the Solar System? Some people say there are nine planets. These include Pluto, which is the furthest from the sun and very, very small. Other people say there are only eight planets, because Pluto is too small to be a planet. Finally, a few people think that there are ten planets. They say there is a hidden planet which is one and a half times the size of Pluto.

**Presenter:** Six.
**Lecturer:** As we all know, the world is running out of oil. If we continue to consume oil at the current rate, there will be no oil left by 2050. Today, I'll examine this issue of global energy shortage in more detail.

**Theme 3: Listening   125**

There are three main solutions to the problem. We could try to change our lifestyles. In particular, we could use cars and planes less. Alternatively, we could try to use energy more efficiently. We could build houses and office blocks in a better way so they lose less heat. Finally, we could try to replace oil as an energy source. We could build more nuclear power stations, and we could develop the technology of renewable sources, like wind, wave and solar power.

### Answers

1. *Types of work*
   1. External – from other people
   2. Internal – from ourselves

2. *Types of memory*
   1. sensory – few secs
   2. short-term – up to 30 secs
   3. long-term – up to lifetime

3. *Moving info to long-term memory*
   1. frequency – use a lot
   2. activity – do something
   3. association – link with old

4. *Global warming*
   1. man-made – air travel, cars, etc.
   2. natural – part of cycle

5. *How many planets?*
   nine – inc. Pluto
   eight – not Pluto
   ten – hidden, 1.5 x Pluto

6. *Energy shortage*
   1. change lifestyle – use cars / planes less
   2. be more efficient – build better
   3. replace oil

### Closure

If you have not already done so, play 🔊 3.9 again with students following the transcript.

## 3.4 Grammar for listening: verb + infinitive

### Objectives

By the end of the lesson, students should be able to:

- listen for two verbs with the pattern (*promise*) + *to do*;
- listen for the object in sentences with transitive verbs.

### Introduction

Point out that it is useful to know the pattern of a verb. This is helpful when listening to a text because the verb will prepare them for the kind of information that comes next.

Remind students about forms after a verb. In Theme 2, students learnt about transitive and intransitive verbs.

Write the following verbs from the table below on the board, and ask students to put them into two groups:
– verbs that are followed by an object (transitive)
– verbs that don't need an object (intransitive)

Ask students to make sentences (linked to topics from the theme) with each verb. Help them with prompts if they are struggling.

### Answers

| transitive | intransitive |
| --- | --- |
| get | go |
| call | sleep |
| do | work |
| see | live |

Possible sentences:

It is important to **get** healthy food.
I have to **call** my friend later.
I hate **doing** chores.
I **saw** my tutor yesterday.

You should **go** to all the lectures.
How long do you normally **sleep** for?
Do you **work** better in the morning or in the evening?
I **live** in a small flat with three other students.

### Methodology note

It is important when listening that students realize that the verbs in the table in Grammar box 13 will usually be followed by a second verb. They may not hear the *to* of the infinitive; that is not important. However, students should try to listen for the other half of the infinitive.

## Grammar box 13

Students study the table. Check understanding. Ask students to close their books. Write the first half of each sentence on the board. In pairs, students take it in turns to read out the first half of each sentence from the board, with the other student trying to give the second half from memory. Monitor and give feedback. Play 3.10, if you wish.

## Transcript

3.10

Presenter: 3.10. Lesson 3.4. Grammar for listening: verb + infinitive. Grammar box 13. Listen to the sentences. How is *to* pronounced?
Voice: The student promised to finish the work yesterday.
I intend to write the essay next week.
Students can't refuse to attend lectures.
You could try to reduce the amount of work.
Everyone must remember to complete assignments on time.
You have to do all the work.

### A Hearing the two verbs

Tell students they are now going to practise listening for two verbs, as they have learnt to do so when studying Grammar box 13. Set the task and go over the example. Play 3.11. Students complete the tables individually, then compare their answers in pairs. Play the CD again if necessary. Elicit answers. Show copies of the transcript, preferably using an electronic projection.

Finally, making sure no copies of the transcript are in sight, ask students to remember the sentences using the correct pairs of words as prompts. This can either be done with students working in pairs or as a whole-class activity.

### Answers

|   | verb     |   | infinitive |
|---|----------|---|------------|
| 7 | forget   | 1 | attend     |
| 5 | learn    | 2 | complete   |
| 2 | need     | 5 | drive      |
| 4 | prefer   | 4 | live       |
| 8 | promise  | 6 | read       |
| 1 | refuse   | 7 | tell       |
| 6 | remember | 3 | watch      |
| 3 | want     | 8 | work       |

## Transcript

3.11

Presenter: 3.11. Exercise A. Listen to each sentence. Number the two words you hear in each case.
Voices: 1. You can't refuse to attend lectures.
2. You need to complete a form in the computer centre.
3. Children often want to watch too much television.
4. Some people prefer to live on their own.
5. Most young people in Britain learn to drive at the age of 17.
6. You must remember to read the notes before each lecture.
7. Sorry. Did I forget to tell you about the next assignment?
8. The student promised to work harder in the future.

## Grammar box 14

Remind students about the work they did on transitive verbs in Lesson 2.4 Grammar for listening, Theme 2, on page 47 of the Course Book. Repeat the procedure for Grammar box 13 above, and play 3.12, if you wish.

## Transcript

3.12

Presenter: 3.12. Grammar box 14.
Voice: Tutors expect you to hand in all assignments.
Books will tell you to get up earlier.
They don't want students to miss lectures.

### B Hearing the object

Set the task and go over the example. Play 3.13. Students complete the activity individually, then compare their answers in pairs. Replay the CD if necessary. Elicit answers. Show copies of the transcript, preferably using an electronic projection.

### Answers

| 1  | students     |
|----|--------------|
| 2  | people       |
| 3  | colleagues   |
| 4  | participants |
| 5  | children     |
| 6  | managers     |
| 7  | us           |
| 8  | the man      |
| 9  | him          |
| 10 | everyone     |

## Transcript

🔊 3.13

Presenter: 3.13. Exercise B. Listen to each sentence. Write the object.

Voices:
1. Lecturers expect students to take notes.
2. Time management books sometimes tell people to get up earlier.
3. Friends sometimes want colleagues to stop revising.
4. The researchers asked participants to complete a questionnaire.
5. Parents teach children to behave correctly.
6. Industrial psychologists help managers to understand the needs of workers.
7. The tutor reminded us to read the reference material.
8. The police forced the man to come out of the building.
9. His wife persuaded him to carry on.
10. My best teacher at school encouraged everyone to do their best.

### C Consolidation

Point out that there are no wrong answers here. The ending must just be logical and grammatically correct. Monitor and assist as necessary. Give feedback, getting students to read out their sentences.

### Answers

Possible endings:
1. I gave the lecturer my essay and she promised *to mark it quickly*.
2. These books are overdue so I have *to take them back to the library today*.
3. This problem is so difficult. I tried *to solve it but I couldn't*.
4. I'm so tired. I don't want *to study this evening*.
5. I asked my friend for help but *he refused to help me*.
6. I forgot to buy milk but *I remembered to get bread*.

### Closure

Tell students to make their own sentences with *expect / tell / want / promise / remember / try*.

## 3.5 Applying new listening skills: Self 1 vs Self 2

### Objectives

By the end of the lesson, students should be able to:
- transfer information from a lecture on management;
- show understanding of facts about managing yourself.

### Introduction

Remind students about the lecture in Lesson 3.2 Real-time listening on page 76 of the Course Book. Tell students that they are going to hear the beginning of sentences. Point out that all the sentences are about managing the 'work = time' equation. Students have to predict the next word or phrase. Read the phrases below, pausing after each one. Ask students to discuss possible endings in pairs. Elicit ideas. Repeat each phrase, if necessary. Continue in the same way with the remaining phrases.

1. *You could try to reduce* (the amount of work.)
2. *Tutors expect you to hand in* (assignments on time.)
3. *They don't want you to miss* (lectures.)
4. *You could try to increase* (the time available.)
5. *Books often tell you to get up* (earlier.)
6. *Previous work is the things that you promised to do* (before.)

### Methodology note

The reflexive pronoun (*myself, yourself*, etc.) is not used as frequently in English as it is in other languages, so you may need to remind students about it. Common expressions are:
*I've hurt / burnt / injured / cut myself.*
*Have you burnt / hurt / cut yourself?*
*Look after yourself.*
*Help yourself / yourselves.*
*I'm going crazy. I'm talking to myself!*
*Let's go by ourselves.*

In this lesson, it is used for the concept of *you must manage yourself*.

### A Activating ideas

Refer students to the visual. Ask:
*What does it show?* (e.g., a happy person and an angry or worried person)

*What does it mean?* (e.g., we all have two sides)

Write *managing yourself* on the board. Ask students what they understand by the term. Students discuss the questions in pairs. Elicit ideas.

### Answers

Answers depend on the students. However, they may suggest the following ideas:

We usually manage other people but we also need to manage ourselves – our time, our money, our work, the way we think and/or behave. We do this by being careful in our actions and our behaviour – even (as the lecture will explain) in our thoughts about ourselves.

> **Methodology note**
>
> Remind students how important the introduction to a lecture is. This is because it often gives the whole structure of the lecture, which can help immensely – particularly if you get lost on one point.

### B Understanding an introduction

Set the task for individual work. Play DVD 3.D. Give feedback, writing the correct headings on the board.

### Answers

Self-management

Theory

Problem

Solution

### Transcript

3.14 DVD 3.D

**Presenter:** 3.14. Lesson 3.5. Applying new listening skills: Self 1 *vs* Self 2

**Lecturer:** Would you like to be a manager when you leave university? Perhaps the answer is yes. Perhaps it is no. But whether or not you want to manage other people at work, there is one kind of manager that we must all become. We must all be managers of ourselves. Today, I want to talk to you about self-management – managing yourself. This is just as important at university as it is at work. Firstly, I'm going to talk about a theory of self-management. How can you actually manage yourself? Then I'll explain the problem which comes from this theory. Finally, I'm going to look at a solution to this problem.

### C Following the lecture

Remind students to listen for signpost language (see Lesson 3.3 Learning new listening skills) and for when the lecturer moves on to the next part of the lecture. Remind students to make a note of any research sources. Play DVD 3.E.

Monitor while students are working. If most students are not making effective notes by the end of the Theory section, then place a good set of notes for this section on the board as feedback. Play one more time the DVD's Theory section to show the relationship between the lecture and the notes. Then continue with playing the rest of the DVD.

Check the meaning of *self-esteem* and explain it is a synonym for *confidence*. Do not give further feedback at this stage.

Explain that you are not going to look at the students' notes yet.

### Answers

Model notes:

Self-management

Theory

Gallway (1974)

everyone = two selves –
- Self 1 confident
- Self 2 doubtful

Problem
see ourselves as Self 2
everything or nothing
pessimistic
feeling = truth
only one right way
single actions = permanent situations

Solution
learn to value ourselves
develop self-esteem

### Transcript

3.15 DVD 3.E

**Presenter:** 3.15. Exercise C. Watch the lecture.

**Lecturer:** OK. So, first, let's look at a theory of self-management. It comes from a fascinating book by a man called Gallway. It was published in 1974. It's actually called *The Inner Game of Tennis* but it's not just about tennis. Many psychologists recognize that the ideas in the book apply to everyday life. In his book, Gallway describes two kinds of people. He says, on the one hand, there is the confident person. On the other hand, there is the doubtful person. Confident … and doubtful. The confident person says, 'I can do A. I remembered to do B. I'm very good at C.' The doubtful person is exactly the opposite. The doubtful person says, 'I can't do X. I forgot to do Y. I'm hopeless at Z.' I'm sure you have all met these two types of people. But ... and this is the important point, Gallway says that we all have the two types of people inside ourself. One side is the confident self – Gallway calls this Self 1. The other side is the doubtful self – Self 2. Which side is truthful? Well, both sides might be truthful. We all have things we can do and things we can't do, things we intended to do, but forgot to do, things we have tried to do, but have failed to do.

Right, so, according to Gallway, we all have two selves. What is the problem with this? But how do other people see us? In some cases, other people see a person as Self 2, the doubtful self. But in most cases, other people see a person as Self 1, the confident self. The point is ... people often see themselves as Self 2.

OK. So is that clear? On the one side, we have the confident self. This is how other people see us. On the other, we have the doubtful self. This is how we often see ourselves. And this is the problem. We see ourselves in a bad way.

What does Self 2 say? Well, firstly, Self 2 believes in everything or nothing. I mean, Self 2 believes things must be perfect, or they are terrible. Self 2 says, 'I made one mistake in that test so I'm hopeless.'

Secondly, Self 2 is pessimistic. The future will always be even worse than the present. Self 2 says, 'I got a C in that assignment so I'll never pass the course.'

Thirdly, Self 2 thinks that a feeling is the same as the truth. In other words, I *feel* this so it is true. Self 2 says, 'I feel ugly so I am ugly.'

Fourthly, Self 2 believes there is only one right way: Self 2 does not believe there can be several ways to be successful. Self 2 says, 'Everyone should have a career plan. I don't have a career plan so there is something wrong with me.'

Finally, Self 2 thinks single actions are the same as permanent situations. To put it another way, Self 2 confuses 'I did' with 'I am'. Self 2 says 'I did badly on that test so I am a bad student.'

What can we do about this? I mean, what is the solution? Gallway says you must learn to value yourself. You must develop your self-esteem. You must recognize when Self 2 is talking, because Self 2 gets in the way of Self 1.

You must try to replace negative thoughts from Self 2 with positive thoughts from Self 1.

- Self 1 says, 'I made one mistake in that test but I got the rest of the answers correct.'
- Self 1 says, 'I got a C in that assignment so I'll have to work harder on the next one.'
- Self 1 says, 'I feel ugly today but I'm sure everyone feels ugly at times.'
- Self 1 says, 'Career plans are a good idea for some people. But I don't want to make one.'
- Self 1 says, 'I did badly on that test so perhaps I didn't revise enough.'

So, to sum up, according to Gallway, we all have two selves. Self 1 is confident. Self 2 is doubtful. People see us as Self 1. But the problem is ... we often see ourselves as Self 2. What's the solution? You must ensure that Self 1 does most of the talking inside your head.

### D Checking understanding

Explain that the point of making notes is so they can then reconstruct the key points from a lecture. If they can answer the questions from their notes, the notes are good. Set the tasks for individual work and pairwork checking.

#### Answers

Model answers:

1. a. Gallway
   b. 1974
   c. a book called *The Inner Game of Tennis*
   d. Answers depend on students.
2. 

| a. Self 2 is ... | doubtful. |
| --- | --- |
| b. Self 2 is the way ... | we see ourselves. |
| c. Self 2 believes in everything or ... | or nothing. |
| d. Self 2 thinks that the future will be ... | worse than the present. |
| e. Self 2 thinks that a feeling is ... | the same as the truth. |
| f. Self 2 believes that there is only ... | one right way. |
| g. Self 2 thinks that single actions are ... | the same as permanent situations. |

3. a. *Self 1 is confident.*
   b. *Self 1 is the way other people see us.*
   c. *Self 1 doesn't believe that everything has to be perfect.* *
   d. *Self 1 thinks that the future will be better than the present.*
   e. *Self 1 thinks that a feeling is not the same as the truth.*
   f. *Self 1 believes that there are many right ways.*
   g. *Self 1 thinks that single actions are different from permanent situations.*
   * **Note:** This one is difficult.
4. Answers depend on students.

### E Transferring information to the real world

Set for whole-class or group discussion. You might want to talk about yourself to start it.

**Closure**

Say some of the sentences from the lecture and ask students to tell you if they correspond to Self 1 or Self 2 talking in each case.

# Speaking: The time thieves

## 3.6 Vocabulary for speaking: Wasting time

### Objectives

By the end of the lesson, students should be able to:
- form and pronounce nouns ending in ~tion;
- show understanding of vocabulary on the topic of time management;
- show understanding of some time management quotations and concepts.

### Introduction

Choose one of the following:

- Write the heading for the section on the board, *The time thieves*, and elicit that the phrase is about the things and/or people that steal or waste your time. Explain that time management is an important business topic and it is the focus of this Speaking section.

- Revise some vocabulary from the Listening section. Write the following words on the board (without the stress marks):

| 'current | re'fuse | our'selves |
| --- | --- | --- |
| 'hopeless | 'ugly | in'tend |
| 'equal | 'urgent | e'nough |
| 'doubtful | 'versus | |

Ask students to discuss the meaning of the words and then decide on the stressed syllable in pairs. Elicit answers and drill each word for the correct stress.

Then, still in pairs, students choose five different words each, taking it in turns to select one word at a time, and then make a sentence with it. Monitor and make a note of common errors. Ask some of the students to tell you one of their sentences. Correct if necessary, then drill the sentence with the class.

### A   Activating ideas

1. Students briefly discuss the question in pairs. Elicit answers.
2. Check understanding of the word *precious*. Students discuss the meaning of the two quotations in pairs. Elicit ideas, prompting students if necessary. When the answers have been elicited, ask students if they agree with the quotations or not.

### Answers

1. They all show ways of wasting time – Facebook and other social networking sites, mobile phones, computer games, iPods.
2. The first quotation refers to time-wasting activities – for example, making a cup of coffee only takes a few minutes. But if we do these activities many times during the day, they add up to hours wasted.

   The second quotation tells us that time thieves are time-wasting activities – time is precious = worth a lot of money. As people have said for centuries, 'Time is money'.

   **Note:** The first quotation comes from www.onlineorganizing.com; the second is from www.canadaone.com/ezine/july05/time_thieves.html.

### B   Understanding new vocabulary in context

1. Check students understand the task. Students complete the activity in pairs. Do not elicit answers at this stage. Play 3.16 so that students can check their own answers.

2. Drill the dialogues, using the recording as a model if you wish. Then students practise in pairs. Monitor for the correct pronunciation of the target vocabulary.

Elicit one or two examples for continuing the dialogues. These can be very simple phrases – for example, these could be the next two lines for conversation 3:
*OK, sorry.*
*That's all right.*

Students then continue writing extra lines in pairs. When they are happy with what they have written, they can practise the extended dialogues. Monitor. Ask two or three pairs of students to read out their extended dialogues for the rest of the class to hear.

### Transcript and Answers

3.16

**Presenter:** 3.16. Lesson 3.6. Vocabulary for speaking: Wasting time. Exercise B1. Listen to each dialogue. Complete it with a word from the list on the right. Make any necessary changes.

One.
**Voice A:** A study group is a good idea because …
**Voice B:** I don't agree. It's a waste of time.

Voice A: Please don't interrupt. I haven't finished.
Voice B: Sorry.

Presenter: Two.
Voice A: Have you done the assignment yet?
Voice B: No, I haven't. I'll do it tomorrow.
Voice A: Don't put it off any more! It's urgent.
Voice B: I've still got plenty of time.

Presenter: Three.
Voice A: Should I write the essay first?
Voice B: Don't distract me!
Voice A: Or should I revise instead?
Voice B: Look! I have to get on with my work.

Presenter: Four.
Voice A: I'm trying to concentrate.
Voice B: Sorry? What do you mean?
Voice A: The television's disturbing me.
Voice B: But this is my favourite programme!

> **Methodology note**
>
> More work is done on stressed syllables in longer words in Lesson 3.8 Learning new speaking skills.

| verb | noun |
| --- | --- |
| distract | *distraction* |
| interrupt | *interruption* |
| concentrate | *concentration* |
| *solve* | solution |
| *quote* | quotation |
| appreciate | appreciation |
| communicate | *communication* |
| recommend | recommendation |
| *introduce* | introduction |
| contribute | *contribution* |
| educate | education |
| inform | information |
| produce | production |
| repeat | repetition |
| transact | transaction |

### C  Word-building

1. Set the task. Students complete the table individually, then compare their answers in pairs. Elicit each answer orally so that you can correct the pronunciation of each word and drill it with the class. Make sure students are using the correct stressed syllable and pronunciation for the ending ~*tion* /ʃən/. The words are all from this course (so far) but you may have to revise the words' meanings as you go along.

2. Divide the class into groups of three. Allocate different words from the table (either the verbs or nouns, or a mixture of both) to each group. Each group makes a sentence with each word. They should then practise it to make sure they have good pronunciation. One person from each group says one of their sentences for the rest of the class to hear. Ask students to write down the sentence they hear. In this way, the class should end up with a good written example for most of the words in the table.

   Point out, if you have not already done so, that the pattern for the nouns is verb +(a/u)tion = noun.

### Answers

Target words in *italics*, including possible extra pairs from this course:

### Closure

Choose one of the following:

1. In pairs, students try to think of more words with the same pattern as the words in Exercise C. For example: *imagination, explanation, application, suggestion.*

2. Review the vocabulary from this lesson for time management and wasting time.

## 3.7 Real-time speaking: Time thieves – people and things

> **Objectives**
>
> By the end of this lesson, students should be able to:
> - recognize their own skills and knowledge gap in reacting to contributions in a tutorial;
> - focus on, and notice, the language and sub-skills for a discussion in a tutorial;
> - apply previously learnt speaking skills to a real-time activity;
> - demonstrate understanding of common core knowledge about time management.

**Introduction**

Exploit the visual. Elicit the fact that the woman is *interrupting* someone in the office. Elicit things that the person in the office could say:
*I can't talk now, I'm busy.*
*Sorry. I'm in the middle of something. Can we talk later?*
*Come in. Have a chat!*

### A  Activating ideas

Revise the meaning of the noun *distraction* and check students understand the two questions.

Students discuss the two questions in pairs. Elicit ideas.

**Answers**
Answers depend on students.

### B  Understanding a model

1. Check students understand the task. Play 3.17. Students complete the 'solutions' column individually, then compare their answers in pairs. Elicit answers.

2. See if students can predict any of the 'problems with solutions' but do not confirm or correct answers yet. Play 3.18. Students complete the second column individually, then compare their answers in pairs. Elicit answers.

**Answers**
Possible notes:

| solutions | problems with solutions |
|---|---|
| tell them to go away | can't be rude |
| stop for a few minutes to talk | interruption disturbs you |
| don't try to study in flat – go to library | ✓ |

**Transcript**

3.17

Presenter: 3.17. Lesson 3.7. Real-time speaking: Time thieves – people and things. Exercise B1. Listen to the first part of a tutorial about interruptions by people.
Lecturer: OK. I asked you to look at time thieves for this tutorial. In particular, I asked you to do some research on interruptions from other students, particularly flatmates. How did you get on? Mark?

Student 1: OK. I asked several people and they all said that other people are the main time thieves. I asked people for solutions. Some people said, um … tell them to go away. So, um, that's the first solution. Other people said that you should stop for a few minutes. You should stop and talk to them for a few moments, then you should get on with your work. So that's number two. A couple of people said that you should not try to study at home, in your flat or house. You should go to the library, instead. That's what I found.

3.18

Presenter: 3.18. Exercise B2. Listen to the second part of the tutorial.
Lecturer: OK. What do we think of those solutions?
Student 2: I agree with the first solution. They know that you have to study so they shouldn't interrupt you.
Student 3: I don't think that's possible. You can't be rude to someone, even if you are studying. I think the second solution is better. Stop for a few minutes and then continue.
Student 4: That's right. You can be polite but then say that you have to study.
Student 1: Yes. I think so, too. That's the best solution.
Student 3: Absolutely. Just have a quick chat.
Student 2: Possibly. But the interruption still disturbs you.
Student 3: I suppose so.
Student 2: OK. I've changed my mind. The last solution is the best one. Go and study somewhere else.
Student 3: I agree.
Student 1: So do I.
Student 4: Me, too.

### C  Studying a model

1. Check students understand the task and go over the example. Students complete the activity individually, then compare their answers in pairs. Elicit answers, preferably using an electronic projection.

2. Drill all or some of the sentences, or play the CDs from the previous exercise, so that students can hear the correct pronunciation once more. Focus on the stressed words and the rhythm of each phrase or sentence. Students can then practise the sentences in pairs.

**Answers**

A: Some people ~~they~~ said: 'Tell them to go away.' ~~Another~~ *Other* people said that you *should* stop for a few minutes.

B: I agree *with* the first solution. They know that you ~~having~~ *have* to study so they should not ~~to~~ interrupt you.

A: I don't think *that* is possible. You can't be rude *to* someone, even if you *are* ~~study~~ *studying*. I think the second solution is better.

B: That's ~~it~~ *right*. You can *be* polite but then *say* that you have *to* study.

Theme 3: Speaking  133

## D Practising a model

1. This activity helps students to focus on, or 'notice', the target grammar and fixed phrases for this section. Check students understand the task. Students discuss the two questions in pairs. Elicit ideas. Students discuss the problems of mobile phones and agree on the best solution. Monitor while students are working.

2. Play 3.19. Ask a few questions to check understanding. Ask students what solutions the students in the tutorial discussed and which one they decided on (tell people not to call). Elicit from students what solution they decided on in their role play in Exercise D1.

   Give feedback on the role play, and tell students that there will be further practice on the language for agreeing and disagreeing in some of the following lessons' tutorials.

### Answers

Answers depend on the students, but here are some ideas:

Problems / distractions:
- people call or send messages
- there are text alerts, e-mails, etc.
- play games, listen to music, etc.

Possible solutions:
- tell people not to ring
- screen calls
- put it on *silent*
- turn it off
- don't take phone with you
- keep focused and don't allow yourself to be distracted

### Transcript

3.19

**Presenter:** 3.19. Exercise D. Listen to the students discussing mobile phones.

**Student 1:** I looked at mobile phones. I talked to a number of students and they all agreed that the mobile phone is a big thief. The problem is that it never stops ringing. I asked people for solutions and some people said, turn it off and other people said tell people not to ring at certain times, when you are studying. A few people said that you should screen the calls. You know, only answer if you need to speak to the person. So, those are my solutions.

**Tutor:** OK. Any thoughts?

**Student 2:** I agree with the first solution. I think that you should turn off the phone when you are studying.

**Student 3:** Absolutely. We shouldn't let mobile phones rule our lives.

**Student 4:** I'm not sure. Mobile phones are for people to contact you in an emergency, so you can't turn them off all the time.

**Student 1:** That's right. You have to keep your mobile on. But you don't have to answer it.

**Student 3:** I suppose so. You could just screen the calls.

**Student 2:** Perhaps. But the call still disturbs you, even if you don't answer it.

**Student 4:** That's true.

**Student 2:** OK. You're right. The second solution is the best one. Tell people not to call during your study period. Then they can still call if it is really an emergency.

**Student 3:** I agree.

**Student 1:** I do, too.

**Student 4:** So do I.

### Closure

If you have not done so already, play the recording of the tutorials from Exercise B once more with the students following the transcript.

## Everyday English: Interruptions

### Objectives

By the end of the lesson, students should be able to:
- use appropriate language to interrupt politely in different situations.

### Introduction

Refer students to the three photographs. Ask: *What is happening in each photograph?*

Possible answers are:
1. A woman is conducting a meeting. Someone has come to the door. / Someone is coming in.
2. Two people are in an office. One of them is talking on a mobile phone.
3. A man is giving a lecture. He is showing the students / people a graph.

## A Activating ideas

Students discuss the questions in pairs. Elicit ideas.

### Answers

Answers depend on the students, but here are some ideas:

1. Maybe there is a message, phone call or an emergency. He may be saying: *Sorry to interrupt / disturb you but …*

2. She may be saying: *Can I call you back? / Could you call me back? / I can't talk at the*

*moment. / Sorry but I'm having a meeting at the moment.*

3. Maybe he/she didn't understand something, disagrees or wants to add something. He/she may be saying: *Excuse me for interrupting ... / Could I interrupt for a moment / second? / Could I just say / add something?*

### B  Studying the models

1. Ask students to cover the conversations. Set the task, and play 3.20. Students make a note of the number of the conversation when they hear one that matches a photograph. Play the conversations again if necessary or allow students to read the transcript. Elicit answers.

2. Students discuss the question in pairs. They can also discuss who 'A' or 'B' is in each case, and possibly give the name of each job. For example, in the first photograph, the woman who is standing up could be a manager and the person interrupting could be a receptionist or a clerk.

   Check understanding of any new language, for example, *I'm flat out.*

3. Check understanding of the words *formal* and *informal*, pointing out that formal language tends to be more polite. Informal language uses shorter forms and colloquial language.

   Students discuss the question in pairs. Elicit ideas.

4. Drill some of the phrases from the conversations, encouraging students to sound tentative in their intonation for the initial statement or question in each conversation.

   Students practise in pairs. Monitor and give feedback. Further practice can be given by asking students to practise the conversations again, either from memory or prompts. They can also substitute some of the other words or phrases if possible and extend the conversations by one or two more lines.

### Optional activity

Review or work on some of the language in the conversations, for example:

- **Formal:**
  *I'm really / very sorry to disturb / interrupt you but ...*

- **Informal:**
  *Is it OK if I + do something?*
  **Possible responses:**
  *That's OK. / Go ahead.*

- **Informal or formal (depending on context, intonation, etc.):**
  *Am I disturbing / interrupting you?*
  **Possible responses:**
  *No, not all. / Well / Actually I am a bit busy.*

- **Formal:**
  *Would you mind + ~ing?*
  **Possible responses:**
  (Tricky for this structure as answering 'yes' would be quite rude!)
  *No, not at all. / Certainly. / Well, actually, yes I would mind.*

- ***Could* is more formal than *Can*:**
  *Can / Could I possibly disturb / interrupt / ask ... ?*

### Answers

- Conversations 1, 3 and 6.
- Answers depend on the students, but the other conversations could be taking place as follows:
  - Conversation 2 – at home, at the university, in the sitting room, etc.
  - Conversation 4 – at home, in the sitting room, etc.
  - Conversation 5 – in rented accommodation or in a student hostel, at the university.
- Conversations 1 and 6 are formal.
  The others are informal.

### Transcript

3.20

**Presenter:** 3.20. Everyday English: Interruptions. Exercise B. Listen to the conversations. Find three conversations that match the photographs above.

One.
**Voice A:** I'm really sorry to interrupt but there's an urgent call for you.
**Voice B:** Who is it?
**Voice A:** The CEO.
**Voice B:** Right. I'd better take it. Excuse me a moment.

**Presenter:** Two.
**Voice A:** Can you help me with this?
**Voice B:** I can't, I'm afraid. I'm flat out.
**Voice A:** It'll only take a minute.
**Voice B:** OK. Pass it over.

**Presenter:** Three.
**Voice A:** Am I disturbing you?
**Voice B:** Well, I am a bit busy at the moment.
**Voice A:** OK. I'll phone back later.
**Voice B:** Thanks. After two.

Theme 3: Speaking  135

Presenter: Four.
Voice A: Is it OK if i put the television on?
Voice B: Well, actually, I'm trying to read.
Voice A: I won't have it on loud.
Voice B: You always say that.

Presenter: Five.
Voice A: Can I disturb you for a moment?
Voice B: Yes, what is it?
Voice A: The Internet connection has stopped working again.
Voice B: Well, phone the maintenance department then.

Presenter: Six.
Voice A: Sorry, could I possibly interrupt?
Voice B: Yes, of course. What's the problem?
Voice A: Well, would you mind repeating that last figure? I'm afraid I missed it.
Voice B: Certainly. It was 15,783,000 dollars.

### C Practising the model

Elicit some ideas for situations when students may need to interrupt. For example:
- in a lecture / tutorial / lesson
- if they need to tell someone there's someone at the door, on the phone, etc.
- if there's a problem or emergency

Go through the introductory phrases in the Course Book and elicit some possible ways to end each one.
- *I'm sorry to disturb you but ...* + sentence
- *Sorry to interrupt but ...* + sentence
- *Do you mind if I ...* + verb (could be past tense for extra politeness, e.g., *opened*)
- *Would you mind ...* + gerund (e.g., *opening*)
- *Is it OK ...* + infinitive (e.g., *to talk now*) OR *if* (e.g., *if I open the window*)
- *Am I ...* + gerund (e.g., *disturbing you*)

Drill the sentences. Elicit some possible ways to extend each conversation.

Students continue in pairs. Monitor and give feedback.

### Answers
Answers depend on students.

### Closure

1. Ask one or two pairs of students to give their conversations to the rest of the class.
2. Ask students to write down one or two of their conversations.

## 3.8 Learning new speaking skills: Tutorial skills

### Objectives

By the end of the lesson, students should be able to:
- pronounce the stress in multi-syllable nouns, adjectives and verbs;
- pronounce target phrases for reacting to contributors in a tutorial.

### Introduction

Write the following two-syllable words from Theme 2 on the board: *reason, honest, reject.*

Remind students that they have already learnt some stress patterns with two-syllable words. Elicit the rules:
- *nouns and adjectives = stress on first syllable*
- *verbs = stress on second syllable*

In fact, 90 per cent of two-syllable nouns and 60 per cent of two-syllable verbs follow this pattern (Avery and Ehrlich, 1992).

Ask students for the stress in these two-syllable words from Lesson 3.6 Vocabulary for speaking:

'sorry (adj)    di'sturb (v)    'essay (n)
a'gree (v)     'study (v)
di'stract (v)  re'vise (v)

### A Reviewing vocabulary

1–2. Set the task. Students discuss the words in pairs. Play 🔊 3.21. Elicit answers. Ask students to give example sentences for two or three of the words. Drill some of the words and sentences.

3. Elicit possible answers for the question but do not confirm or correct any of them at this stage. Give students two or three minutes to read the Pronunciation Check. Elicit the pronunciation of the three example words, then play 🔊 3.23 or read them out loud to the class yourself. Ask questions to check understanding:
*Where is the stress in words like* quotation? (two syllables from the end)
*Where is the stress in multi-syllable words?* (three syllables from the end)

Now elicit the answer to the question in the Course Book (see below).

Answers

1/2.

| a. di'straction | appreci'ation | contri'bution |
| b. 'preference | 'emphasis | 'possible |
| c. a'pologize | im'possible | al'ternative |
| d. a'nnoying | a'greement | re'member |

3. a. two syllables from the end (because all words end in ~tion)
   b. stress on first syllable (because they are all three-syllable words)
   c. stress on second syllable (because they are all four-syllable words)
   d. stress on second syllable (irregular stress patterns)

## Transcripts

🔊 3.21

Presenter: 3.21. Lesson 3.8. Learning new speaking skills: Tutorial skills. Exercise A2. Listen and check your answers.
Voice: a. distraction, appreciation, contribution
b. preference, emphasis, possible
c. apologize, impossible, alternative
d. annoying, agreement, remember

🔊 3.23

Presenter: 3.23. Pronunciation Check.
Voice: quotation, interruption, emphasize, sincerity, efficiency, forgiveness, improvement

### B  Identifying a key skill

If you wish, you could replay the tutorial extracts from Lesson 3.7 Real-time speaking before you start this activity. Students could also follow the transcript. Pause after each student in the tutorial has spoken, and elicit if they are agreeing or disagreeing with the previous speaker.

1. Give students time to read the Skills Check. Check students understand the following: *partly, holding to your opinion, politely, changing your mind.*

2. Set the task. Students complete the activity individually, then compare their answers in pairs. Elicit answers and then drill some of the phrases.

3. Play 🔊 3.23 for repetition practice. Alternatively, model the phrases yourself. Make sure students use suitable intonation patterns, stress the correct words, and sound tentative or more certain when necessary.

Answers

2. Agreeing = Absolutely.
   Partly agreeing = I suppose so.
   Disagreeing politely = I'm not sure.
   Holding to your opinion = I still don't believe that …
   Changing your mind = Yes. Actually, that's true.

3. The following should sound positive, strong and with appropriate intonation:
   *I agree with you …*
   *That's right.*
   *Absolutely.*

   The following should sound tentative with appropriate intonation:
   *Possibly.*
   *Perhaps …*
   *You could be right.*
   *I suppose so.*
   *I don't really agree with you …*
   *I'm not sure.*

   The following should be polite but firm:
   *I still think that …*

   The following should sound firmer:
   *I still don't believe that …*
   *I've changed my mind. Now, I think …*
   *OK, you're right.*
   *Yes. Actually that's true.*

## Transcript

🔊 3.22

Presenter: 3.22. Exercise B3. Listen and repeat some of the phrases. Copy the intonation patterns.
Voice: I agree with you …
That's right.
Absolutely.
Possibly.
Perhaps …
You could be right.
I suppose so.
I don't really agree with you …
I'm not sure.
I still think that …
I still don't believe that …
I've changed my mind. Now, I think …
OK, you're right.
Yes. Actually, that's true.

### C  Practising a new skill

1. Check students understand the task. Students complete the activity individually. Help students understand the vocabulary or any opinions they are uncertain of.

2. Divide the class into groups of four. Check students understand the task. Monitor and give help where necessary. Give feedback.

## Closure

You can give some more opinions to students (still in groups), as in Exercise C. For example:
* *Rote learning can be helpful for vocabulary.*
* *You need to rehearse new information in order to remember it.*
* *You should take regular breaks when you are revising.*
* *You shouldn't try to change your friends. You should accept them the way they are.*

You can give these opinions orally, write them on the board, or hand them out on slips of paper to individuals who can then read them out to the other students in their group.

Ask students to react to, agree or disagree with the statements.

### 3.9 Grammar for speaking: Tense agreement in short responses

### Objectives

By the end of the lesson, students should be able to:
* pronounce correctly the tense forms for agreeing and disagreeing;
* demonstrate understanding of the grammar rules for tense agreement in short responses.

### Introduction

Write the heading of the lesson, *Tense agreement in short responses*, on the board. Elicit the meaning of *responses*.

Elicit the meaning of the verb *agree*, which the students are already familiar with. Write some example sentences on the board:
*I agree with you.*
*I don't agree with the article.*

Now explain the meaning of the verb *agree* in its grammatical sense. Write the following sentences on the board:
1. He works in a bank.
2. Have you got a car? Yes, I have.

Explain that in the first sentence, the verb *works* must **agree** with the subject. We cannot say *He work in a bank*.

In the second example, the answer *Yes, I have* must **agree** with the verb in the question. We cannot say *Yes, I do* or *Yes, I am*, for example.

### Grammar box 15

Ask students to study the table. Go through the examples, pointing out how the verb in each response agrees with the verb in the statement. Practise the pronunciation of the words *either* and *neither*. Each word has two possible pronunciations – /[n] iːðə (r)/ or /[n] aɪðə (r)/ – so decide which one you wish to teach.

Ask students to study the word order of the responses. Use the board to highlight the word order – in particular the position of the pronoun *I* – for example:

| 1 | 2 | 3 |
|---|---|---|
| I | do | too. |
| So | do | I. |

Point out that this is a very unusual pattern – in English, 99.9 per cent of the time, the subject comes in front of the verb.

Repeat the procedure for the negatives.

Point out how *too* and *neither*, in the phrases *Me too* and *Me, neither*, come at the end.

Get students to tell you how the short responses are constructed, i.e., use auxiliary, or bring in the appropriate auxiliary if no auxiliary in the statement.

Elicit responses for Statements 3 and 4 in the table. If you wish, play 3.24. Then give students time to write the correct responses in.

Spend a few minutes drilling the statements and eliciting possible responses.

### Answers
See next table.

### Transcript
3.24

Presenter: 3.24. Lesson 3.9. Grammar for speaking: Tense agreement in short responses. Grammar box 15.

One.
Voice A: I agree.
Voice B: I do, too.
Voice C: So do I.
Voice D: Me too.

Presenter: Two.
Voice A: I don't agree.
Voice B: I don't either.
Voice C: Neither do I.
Voice D: Me neither.

| statement | choice of short responses | | |
|---|---|---|---|
| 1. I agree. | I do, too. | So do I. | Me, too. |
| 2. I don't agree. | I don't, either. | Neither do I. | Me, neither. |
| 3. I researched mobile phones. | *I did, too.* | *So did I.* | *Me, too.* |
| 4. I didn't look at interruptions. | *I didn't, either.* | *Neither did I.* | *Me, neither.* |

Presenter: Three.
Voice A: I researched mobile phones.
Voice B: I did, too.
Voice C: So did I.
Voice D: Me too.

Presenter: Four.
Voice A: I didn't look at interruptions.
Voice B: I didn't, either.
Voice C: Neither did I.
Voice D: Me neither.

### A  Agreeing with statements

Divide the class into groups of three. Set the task. Students complete the conversations in their groups. Stress that Student C must use a different form of a short response from Student B. This is a form of lexical cohesion – avoid repetition. When they have finished, ask some of the groups to read out their dialogues to the class. The rest of the class listens and says if they had the same or different conversations. If they are different, then they should read out their conversation.

Drill a few of the phrases from the dialogues. Then students practise the conversations, still in their groups of three. Monitor. Give feedback.

Finally, ask the students to practise the conversations once more. However, this time, only Student A can have the Course Book open. The others must give a suitable response, but remind them that they can only *agree* at this stage. Students should take it in turns to be Student A.

Monitor once more and give feedback.

### Answers

1. A: I think mobile phones can waste a lot of time.
   B: *So do I. / I do, too. / Me too.*
   C: *So do I. / I do, too. / Me too.*
   A: But I don't think you should turn them off during study periods.
   B: *Neither do I. / I don't, either. / Me, neither.*
   C: *Neither do I. / I don't, either. / Me, neither.*

2. A: I am going to put my mobile on silent during study periods.
   B: *So am I. / I am, too. / Me too.*
   C: *So am I. / I am, too. / Me too.*
   A: And I will tell people not to phone me at those times.
   B: *So will I. / I will, too. / Me too.*
   C: *So will I. / I will, too. / Me too.*

### Grammar box 16

Ask students to study the table. Go through the examples, pointing out how the verb in each response agrees with the verb in the statement.

Ask students to discuss the pattern of the short responses in pairs. Elicit ideas. Summarize on the board as follows, making sure students know the words *positive* and *negative*:

| statement | response | |
|---|---|---|
| + | + | – |
| I **think** it's a good idea. | Do you? | I don't. |

| statement | response | |
|---|---|---|
| + | + | – |
| I **don't think** it's a good idea. | Don't you? | I do. |

Point out that, again, all the verbs are in the same tense – in other words, they *agree*.

Students complete the table. If you wish, play 3.25. Elicit answers. Drill the responses, making sure students use the correct intonation pattern.

### Answers

| statement | short responses | |
|---|---|---|
| 1. I think it's a good solution. | Do you? | I don't. |
| 2. I don't think that's a good idea. | Don't you? | I do. |
| 3. I looked at interruptions. | *Did you?* | *I didn't.* |
| 4. I didn't find anything on the Internet. | *Didn't you?* | *I did.* |

## Transcript

🔊 3.25

Presenter: 3.25. Grammar box 16.

              One.
Voice A: I think it's a good solution.
Voice B: Do you? I don't.

Presenter: Two.
Voice A: I don't think that's a good idea.
Voice B: Don't you? I do.

Presenter: Three.
Voice A: I looked at interruptions.
Voice B: Did you? I didn't.

Presenter: Four.
Voice A: I didn't find anything on the Internet.
Voice B: Didn't you? I did.

### B  Disagreeing with statements

Note that this activity should be done in pairs only, despite the fact that the original activity was done in groups of three.

Elicit and practise an example exchange with the class:
*I think mobile phones can waste a lot of time. Do you? I don't.*

Students continue in pairs. Monitor and give feedback.

### Answers

1. A: I think mobile phones can waste a lot of time.
   B: *Do you? I don't.*
   A: But I don't think you should turn them off during study periods.
   B: *Don't you? I do.*
2. A: I am going to put my mobile on silent during study periods.
   B: *Are you? I'm not.*
   A: And I will tell people not to phone me at those times.
   B: *Will you? I won't.*

### C  Agreeing and disagreeing with statements

Check students understand the task. There are different ways you could do the activity:

- Play 🔊 3.26. Pause after each line. Elicit different responses from various students around the class. Replay the CD and repeat the activity if necessary.
- Divide the class into pairs. Play 🔊 3.26. Pause after each line. In each pair, Student A repeats the statement from the recording. Student B gives a suitable, truthful response.

Replay the CD and repeat the activity so that students can swap roles.

### Answers

Answers depend on students.

## Transcript

🔊 3.26

Presenter: 3.26. Exercise C. Listen to some statements. Give a truthful response.
Voices: 
1. I have two brothers.
2. I live close to this institution.
3. I'm quite good at English.
4. I'm a morning person.
5. I'm going to go abroad for my next holiday.
6. I don't like the weather at the moment.
7. I didn't go to any lectures last week.
8. I'm looking forward to the exams.
9. I'll probably get a job straight after university.
10. I probably won't work in this country.

> **Methodology note**
>
> Examples should begin with *I* ... Note that it may be quite tricky for students to agree with statements such as *English is my favourite subject (Mine too. / It's my favourite too.)*

### D  Transferring skills to the real world

Set the task. Elicit a few ideas about possible statements from the class. For example:
*I don't like getting up early.*
*I really enjoy History / English / Art lessons.*
*I'm staying in this evening.*
*I thought the last assignment was really difficult.*
*I don't understand this word / lesson / sentence / grammar point.*
*I'm not going to do any work this weekend.*

Monitor while students are working in pairs and give feedback afterwards.

### Closure

You can use your feedback for Exercise D as Closure.

Alternatively, you could build up and extend the two tables in Grammar boxes 15 and 16 by adding examples of more tenses.

### 3.10 Applying new speaking skills: Time thieves – self

#### Objectives

By the end of the lesson, students should be able to:
- take turns in a tutorial in order to express agreement or disagreement;
- evaluate more common core knowledge about time management.

#### Introduction

Exploit the visual. Ask students if they can add anything else to each heading:
- people – talking, laughing, making a lot of noise, etc.
- things – e-mails, noises from street including workmen, etc.
- self – motivation, confidence, etc.

#### A  Previewing vocabulary

Check students understand the task. Students complete the activity individually, then compare their answers in pairs. Elicit answers. Drill each phrase. Elicit some example sentences for a few of the phrases in order to further check understanding. Drill the elicited sentences if you wish.

#### Answers

| 1. turn on | 8 | short breaks |
| 2. check | 7 | a cup of coffee |
| 3. go on | 9 | to sleep |
| 4. break down | 5 | a time limit |
| 5. set | 3 | Facebook |
| 6. give | 1 | your computer |
| 7. have | 10 | your best time of day |
| 8. take | 2 | your e-mails |
| 9. go | 4 | activities into parts |
| 10. find out | 6 | yourself a reward |

#### Methodology note

Students will need to know how to make a tally chart (see Lesson 2.17 Real-time writing in and Lesson 2.20 Applying new writing skills in Theme 2). For example, students will need to make something like this:

| solution | tally | total | order |
|---|---|---|---|
| don't turn on computer | ////  /// | 8 | 1 |
| set time limit for e-mails, etc. | /// | 3 | 3 |
| break down activities / give rewards | //// | 4 | 2 |

For step 2 of the group work, you have a choice of methods. You could organize it as a general 'milling' activity if your class is not too large. Alternatively, you could re-divide the class into more formal groups of four, six, eight or ten, etc., making sure there is an even number from each of the original Groups A and B.

In step three, students should collate all their results before ranking the results.

#### B  Researching information

Ask students to study the assignment task. Check students understand the task and make sure they realize it is primarily a spoken activity, not a written one.

1. Divide the class into two groups, A and B. Ask them to read their relevant texts and complete the table. Monitor and give help where necessary.
2. Make sure students understand the task and re-divide the class into new groups if you wish. Check students know how to use a tally chart (see Methodology note above).
3. Check students understand the task. Monitor and give help where necessary.

#### C  Taking part in a tutorial

Point out that the name of this task is *Taking part in a tutorial*. Discuss what this means, including the idea that it is important for everyone to contribute in a tutorial.

Set the task – but before students start, remind them of the language of agreeing and disagreeing from the previous lessons in this section. Explain that, if they wish, they can also suggest different solutions to the ones given in the earlier texts.

Make sure students are in the correct groups, and that there are two students from Group A and two from Group B.

Monitor during the activity. Make a note of how well students 'take turns', listen to each other and contribute to the discussion, as well as how well they use the target language.

**Closure**

Give feedback on the notes you made while monitoring Exercises B and C.

# Reading: Decisions, decisions, decisions

**3.11 Vocabulary for reading: The language of problems and solutions**

### Objectives

By the end of the lesson, students should be able to:

- recognize and understand target vocabulary from the Reading section;
- show understanding of target verb + preposition collocations;
- show understanding of different parts of speech for the target vocabulary.

| 1. attend | miss |
| --- | --- |
| 2. calm | stressed |
| 3. confident | doubtful |
| 4. current | previous |
| 5. either | neither |
| 6. refuse | agree |
| 7. remember | forget |
| 8. ugly | beautiful |
| 9. waste | use |
| 10. work | rest |

**Introduction**

Refer students to the photograph. Ask them to describe it, then to explain its connection with decisions. They will probably struggle and you will have to explain that people often fail to solve a problem because they do not recognize there is a huge problem lying behind a small problem. In other words, there is an elephant in the room which they do not see.

### Methodology note

Remind students it is important to learn a complete phrasal verb or the dependent preposition that goes with a verb for a particular meaning. When they are reading phrasal verbs or verbs with dependent prepositions, they must be able to predict the preposition that will be needed to complete the meaning.

**A  Reviewing vocabulary**

Some of these words are directly connected to problems and solutions, others are not.

Check students understand the task and go over the example. Students continue in pairs. Elicit answers. If you wish, you can also ask students to make a note of the part of speech for each word.

### Optional activity

Students write a sentence for some of the words.

**Answers**

See next table.

**B  Predicting prepositions in context**

Set the task. Students complete the activity individually, then compare their answers in pairs. Elicit answers. Ask follow-up questions to further check understanding of the target vocabulary.

Ask students to close their books, or cover the exercise. Do one or both of the following activities:

- Say the verb and ask students to give you the preposition, e.g.,
  T: *approve* …
  Ss: … *of.*
- Write each verb + preposition on the board, e.g., *approve of*. Students write or say the complete sentence, then open their books to check and correct their work.

### Optional activity

This can either be done in class or set for homework. Students write a new sentence for each verb + preposition.

Theme 3: Reading  143

Answers

1. People sometimes don't approve *of* the actions of a friend.
2. The scientist thought *of* a possible solution.
3. Let's go back *to* the first problem.
4. How can we deal *with* this issue?
5. Let's work *through* an example.
6. The researchers had to come up *with* another idea.
7. If you are sure that you are right, you should stick *to* your opinion.
8. Many people agree *with* this point of view.
9. People sometimes make fun *of* new ideas.
10. A manager needs someone to rely *on* inside the organization.

### Methodology note

This activity partly highlights a useful technique for guessing words in context. However, this exercise also demonstrates the importance of working out the part of speech of a new word and – at times – of looking at words' endings to help with this identification. Word endings are not very informative in English though, so this last strategy is only of limited value.

### C  Understanding new words

Point out to students that sometimes new words in a text are built from words which they already know. Go over the example. They can work out that the noun *decisions* must come from the verb *decide*, and therefore they can guess the meaning of the noun in context.

Set for individual work and pairwork checking.

Answers

See next table.

### Closure

Write the underlined words from Exercise C on the board. Ask students to try to remember the complete sentences.

| | |
|---|---|
| 1. The manager found it difficult to make <u>decisions</u>. | *decide* |
| 2. We can <u>define</u> the word *style* in a number of ways. | *definition* |
| 3. You need to <u>evaluate</u> each solution carefully. | *value* |
| 4. It is easy to <u>identify</u> the cause of the problem. | *identity* |
| 5. People in <u>management</u> are responsible for many problems inside companies. | *manage* |
| 6. The students have a <u>participatory</u> role in the process. | *participate* |
| 7. There is a small <u>possibility</u> of finding a peaceful solution. | *possible* |
| 8. In <u>reality</u>, the people would never accept this answer. | *real* or *really* |
| 9. There is a <u>saying</u> in English: 'Measure three times, cut once.' | *say* |
| 10. I would like to <u>summarize</u> the main issues in this essay. | *sum* |

Write the underlined words from Exercise C on the board. Ask students to try to remember the complete sentences.

### 3.12 Real-time reading: 'Digest' problems to make good decisions

### Objectives

By the end of the lesson, students should be able to:

- predict content from topic sentences;
- show understanding of a text about making decisions in business management;
- show understanding of target vocabulary in context.

### Introduction

Use Exercise A as the introduction.

### A  Activating ideas

Divide the class into pairs or small groups. Students discuss the questions. Elicit ideas.

Exploit the visual of the signpost and discuss what it shows.

Discuss the main heading and subheading of the article (on page 89 of the Course Book) and elicit possible ideas for what the text will be about. Remind students that this is all about *preparing to read*.

Answers

Answers depend on students.

### B  Understanding paragraph structure

Make sure the text is covered for this activity.

Set the task. Students complete the activity individually, then compare their answers in pairs. During the pairwork phase, encourage students to discuss their reasons for choosing the next sentence.

Finally, students uncover the article so that they can check their answers with the text.

Answers

| 1. How do you make decisions? | 5 | However, there is an old saying in business … |
|---|---|---|
| 2. We can summarize the process of good decision-making in the acronym DIGEST. | 4 | First, the problem. |
| 3. Firstly, **define** the problem – say what you are really trying to do. | 2 | What does DIGEST mean? |
| 4. Let's work through an example of the process in action. | 1 | A lot of the time people make decisions without really thinking about it. |
| 5. You will not make perfect decisions every time, even with this decision-making process. | 3 | Secondly, **imagine** a successful solution. |

**Methodology note**

If your students are working towards the IELTS exam, then point out that this activity is very similar to one of the question types from the exam. In IELTS, students are required to answer if the information is *true*, *false* or *not given*.

### C  Understanding the text

Students should read through the sentences first, then look at the text to find the correct answer. Students complete the task individually, then compare their answers in pairs. Elicit answers.

At this point, allow students a few minutes to ask you about any vocabulary or phrases they may still not understand.

Answers

| 1. Using *instinct* means not really thinking about something. | T |
|---|---|
| 2. Good decision-making only really matters in business. | F |
| 3. DIGEST is the acronym for a decision-making process. | T |
| 4. The writer has chosen the acronym because *digest* means 'to break down food in the stomach'. | F |
| 5. *Generate alternative solutions* means 'think of different answers to the problem'. | T |
| 6. The writer thinks you should involve other people in generating alternatives. | ? |
| 7. You should evaluate each solution as you think of it. | F |
| 8. The creative side of the brain is the left side. | ? |
| 9. The last stage of the process is selecting the best solution. | F |
| 10. The writer thinks it is better not to make a decision than to make a bad one. | F |

### D  Developing critical thinking

Go through the example situation with the class and check they understand it. Students should imagine themselves in the same situation, or a similar one.

Students work in pairs. Monitor. Elicit decisions from some of the pairs of students.

The activity could be continued with other simple problems or situations, for example:
– not enough money to buy or do something important;
– finding a part-time job.

Answers

Answers depend on students.

**Closure**

You could use Exercise D for Closure, or briefly recap some of the vocabulary from the lesson.

## 3.13 Learning new reading skills: Brackets, italics, dashes ...

### Objectives

By the end of the lesson, students should be able to:
- recall vocabulary from the previous lesson;
- identify text markers and their purpose in a written text;
- demonstrate understanding of the MBO style of management.

### Introduction

Exploit the visual, then ask students to reread the article about decision-making from the previous lesson.

### A  Reviewing vocabulary

If your students have not reread the article from the previous lesson (see introduction above), then briefly remind them about it now. Set the task. Students discuss in pairs. Elicit answers.

#### Answers

| 1. Define | the problem. |
| 2. Imagine | a successful solution. |
| 3. Generate | alternative possibilities. |
| 4. Evaluate | the possibilities. |
| 5. Select | the best one. |
| 6. Tell | people your decision. |

### Methodology notes

This lesson may be even more important for speakers of languages which have a different alphabet. These students may have not been fully aware of different typefaces, for example, and their purpose. You may need to keep reminding students from these backgrounds about non-text markers throughout the course.

### B  Identifying a new skill

1. Ask the students to read the Skills Check box and answer the question. Tell students they should learn the name of each text marker. Help them to do this by drawing each marker on the board and, with books closed, eliciting the correct name for it.

2. Set the task and go over the example. Students work in pairs. Monitor. Elicit answers, preferably using an electronic projection.

#### Answers

1. They are not words themselves. They are marks, such as brackets, speech marks, etc., and font changes, such as bold or italics.

2.

| What does DIGEST mean? | DIGEST = acronym. It stands for the mnemonic Define, Imagine, etc. |
|---|---|
| In general English, it has a number of meanings, including 'to break down food in the stomach', | 'to break down ...' = speech marks = definition |
| Firstly, **define** the problem – say what you are really trying to do. | define = bold = important word |
| This is usually easy. (If it isn't, go back to the first stage again and re-define the problem.) | (If it isn't, ...) = brackets = extra information |
| The more people you *tell* about your decision, the harder it is to change your mind later. | tell – italics = important word |
| You could take a bus, but don't like public transport ... | transport .. = suspension dots = this sentence is not complete |

### Methodology notes

These days, acronyms are defined as any abbreviation based on initial letters – they do not have to be pronounceable. Students are not expected to know or learn the exact word that each letter of the acronym stands for. They should, however, recognize the general meaning of the acronym when they find it in a text.

### C  Practising a new skill (1)

Set the task and go over the example; students do not have to explain what each letter stands for. If students find it difficult, write the following list on the board for students to refer to:

*an organization*
*a country*
*a qualification*
*a job*
*a piece of technology*

Students discuss what the acronyms are in pairs.

Elicit answers. Discuss what other acronyms students know for their town, country, university, etc. With a more able class, you might like to find out if they know the actual words.

#### Answers

| abbrev. | type | actual words |
| --- | --- | --- |
| WHO | organization | World Health Organization |
| UN | organization | United Nations |
| NASA | organization | National Aeronautics and Space Administration |
| EU | group of countries | European Union |
| UK | country | United Kingdom |
| USA | country | United States of America |
| MBA | qualification | Master of Business Administration |
| SMS | text messaging system | Short Message Service |
| BBC | organization, broadcaster | British Broadcasting Corporation |
| PC | type of computer | Personal Computer |
| ISP | organization for e-mail, Internet | Internet Service Provider |
| CEO | job title | Chief Executive Officer |

### D  Practising a new skill (2)

Explain that this is a text about a style of management. Set the task and check understanding. Students should first read all the sentences and think about possible answers, before looking at the phrases at the bottom of the page.

Elicit answers, preferably using an electronic projection. Ask a few questions to check understanding of the information in the text:

*What is MBO?* (a style of management)
*What does the saying mean?* (tell people what the goal is, not how to do it)

#### Answers

| 1. There is a style of management called MBO … | 6 | and may damage the relationship between workers and managers. |
| --- | --- | --- |
| 2. It is based on the saying … | 2 | 'Give a person a map, not a route.' |
| 3. If a worker knows the objective of a job, his/her decision will be as good as the manager's … | 1 | (Management By Objectives). |
| 4. In MBO, managers set the objectives but decisions are made by everyone … | 4 | it is called *delegation*. |
| 5. The key to successful MBO is giving workers … | 3 | perhaps better. |
| 6. If managers don't really give power away, MBO will not work … | 5 | power. |

### Closure

Choose one of the following:

1. Check the names for the different kinds of non-text markers once more.

2. Discuss the MBO style of management with the class:
   - Do they agree with the principles?
   - Would they like to be managed in this way?
   - What other styles of management do they know about?

## 3.14 Grammar for reading: Identifying missing subjects and verbs

### Objectives

By the end of the lesson, students should be able to:

- demonstrate understanding of sentences with missing subjects and verbs.

## Introduction

Revise the meaning of the word *instinct* (from the article in Lesson 3.12 Real-time reading).

> **Methodology note**
>
> You will probably need to show at some point the use of the words *and* / *or* in joining negative sentences. Compare the following:
> *The lecturer does not know **and** the lecturer does not care about your problems.* (*Or* would be incorrect in this sentence.)
> *The lecturer does not know **or** care about your problems.* (*And* would be incorrect in this sentence with the missing subject and auxiliary in the second half.)

## Grammar box 17

Ask students to study the table of information. Ask different students to read out each full sentence with the joining word. The rest of the class follows in their books, e.g.,
*People use their instinct and hope that they have done the right thing.*

For consolidation, elicit how the joining words are used:
- *and* = two positive ideas
- *or* = two negative ideas
- *but* = one positive and one negative idea (or it can be a 'surprising' piece of information)

Now elicit what the missing parts of speech are in each sentence.

### Answers

| sentence 2 | what is omitted |
| --- | --- |
| ~~They~~ hope that they have done the right thing. | subject |
| ~~You~~ keep arriving late. | subject |
| ~~The lecturer does not~~ care about your problems. | subject, auxiliary, negative particle |
| ~~You could~~ go in your father's car. | subject, modal auxiliary |
| ~~Decision making is~~ a process. | subject, verb *be* |
| ~~You must not~~ criticize them. | subject, modal auxiliary, negative particle |

## A  Identifying missing subjects

Check students understand the task and go over the example. If necessary, do the second sentence with the class, as well as a further example. Students complete the activity individually, then compare their answers in pairs. Elicit answers.

### Answers

1. Perhaps you have lectures every morning and ~~you~~ keep arriving late.
2. Thomas Harris was born in California but ~~Harris~~ studied medicine at the University of Arkansas.
3. People are often happy to work in groups and ~~people~~ respect the contributions of other people.
4. Most children do not make many decisions inside a family but ~~most children~~ accept the decisions of parents.
5. Adolescents sometimes don't accept their parents' decision and ~~adolescents~~ rebel.
6. Every moment, we pay attention to sensory memories or ~~we~~ ignore them.
7. Loftus and Palmer showed students a film and ~~Loftus and Palmer~~ asked them to complete a questionnaire about it.
8. Charles Dickens, the English novelist, left school at 12 and ~~Charles Dickens~~ went to work in a factory.
9. Mobile phones are very useful but ~~mobile phones~~ can also waste a lot of time.
10. The aural learner does not respond well to written information but ~~the aural learner~~ learns from lectures and tutorials.

## B  Identifying the missing subject and modal auxiliary

Check students understand the task and go over the example. Students discuss in pairs. Elicit answers.

### Answers

1. Managers have to communicate their ideas and ~~managers have to~~ ensure that workers understand them.
2. Directors should provide regular and full information and ~~directors should~~ keep workers up-to-date.
3. In order to remember information, you must take it out of memory and ~~you must~~ use it again and again.

4. Humans cannot remember every event in their lives or ~~humans cannot~~ name all their childhood friends.
5. Doctors in the past could not treat many diseases or ~~doctors could not~~ save people from fatal infections.
6. In this report, I am going to discuss the reasons for the problem and ~~I am going to~~ suggest possible solutions.
7. Soon, the world will not have enough oil for global needs or ~~the world will not~~ have enough renewable energy sources to meet demand.
8. People may not be able to use cars or ~~people may not be able to~~ travel by air as much as today.

**Closure**

Students' books closed. Choose one of the following activities:

1. Dictate some of the sentences from the exercises.
2. Write the first half of some of the sentences from the exercises on the board. Students copy and complete, either using their own words or by recalling the actual words from the exercise.

---

**3.15 Applying new reading skills: Are you an autocrat or a democrat?**

**Objectives**

By the end of this lesson, students should have:

- use reading sub-skills and vocabulary from the theme to deal with a text about management styles;
- recognize and develop target vocabulary from the Reading section.

**Methodology notes**

You could use flashcards for the introductory task. Expose letters in turn until students predict the correct word.

**Introduction**

Write the first few letters of the following words on the board. Say they are all connected with decision-making. Ask students to tell you the full word in each case.

dem ocrat / ic
aut ocrat / ic
part icipate / tory
gen erate
ide ntify
log ical
eva luate
pos sibility

**A**  Reviewing vocabulary

These phrases are all from the article in Lesson 3.12 Real-time reading. Set the task. Students complete the activity individually, then compare their answers in pairs. Elicit answers.

Ask students if they can remember the complete sentence from the article for each phrase. If not, they can refer back to the text (see page 89 of the Course Book) and try to find it.

**Optional activity**

Students write a sentence for some of the phrases.

Answers

| 1. the right | 7 | one |
| 2. everyday | 5 | say |
| 3. an old | 4 | brain |
| 4. the human | 8 | thinking |
| 5. let's | 1 | thing |
| 6. at the same | 3 | saying |
| 7. one by | 2 | lives |
| 8. without | 6 | time |

**B**  Activating ideas

Tell students this lesson continues the idea of management and decision-making. If you wish, spend some time revising the DIGEST approach to decision-making; you could also ask students to reread the article from Lesson 3.12 Real-time reading (see also notes for Exercise C below).

Exploit the visuals. Tell students to use them in order to predict some of the lesson content regarding autocratic and democratic management styles.

Students discuss the two questions in pairs. Elicit ideas.

### Answers

1. Answers depend on students.
2. The title suggests there are two different management styles:
   - autocratic: the manager tells his/her staff what to do without consulting them
   - democratic: the manager consults with his/her staff in all stages except defining the problem and telling people the decision

   [in fact, the article will cover three management styles; the third is participatory: the manager consults with his/her staff in some stages]

### C Understanding a text

Remind students about the DIGEST process for decision-making from Lesson 3.12 Real-time reading, if you have not already done so (see notes for Exercise B above). Elicit what each letter stands for:
- **D**efine the problem
- **I**magine a successful solution
- **G**enerate alternative possibilities
- **E**valuate the possibilities
- **S**elect the best one
- **T**ell people your decision

Remind students about non-text markers (they carry meaning but they are not actually words, e.g., bold or italics).

### Para 1
1. Set for individual work and pairwork checking. Give feedback orally.
2. Set for pairwork. Work through the first example – see Answers below.

### Paras 2–5
Briefly discuss the three tables for each management style but try not to pre-empt the text too much.

Deal with each paragraph separately; students read a paragraph, then compare their ideas for the activity in pairs. Elicit ideas. Move on to the next paragraph.

When you get to Paragraph 3, check students understand the text and the task before they complete the table. The stages of the task are:

1. Students must imagine they are organizing a social event.
2. Students individually complete the DIGEST table. They should tick who does each stage.
3. Students show their completed table to others.

### Optional activity

Focus on the following sentences from the text. They all have a missing subject and/or auxiliary in the second half of each sentence (see Lesson 3.14 Grammar for reading). Write the sentences on the board, or use an electronic projection. Ask students to find the missing subjects and/or auxiliary, and underline them in the text. Elicit the missing words.

1. In an *autocratic* style, the manager does not ask for any help or involve the workers at any stage in the process.
2. They involve the workers in some stages but retain control of the decision-making.
3. You could make all the decisions yourself or ask the other students to help you at any stage.
4. They may agree with your ticks or think that you have not been honest about your *real* management style.
5. But in reality, you will only accept your *own* possibilities and make fun of any other suggestions.
6. You can decide to change your style completely or for particular situations.

### Answers

#### Para 1

1. A management style is how we manage other people.
2. Non-text markers from Para 1:

| 'I have no idea. I am not a manager.' | ' ... ' = speech |
|---|---|
| *style* and *job* | italics = stressed words |
| see *Digest* ... in this publication | suspension dots = the actual title is longer |
| DIGEST | capital letters = acronym |

#### Para 2
autocratic = nothing!
participatory = G and E – generate and evaluate
democratic = everything except define the problem and tell people of the decision

## Para 3
Answers depend on students.

## Para 4
Answers depend on students – get students to tell you if they agree with their partner's assessment.

## Para 5
Because the autocratic style does not work in that situation.

### D  Developing critical thinking

Students discuss in pairs or small groups. Elicit answers.

**Answers**

Answers depend on the students, but here are some ideas:
1. autocratic – decisions made more quickly; decisions can be based on one idea, one way of achieving objectives
2. participatory – workers feel part of the decision
3. democratic – staff feel fully involved

### E  Developing vocabulary

1. Check students understand the task. Students complete the activity individually, then compare their answers in pairs. Discuss the meaning of each phrase. Point out that the verb *retain* is a formal word. Elicit the more informal synonym *keep*.
2. Go over the examples. Students can discuss the task in pairs or small groups. Elicit ideas. Some verbs will have a different meaning depending on the collocation, e.g.,
   My father **managed** a big bank in the city centre.
   I **managed** the assignment but it wasn't easy.
   You may, therefore, wish to keep to the meanings as used in the text.

**Answers**

1. 

| miss | the point |
|---|---|
| make | fun of / a decision |
| retain | control |
| achieve | your objectives |
| change | your style |
| involve | the workers / other people |
| organize | a social event |
| manage | his wife or her husband |

2. Here are some suggestions:

| verb | common collocations / phrases |
|---|---|
| miss | the bus; my family; a chance; an opportunity; the ball |
| make | a meal; a cup of coffee; a mistake; a suggestion; a comment; an arrangement |
| retain | facts; a receipt; an invoice; water; liquid |
| achieve | results; a good rate; success; a record |
| change | money; appearance; your mind; your opinion; your clothes; jobs; car; name; address; phone number; money; the subject |
| involve | everyone; children; yourself |
| organize | people; work; a party; information; your thoughts |
| manage | an organization; a business; the staff; the employees |

### Closure

Use Exercise E2 for Closure, or the optional activity suggested in Exercise C.

---

**Knowledge quiz: Grammar auction game**

**Objectives**

By the end of the lesson, students should be able to:
- review target grammar from the theme;
- discriminate between correct and incorrect forms;
- discuss and explain decisions in a group.

**Methodology notes**

Grammar auctions are great fun, but with a large or noisy class you will need to make sure you keep the students under control!

You can use toy money from a Monopoly game, for example, or use coloured counters to represent different denominations. If you do not use toy money or counters, you will need to keep a careful check of how much money each group is spending. Use the board to keep track: draw columns with the name of each group at the top. Make a note of the amount for each successful bid and the remaining balance. If you like, you can ask a student to be your assistant to do this.

It's a good idea to use an electronic projection of the sentences, so that students can refer to them as the auction goes on.

You may find there are too many sentences for one lesson, so do half of them in this lesson and leave the others for another time.

The most important thing is for the teacher to keep a straight face throughout and not to give any indication as to which sentences are correct until the very end!

The activity could easily be adapted – for example, you can use other sentences, vocabulary definitions or even spellings.

**Closure**
Announce the winning group. Give feedback by eliciting how to correct the incorrect sentences.

### Answers
Mistakes and correct answers in *italics*.
See table opposite.

**Introduction**
Explain the idea of a grammar auction. If you like, you can also spend a few minutes revising some vocabulary from the sentences for the auction.

Give students some phrases to use:
*I am sure this sentence is correct.*
*I don't think this one is right.*
*Let's bid for this one.*

**Grammar auction**
1. Divide the class into groups of five or six students. Name each group A, B, C, etc., or get students to come up with more imaginative team names!

2. In their groups, students decide which sentences are correct or incorrect. Monitor and help with vocabulary if necessary, but do not give any further help.

3. The teacher is the auctioneer. Make sure students are clear on the rules for bidding. Remind them that they should only bid for sentences which they think are correct. Ask students for bids for the first sentence. Make a note of which group wins the sentence. You can either tell the class at this point if the sentence was in fact correct or not, or leave this until the end.

4. Continue with the remaining sentences.

| | | |
|---|---|---|
| 1. A basic idea *is linking* psychology and sociology. | ✗ | links |
| 2. After practising psychiatry in Montreal, he moved to New York. | ✓ | |
| 3. At one time, people believed that the Earth is flat. | ✓ | |
| 4. Books *sometimes will* tell you *get up* earlier. | ✗ | will sometimes; to get up |
| 5. Did you remember to get some coffee? | ✓ | |
| 6. *During* he was at university, the Second World War started. | ✗ | While |
| 7. Have you met your tutor yet? | ✓ | |
| 8. How long *you have* been here? | ✗ | have you |
| 9. I am doing Business Studies and so *you are*. | ✗ | are you |
| 10. I couldn't find any information on the Internet. | ✓ | |
| 11. I forgot *returning* the books to the library. | ✗ | to return |
| 12. I think you should apologize to her. | ✓ | |
| 13. I thought the deadline *is* next week. | ✗ | was |
| 14. If you like hearing new information, you are probably an aural learner. | ✓ | |
| 15. Look at each possibility carefully and evaluate it. | ✓ | |
| 16. Many parents make their children study. | ✓ | |
| 17. Miller explained how short-term memory works. | ✓ | |
| 18. Parents often allow adolescents *take* more responsibility. | ✗ | to take |
| 19. Pronunciation of words involves the sounds of individual letters. | ✓ | |
| 20. Psychiatrists accept that people play games. | ✓ | |
| 21. She didn't do the work and neither did I. | ✓ | |
| 22. Some managers do not ask for help *and not* involve their workers at any stage. | ✗ | or |
| 23. The red line on the graph shows the loss of information. | ✓ | |
| 24. The student promised *finishing* the work last week. | ✗ | to finish |
| 25. There *is* four main components of knowing a word. | ✗ | are |
| 26. Visual learners like colour *because* they should highlight key words in their notes. | ✗ | so |
| 27. We'll see if *is this idea* true. | ✗ | this idea is |
| 28. You could take a train or *could go* by bus. | ✗ | go |
| 29. You should not waste time at work on social network sites or with personal phone calls. | ✓ | |
| 30. You will forget nearly everything if you *won't* rehearse new information. | ✗ | don't |

# Writing: For and against

### 3.16 Vocabulary for writing: City and town

**Objectives**

By the end of this lesson, students should be able to:
- demonstrate understanding of target vocabulary in context;
- relate information in a table to the advantages and disadvantages of relocation.

**Introduction**

In preparation for Exercise A, spend a few minutes looking at the verb *grow*. Students will already 'know' the verb in its most common meaning, for example, *children growing into adults*.

Write the following sentences on the board:
- My daughter has **grown** five centimetres in the last six months.
- Britain is too cold to **grow** bananas.
- If my nails **grow** too long, I can't type.
- There is a **growing** interest in the environment.
- I'm scared of **growing** old.
- The retail industry stopped **growing** during the economic recession.

Discuss the meaning of the verb *grow* in each sentence. Synonyms include: *produce, develop, expand, increase, become, get*.

### A Activating ideas

Ask students to study the rubrics. Ask questions to check understanding:
*What is the name of the company?* (Acme Engineering Ltd)
*What does Ltd mean?* (*limited* – it means it is not a private company; it is owned by a group of people)
*Where are they considering relocation from?* (Causton)
*Where are they relocating to?* (Bellport)
Exploit the map and photos of Bellport and Causton:
- Discuss the location of the two places. (Bellport is by the sea, Causton is nearer the airport)
- Elicit which place is the bigger of the two. (Bellport)
- Elicit what the surrounding area of each place is like. (Bellport = industrial city, Causton = in the country)
- Elicit which photo shows each place. (Bellport = bottom photo, Causton = top photo)

Set questions 1 and 2 for pairwork discussion. Check the meanings of *benefits* and *drawbacks* (advantages and disadvantages).
Elicit ideas.

**Answers**

Answers depend on the students, but here are some ideas for question 1:
Bellport – access to sea and motorway, more exciting place to live
Causton – access to airport, quieter place to live

### B Understanding new vocabulary in context

Check students understand the task. Ask students to try to work out the meaning of any new words in the sentences from context as they do the exercise. Students complete the activity individually, then compare their answers in pairs. Elicit answers. Check the meaning of the new vocabulary:
*raw materials* vs *finished goods*
*export* vs *import*
*grant* vs *loan*
*salary*
*units*
*rent*

**Answers**

1. There are <u>more</u> / fewer people in Bellport than Causton.
2. Bellport has more *employment* / <u>unemployment</u> than Causton.
3. Bellport is a good location for importing <u>raw materials</u> / *finished goods* by sea.
4. It is difficult to *import* / <u>export</u> finished goods by air from Bellport.
5. The average <u>salary</u> / *rents* is higher in Bellport than in Causton.
6. There are many *shop* / <u>factory</u> units for rent in Bellport.
7. Shop rents are <u>higher</u> / *lower* in Bellport than Causton.
8. There are incentives to relocate in Bellport, such as set-up <u>grants</u> / *loans*.

## C Using new vocabulary

Check students understand the task, especially that the relocation is the other direction from the one in Exercise A – from Bellport to Causton. Go over the example. If necessary, briefly revise with the class the rules for writing sentences with comparative adjectives. With a more able class, you can ask them to cover the sentences in Exercise B. Students complete the activity individually. Monitor while students are working. Elicit answers, preferably using an electronic projection.

Make sure students have spelled target vocabulary and used comparative adjectives correctly.

### Answers
Model answers:
1. There are fewer people in Causton than Bellport.
2. Causton has less unemployment than Bellport. / Causton has more employment than Bellport.
3. Causton is not a good location for importing goods by sea.
4. It is easy to export finished goods by air from Causton.
5. The average salary is lower in Causton than in Bellport.
6. There are few factory units to rent in Causton. / There are many shop units to rent in Causton.
7. Shop rents are lower in Causton than Bellport.
8. There are no incentives to relocate in Causton.

## Closure
Give the meanings of some of the target vocabulary and ask students to tell you the words, e.g.,
T: *What's another word for* advantages?
Ss: *Benefits.*

## 3.17 Real-time writing: Relocation – for and against

### Objectives
By the end of this lesson, students should be able to:
- analyze the discourse structure of a For and against report;
- produce a paragraph of recommendation in writing.

### Introduction
Put students into pairs. Give them two minutes to look at the table in Lesson 3.16 Vocabulary for writing (see page 172 of the Course Book). Student A looks at the information for Causton and Student B looks at the information about Bellport.

Then get students to close their books and compare the two places.

After a few minutes of pairwork, ask some questions to check understanding:
- *Where is Bellport / Causton located?*
- *Which is bigger?*
- *Which town has the most unemployment?*

Remind students of the verb *relocate* (re + locate = locate again = move) and the noun *relocation*.

Point out that they are going to look at an essay about relocation in this lesson.

### A Activating ideas
This activity is not just for vocabulary revision but involves critical thinking, too.

Set the task and go over the example. Students can change the form of the words if they wish, e.g., singular to plural, verb + ~ing, etc.

Students can write sentences individually. Alternatively, they can discuss each word in pairs and agree on a good sentence. Monitor and give help where necessary. For feedback, ask some students to read out their sentences.

### Answers
Answers depend on students, but here are some suggestions:
1. There is better *access* to a motorway, an airport or a seaport.
2. There is less *competition* in the area.
3. There are more *customers* in the new location.

4. The location is better for *exporting* finished goods.
5. The location is better for *importing* raw materials.
6. There are government *incentives*.
7. The rental costs for *premises* are lower.
8. Average *salaries* are not as high.
9. The rate of *unemployment* is higher.

> **Methodology note**
>
> The research and writing activities in this lesson, as well as in Lesson 3.20 Applying new writing skills, can be used as introductions to case study work. Case studies are often used in the field of business and management. However, in classic case studies, decisions have already been taken and are evaluated by students.

### B Gathering data

Exploit some of the information in the tables and figures on page 97 of the Course Book.

Set the task. Students complete the activity individually, then compare their answers in pairs. Elicit answers, preferably using an electronic projection. Point out to the class that this information will help form the first paragraph of the text.

#### Answers
1. Acme Ltd is a small engineering company.
2. It is located in the town of Causton which has a population of 10,000.
3. The company employs 14 people, including three skilled workers and ten unskilled workers.
4. The company occupies premises of 5,000 square metres.
5. The company imports its raw materials by sea.
6. The company sells 75 per cent of its finished goods in Britain and exports 25 per cent of its finished goods to Europe.
7. Sales to Britain have increased from 4,425 units to 5,320 units in the last three years.
8. Exports have risen from 580 units to 1,800 units.
9. The company needs skilled and unskilled workers and cannot recruit them. The company needs additional factory units and cannot rent them.

### C Choosing the discourse structure

1. Give students time to read through the assignment. Ask one or two questions to check understanding:
   - *Which company is thinking about relocation?* (Acme Ltd)
   - *Where to?* (Bellport)
   - *What should your report contain?* (the arguments for and against relocation, a recommendation)

   Set the task. Elicit the answer.

2. Set for individual work and pairwork checking. Give feedback by putting the five sections of the essay on the board in the correct order.

#### Answers
1. The essay should be *For and against*.
2.

| 1 | Purpose of report |
| 4 | Points against |
| 3 | Points for |
| 5 | Recommendation |
| 2 | Background |

> **Methodology note**
>
> Note that this type of essay does not usually have paragraph headings but it does have a clear paragraph structure.

### D Writing the essay

1. Refer students to the five paragraph topics on the board from Exercise C2. Then ask them to look at the essay on the facing page. Point out that the final part of the essay – the recommendation – is not there, as they will write that themselves later. Ask them to find where they should divide up the essay to make four paragraphs with the topics from Exercise C2. Give feedback, ideally using an electronic projection.

2. Students discuss in pairs. Elicit ideas. Write some notes about each point on the board.

3. Remind students of the meaning of the word *recommendation*. Once again, ask students to discuss the two questions in pairs. Then elicit ideas. If you like, you can add notes to the ones already on the board from the

previous activity. Monitor and make a note of common errors.

**Less able classes:** Build up the final paragraph on the board, with students' pens down. Erase some of the words when the paragraph is complete. Students copy and complete the paragraph.

**More able classes:** If necessary, start the class off by eliciting the first sentence or two and writing them on the board. Then leave students to complete on their own.

### Optional activity

The following information can be deduced from the data supplied and could also be inserted into the model answer. Write the following sentences on the board and ask students which paragraph each sentence should go in, and where exactly it should be placed in that paragraph (see Answers below).

- *Finally, the current location of Causton is better for the international airport. This will become more important if exports by air continue to grow.*
- *In particular, Acme Engineering is selling more goods overseas. Export sales have risen by more than 1,200 units in the last three years.*
- *Thirdly, Acme Engineering imports raw materials by sea. Bellport is on the coast and has regular sailings to Europe and elsewhere.*

### Answers

See table below. Target text in *italics*, including the extra information (in *underlined italics*) which has been placed in the best location in the paragraph.

### Closure

Give feedback on the errors you noted while monitoring.

| | |
|---|---|
| purpose of report | The purpose of this report is to make a recommendation to the owner of Acme Ltd. The company is considering relocation from Causton to Bellport. In this report, I examine the case for and the case against relocation and make a recommendation. // |
| background | Acme Engineering is a small engineering company. It is located in the small town of Causton, which has a population of 10,000. The company employs 14 people, including three skilled workers and ten unskilled workers. The company occupies premises of 5,000 square metres. It imports raw materials by sea. It sells 75 per cent of its finished goods to customers in Britain, and exports 25 per cent of its finished goods to Europe. The company is expanding rapidly. In the last year, total sales have increased by 46 per cent. *In particular, Acme Engineering is selling more goods overseas. Export sales have risen by more than 1,200 units in the last three years.* The company now needs skilled and unskilled workers to deal with the increase in demand. It also needs additional factory units but cannot rent them in Causton. // |
| points for | There are several factors in favour of a move to Bellport. Firstly, Acme Engineering should find it much easier to recruit staff in Bellport, because the town is much larger than Causton. In addition, the unemployment rate in Bellport is 10 per cent whereas it is only 3 per cent in Causton. Secondly, the company needs to acquire more factory space. There are more factory units to rent in Bellport than Causton. *Thirdly, Acme Engineering imports raw materials by sea. Bellport is on the coast and has regular sailings to Europe and elsewhere.* (Note that this would make the next item *Fourthly, …*) Thirdly, the company sells most of its finished goods inside Britain at the moment. There is a major motorway close to Bellport which links the city to London and the rest of the country. Finally, there is a relocation grant of £2,000 per person. This is a government incentive to bring business to Bellport. // |
| points against | There are also two factors against relocation to Bellport. Firstly, salaries are not as high in Causton as in Bellport. The company will pay about 25 per cent more in salaries if they relocate. Secondly, rental costs of factory units are higher in Bellport than Causton. The company will pay 100 per cent more in rent for the same size of unit. *Finally, the current location of Causton is better for the international airport. This will become more important if exports by air continue to grow.* |
| recommendation (model answer) | I recommend relocation to Bellport. The company will be able to recruit more staff and acquire additional factory space in the city. It will also benefit from cheaper import costs and cheaper transportation costs inside Britain. These benefits outweigh the drawbacks, which include higher salary costs and higher rental costs. |

### 3.18 Learning new writing skills: The For and against essay

**Objectives**

By the end of this lesson, students should be able to:
- identify and follow a plan for essay type 3 (For and against);
- compare places and things using common writing patterns.

**Introduction**

Choose one of the following:
- Use Exercise A.
- Ask students to reread the essay about the relocation of Acme Engineering from the previous lesson.

**A**  Reviewing vocabulary

Check students understand the task, then set for individual work and pairwork checking.

**Answers**

Answers depend on students.

**Methodology note**

Remind students that they should not write numbers or headings for this kind of essay; the five points for each paragraph topic are for guidance only.

**B**  Identifying a new skill (1)

Exploit the visual and use it to introduce the idea of a construction company and a house-building project. Remind students about the two towns of Bellport and Causton (if you have not already done so – see introduction above) and find out what they can remember about them.

Set the task. Give students time to read the information in Skills Check 1. Elicit answers. Elicit the names for the five sections of the essay plan and check understanding. Remind students that they studied them before in Exercise C2 from the previous lesson.

**Answers**

For and against essay; five sections.

**C**  Practising a key skill (1)

Ask students to read the assignment instructions again. Check understanding:
- *What is 'Allen Homes'?* (a building company)
- *What decision do they have to make?* (whether to build houses in Bellport or Causton)
- *What is the assignment?* (to write a report with arguments for and against)

Set the task and check students understand they need to match each sentence (1–5) to the points in Skills Check 1. Students complete the activity individually, then compare their answers in pairs. Elicit answers.

**Answers**

| 1. Allen Homes is a large construction company which employs 1,500 people. | background |
| 2. Land prices in Causton are much higher than in Bellport. | points against |
| 3. There are fewer houses to buy in Causton than in Bellport. | points for |
| 4. In this report, I examine the case for and against a house-building project in Causton. | purpose of essay |
| 5. The company should build new houses in Causton because the demand is much higher in that location. | recommendation |

**Methodology note**

Students should already be aware of the grammar rules for comparing with adjectives. However, if necessary, you can do some quick revision here.

The main point of this Skills Check, though, is to remind students of different ways of comparing so that they can vary their writing.

**D**  Identifying a key skill (2)

Ask students to study Skills Check 2. Alternatively, you can ask students to close their books and dictate each sentence to them. Then students reopen their books and check their writing with the sentences in the Skills Check.

Set the task. Students complete the activity individually, then compare their answers in pairs. Elicit answers.

Answers

|  | adjective | noun |
|---|---|---|
| much | ✓ | ✓ |
| more | ✓ | ✓ |
| less |  | ✓ |
| fewer |  | ✓ |
| not as ... as | ✓ |  |

### E  Practising a key skill (2)

Set the task. Students complete the activity individually. Monitor. Show the correct answers on the board, preferably using an electronic projection. Students correct their own writing.

Answers
1. Causton is much smaller than Bellport.
2. Bellport is not as attractive as Causton.
3. The unemployment rate is lower in Causton than in Bellport.
4. There are fewer factory units to rent in Causton than in Bellport.
5. Salaries are much lower in Causton.
6. Raw materials are imported by sea whereas finished goods are exported by air.

### Closure
Ask students to produce sentences with similar patterns to the ones shown in Skills Check 2 about two towns that they know – either in their own country or in the UK. For example:
*London is much larger than Southampton.*

---

### 3.19  Grammar for writing: Describing trends

**Objectives**

By the end of the lesson, students should be able to:
• discriminate between the three tenses *past simple*, *present perfect* and *present continuous* in order to describe the information given in a graph.

---

**Methodology note**

Describing a graph is part of the writing section of the IELTS exam, so this lesson will be useful to students taking that exam. In IELTS, students usually have to describe graphs that contain information from some years ago. In this lesson, students describe current or recent information, which therefore entails the use of different tenses. Nevertheless, the activities still give useful practice for IELTS through:
• interpreting information in a graph;
• using key verbs and phrases for graphs – e.g., *rise / fall (or drop); go up / go down; slightly / sharply*, etc.

### Introduction
Check students understand the meaning of the word *trends* (direction, movement).

### Grammar box 18
Briefly revise the forms of the present continuous and present perfect tenses if necessary. Elicit and revise the forms and spellings of past participles, especially:
*increase – increased*
*rise – risen*
*fall – fallen*
*go – gone*
*improve – improved*
*drop – dropped*

**Methodology notes**

You do not need to do the text as a gap-fill exercise if you prefer not to. You could do it as a dictation, or even as 'wall' or 'running' dictation.

Note that the text and information are not about Acme Engineering this time, but about a different company in Bellport.

### A  Describing a graph (1)
1. Make sure students understand that the graph shows information for the current year, hence the use of the present perfect tense. Spend a few minutes exploiting the graph.

Theme 3: Writing  159

Set the task. Students complete the activity individually, then compare their answers in pairs. Elicit answers, preferably using an electronic projection. Check students have used the passive voice correctly for *were sold*. Check the spelling of the past participles. Elicit the meanings of *slightly* and *sharply*.

Discuss with the class why each tense has been used and build up a list of key phrases to go with each of the two tenses on the board. You could also add a few more common key phrases for each tense if you wish (see words in non-italics in the table below).

| present perfect | past simple |
|---|---|
| in the last X months ... | in the (first) month(s) of the year |
| since (month) ... | in (January) |
| now | last month |
| recently | last week / year |
| for the last X months / years | |
| up to now | |
| in this period | |

2. The task can either be set for individual work or you can do it with the class as a whole, building the text up on the board.

   Another method is to provide the class with two or three prompts for each sentence, then ask students to complete the text. Students can check their writing with the information in the Course Book when they have finished.

### Answers

1. Bellport Goods Ltd has not had a very good start to the year. In the last five months, sales to Britain *have risen* (rise) from 139 to 172 per month. However, sales to the EU *have fallen* (fall) sharply since January. In the first month of the year, 151 units *were sold* (sell) whereas last month we only *sold* (sell) 115. Sales to the rest of the world *have* also *gone down* (go down) slightly this year. Overall, the company *sold* (sell) 465 units in January but monthly sales *have* now *dropped* (drop) to 452.

2. Model answer:

   Sales to Britain have risen in the first five months of the year from 139 units to 172. However, sales to the EU and the rest of the world have both fallen in this period. Sales to the EU have gone down from 151 to 115 units, while rest of the world sales have dropped from 175 to 165 units.

### B Describing a graph (2)

Ask students to cover the text and graph. Revise the acronym WHO and what it means (World Health Organization – part of the UN). Teach the phrase *life expectancy*. If possible, show some photographs of older people from developing countries and from the developed world and ask students to predict life expectancy rates for each group. Now ask students to uncover the graph. Ask:
T: *What does the graph show?*
Ss: *Life expectancy at birth.*
T: *What does the red line show?*
Ss: *Life expectancy in developing countries.*

Discuss the information shown and ask students if they find any of it surprising. Discuss the meaning of the phrase *life expectancy at birth*. Elicit some possible sentences to describe the trends shown in the graph, e.g.,

- *Life expectancy is rising / increasing in both developed and developing countries.*
- *People are living longer.*
- *It is rising slowly in developed countries.*
- *It is rising more quickly in developing countries.*

1. Set the task. Point out that this time they must choose between the present continuous and the present perfect tense. Explain that in this situation, we normally give a time reference with the present perfect tense.

   If necessary, write the infinitives of the missing verbs on the board. Write them either in the correct order or mix them up, depending on the level of your class. Here is the correct order:
   rise
   live
   go down
   go up
   improve
   jump
   rise

2. Students complete the task individually, then compare their answers in pairs. Elicit answers, preferably using an electronic projection.

Answers

1. Possible verbs:

   Life expectancy *is rising* all over the world. People *are living* longer in the developed world and in the developing countries. This is because the death rate *is going down* and the birth rate in most countries *is going up*. Overall, the figure *has improved* by ten years, from 57 in 1970 to 67 this year. In developing countries, life expectancy *has jumped* by 11 years in the last 40 years, from 42 to 53. The figure in developed countries *has* only *risen* by half that amount, but from a starting figure of 71.

2. See text above.

### C Writing about general trends

Check students understand the task. Do an example with the class and elicit some possible sentences.

Students complete the task individually. Monitor and give help where necessary.

Ask a few students to read out their sentences to the rest of the class.

Answers

Answers depend on students.

## Closure

Give students a test on the past tense and past participle of irregular verbs as follows:

| infinitive | past | past participle |
|---|---|---|
| is | was | been |
| rise | rose | risen |
| fall | fell | fallen |
| grow | grew | grown |
| go | went | gone |
| sell | sold | sold |
| buy | bought | bought |
| make | made | made |
| pay | paid | paid |
| cost | cost | cost |

## 3.20 Applying new writing skills: Opening a new branch

### Objectives

By the end of the lesson, students should be able to:
- use vocabulary, grammar and sub-skills from the Writing section in order to produce a For and against report;
- use the TOWER process to produce a final written draft.

### Introduction

Use Exercise A as the introduction.

### A Previewing vocabulary

1. Check students understand the task. Students discuss in pairs. Elicit answers.
2. Exploit Figure 1. Ask students what a warehouse is for (storing goods, etc.). Set the task. Students complete the activity individually, then compare their answers in pairs. Elicit answers.

Answers

1. The pairs of words are opposites.

| for | against |
|---|---|
| advantage | disadvantage |
| benefit | drawback |
| positive | negative |
| strength | weakness |

2. Supastores Ltd is a *retail* company. It has a number of *branches* across the south of England. The branches *are supplied* daily. The goods are transported by *road* from a *warehouse* near London.

### Methodology note

Remind students about the TOWER approach to writing again (taught in Level 1 of *Progressive Skills in English*):
- Thinking about what you're going to write
- Organizing your ideas
- Writing a first draft
- Editing the first draft
- Rewriting in order to produce a second draft

Theme 3: Writing  161

Notice that Exercises B–E are named according to the TOWER stages.

## B Thinking and organizing

Ask students to read the assignment and check understanding:
- *What kind of report do you have to write?* (For and against)
- *What is it about?* (opening a Supastore branch in Bellport)

Ask students to study the notes, then check understanding:
- *What's the name of the company?* (Supastores Ltd)
- *How many branches has it got?* (more than 50)
- *Where are the branches?* (in the south of England), etc.

Tell students to study the graph and ask them to describe the trends shown, for example:
- *Total sales are increasing steadily.*
- *There has been a big increase in sales this year.*
- *The company income is rising / going up.*

Now set the task. Tell students they can look back at the previous lessons from this section in order to gather information for the table.

Students complete the table individually. Elicit answers, preferably using an electronic projection of the completed table.

### Answers

| for | against |
|---|---|
| 1. easier to recruit staff because larger and higher unemp. rate | 1. salaries higher |
| 2. higher sales because larger population | 2. rental costs of shops higher |
| 3. motorway closer so transport cheaper | 3. fewer shop units |
| 4. set-up grant | |

### Methodology note

You may need to remind students about topic sentences, especially if they have not studied Level 1 of *Progressive Skills in English*. Topic sentences are usually the first sentence of a paragraph and they introduce the topic of that paragraph. When reading, a lot of information can usually be predicted simply by reading the topic sentence. Topic sentences often summarize the information in a text.

## C Writing a For and against essay

Briefly revise the essay from Lesson 3.17 Real-time writing about the relocation of Acme Engineering Ltd. Allow students to reread the model answer (see Exercise D, page 157 above). Elicit where each new paragraph starts and what the topic sentence is for each one. Highlight some of the target sentence patterns.

1. Elicit a topic sentence for the first paragraph and write it on the board (see model answer below – Exercise E). Divide the class into pairs. Each pair of students should work on the remaining four topic sentences. Monitor and give help where necessary.

   Elicit the topic sentences and write them on the board.

   **Less able classes:** Write the first few words of each topic sentence on the board and ask students to copy and complete.

2. You can start the essay off on the board with the first one or two sentences (following the topic sentence) from the model answer. Monitor while students are writing their first draft and make a note of common errors. Give feedback on some of the common errors before moving on to the next stage.

### Answers
See Exercise E.

## D Editing

Remind students of things to check for: spelling, correct tenses, etc. Monitor and help as necessary.

## E Rewriting

The final version of the report can be written in class or set up for homework. If done in class, monitor and make a note of common errors.

### Answers

See next table. Model answer, with topic sentences in *italics*:

| purpose of report | *The purpose of this report is to make a recommendation to the management of Supastores Ltd.* The company is going to open a new branch. They are considering Bellport and Causton. In this report, I examine the case for and the case against Bellport and make a recommendation. |
|---|---|
| background | *Supastores is a large retail company.* It has over 50 branches across the country. The company employs, on average, ten people in each branch. All are unskilled except for the manager. On average, each branch occupies premises of 500 square metres. It is supplied daily by road from a warehouse near London. The company is expanding. In the last three years, total sales have increased from £734,000 to £1,056,000. Last year sales rose by 18 per cent and this year, they have gone up by 22 per cent. |
| points for | *There are many factors in favour of opening a branch in Bellport.* Firstly, it is easier to recruit staff in Bellport because the town is much larger than Causton. In addition, the unemployment rate in Bellport is 10 per cent whereas it is only 3 per cent in Causton. Secondly, they will get higher sales in Bellport because the town has a much larger population. Thirdly, Supastores supplies its branches by road. The motorway from London is much closer to Bellport than Causton. Finally, there is a set-up grant of £10,000 per unit in Bellport. This is a government incentive to bring business to the town. |
| points against | *There are several factors against opening a branch in Bellport.* Firstly, salaries are higher in Bellport. Secondly, rental costs of shop units are also higher there. Finally, there are fewer shop units in Bellport. |
| recommendation | *I recommend opening the new branch in Bellport.* The company will be able to recruit staff easily and attract a large number of customers. It will also benefit from cheaper transportation costs from their warehouse. These benefits are greater than the drawbacks, which include higher salary costs, higher rental costs and the difficulty of finding a suitable shop unit. |

**Closure**

Give feedback to the whole class on the common writing errors you noted while monitoring. If students have completed their work in class, you can give out copies of the model answer. Go through the model answer with the class.

**Portfolio: Self-management**

**Objectives**

By the end of this lesson(s), students should have:

- revised target vocabulary from the theme;
- used integrated skills to practise language and revise knowledge from the theme;
- practised questions to check information;
- used integrated skills to talk and write about self-management;
- learnt more common core knowledge about self-management.

**Introduction**

Exploit the visuals. Ask how each person feels and elicit some adjectives:
*angry*
*upset*
*embarrassed*
*ashamed*
*stressed*
*tired*
*depressed*

Ask students: *What do you do when you feel angry / upset?* etc.

Elicit ideas, such as go for a walk, punch a pillow, talk to a friend, etc.

**Methodology note**

*Awake (awoke / awoken)* used to be the verb as well as the adjective but its usage as a verb is now rare. We do not normally say *He awoke ...* but *He woke up*.

We sometimes use *sleeping* as the noun from *sleep*. The adjective *asleep* can only be used predicatively (after a verb), i.e., *He is asleep*. When we want to use an adjective attributively (in front of the noun), we must use *sleeping*, i.e., *The sleeping man ... Let sleeping dogs lie ...*

Note that the adjective *sleepy* means *tired* as in *I'm feeling sleepy*.

**A** Activating ideas

Write the word *sleep* on the board. Point out that this can be a noun or a verb.

- Ask for the adjective, i.e., *How do we finish the sentence 'He is ...'* = *'He is ... asleep.'*
- Ask for the opposite word = *awake*.
- What is the verb? = *wake up*.
- What is the noun? = *wakefulness* (this is rare but it is the only noun that exists; students do not need to learn this word).

Divide the class into pairs or small groups. Monitor while students are discussing the questions. Elicit some of their ideas.

**Answers**
Answers depend on students.

**B** Gathering and recording information (1)

1. Refer students to the questions. Set the task for pairwork. Give students plenty of time to discuss the questions. Elicit a few responses, but do not confirm or correct at this stage. Play 3.27. Students complete the activity individually, then compare their answers in pairs. Elicit answers. Check understanding of some of the vocabulary in the transcript but do not spend too long on this.
2. Set the task. If students find it difficult, write the summary on the board in prompt form. Students copy and complete the full sentences. If you wish, give out copies of the transcript at this point.

**Alternative presentation**
If you are able to arrange it, allow different groups of students to listen to the five different parts of the lecture, then put them together to exchange information and get a composite set of notes.

**Answers**
1. See next table.
2. Model answer:
   Sleep is a physical and mental state. Teenagers need 9.5 hours of sleep each night but they often get much less. During sleep, the body rests and the senses shut down but the brain remains active and organizes long-term memory. Sleep follows the circadian rhythm which is controlled by

| question | information |
|---|---|
| a. What is sleep? | physical and mental state – person rests body |
| b. How much sleep does a teenager need? | 9.5 per night |
| c. How much sleep does a teenager get, on average? | 7.4 per night |
| d. Why do teenagers need more sleep than young children and adults? | – teenagers = large number of changes happening to bodies<br>– if not enough sleep: get angry; hard to concentrate; feel stressed bec. always late |
| e. What happens if we don't get enough sleep? | ability to do simple tasks goes down – mental and sporting |
| f. What happens to our bodies during sleep? | rests body; senses shut down; not aware of changes; muscles lose power; heart rate decrease; body temp. down; breathing falls |
| g. What happens to our brains? | – no decrease; brain active<br>– brain organizes long-term memory<br>– fixes information learnt during the day |
| h. Why do we need sleep? | helps brain and body to work better during wakefulness |
| i. What controls sleeping and wakefulness? | – circadian rhythm – controlled by melatonin<br>– children / adults = ready for sleep at 10<br>– 13/14 = ready for sleep at 12 midnight / 1 a.m.<br>– situation worse now with computers and TVs in bedroom = light = stop release of mel. |
| j. How can we manage sleep? | turn down the lights in bedroom; turn off computer and TV one hour before sleep |

melatonin. We can manage sleep by turning down lights and turning off computers and televisions so that melatonin is released.

**Transcript**

3.27

Presenter: 3.27. Portfolio: Self-management. Exercise B1. Listen to a lecture about sleep.

Lecturer: ... How much sleep do you get each day on average? If the answer is nine or ten, you are very unusual. The average for American teenagers, for example, is 7.4 hours per night. According to scientists, this is far too little. The average teenager needs about nine and a half hours of sleep. This is more than a young child, and more than an adult. Teenagers need more sleep because there are a large number of physical changes happening to their bodies. If they do not get enough sleep, they suffer many bad effects of sleep deprivation, for example, they get angry easily, they find it hard to concentrate in class and they may feel stressed because they are always late for school.

… Sleep is a physical and mental state in which a person rests their body. During periods of sleep, most senses, such as sight and smell, shut down and you are not aware of changes in the outside world. Your muscles lose power and you do not move around very much. This is why you do not normally fall out of bed. When you go to sleep, there are physical effects, too. For example, your heart rate decreases, your body temperature goes down and your breathing rate falls. However, surprisingly perhaps, there is no decrease in brain activity. In other words, your brain is as active when you are asleep as when you are awake.

… Researchers do not know the exact function of sleep, but clearly the body needs periods of complete rest. The harder you work during the day, the more sleep you need. There is also evidence that the brain uses a period of sleep to organize long-term memory and to fix information learnt during the day. A few studies have shown that it is a good idea to learn words from another language just before you go to sleep. The period of sleep seems to fix the words in your memory. Sleep may even help your brain and your body to work properly during periods of wakefulness. Studies have shown that if you do not get enough sleep, your ability to do even simple tasks goes down. This effect is not just on mental activity, but sporting tasks as well.

… All animals, including humans, have a pattern of sleeping and waking. It is called the circadian rhythm, spelt C-I-R-C-A-D-I-A-N R-H-Y-T-H-M. The rhythm is controlled largely by a chemical called melatonin – M-E-L-A-T-O-N-I-N. There is a difference in the sleep patterns of teenagers compared with the sleep patterns of younger children and adults. When you are young and when you pass your teens, you are normally ready to go to sleep at around 10 p.m. That is because melatonin is released into the blood at this time. But the sleep pattern changes at about 13 or 14. The melatonin is released later, sometimes as late as 1 a.m. Teenagers often don't feel tired until that time, then, of course, they have to get up five or six hours later to go to school.

… There is a chemical which prepares you for sleeping. It is called melatonin - M-E-L-A-T-O-N-I-N. The chemical is produced at about 10 p.m. in children and adults. But in teenagers, it is released later, at about midnight. This is why teenagers often go to bed so late. This later release of the melatonin has probably always happened in teenagers. However, the situation is worse nowadays because teenagers often have computers and televisions in their bedrooms. Researchers believe that the light from this equipment tells the brain that it is still daytime and so the brain does not release the sleep chemical. You can manage the production of melatonin by turning down the lights in your bedroom and turning off your computer and television one hour before you want to go to sleep.

## C Gathering and recording information (2)

1. Explain that you are going to give students one of two texts. Write the titles on the board:
*Managing anger*
*Managing stress*

Elicit questions which you could ask about both of these topics. Write the questions on the board. Make sure that by the end of the process you have the following questions (simply add them if students do not come up with them):
- *What is it?*
- *Why do we need it?*

(**Note:** The idea that we might need anger and stress may be strange to some students.)
- *What causes it?*
- *What is the result?*
- *How can we manage it?*

2. Students can work in pairs, as suggested in the Course Book, or you can set the task for group work as follows.

Put the students into two groups, numbered 1 and 2. Refer each group to one of the texts:
Group 1 – should read *Managing anger* on page 102
Group 2 – should read *Managing stress* on page 103

Students make notes individually. Then allow them to discuss and check the final notes with the other students in their group. Monitor and assist each group. During this stage, refer students back to the text if they have missed any key points. Use the model notes (see below) and check them against the notes that are emerging from each group.

Put the students into new groups. Each group must have at least one person from each original group, 1 and 2. Each student must give the relevant information of his/her research and the other students take notes. Encourage listeners to ask questions if they are not sure of any of the information. Monitor and assist each group. Once again, use the model notes to ensure that the groups are producing good notes of all research.

3. The questions can be discussed either in pairs or groups. After a few minutes' discussion, elicit ideas.

### Answers

Model notes: see table on next page.
3. Answers depend on students.

|  | anger | stress |
| --- | --- | --- |
| What is it? | *emotional state* | *emotional state* |
| Why do we need it? | *helps you stand up to someone* | *helps you concentrate; achieve better results* |
| What causes it? | *irritating behaviour; stress; depression* | *change; not in control* |
| What is the result? | *heart rate increases; adrenaline flows into your blood* | *heart rate increases; adrenaline flows into your blood; stomach upset; feeling of fear; immune system weakens* |
| How can we manage it? | *e.g., BRIGHTEN process*<br>• *breathe*<br>• *repeat 'calm down'*<br>• *imagine*<br>• *go through good things*<br>• *highlight cause*<br>• *think of solution*<br>• *explain feeling*<br>• *never act immediately* | *e.g., RELAX process*<br>• *rehearse stressful situations*<br>• *eat regularly and sensibly*<br>• *learn to break down tasks*<br>• *assert yourself*<br>• *exercise* |

### D Giving a talk

Spend a few minutes revising the information from this section's previous lessons.

Encourage students to start by making a spidergram in order to organize all the information. Students do not have to refer to every single topic in their talks, but they should refer to at least three or four of them.

Elicit ideas for how students should organize the talks. For example, students could say which – in their opinion – are the most important areas of self-management for a particular job or situation. Or they could make notes for the topics that most relate to them.

Elicit some ways in which students can begin their talk, e.g.,
*I am going to talk about self-management. In particular, I want to look at managing stress and anger …*

Monitor while students are making notes and give help where necessary.

Students should then spend some time working in pairs and practising their talks.

Finally, put students into larger groups of four or five to give their final talk. Monitor and give feedback.

### Answers
Answers depend on students.

### E Writing

This can be done in class or set up as homework.

Spend a few minutes discussing each of the two writing tasks. Elicit ideas, as well as an approach, for each topic. Tell students how many words you want them to write. Remind students to try to practise vocabulary and common patterns from the theme.

### Answers
Answers depend on students.

### Closure

If there is no time for writing the article in class, set an appropriate deadline for the task.

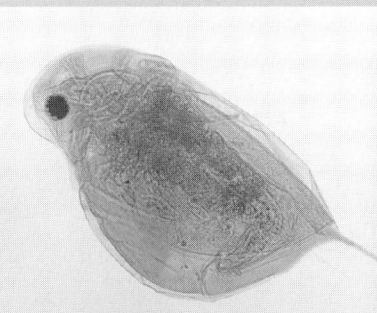

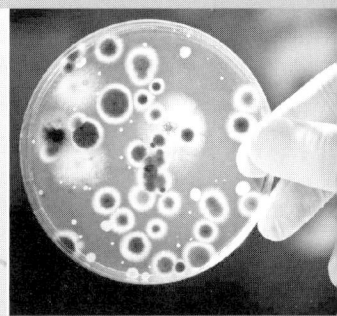

# Theme 4

## Natural cycles

- Greening the desert
- Oxygen and carbon
- Chains, webs and pyramids
- Energy and the oceans

# Listening: Greening the desert

## 4.1 Vocabulary for listening: Desert regions

### Objectives

By the end of the lesson, students should be able to:
- recognize the meaning and pronunciation of target vocabulary;
- demonstrate understanding of information about deserts.

### Introduction

If possible, show some pictures of deserts; make it clear there are different types of desert – such as scrubland, as well as the well-known dune type. You can also show some pictures of oases and desert wildlife if possible, as well as some of nomads or Bedouin people.

If you are not able to show pictures, then use Exercise A as the introduction.

### A Activating ideas

Exploit the visual of the map of desert regions (without pre-empting the questions). You could use it to revise the names of the continents and oceans.

Set the task. Students discuss the questions in pairs. If students find question 1 difficult, write the names of the deserts on the board (see Answers below) at random, and ask students to match them with the correct continent.

Elicit answers. It does not matter if students cannot name many plants or animals, so try not to spend too long on the answers to questions 2 and 3.

### Answers

1. Possible answers (there are also others):
   - North America: Mojave / Mohave
   - South America: Atacama in Chile / North West Desert in Brazil
   - Africa: Sahara / Namib
   - Asia: Gobi
   - Australia: Gibson / Great Victoria
   - Europe / Antarctica: No deserts
2. The Sahara.
3. Cactus (many different types), palm tree, dragon tree, aloes, succulents, yucca.
4. There are many different animals including birds (ostriches, vultures), mammals (camels, foxes, rats, meerkats, hyenas, etc.), reptiles (snakes, lizards), arthropods (spiders, scorpions, ants, butterflies) and amphibians (toads). There are even fish in some deserts!

### B Understanding key vocabulary (1)

Set the task and make sure students understand they must use the correct form of each verb.

Give students time to complete the sentences. Then play 4.1 so that students can check their answers. Elicit answers.

Go over any problem areas. Point out the pronunciation of the word *drought* and elicit the meaning. Ask students which facts they found most surprising.

### Optional activities

Tell students to close their books. Ask students to remember each fact from Exercise B. If students are finding it difficult, write some prompts on the board to help them. If you wish, divide the class into pairs and set up conversations as follows:
S1: *Did you know that deserts cover one-third of the Earth's surface?*
S2: *No. I didn't know that. It's amazing.*

### Transcript and Answers

 4.1

Presenter: 4.1. Theme 4: Natural cycles
Lesson 4.1. Vocabulary for listening: Desert regions
Exercise B. Listen and complete the facts below about deserts. Use verbs from the box. Make any necessary changes.

Voice:
1. Deserts cover one-third of the Earth's surface.
2. Thirteen per cent of the world's population live in deserts.
3. A drought lasted for over 40 years in the Atacama desert in Chile.
4. Water evaporates 20 times faster in deserts.
5. Wind has sometimes carried sand from the Sahara to the UK.
6. The Sahara Desert occupies around eight per cent of the world's land area.
7. About 1,200 different types of plants – flowers and trees – grow in the Sahara.
8. The Sahara is expanding southwards at an average of nearly one kilometre a month.

### C Understanding key vocabulary (2)

1. This is a new type of activity so it will need careful setting up. Students will listen to a definition and then try to find the word with that meaning in the word list. Students should number each word (or underline, or circle). If they cannot find the word – because it is new for them, or for other reasons – it does not matter. Students will then hear the word with the correct pronunciation. If you wish, you can pause 4.1 after the correct word has been given, and elicit the definition. This will help students to remember the meaning of the new word.

2. Divide the class into pairs. Students tell each other the definition for each word.

### Transcript

4.2

**Presenter:** 4.2. Exercise C. Listen to each definition. There will be a pause ... find the correct word in the list on the right as quickly as you can. Then you will hear the pronunciation of the word.

**Voice:**
1. It's an adjective. It means 'very big'. [PAUSE] The word is *huge*.
2. It means 'at an angle'. It's the opposite of *straight*. It can be a verb or a noun. [PAUSE] The word is *tilt*.
3. This is a verb. It means 'to go back' or 'move back'. [PAUSE] The word is *reverse*.
4. This is another verb. It means 'to tell people something important'. [PAUSE] The word is *announce*.
5. This word is a noun. It is a sign, something that helps us understand a problem. The word is often used in detective stories. [PAUSE] The word is *clue*.
6. This word is a noun. It is similar in meaning to the word clue. It means 'facts' or 'confirmation that something is true'. [PAUSE] The word is *evidence*.
7. This word is a verb. We use it with words such as *water* and *rivers*. It means 'to move'. [PAUSE] The word is *flow*.

### Closure

1. Ask students to make sentences with the words from Exercise C.

2. Ask students to suggest a synonym for each of the following:
   *raise* (grow)
   *reverse* (go back)
   *expand* (get bigger)
   *occupy* (fill)
   *huge* (very big)
   *comprise* (contain)

## 4.2 Real-time listening: Desertification

### Objectives

By the end of the lesson, students should be able to:
- use real-time / top-down listening skills, in order to identify and retain key information in a lecture about desertification;
- use previously learnt sub-skills about understanding an introduction;
- recognize target vocabulary from the Listening section.

### Introduction

Spend a few minutes discussing climate change, especially the reduction in the amount of water available in some countries. Students may be aware of rivers and lakes, etc., in their country(ies) that are much smaller than before.

### A Activating ideas

1. Students discuss in pairs. Elicit answers. Say aloud some of the key words so the class can hear the correct pronunciation: *oasis, Sahara, Saharan, dune, pipeline, desert, rock paintings, giraffes, deer*, etc. (Students do not need to learn the words for the animals.)

2. Elicit answer. Students may be puzzled by the rock paintings of animals. Try not to pre-empt the lecture too much but note that the rock paintings show there was once water in the Sahara.

3. Say the word *desertification* for the class to hear and elicit its meaning. Check the meaning of *fertile*. Set the task for pairwork. After a few minutes, ask some of the students to read out the words in their lists.

### Answers

1.

| A. old map of Africa including Sahara showing rivers and lakes – c.100 CE by Ptolemy | B. rock paintings showing giraffes, bison, cows, deer – from the Sahara |
|---|---|
| C. modern map showing extent of Sahara now | D. Saharan sand dunes |
| E. oasis in the Sahara with standing water – very rare now | F. pipelines carrying water across the desert |

Theme 4: Listening 169

2. They are all from, or about, the Sahara.

3. Answers depend on the students, but here are some ideas:

| | |
|---|---|
| agriculture | farming |
| animals | increase |
| area | land |
| climate | plants |
| desert | rain |
| die | size |
| drought | weather |
| dry | |

## B Understanding an introduction

Play DVD 4.A and elicit answers. The suggested answers are below. However, students may have different headings, for example:

*The Sahara*
*1. size and location*
*2. history*
*3. desertification*

### Answers

The Sahara
1. description
2. history
3. explanation

### Transcript

4.3 DVD 4.A

**Presenter:** 4.3. Lesson 4.2. Real-time listening: Desertification

**Lecturer:** This is the first of two lectures about the Sahara Desert. Firstly, in this lecture, I'm going to describe the Sahara. – size and location. Secondly, I will talk about the history of the Sahara. This is actually quite surprising. Next, I will explain what happened to the Sahara. The events there are a special case of desertification. Finally, I will tell you about desertification more generally. How does it happen?

### Methodology note

When giving feedback for this exercise:

1. Deal with the issue of the tilt of the Earth. If students have been following the whole of the *Progressive Skills in English* course, this will be familiar to them. If not, simply point out – using a diagram of the globe – that the Earth is tilted, with the northern half closer to the Sun. This tilt has changed – it has now actually become less – but because the interaction between the position of the Earth and the climate is so complex, the smaller tilt = hotter and drier Sahara.

2. Check students understand the word *pharaohs*. If not, mention Tutankhamen or the pyramids and they should realize what it means.

## C Understanding a lecture (1)

Give students time to read through the questions and discuss answers in pairs before they listen to the DVD.

Check understanding of the phrase *tilt of the Earth* in question 8.

Elicit the pronunciation of some of the numbers and figures in the answers.

Play DVD 4.B. Students complete individually then compare their answers in pairs. Elicit answers.

### Answers

See table below.

| | a | b | c |
|---|---|---|---|
| 1. Where in Africa is the Sahara? | in the centre | in the north ✓ | in the south |
| 2. What is the area of the Sahara? | 9 m. km² ✓ | 90 m. km² | 900 m. km² |
| 3. Where does the name *sahara* come from? | from Arabic | from Sanskrit | perhaps from Arabic or Sanskrit ✓ |
| 4. How do we know that people lived in the Sahara thousands of years ago? | rock paintings of animals and fish ✓ | bones of animals and fish | stories about animals and fish |
| 5. How much rain does the area get now? | < 5mm ✓ | 5mm | > 5mm |
| 6. How many people lived in the Sahara 5,000 years ago? | thousands | tens of thousands ✓ | hundreds of thousands |
| 7. Who farmed the Sahara 2,000 years ago? | Egyptians | Greeks | Romans ✓ |
| 8. How much did the tilt of the Earth change 9,000 years ago? | just under 2° | 0.5° | just over 0.5° ✓ |

## Transcript

4.4 DVD 4.B

Lecturer: Firstly, some facts about the Sahara. The Sahara is the largest desert in the world. It occupies most of the northern third of the continent of Africa, which, of course, is a huge continent. The Sahara covers nine million square kilometres. It comprises most of the land area of the Arab countries of Algeria, Libya, Egypt and the Sudan, as well as Mauritania, Mali, Niger and Chad. It is shaped like a rectangle. It is about 1,600 kilometres north to south and, incredibly, it is 5,000 kilometres east to west.

What is the history of the Sahara? Perhaps there is a clue in the name *Sahara*. Some people believe that the name comes from the Arabic word for desert, *sahra*, spelt S-A-H-R-A. But there is another theory. It is possible that the name comes from the word *sagara*. That's S-A-G-A-R-A. This is from the ancient language of Sanskrit. People spoke Sanskrit more than 3,000 years ago. In Sanskrit, *sagara* means 'big sea' or 'ocean'.

This theory is not impossible. There was water once in the Sahara – a great deal of it. It has been known for many years that large animals once lived in the area. Rock paintings show a large number of different types of animals, including giraffes, cows and deer. There are even some which show fish. But recently scientists made an astonishing discovery in the Sahara in southern Libya. They found the bones of crocodiles and hippopotamuses. Just think about that. Crocodiles and hippos. These are animals that live in large rivers and lakes.

This is not the first piece of evidence that there was once water in the Sahara. Many years ago, scientists found signs of a huge lake in the Sahara, in northern Sudan. Traces of rivers exist that once flowed hundreds of miles into the Nile. But now, the same region gets less than five millimetres of rain each year. Five millimetres! That amount would hardly cover the bottom of a glass.

So it is certain that there was water in the Sahara, lots of it, in the distant past. It is also known that there were tens of thousands of people living in the Sahara five or six thousand years ago. These people were mainly farmers. Some evidence lives on in records from Ancient Rome. Most of the Sahara was already desert by the time of the Romans, about 2,000 years ago. But a small area along the Mediterranean coast still had good agricultural land. In fact, this area was so important to the Romans for agriculture that it was called 'the bread basket of Rome'.

We have seen, then, that the Sahara had lakes and rivers, and thousands of inhabitants. These people grew crops. What happened to the area? The changes in the Sahara are an example of desertification. But how did it happen? How did the Sahara change from a rich agricultural area with lakes and rivers, to the biggest desert on the planet? The main cause was a change in the tilt of the Earth. Nine thousand years ago, the earth's tilt was just over 24 degrees. At present, it is just under 23.5 degrees. It took about 3,000 years for the tilt to reach its present position. The tiny change in the tilt changed the climate of the Sahara. It did not happen overnight but from start to finish, it only took a few hundred years.

The Sahara is a very special case, because of the change in the tilt of the Earth. But it is now understood that climate change in a particular area can happen without a major event, like the Earth's tilt changing. We call the process a *vicious circle*. It works like this. One year, there is slightly less rain than the year before. This means that the plants do not grow quite as well. This in turn means that the leaves of the plants hold less water close to the surface … which means there is less evaporation into the air … which means there is less rain the next year, and so on.

The ancient people of the Sahara left the areas which are now Libya and western Egypt. They arrived at the Nile … and the age of the Pharaohs began.

Next week, I'm going to talk about reversing the process. Can we green the desert – even a desert the size of the Sahara?

### D  Understanding a lecture (2)

Students discuss the questions in pairs. If necessary, play DVD 4.B one more time. Elicit answers.

Further help is given with the phrase *vicious circle* in the next activity, but you can explain that it is a situation or a process that is difficult to get out of.

### Answers

Possible answers in *italics*:

| 1. sagara | *Sanskrit; origin of name 'sahara'?* |
|---|---|
| 2. giraffes, cows and deer | *animals in rock painting = shows there were rivers, lakes* |
| 3. crocodiles and hippos | *bones found = shows they lived there* |
| 4. the Nile | *where the people of the Sahara went to* |
| 5. Mali, Niger and Chad | *countries in the Sahara* |
| 6. the bread basket of Rome | *name given to the area 2,000 years ago* |
| 7. a vicious circle | *the name for the kind of process involved in desertification* |
| 8. the Pharaohs | *the age which followed desertification* |

### E  Understanding a lecture (3)

1. Students discuss the diagram in pairs. Reassure them not to worry if they cannot complete the diagram at this stage.

2. Play 4.5 so that students can listen to the last part of the lecture again. Elicit answers, preferably using an electronic projection.

Theme 4: Listening  171

### Optional activity

Ask students to add drawings to the diagram. If you have a student who is particularly good at drawing, ask him/her to come to the board and draw them.

Answers

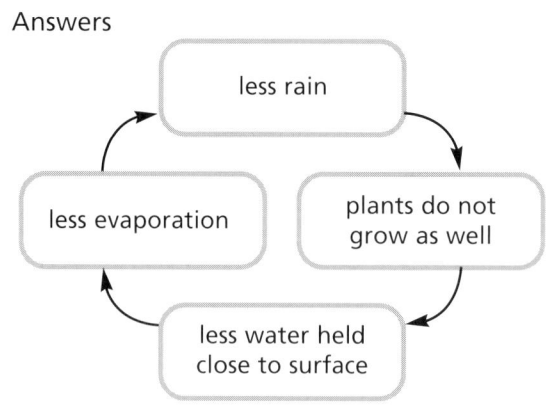

```
        less rain
           ↓
    plants do not grow as well
           ↓
    less water held close to surface
           ↓
      less evaporation
           ↑ (back to less rain)
```

Figure 1: *A vicious circle*

### Transcript

🔵 4.5

**Presenter:** 4.5. Exercise E2. Listen to that part of the lecture again and check your ideas.

**Lecturer:** The Sahara is a very special case, because of the change in the tilt of the Earth. But it is now understood that climate change in a particular area can happen without a major event, like the Earth's tilt changing. We call the process a *vicious circle*. It works like this. One year, there is slightly less rain than the year before. This means that the plants do not grow quite as well. This in turn means that the leaves of the plants hold less water close to the surface … which means there is less evaporation into the air … which means there is less rain the next year, and so on.

### Closure

Choose one of the following:

1. Tell students to imagine that their friend could not go to the lecture. Ask them to tell him/her the lecture's main points.

2. Give out copies of the transcript for Exercises B and C. Play the DVDs of the lecture once more with students following the transcript.

## 4.3 Learning new listening skills: Numbers

### Objectives

By the end of the lesson, students should be able to:
- recognize a word from the stressed syllable;
- predict and identify units and numbers in a lecture.

**Note:** Leave enough time for Exercise D at the end of the lesson.

### Introduction

Review the information from the lecture about desertification in the previous lesson.

**A**   Reviewing vocabulary

1. Students work in pairs. Elicit answers.

   **Less able classes:** Give students the first letter of each word/answer and allow them to look back at Lesson 4.2 Real-time listening.

2. Students discuss in pairs. Do not elicit answers at this stage.

3. Check students understand the task. Play 🔵 4.6. Students discuss answers in pairs. If necessary, play the CD again. Elicit answers.

Answers

| a. very, very old | 'ancient | 1 |
| --- | --- | --- |
| b. Earth, Mars, Jupiter | 'planet | 3 |
| c. the normal weather in a particular place | 'climate | 7 |
| d. people who grow things or keep animals | 'farmers | 2 |
| e. water going up from the ground to the clouds | evapo'ration | 5 |
| f. a very big sea | 'ocean | 9 |
| g. small signs of something | 'traces | 8 |
| h. scientists look for this | 'evidence | 4 |
| i. a person who looks for facts about the world | 'scientist | 10 |
| j. finding something for the first time | dis'covery | 6 |

## Transcript

🔊 4.6

Presenter: 4.6. Lesson 4.3. Learning new listening skills: Numbers. Exercise A. Listen and number the words. You will only hear the stressed syllable.

Voice:
a. an[cient]
b. far[mers]
c. pla[net]
d. e[vidence]
e. [evapo]ra[tion]
f. [dis]co[very]
g. cli[mate]
h. tra[ces]
i. o[cean]
j. sci[entist]

| unit | abbreviation |
|---|---|
| 1. millimetres | mm |
| 2. centimetres | cm |
| 3. kilometres | km |
| 4. square kilometres | km² |
| 5. litres (per second) | l (p.s.) |
| 6. degrees | °(N / E) |
| 7. millions of years ago | mya |
| 8. degrees Celsius | °C |

### B  Identifying a new skill

Give students time to read the Skills Check. Ask some questions to further check understanding:
*Give me some examples of units.* (thousands, litres, degrees, etc.)
*Is minute a unit?* (yes)
*Is volume a unit?* (no)
*What can we use centimetres for?* (length, width, etc.)
*What about litres?* (volume)

Check the pronunciation of some of the words: *height*, *area*, etc.

Highlight the spelling of words such as *length, width, depth, height, litres*.

Set the task for pairwork. First, drill and practise the example question, as well as some other possible questions. Once students are working in pairs, monitor and give feedback.

### Answers
Answers depend on students.

### C  Practising a new skill (1)

Go over the rubrics and check students understand the task. They should make a note of the unit in each sentence by writing down its abbreviation. Reassure students they do not need to understand every sentence in order to do the activity.

Play 🔊 4.7. Students complete the activity individually, then compare their answers in pairs. Elicit answers, preferably using an electronic projection. Replay the CD if you wish.

### Answers
See next table.

## Transcript

🔊 4.7

Presenter: 4.7. Exercise C. Listen to some sentences. Which unit(s) do you hear in each sentence?

Voices:
1. A house fly is about ten millimetres long.
2. Atmospheric pressure supports a column of mercury about 76 centimetres.
3. The distance from New York to London is just over 5,500 kilometres.
4. The area of Mexico is just under two million square kilometres.
5. The discharge from the Amazon into the Atlantic Ocean is about 100 million litres per second.
6. New Delhi in India lies at latitude 28° north and 77° east.
7. Mammals appeared on Earth about 65 million years ago.
8. The boiling point of water is 100 degrees Celsius.

### D  Practising a new skill (2)

1. Students discuss the questions in pairs. Elicit ideas but do not confirm or correct any of them at this stage.
2. Play 🔊 4.8. Students discuss answers in pairs. Elicit answers, preferably using an electronic projection. Replay the CD if necessary.

### Answers

Note that the kind of numbers and their predicted size depend on the students, but here are some ideas for the kind and actual sizes of the numbers in the extracts:

See table on following page.

Theme 4: Listening  173

| lecture | kind | size in extract |
|---|---|---|
| Global warming: the effect on sea level | degrees Celsius, dates, cm, mm | in last century: temp = <1 degree °C sea level = 10–20 cm during 21st C: 3 degrees °C sea level = 50 cm |
| Brazil: an introduction | area in million square km? long, lat – degrees | 78.5 m km2 Equator to 30 deg S Long 35 deg W to 75 deg W |
| Mary Ainsworth: life and theories of child development | dates | 1913 b. 1935 BA 1936 MA 1939 PhD 1960 famous exp. |
| The US economy | population, in millions? money, in billions of dollars? change, in percentage; dates | 2008 economy: > $14 trillion pop: > 300 million in 2008 output per person: $50,000 p.a. US = 10th ↑3% p.a. last 10 yrs. |

## Transcript

🔊 4.8

Presenter: 4.8. Exercise D2. Listen to an extract from a lecture. Record the information.

Global warming: the effect on sea level

Lecturer 1: According to researchers, global surface temperature increased by just under one degree Celsius during the last century. During this same period, sea levels rose between 10 and 20 centimetres. It is believed by most scientists that the Earth will continue to get warmer. A recent report suggests that temperatures will probably rise around three degrees Celsius during the 21st century. If global warming happens at this level, sea levels will rise around 50 centimetres by 2100. More than 70 per cent of the world's population live in coastal areas. If sea levels rise one metre, the cities of London, New York and Bangkok will be under sea level.

Presenter: Brazil: an introduction

Lecturer 2: Brazil is a vast country in South America. In fact, it is the fifth largest country in the world. It occupies half of the continent. It stretches from the Equator to latitude 30 degrees south, and from longitude 35 degrees west to 75 degrees west. The total area of the country is over eight and a half million square kilometres.

Presenter: Mary Ainsworth: life and theories of child development

Lecturer 3: One of the most important theories of child development was suggested by a psychologist, Mary Ainsworth. Ainsworth was born in 1913 in Ohio, USA. She earned a BA from the University of Toronto in 1935, an MA in 1936 and a PhD in 1939. She did her famous experiments with children in the 1960s.

Presenter: The US economy

Lecturer 4: The economy of the United States is the largest national economy in the world. It was worth just over $14 trillion in 2008. A trillion is a thousand billion. The US has a large population – just over 300 million in 2008, but the output per person is nearly $50,000 per year. This means the US is in tenth position in the world in this statistic. The US economy has grown by an average of around three per cent per annum for the last ten years.

### Closure

Give out copies of the transcript for Exercise D. Replay the CD with students following the transcript.

### 4.4 Grammar for listening: Replacement subject: *it*

### Objectives

By the end of the lesson, students should be able to:

- recognize the certainty of statements with introductory phrases (*it's* + past participle / adjective);
- recognize the attitude of the speaker with introductory phrases (*it's* + adjective).

### Introduction

Revise some of the information that students learnt about the Sahara and its history from Lesson 4.1 Vocabulary for listening and Lesson 4.2 Real-time listening.

### Methodology note

It may be worth noting that the degrees of certainty given are only a guide and very much depend on, among other things, the intonation of the speaker.

### Grammar box 19

Students' books closed. Choose one of the statements from the tables and write it on the board: *There was once water in the Sahara.*

Ask students how certain the statement is (100%). Show how by putting phrases in front of the

statement, we can make it sound less certain, e.g.,
*It's possible that there was once water in the Sahara.*

Elicit other ways to make the statement less certain:
- *Maybe ...*
- *It's probable that ...*
- *It's not true that ...*
- *I don't think / believe (that) ...*

Now ask students to open their books and go over **Table 1**.

Ask different students to read out a full sentence each from Table 1 (with the introduction), while the rest of the students follow in their books.

Check students understand the meaning of *unlikely*.

Elicit which introductory phrases in the table are 100%, 40–60% or 5–10% certain.

Elicit which introductory phrases use past participles (*known, believed, said*) and which use adjectives (*possible, unlikely*). Point out that it's possible to use the 'opposite' adjectives as well:
*It's **impossible** that ...*
*It's **likely** that ...*

Now students look at **Table 2**. Ask different students to read out a full sentence each from the table. Point out that the introductory phrases here show the attitude or feelings of the speaker.

Tell students that the word *that* in the introductory phrases is unstressed /ðət/ and difficult to hear. However, emphasize how important it is for students to listen for the adjective or past participle in the introductory phrases, as these can change the meaning of a statement. For example, compare the following statement:
- *We can green the whole of the Sahara.* (100% certain)
- *It's unlikely that we can green the whole of the Sahara.* (5–10% certain)

You may wish to play 4.9 and further discuss the importance of speakers' intonation.

## Transcript

4.9

Presenter: 4.9. Lesson 4.4. Grammar for listening: Replacement subject: *it*
Grammar box 4.9.

Table 1.
Voices: It's known that there were tens of thousands of people in the Sahara once.
It's believed that there was once water in the Sahara.
It's said that the people from the Sahara founded Ancient Egypt.
It's possible that the name comes from the word *sagara*.
It's unlikely that we can green the whole of the Sahara.

Presenter: Table 2.
Voices: It's surprising that the Sahara was once green.
It's astonishing that crocodiles and hippopotamuses once lived in southern Libya.
It's obvious that people once lived in these areas.

### A  Understanding certainty

Check students understand the task and go over the example. Set the task and play 4.10. Students complete the table individually, then compare their answers in pairs. Play the CD again, if necessary. Elicit answers.

Ask students what new adjectives or past participles they heard in the introductory phrases on the CD (*certain, expected, accepted*).

Ask students if they found any of the information surprising – for example, that the population of the Earth will reach nine billion by 2050.

### Optional activities

Find out if students can remember any of the information/sentences they heard on the CD. If necessary, write a few prompts on the board.

### Answers

|   | 100% | 40–60% | 5–10% |
|---|------|--------|-------|
| 1 |      | ✓      |       |
| 2 | ✓    |        |       |
| 3 | ✓    |        |       |
| 4 |      | ✓      |       |
| 5 |      |        | ✓     |
| 6 |      | ✓      |       |
| 7 | ✓    |        |       |
| 8 |      |        | ✓     |

## Transcript

4.10

Presenter: 4.10. Exercise A. Listen to some sentences. For each sentence, decide if the statement is 100%, 40–60% or 5–10% certain.
Voices: 1. It's believed that oil will run out in about 100 years.
2. It's certain that the population will reach nine billion by 2050.
3. It's known that the Earth is more than four billion years old.
4. It's likely that global temperatures will continue to rise.
5. It's possible that scientists can reverse global warming.
6. It's expected that fresh water supply will be a big problem in the future.

7. It's accepted nowadays that the Earth goes round the Sun.
8. It's unlikely that we will ever completely solve the problem of aging.

### B  Understanding attitude

Check students understand all the adjectives in the first column of the table. Ask students, in pairs, to discuss some possible matches before listening to the recording. However, point out that there is no 'right' answer because this is the speaker's attitude.

Set the task. Play 🎧 4.11. Students compare their answers in pairs. Elicit answers. Play the CD once more if necessary.

#### Answers

| 1. amazing | 4 | some people believe in ghosts. |
|---|---|---|
| 2. terrible | 2 | malaria kills a million people every year. |
| 3. strange | 8 | many children do not get enough to eat. |
| 4. funny | 5 | footballers get so much money. |
| 5. ridiculous | 7 | people live longer than 50 years ago. |
| 6. incredible | 1 | lightning travels from the ground to the sky. |
| 7. wonderful | 6 | people have walked on the Moon. |
| 8. awful | 3 | we accept so many deaths in road accidents every year. |

### Transcript

🎧 4.11

Presenter: 4.11. Exercise B. Study each statement, then listen to each one. Match the adjective and the statement.

Voices:
1. It's amazing that lightning travels from the ground to the sky.
2. It's terrible that malaria kills a million people every year.
3. It's strange that we accept so many deaths in road accidents every year.
4. It's funny that some people believe in ghosts.
5. It's ridiculous that footballers get so much money.
6. It's incredible that people have walked on the Moon.
7. It's wonderful that people live longer than 50 years ago.
8. It's awful that many children do not get enough to eat.

### C  Consolidation

Check students understand the task. You can elicit ideas from individuals, or students can work in pairs. Finally, students could write down a few of their sentences.

#### Answers

Answers depend on students.

### Closure

Students write down some of their sentences from Exercise C, if they have not already done so.

## 4.5 Applying new listening skills: Greening projects

### Objectives

By the end of the lesson, students should be able to:
- apply vocabulary and sub-skills from the Listening section in order to understand a lecture about greening projects;
- show understanding of knowledge about greening projects.

### Introduction

Elicit the meaning of the word *green* as a verb; *to green* = to make a place green by growing plants, trees, etc.

Revise the information and vocabulary from the lecture in Lesson 4.2 Real-time listening from page 108 of the Course Book. Remind students of the meaning of *vicious circle* and go over Figure 1 in Lesson 4.2 once more.

### A  Activating ideas

Exploit the pictures and elicit where each place is:
- Libya – North Africa
- The Gobi Desert – Mongolia in Northern China
- The UAE – Arabian Gulf

1. Students discuss the question in pairs. Elicit ideas. If students are stuck for ideas, you can offer prompts by asking questions such as:
   - *What sort of climate do they have in each place?*
   - *How much rainfall is there?*
   - *What problems does the dry climate cause?*

Students should at least mention that all three places are hot and dry, and are therefore short of water.

2. Remind students of the meaning of *desertification* and revise the information for the lecture in Lesson 4.2 Real-time listening if you have not already done so. Elicit the name of the figure, *a virtuous circle*. Explain that this is the opposite of a *vicious circle*. Students do not need to learn the word *virtuous*. Also check understanding of the phrase *to reverse the process*.

Set the task – this should be clear as the information in Figure 1 is the reverse of the figure in Lesson 4.2. Elicit answers, preferably using an electronic projection of the completed figure.

### Answers

1. Answers depend on the students, but here are some ideas:
   - using pipelines to carry water
   - planting trees in the desert / irrigation
   - planting trees in the city

2. 

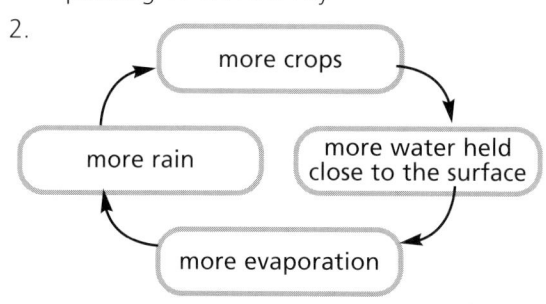

```
        more crops
       ↗         ↘
  more rain    more water held
       ↖         close to the surface
              ↙
        more evaporation
```

Figure 1: *A virtuous circle*

### B  Preparing for a lecture

Set the task and elicit one or two ideas as examples. Check students understand the phrases in the first column of the handout. Students continue discussing ideas in pairs. Elicit ideas but do not confirm or correct at this stage.

### Answers

Answers depend on students.

### C  Following the lecture

Set the task. Play DVD 4.C. Students discuss answers in pairs. Elicit answers, preferably using an electronic projection of the completed handout. Check students are using correctly the abbreviations for measurements in their written answers (they might need help with cubic metres [m³]), and that they also know the full word for each abbreviation.

### Answers

| Great Man-made River Project | |
|---|---|
| 1. Start date | 1984 |
| 2. Length of pipelines | 3,500 km |
| 3. Volume of water per day | 6.5 m. m³ |
| 4. Number of people supplied | 60 m. |
| 5. Extra farmland produced | 1,500 km² |
| **The Gobi Desert Tree Project** | |
| 6. Start date | late 1990s |
| 7. Area of desert | 1.3 m. km² |
| 8. Speed of desertification p.a. | 1,000 km² |
| 9. Area of tree planting | 18 km² |
| 10. Evaporation of surface water p.a. | 3,200 mm |
| **UAE Greening Project** | |
| 11. Start date | late 1980s |
| 12. Number of city parks | 39 |
| 13. Area of city parks | 4 km² |
| 14. Number of trees planted | >1.5 m. |
| 15. Temperature fall (Abu Dhabi) | 2°C |

### Transcript

🔊 4.12  DVD 4.C

**Presenter:** Lesson 4.5. Applying new listening skills: Greening projects

**Lecturer:** We heard in the last lecture how the Sahara became a desert. Can we reverse the process? Can we make the Sahara green again? In this lecture, we are going to hear about some small steps towards greening the Sahara. First, I'll talk briefly about the Sahara in general. Then I'll describe an amazing project from Libya. Next, we'll look at projects in two other desert areas: the first is in northern China, and the other is in the Gulf – in Abu Dhabi state, to be precise. Finally, we'll return to the initial question – can we green the Sahara?

OK. So, the Sahara. It is possible that we can turn the Sahara green – or at least parts of it. The desert itself can help. How? It is clear that the Sahara was once green. We have the evidence of rock paintings, for example. We also have evidence from modern geology. There is water 2,000 metres under the surface. This water fell on the Sahara when it was a huge forest and agricultural area. Science is helping to raise this water to the surface and people are returning to the ancient oases in Egypt and Libya.

But these new wells are only the beginning of the story. It is known that there is a huge amount of water under the desert in Libya. In 1984, the Libyan government announced the start of an amazing project. It is called the Great Man-made River. The idea is simple. A number of pipelines will carry water across the desert. The figures are huge. The pipelines will be 3,500 kilometres long. According to the plans, they will carry 6.5 million cubic metres of water per day. That's enough water for 60 million people. By the end of the project, this water will produce an extra 1,500 square kilometres of agricultural land. That's an area the size of Greece or Bangladesh.

But can we do more. Let's look at desert areas in other parts of the world. Firstly, China. The Gobi desert is one of the largest deserts in the world. It is called in Chinese *han hal* or 'dry sea'. It is mainly a rock desert. The Chinese government started a project there in the late 1990s. It has an extreme range of temperature – from minus 40 degrees centigrade in winter to plus 40 degrees centigrade in summer. It occupies an area of 1.3 million square kilometres. It is said that sand from the Gobi sometimes reaches the capital Beijing, which is 1,000 kilometres to the southeast. The desert is growing at the rate of 1,000 square kilometres per year. Scientists planted 18 square kilometres of fast-growing trees. But the area only receives 100 millimetres of rain each year, and evaporation from surface irrigation is 3,200 millimetres per year. Scientists had to find a better way of supplying water to the plants. So scientists devised an underground irrigation system, which supplies water to the roots of the plants. It is unlikely that the Gobi desert will stop growing in the near future but in many years' time, it is possible.

Secondly, the United Arab Emirates. In the late 1980s, the government started an enormous project of tree planting. Now, in the UAE, huge green belts exist around the main cities. Inside the cities, there are now 39 public parks. They occupy an area of nearly four square kilometres. They have planted more than 1.5 million trees. The result is beautiful. But the greening of the UAE is not just to make the country more beautiful. The green belts also protect the cities from sandstorms. There is an even bigger benefit. It is likely that the trees are also affecting the climate. In Abu Dhabi, it is said that maximum summer temperatures are two degrees centigrade lower. And it is clear that in Al Ain, in the south of the country, the advance of the desert is over.

So can we green the Sahara? It will be a huge project – the biggest project ever on the planet. But if we can learn the lessons from small successes, perhaps we can green the Sahara. It would take over 200 years, but it is amazing that there might be crocodiles and hippos once again in the lakes and rivers of the Sahara rainforest in the distant future. Perhaps the Sahara can be the bread basket of the world in the 23rd century.

## Transcript

4.13

Presenter: 4.13. Exercise C2. Listen and check your answers.

[REPEAT OF SCRIPT FROM 4.12]

## Closure

1. Discuss the information from the lesson:
   - *Is any of the information surprising?*
   - *Are these projects useful / successful / too expensive, in your opinion?*

2. Give out copies of the transcript for Exercise C. Play the DVD once more with students following the transcript.

## D  Understanding certainty

1. Set the task. Students should work out the answers by using their memory of the lecture and/or their common sense. Students discuss the answers in pairs. Do not elicit answers at this stage.

2. Play 4.13 which contains the sentences extracted from the lecture. Elicit answers.

### Answers
certain = b, c and h

# Speaking: Oxygen and carbon

## 4.6 Vocabulary for speaking: O, H, C

### Objectives

By the end of the lesson, students should be able to:

- demonstrate understanding of, and pronounce, target vocabulary from the Speaking section;
- demonstrate understanding of knowledge about:
  - the states of water
  - three of the building blocks of life – oxygen, hydrogen and carbon.

### Introduction

Choose one of the following:

1. If your students are not very scientific, you may like to bring in some items made of carbon (not difficult as all living things contain carbon!). For example, you can bring in sugar, diamonds (they do not have to be real!), a pencil (both the wood and the graphite types contain carbon), any food, a flower or plant, a printer ink cartridge, a visual of a petrol station or a fuel sign, etc.

   Put the items on a desk or table, and elicit what they have in common.

   Explain that carbon is one of the four 'building blocks' of life. Try to elicit the other three: *hydrogen*, *oxygen* and *nitrogen*. Point out that nitrogen is dealt with later in the theme.

2. Elicit the connection between all the pictures: it is water. Water contains two of the 'building blocks of life' – oxygen and hydrogen.

   Exploit the visuals and elicit the following vocabulary: *ice, iceberg, snow, clouds, river, waves, drops, drought, condensation*, etc.

### A Activating ideas

1. Students discuss in pairs. Elicit answer. Check the meaning and the pronunciation of all the words in the box.
2. Set the task. Students work in pairs. Elicit ideas but do not confirm or correct at this point.
3. Play 4.14. Elicit answers. Check understanding of the words *state*, *matter* and *exist* in this context.

### Optional activity

Students restate the information about water, using the words in the box as prompts. Elicit sentence by sentence, either as a whole-class activity or in a more student-centred way with students working in pairs. Faster students may be able to give the whole extract as a talk.

### Answers

1. All the words are connected with water.

2–3.

| liquid | gas | solid |
|---|---|---|
| lake, river, sea, ocean, condensation, rain | clouds, vapour | ice, snow |

### Transcript

4.14

Presenter: 4.14. Lesson 4.6. Vocabulary for speaking: O, H, C. Exercise A3. Listen to part of a lecture. Check your ideas.

Lecturer: So, as I was saying, there are three states of matter on Earth. The three states are solid (like rocks and stones), liquid (like oil or milk) and gas (like oxygen or hydrogen). Now, let's think about water for a moment. Water is very common on Earth but it is a very special thing indeed. Why? Because water is the only substance that can exist in all three states in the natural world. It exists as a gas, in vapour in the clouds. It exists as a liquid, in lakes, rivers, seas and oceans. It also exists as a liquid in condensation, for example, water droplets on a cold mirror in a hot bathroom. Finally, it exists as a solid in ice and snow.

### B Understanding new vocabulary in context (1)

1. If you prefer, students can complete Figure 1 first and then listen to 4.15 to check their ideas. If necessary, give students the first letter of each answer as a prompt. Students complete Figure 1 individually, then compare their answers in pairs. Elicit answers, preferably using an electronic projection of the completed figure.

2. Check students understand the task. Play 4.16. Pause after each definition and elicit the answer from the vocabulary list. Practise the pronunciation of each word and elicit where the stressed syllable is in each case.

   Write each correct answer on the board as you go along. Point out that three of the nouns describing the process end in ~tion: evapo'ration, conden'sation, subli'mation.

Also point out that two nouns look like verbs because they end in ~ing: freezing, melting.

When all the correct answers have been elicited, point to each word on the board and try to elicit the definition. (This is quite difficult, so it is best used for more able classes only.)

3. In this activity, students should try to reproduce Figure 1 from memory. It is best for students to work in pairs because in this way they will also have to pronounce the target vocabulary in context, in order to complete the task.

Monitor. Give feedback, preferably using an electronic projection.

### Answers
1.

( sublimation )

( melting )   ( evaporating )

( freezing )   ( condensation )

**solid      liquid      gas**

Figure 1: *Changing states of water*

2. a. freezing
   b. melting
   c. evaporation
   d. condensation
   e. sublimation

### Transcripts

🔊 4.15

**Presenter:** 4.15. Exercise B1. Listen to the next part of the lecture. Complete Figure 1 with words from the list on the right.

**Lecturer:** So, water can exist as a liquid, as a solid and as a gas. But how can we convert water from one state to another? We can covert liquid water to ice by freezing. Sunlight can convert liquid water to water vapour by evaporation. Melting is the process of converting ice to liquid water. Condensation is the process of converting water vapour to liquid water. This happens on a cold mirror in a hot bathroom, for example. A solid normally changes to a liquid and then to a gas. But water can also change straight from ice to water vapour by the process of sublimation. This happens when the sun shines on ice or snow.

🔊 4.16

**Presenter:** 4.16. Exercise B2. Listen to definitions of key words from Figure 1. Say the word in each case.

**Voice:**
a. It is the process of converting liquid water into a solid.
b. It is the process of converting ice into water.
c. It is the process of converting water into water vapour …
d. The process of converting water vapour into liquid water is called …
e. Water can change straight from ice to water vapour. This process is called …

**Methodology note**

Do not spend too long on Exercise B1 if you have a lot of science students (or students who already have this general knowledge). It is more important for them to hear and use the correct pronunciation of the target words in Exercises B2 and B3. If you prefer, you can start with Exercise B2 (listening to the lecture) and then move on to the other activities.

### C  Understanding new vocabulary in context (2)

1. Students cover the words in the right-hand column and try to guess what some of them are. Then students do the matching activity in pairs. Do not elicit answers at this stage.

2. Play 🔊 4.17. Students check their answers. Refer students to Figure 2, which shows two of the forms of carbon.

3. Elicit answers, checking students' pronunciation as you go along. Finally, tell students to cover the symbols in the table and ask them to try and write them from memory.

### Answers

| 1. O | 7 | sugar |
| --- | --- | --- |
| 2. C | 1 | oxygen |
| 3. H | 5 | carbon dioxide |
| 4. $H_2O$ | 6 | petrol |
| 5. $CO_2$ | 3 | hydrogen |
| 6. $C_8H_{18}$ | 4 | water |
| 7. $C_6H_{12}O_6$ | 2 | carbon |

180  Theme 4: Speaking

## Transcript

🔊 4.17

Presenter: 4.17. Exercise C2. Listen to the next part of the lecture and check your answers.

Lecturer: OK. We've talked about water, which is, of course, vital to life. In fact, water contains two of the four building blocks of life. The chemical formula for water is $H_2O$, which means it contains hydrogen and oxygen. Carbon is the third building block. It has the chemical symbol C. Carbon takes many forms, including coal, and diamond. If carbon and hydrogen are combined in a particular way, they make petrol. If carbon and hydrogen and oxygen are combined in a particular way, they make sugar. Petrol, water and sugar. Three very different substances, but all made from three of the building blocks of life.

### D  Using new vocabulary

Students ask and answer the questions in pairs. Monitor and give help where necessary, especially with pronunciation.

Elicit ideas but do not give extra answers yourself if students do not come up with them (as in some cases these points are taught later in the theme). Practise the pronunciation of the target vocabulary.

#### Answers

In some cases, answers depend on the students (possible answers given):

| | |
|---|---|
| 1. What produces oxygen? What consumes it? | plants produce oxygen during photosynthesis; animals consume oxygen during breathing |
| 2. What produces $CO_2$? What consumes it? | the converse of #1 |
| 3. Where is most of the $H_2O$ in the world? Where is the rest? | in the oceans; the rest is in the atmosphere, in the ground, and in animals and plants |
| 4. How were fuels like petrol and coal made millions of years ago? | from dead plants and animals being compressed under the ground |
| 5. What are these fuels called? Why? | fossil fuels – because they are as old as fossils of animals and plants |
| 6. What living things make sugar from carbon dioxide and sunlight? | plants – see answers for #1 and 2 above |

### Closure

Play all three lecture extracts again for students to hear as a complete lecture. Give out copies of the transcript so that students can follow it while they listen to the recordings.

## 4.7  Real-time speaking: The oxygen cycle

### Objectives

By the end of the lesson, students should be able to:
- use existing skills to explain a process from the oxygen cycle;
- demonstrate understanding of knowledge about the oxygen cycle.

### Introduction

As this is quite a long lesson, use Exercise A for the introduction.

### A  Reviewing vocabulary

1. Elicit the part of speech for each word. Set the task. Students complete the activity individually, then compare their answers in pairs. Elicit answers and practise pronunciation. Point out the change of vowel sound for the stressed syllables in these related verbs and nouns (from /uː/ to /ʌ/):
   produce, production
   consume, consumption

2. Students complete the task individually. Elicit answers. Point out that we usually stress the preposition in phrasal verbs.

#### Answers

| | |
|---|---|
| pro'duction | con'sumption |
| pro'duce | con'sume |
| give 'out | take 'in |
| re'lease | ab'sorb |

### Methodology note

If your students did Level 1 of *Progressive Skills in English*, you might like to spend a few minutes revising the water cycle at this point.

Theme 4: Speaking   181

## B Activating ideas

Remind students of the meaning of the word *cycle* in this context (a repeated series of events, often with a circular nature – so the cycle never ends).

Ask students to study the assignment extract and elicit the meaning of *scientific term*.

Find out how much, if anything, students know about the oxygen cycle. They may know a little about the process of photosynthesis.

### Answers
Answers depend on students.

## C Understanding a model

Exploit the diagram without pre-empting the talk on the DVD too much. If possible, establish the following points:
- *the diagram is in two halves – production and consumption*
- *vocabulary – sun, sunlight / sunshine, shine, atmosphere*

Pronounce the words in the diagram for the students to hear.

Explain that the words in the diagram are *scientific terms*; these will be explained in the talk.

Set the task and play [DVD] 4.D. Elicit answers, preferably using an electronic projection. If students do not find one or more of the answers, play the relevant section of the DVD again.

Discuss any other aspects of the DVD that may be useful. For example:
- *In what ways did the student on the DVD refer to the diagram?*
- *What gestures or other types of emphasis did the student use?*

### Optional activities

Spend a few more minutes exploiting the DVD. For example:
- true / false statements about the processes;
- explain one of the processes, students give you the scientific term.

### Answers
The three mistakes the student makes are:
- 'There are *four* main production processes for oxygen' – should be *three*
- 'This process is called *breathing* ' – should be *respiration*
- '*Carbon dioxide* is required for the process' – should be *oxygen*

## Transcript

🔊 4.18  [DVD] 4.D

**Presenter:** Lesson 4.7. Real-time speaking.

**Student:** Today, I'm going to talk about one of the natural cycles on Earth. It is called the *oxygen cycle*. First, I'll tell you about oxygen on Earth. Then I'll talk about the production processes in the oxygen cycle. Finally, I'll describe the consumption processes of the cycle.

Firstly, where is oxygen stored on Earth? The Earth's oxygen is stored in three places. Most of the oxygen is buried in the ground, but some of it is in the atmosphere, and the rest is in the bodies of living things. The most important oxygen, of course, is the gas in the atmosphere.

There are four main production processes for oxygen. The first process is called photosynthesis. In this process, sunlight shines on the leaves of a plant, and the plant uses the light energy. It converts it into sugar and oxygen. The sugar feeds the plant, and the oxygen is released into the atmosphere.

Oxygen is also produced from water vapour in the atmosphere. Sunlight shines on the vapour and oxygen is released into the atmosphere. This process is called photolysis.

Finally, oxygen is released by rainfall on mountains and rocks. This is called weathering.

There are also three main consumption processes for oxygen. Oxygen is consumed from the atmosphere by animals and plants. This process is called breathing. Oxygen is taken in, and carbon dioxide given out.

Oxygen is also consumed from the atmosphere during decomposition. This is the process of breaking down dead animals and plants. Animals and plants die, and bacteria decompose them. Carbon dioxide is required for the process.

Finally, oxygen is required for combustion to take place. Combustion is also called *burning*, and requires oxygen, heat and a fuel of some kind.

So, to sum up ... Some of the oxygen in the atmosphere comes from photosynthesis, some comes from photolysis and some from weathering. Some of the oxygen in the atmosphere is consumed by respiration, some is consumed by decomposition and some by combustion.

### Methodology note

There are several different ways of exploiting Exercise D4. For example, you could divide the class into groups of three. Half of the groups work on the production part of the cycle, the other half work on the consumption part. Each student will work on one process as follows:

- Production groups
  S1 – photolysis
  S2 – photosynthesis
  S3 – weathering

- Consumption groups
  S1 – respiration
  S2 – combustion
  S3 – decomposition

Show DVD 4.D again and ask students to focus on their relevant section of the talk. Do this before students start to make notes for their section of the cycle.

Finally, combine the 'production' and 'consumption' groups into larger groups of six students. In their groups of six, students give the complete talk.

If this is too complicated, then try this alternative: prepare two 'opposite' processes with the class, for example *weathering* and *decomposition*. Then divide the class into pairs. Student 1 explains the *weathering* process, whereas Student 2 explains the *decomposition* process. If there is time, repeat this with another pair of 'opposite' processes.

## D  Practising a model

1. If possible, use an electronic projection to show the extract on the board. Elicit and then highlight the answers for the three points.

2. Remind students about sense groups (see Lesson 1.6 Vocabulary for speaking in Theme 1 on page 17 of the Course Book). Do an example with the class. Students complete the task individually, then compare their answers in pairs. Elicit answers.

3. Drill the sentences from the extract. Students then cover the extract and work in pairs to say the sentences again from memory. If necessary, put prompts on the board.

4. Select one of the other processes, for example, *weathering*. If you wish, you can play the relevant section of the DVD again. Elicit some sentences about the appropriate process and drill them. Write prompts on the board. In pairs, students then practise giving the talk. Monitor and give feedback.

Repeat with one or more of the other remaining processes, or students can attempt the whole talk.

See also the Methodology note above for other ways to exploit this activity.

**Less able classes:** Photocopy and cut up sections of the transcript (as for 'jigsaw' reading). Give different sections to different students. Students divide their sentences into sense groups and practise saying their section. Give help where necessary. Divide the class into groups, with one student for each section, if possible. Students take it in turns to present their section to the other students in their group, so that together they produce the complete talk. Encourage students to try to look up from their piece of paper as much as possible. (If students can learn their section by heart in the time available, so much the better.)

## Answers

1–2. Process is underlined; scientific term is highlighted ; explanation is in *italics*; sense groups with /.

<u>Oxygen is produced by green plants</u>. / *Sunlight shines / on the leaves / of a plant, / and the plant converts the light energy / into sugar / and oxygen.* / This process is called  photosynthesis . / *The sugar feeds the plant / and the oxygen is released / into the atmosphere.*

## Closure

Give out copies of the transcript if you have not already done so. Play the DVD one last time if you wish.

### Everyday English: Making arrangements

**Objectives**

By the end of the lesson, students should be able to:

- use appropriate language to make arrangements in different situations.

**Introduction**

Write the title of the lesson on the board, *Making arrangements*, and elicit the meaning.

Point out the collocation of *make* + *arrangements*. We usually use the word *arrangements* in the plural. Elicit the verb form *arrange*.

### A  Activating ideas

Exploit the visuals. Ask:
*Why are they good meeting places?* (easy to find, etc.)
*What are other good meeting places in this university / town?*

Focus on the exercise. Give students a minute or two to discuss the questions in pairs. Elicit answers.

**Answers**

Answers depend on the students, but here are some ideas:

1. friends, tutor, other students, girl/boyfriend, family members, colleagues
2. time, place, exchange mobile phone numbers, possibly decide on activity, e.g., which film to watch, etc.

### B  Studying the models

1. This is a new type of activity so it might need more careful setting up. Explain to the class that they will hear six conversations about making arrangements to meet. They should listen to the conversations and decide who the people are, and where they are arranging to meet. Make sure the conversations in the students' Course Books are covered.

   Play 4.19. Pause after each conversation. Give students a minute to discuss ideas, then elicit answers. Students' answers may vary; accept anything reasonable.

2. Students uncover the conversations. Set the task. Students complete the activity individually, then compare their answers in pairs. Play 4.20 so that students can hear the conversations one more time and check their ideas. Give feedback, preferably using an electronic projection of the completed conversations.

   Check students understand any new vocabulary and phrases, including:

- *I can't make it.*
- *I won't (be late).*
- *available*
- *look forward to +~ing*

There are a number of language points you could focus on and highlight, including:

- prepositions
- times
- phrases using the infinitive with *to*; *free* + *to do something*, *come* + *to do something*, *need to do*
- key phrases for making arrangements:
  *Are you free ...*
  *Shall we meet ...?*
  *Where are we meeting?*
  *I'll meet you at ...*

**Answers**

1. 1. A = student, B = lecturer, meeting place = tutorial room / staff room / lecture or class room
   2. A = student, B = student, meeting place = library
   3. A = student, B = receptionist, meeting place = fees office / reception
   4. A = student / friend, B = student / friend, meeting place = clock tower
   5. A = landlord, B = student / tenant, meeting place = main entrance
   6. A = student / flatmate, B = student/ flatmate, meeting place = main entrance

2. 1. see
      giving
   2. to do
      make
      meet
   3. give
      to make
   4. see
      meet
      'll
      won't
   5. would
      meet
      meeting
   6. to see
      meeting
      see

## Transcripts

🔊 4.19

**Presenter:** 4.19. Everyday English: Making arrangements. Exercise B1. Listen and choose possible people and meeting places from the boxes above.

One.
**Voice A:** I'd like to ask you something about the assignment.
**Voice B:** Sure. Can you come and see me this afternoon?
**Voice A:** Yes. What time is best?
**Voice B:** I'm giving a lecture until 2.30. I'm free after that.

**Presenter:** Two.
**Voice A:** Are you free to do some research today?
**Voice B:** No I can't make it. I'm busy all day.
**Voice A:** What day is good for you?
**Voice B:** Can we meet tomorrow in the library?

**Presenter:** Three.
**Voice A:** Can someone here give me some advice about fees?
**Voice B:** Yes. You need to make an appointment. What about tomorrow, 9.30?
**Voice A:** Yes, that's fine.

**Presenter:** Four.
**Voice A:** I'll see you on Monday evening about seven then.
**Voice B:** Yes. Shall we meet at the clock tower in town?
**Voice A:** Great! I'll be there. And don't be late!
**Voice B:** I won't.

**Presenter:** Five.
**Voice A:** I can show you the flat tomorrow, if you like.
**Voice B:** Yes, that would be great. What time?
**Voice A:** I'll meet you at the main entrance at 10 o'clock.
**Voice B:** Right. Look forward to meeting you then.

**Presenter:** Six.
**Voice A:** Are you coming to see this flat tomorrow?
**Voice B:** Yes, of course. Where are we meeting the landlord?
**Voice A:** At the main entrance at 10.
**Voice B:** OK. I'll see you there just before 10.

🔊 4.20

**Presenter:** 4.20. Exercise B2. Listen again and complete the conversations with verbs from the box below. You can use a verb more than once.
[REPEAT OF SCRIPT FROM 🔊 4.19]

**C** Practising the model

Choose some sentences or phrases for choral and individual drilling.

1. Set the task. Elicit examples for the first set of words in italics in Conversation 1:
   *I'd like to ask you something about ... the assignment / the lecture / the tutorial / my talk.*
   Students work in pairs. Monitor and give feedback.

2. Go over the example given. Elicit some sentences for a conversation based on the scenario.

Elicit further ideas for new situations. For example:
*Meeting another student for a coffee after the lecture.*
*Meeting the manager of a café / bar / shop about a possible part-time job.*
*Arranging to meet a friend to play squash / tennis or go to the gym.*

Monitor and give help where necessary. Give feedback.

## Closure

Choose one of the following:

1. Ask students to write down one or two of their conversations from Exercise C (C1 or C2).

2. Explain that meet can have different meanings. Write these sentences on the board and ask students to discuss in pairs the different meanings:
   - *We arranged to **meet** in front of the cinema.* (be at the same place)
   - *I haven't **met** my science tutor yet.* (see somebody for the first time)
   - *It's nice to **meet** you.* (when meeting someone for the first time)
   - *My father will **meet** me at the airport.* (when you arrive somewhere)
   - *The Drama club **meets** once a week.* (group is together at same place and time)

### 4.8 Learning new speaking skills: Specialist terms

**Objectives**

By the end of the lesson, students should be able to:
- pronounce the schwa sound in unstressed syllables;
- produce common intonation patterns in sentences;
- explain specialist terms in a talk.

## Introduction

Use Exercise A as the introduction.

Theme 4: Speaking 185

## A Reviewing vowel sounds

1. Refer students to the words in each row. Briefly revise the meanings of two or three of them. Check students' pronunciation. Play 🎧 4.21. Students discuss the question in pairs. Elicit ideas but do not confirm or correct at this stage.

2. Refer students to Pronunciation Check 1. Revise the meaning of *stressed* and *unstressed syllables*.

Give students time to read the Pronunciation Check. Read out the example words in the tables, and/or play 🎧 4.22.

Write some more words on the board and ask students to tell you where the schwa sound is in each:

en*e*rgy
ox*y*gen
hydr*o*gen
carb*o*n
nat*u*ral
pr*o*duction
c*o*nsumpti*o*n
vap*ou*r

### Answers
All the words contain the schwa sound.

## Transcripts

🎧 4.21

Presenter: 4.21. Lesson 4.8. Learning new speaking skills: Specialist terms. Exercise A1. Listen. What do the words in each row have in common?
Voice:
a. animals, natural, amount
b. release, weathering, required
c. combustion, convert, consume

🎧 4.22

Presenter: 4.22. Pronunciation Check 1
Voice: sugar, water, atmosphere, supply ocean, precipitation, vapour

## B Reviewing intonation

1. Students discuss in pairs but make sure they realize the focus here is *intonation*. Elicit ideas but do not confirm or correct just yet.

2. Refer students to Pronunciation Check 2. Ask one or two students to read out the information, with the rest of the class following in their books. Emphasize that using full stops and commas in the correct places (when writing a talk, for example) will help with using common intonation patterns.

Say the two example sentences, with the correct intonation, for the class to hear. Play 🎧 4.23, if you wish. Highlight the present simple verb forms used, and the fact that *is released* is a passive verb. Drill the two sentences.

3. Refer students back to the sentences in Exercise B1. Ask one or two students to read them out. Highlight the verb forms used once again; in this case, they are all present simple passive forms. Drill the sentences.

### Answers

The process is called respiration. Oxygen is taken in, and carbon dioxide is given out.

### Transcript

🎧 4.23

Presenter: 4.23. Pronunciation Check 2
Voice: Sunlight shines on the leaves, and the plant uses the light energy.
The sugar feeds the plant, and the oxygen is released.

## C Identifying a new skill

1. Revise the meaning of the word *term* in this context. Ask students to study the Skills Check box. Read the first example aloud with students following in their books. Point out that the explanation is given **after** the term in this example. Write the example on the board, or use an electronic projection. Highlight the verb forms used (present simple). Elicit the correct intonation patterns required (see Pronunciation Check 2), and play 🎧 4.24 if you wish. Draw arrows to show the intonation. Drill the first example sentence. Students then practise the example sentence in pairs. Monitor and give help where necessary.

Repeat the procedure with the second example sentence given in the Skills Check, but this time point out that the explanation is given **before** the term is used.

2. Set the task. Elicit the answers for the first part of the task. If you want, you can give students a few minutes to mark up the sentences for intonation patterns (and the schwa sound if you wish). In pairs, students take it in turns to give each explanation. If possible, the explanations should be given

without reading the sentences aloud – write prompts on the board instead. Monitor and give feedback.

### Answers

Target words in *italics*:

> Oxygen is consumed from the atmosphere by animals and plants. This process is called *respiration*.

> Oxygen is also consumed from the atmosphere during *decomposition*. This is the process of breaking down dead animals and plants.

> Finally, oxygen is required for *combustion* to take place. *Combustion* is also called burning.

### Transcript

🔊 4.24

**Presenter:** 4.24. Skills Check. Examples:
**Voice:** The first process is called photosynthesis.
In this process, sunlight shines on the leaves of a plant, and the plant uses the light energy.
Sunlight shines on the vapour, and oxygen is released into the atmosphere.
This process is called photolysis.

### Methodology note

There are several different ways this activity can be exploited other than the one given in the Course Book. For example, students can work on the definitions in Exercise D2 in groups and help each other to make notes. Then the class can be re-divided into pairs for Exercise D3.

Another alternative is this: give the definitions out and ask students to learn them for homework. Students can explain the definitions to each other in the next lesson.

Finally, if you prefer, you could replace the words and definitions with your own set of examples.

### D Practising a new skill

1. Briefly revise one or two points about each topic: *learning*, *apologizing* and *time management* (covered in the three previous themes). Pronounce the six specialist terms for the students to hear. Explain that students do not have to learn these words. Students, in pairs, quickly ask each other if they know any of the words.

2. Check students understand the task and set carefully. Note that these terms are not about *processes*, so the explanations have slightly different patterns from the ones in the earlier exercises.

   Go around the class and give help where necessary while students are reading the definitions. Students should make notes for each explanation. (See also the Methodology note above.)

3. Remind students to use the appropriate intonation. Monitor while students are giving the explanations. Give feedback.

### Closure

Give feedback on Exercise D if you have not already done so.

## 4.9 Grammar for speaking: Avoiding repetition

### Objectives

By the end of the lesson, students should be able to:
- use ellipsis (omit items) in repeated structures;
- use *some* as the subject of target structures.

### Introduction

Elicit any information students have learnt about oxygen so far in this section.

### Grammar box 18

Explain that the sentences in **Table 1** are about the element oxygen. They are from the lecture they listened to in Lesson 4.6 Vocabulary for speaking.

Theme 4: Speaking 187

Read the example sentences from the table aloud with the students following in their books. Elicit the name of the tenses used for the verbs *is stored* and *is buried* (present simple passive tense).
Ask students to read the explanation under the table. Offer further help with understanding by referring back to the example sentences.

Remind students about the intonation patterns they learnt about in Lesson 4.8 Learning new speaking skills. Drill the example sentences and check students are using the correct intonation. Play 4.25, if you wish.

Write prompts for each sentence on the board. With the table covered (or with the books closed), students practise the sentences in pairs.

Ask students to study **Table 2** and the information. Read out the three example sentences in full, to show how repeating words is unnecessary and boring. Now say the sentences with the words omitted for comparison.

Drill the target sentences and phrases, and give further practice as for Table 1 above.

### Transcript

4.25

**Presenter:** 4.25. Grammar box 18.

Table 1.
**Voice:** The Earth's oxygen is stored in three places.

Most of the oxygen is buried in the ground … but some of it is in the atmosphere, and the rest is in the bodies of living things.

**Presenter:** Table 2.
**Voice:** Some of the oxygen in the atmosphere comes from photosynthesis. Some comes from photolysis, and some from weathering.

### A  Using *some* as subject (1)

Ask students to read the rubrics. Teach *water storage*.

Give students a minute or two to study the four figures. Elicit answers to the three questions. Drill some of the sentences for the answers. Students practise the questions and answers in pairs. Monitor and give feedback.

#### Optional activities

1. Students prepare a talk about water storage on Earth (see model answer below). Students give the talk in small groups.

2. Students write down the answers to the questions and/or write out the talk in full.

### Answers

Answers depend on the students, but here are some suggestions:

| | |
|---|---|
| 1. Most of the water on Earth is salt water in the oceans. What is the rest of the water? | The rest of the water is fresh water |
| 2. Where is most of the fresh water on Earth? | Most of the fresh water on Earth is in the ground. Some of it is in ice and snow. |
| 3. Where is the surface fresh water on Earth? Where is the other fresh water on Earth? | Most of the surface fresh water on Earth is in lakes. Some of it is on the soil surface and some in swamps and rivers. Most of the other fresh water on Earth is in the atmosphere. A small amount is in animals and plants. |

### Possible talk (if you decide to do this):

Ninety-seven per cent of the water on Earth is stored in the oceans. This is salt water. But there is also a small amount of fresh water on Earth. Some of it is stored in ice and snow, and some in the ground. Less than one per cent of the Earth's water is on the surface. Some fresh water is in lakes and rivers, and some of it is in swamps. A very small amount is not in the oceans, or on the surface. Some of it is in the atmosphere, and some in animals and plants.

### B  Using *some* as subject (2)

1. Check students understand the information and the word *renewable*. Remind students of the meaning of the phrase *fossil fuels*. Ask two or three questions to check understanding:
   *What do the three figures show?* (world energy usage)
   *What does the first figure show?* (the usage of fossil fuels)
   *Which type of fuel is used the most?* (fossil fuel)

2. Set the task. Elicit a few sentences as examples. Drill the sentences. Remind students to use the correct intonation, as well as the correct forms.

   Divide the class into groups of three. Students prepare together a talk about the usage of fossil fuels. They should make notes. Number the students 1–3 in their

188  Theme 4: Speaking

groups. Student 1s explain the information in Figure 1, Student 2s give the information for Figure 2, and so on. Then students can repeat the talk, but change the figure they talk about. Monitor and give feedback.

### Answers
Model answer:

*Eighty five per cent of the energy usage in the world comes from fossil fuels. Some of the energy comes from oil, some of it from coal and some from gas. 'Old' renewables provide 13 per cent of the energy. Some of it is from nuclear power, some from wood and biomass and the rest from hydro. Two per cent of energy comes from 'new' renewables. Half of it is from solar power, some from wind power and the rest from geothermal.*

### Closure
Students write out their talk in full for the figures in Exercise B.

## 4.10 Applying new speaking skills: The carbon cycle

### Objectives
By the end of the lesson, students should be able to:
- work collaboratively to produce a talk using researched information about the oxygen cycle;
- use target vocabulary, sub-skills and language patterns from the Speaking section with accuracy and fluency.

### Introduction
Revise the oxygen cycle with the class.

Revise the symbols and formulas for the elements and compounds from Lesson 4.6 Vocabulary for speaking on page 113 of the Course Book. For example, carbon dioxide = $CO_2$.

### A Reviewing vocabulary

1–2. Set Exercises A1 and A2 together. Students discuss in pairs. Do not elicit answers at this point.

3. Play 4.26. Elicit answers. Practise pronunciation and elicit the stressed syllables on each word from the box:
'breathing
'chimneys
ex'haust gas
'jet
'leaves
bac'teria
vol'cano
'fossils

### Answers
1.

| exhaust gas | breathing | bacteria | chimneys |
|---|---|---|---|
| leaves | volcano | jet | fossils |

2. The picture with fossils is the odd one out. All the others produce/release $CO_2$. Fossil layers contain carbon.

### Transcript
4.26

Presenter: 4.26. Lesson 4.10. Applying new speaking skills: The carbon cycle. Exercise A3. Listen and check your answers.

Lecturer: Last week, we looked at the oxygen cycle. This week, the carbon cycle. In some ways, the carbon cycle is the opposite of the oxygen cycle. Many things produce oxygen. Those same things often consume carbon, often in the form of $CO_2$. Many things consume oxygen. Those same things often produce $CO_2$. Burning fossil fuels consumes oxygen and produces $CO_2$. So there is $CO_2$ in exhaust gas from cars and from jet planes, and in smoke from chimneys. There is also $CO_2$ in the gas from volcanoes. There is $CO_2$ in the gas from breathing. Finally, $CO_2$ is released when things die. After death, bacteria produce $CO_2$ as they destroy the bodies of living things. Some is absorbed by the leaves of plants during photosynthesis and some is absorbed by the surface of the oceans.

### B Researching information

1. Discuss the assignment. Explain that the carbon cycle is the reverse of the oxygen cycle. Elicit any ideas that students might already have about the cycle. Reassure them that they will have plenty of help if they do not have many ideas at the moment.

2. Explain to students that the information about carbon will help with their talk.

Students discuss the question in pairs. Students may be very surprised at the huge amount of carbon that is stored in rocks. Elicit ideas. Make sure students use language and patterns from Lesson 4.9 Grammar for speaking, e.g.,
*Most carbon is stored in rocks.*
*Some / a little is stored in plants.*

3. Students study the resources on page 174 of the Course Book. Ask students to only study the diagram at this point and to discuss the meaning of the terms in pairs. Pronounce the words in the diagram and get students to repeat them. Make sure that they can stress the words correctly:
respi'ration
out'gassing
com'bustion
decompo'sition
photo'synthesis
ab'sorption
com'pression

Reassure them it does not matter if they do not know many of these terms at this point. Elicit ideas but do not confirm or correct any of them yet.

Now students read the information below the diagram on page 174 to check their ideas. Pronounce the new scientific terms for the students to hear and get them to repeat each one. Remind students about the schwa sound (see Lesson 4.8 Learning new speaking skills).

Ask some questions to check understanding:
*What's the scientific word for 'breathing'?* (respiration)
*What happens when animals and plants die?* (carbon dioxide is released / produced)

### Answers

2. Model answer:

Most of the carbon on Earth is stored in rocks. Some carbon is stored in the oceans, some of it is in the atmosphere, some is in the soil, some in the atmosphere and some in plants.

### Subject note

Plants 'breathe' the same as people and other animals do, i.e., oxygen in, $CO_2$ out. During the day, though, they also photosynthesize so the net effect of a plant is to add oxygen to the atmosphere.

### Methodology note

The activities have deliberately been left fairly open here in order to encourage learner independence. In their groups, students should decide how to organize the talk. For example, who is going to give each piece of information for the talk and in which order.

If you have a very fast class, you could ask students to work in pairs or small groups. Each student should give the complete talk.

If students wish, they can also add information from their own knowledge.

### C Preparing a talk

1. Students should work in groups to give the complete talk, with each student preparing to speak for one or more sections. Give suggestions to each group about how they can organize themselves, if necessary. Make sure all students are participating.

2. Remind students that it is better not to read complete sentences aloud. Elicit one or two ideas for notes or PowerPoint slides, then leave students to continue on their own. Monitor and give help where necessary.

3. Explain that the information as given is only the essential facts. The talk needs 'signposts' and so on to guide the listener. Monitor while students consider where to add 'signposts'.

4–5. Elicit some possible sentences for an introduction and conclusion (see model answer below).

Students then continue in groups and decide which student is going to give the introduction and conclusion.

### Answers

Model answer with introduction, conclusion and linkage: see next table.

| |
|---|
| Today, I'm going to talk about one of the natural cycles on Earth. It is called the carbon cycle. First, I'll tell you about carbon on Earth. Then I'll talk about the production processes in the carbon cycle. Finally, I'll describe the consumption processes of the cycle. |
| Firstly, where is carbon stored on Earth? The Earth's carbon is stored in four places. Most of the carbon is dissolved in the oceans, but some of it is in the atmosphere, some is in fossil fuels deep underground, and the rest is in the bodies of living things. |
| There are also four main production processes for carbon. Carbon is released into the atmosphere by animals and plants. This process is called respiration. Carbon dioxide is given out and oxygen is taken in. |
| Carbon dioxide is also released into the atmosphere during decomposition. This is the process of breaking down dead animals and plants. Animals and plants die, and bacteria decompose them. Carbon dioxide is released into the atmosphere and carbon is absorbed into the ground. |
| Thirdly, carbon dioxide is released during combustion. Combustion is also called burning. |
| Finally, carbon dioxide is released into the atmosphere by a process called outgassing. This happens when gas escapes from a volcano, for example. |
| So to sum up. Some of the carbon in the atmosphere comes from photosynthesis, some comes from decomposition, some from combustion and some from outgassing. |
| There are two main consumption processes for carbon dioxide in the atmosphere. The first process is called photosynthesis. In this process, sunlight shines on the leaves of a plant, and the plant uses the light energy. It converts it into sugar and oxygen. During the process, carbon dioxide is consumed from the atmosphere. |
| Carbon dioxide is also dissolved in the oceans in a process called absorption. Carbon dioxide is absorbed at the surface and carried down to the deep ocean. |
| So to sum up. Some of the carbon dioxide in the atmosphere is produced by respiration, some is produced by decomposition, some by combustion and some by outgassing. Some of the carbon dioxide in the atmosphere is consumed by photosynthesis and some is dissolved in the oceans by absorption. |

2. Each group presents their talk to the class. They can refer to slides and diagrams if they wish. The rest of the class should listen to each talk, and compare differences and similarities with their own talk.

**Closure**

1. Give feedback on the talks.

2. Give out copies of the model talk for students to study.

**D**  Rehearsing and giving a talk

1. Remind students about intonation patterns and the schwa sound, both from Lesson 4.8 Learning new speaking skills. Drill some sentences from the talk if you wish. Students work in twos or threes within their groups, and practise saying their section of the talk. Monitor and give help where necessary.

# Reading: Chains, webs and pyramids

## 4.11 Vocabulary for reading: Climate areas

### Objectives

By the end of the lesson, students should be able to:
- recognize and understand target vocabulary from the Writing section;
- show understanding of information about climate areas.

### Methodology note

The introductory activity is about recognizing more formal or scientific versions of everyday words. It is at the base of the whole of this theme but comes particularly into focus here with work on encyclopedia entries.

### Introduction

Set the task suggested here and go over the example (see below). Students then continue in pairs. If necessary, they can look back at the previous sections of this theme.

Write the following words on the board:

| absorb | ~~air~~ | ~~atmosphere~~ | breathing |
| break down | burning | change | combustion |
| convert | decompose | give out | release |
| respiration | surface | take in | top |

Tell students to find pairs of words, e.g., *air + atmosphere*.

Elicit answers, writing the pairs of words in two lists as shown in Answers below – the order of words is not important but informal/vague words must be on the left. When students have given you all the pairs, ask them to explain the way you have listed them in the table on the board. Finally, add the headings as shown in Answers. Point out that the specific word is more likely in an academic text.

Test the students by giving one word from each pair and eliciting the other.

### Answers

| general | specific |
|---|---|
| breathing | respiration |
| burning | combustion |
| break down | decompose |
| take in | absorb |
| change | convert |
| top | surface |
| *air* | *atmosphere* |
| give out | release |

### A  Understanding world maps

Write the title of the lesson on the board, *Climate areas*. Discuss the difference in meaning between the two words *climate* and *weather* (*climate* = typical *weather* in a region or area).

Exploit the visual. Ideally, display the map, point at areas and ask questions to see how much information students can give you. Try to elicit names of continents, oceans and large countries.

1. Set for individual work and pairwork checking. Give feedback.

2–4. Set for pairwork. Give feedback orally.

### Answers

1. See map on next page.
2. They indicate climate areas, e.g., white = polar
3–4. Answers depend on students.

### B  Understanding new words in context

Make sure students understand the exercise. Go over the example. Set for individual work and pairwork checking. Give feedback orally. Get students to close their books and tell you the description for each climate area. Give prompts as necessary.

Figure 1: *World climate areas (worldclimate.com)*

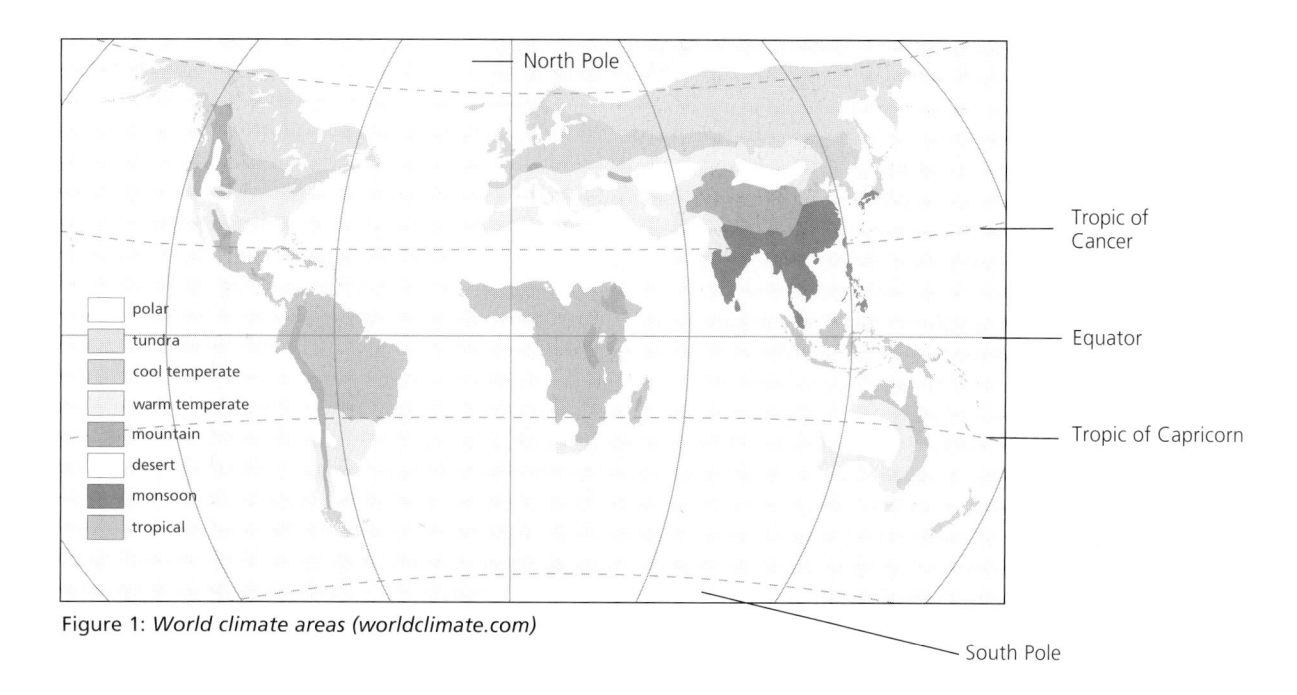

### Answers

| | |
|---|---|
| desert | An area with less than 25 cm of rain a year. These areas have hot days and cold nights. |
| polar | An area near the North Pole or the South Pole with a maximum temperature of 10°C. |
| temperate | An area with generally mild summers and mild winters but there can be extremes of temperature. These areas are divided into cool and warm. |
| tropical | An area normally between latitude 10 degrees north and 20 degrees south of the Equator. These climates have an average temperature around 25°C and at least 150 cm of rain a year. |
| tundra | An area near the North Pole with no trees. The area under the surface of the earth is permanently frozen. |
| monsoon | A tropical area with very high rainfall in the summer season. |
| mountain | An area of very high land with cold winters and mild summers. |

**C** Developing critical thinking

Set task for small groups. Give help, making sure that students can find the approximate position of their country on the small-scale map. Give feedback orally. Encourage students to disagree with the climate descriptions if you sense that they want to. The map shows very broad divisions and individual areas, including whole countries, may not fit the broad classification.

### Answers

Answers depend on students.

### Closure

While students are doing Exercise C, write on the board the beginnings of words from this lesson. Get students to identify the following words at speed:
*cli* (mate)
*des* (ert)
*fro* (zen)
*max* (imum)
*mon* (soon)
*mou* (ntain)
*pol* (ar)
*sea* (son)
*sum* (mer)
*sur* (face)
*tem* (perate / perature)
*tro* (pical)
*tun* (dra)

Alternatively, use flashcards of these words. When you are asking students to identify them, only expose the first three letters.

### 4.12 Real-time reading: Chains and webs

#### Objectives

By the end of the lesson, students should be able to:
- use existing skills to deal with an encyclopedia text with internal links;
- demonstrate understanding of knowledge about food chains and webs.

**Introduction**

Use Exercise A as the introduction.

#### A  Activating ideas

Students discuss the questions in pairs. Elicit ideas. Discuss the meaning of some phrases, or ask students to use dictionaries to find more phrases and meanings, such as:

- *a **chain** of events / thoughts – hotel / supermarket **chain***
- *the two ideas were **linked** – weakest **link** – road / rail / telephone / computer **links***
- *a **web** of lies – the **web** (computer network)*

**Answers**

1. A chain and a spider's web.
2. There are a couple of links in the first photo, there are hundreds in the second.
3. The words have different meanings in everyday English but we often use them to talk about joining ideas, events, etc.

#### B  Understanding text organization

Briefly discuss encyclopedias:
*Do students ever use them?*
*In English? In their own language?*
*In book form? Online?*
*How are they organized?*
*What are they for?*

Check students understand the task. Students complete the activity individually, then compare their answers in pairs. Elicit answers.

**Answers**

1. Alphabetically.
2. In a science encyclopedia or a specialist dictionary.
3. It means there is more information about this item in the book.

#### Methodology note

1. Exercise C focuses on only reading a text's relevant sections and ignoring any irrelevant information. The idea that it is not necessary to read every word on a page may be new to students and it may take them some time to get used to. In this lesson – which introduces the idea – the sections which are to be read are highlighted.

   At some point during the activity, make sure students realize that they have been working with only some of the text on the page – make the point that this is how they should always do research, by only reading the relevant information.

2. The meanings of the words *ecology*, *environment* and *ecosystem* are often used interchangeably and with a good deal of overlapping in both everyday and academic contexts. In the 'encyclopedia extract' we have defined the words very carefully in order to avoid confusion and for the purposes of the lesson. In particular, we have used the subject-specific definition of *an environment*, as opposed to the general usage of *the environment* = everything on our planet.

#### C  Preparing to read

Ask students if they would like to study Biological Sciences. What topics do they think this subject is likely to cover? (ecology of forests, conservation, landscape, marine ecology, etc.)

Students read the information about the lecture. Students may already 'know' the word *environment*.

Elicit ideas for the difference between the two words *environment* and *ecosystem* but do not confirm or correct at this stage.

Set the task for writing research questions. Remind students about research questions if necessary. Students complete the task individually. Elicit possible questions and write them on the board.

**Answers**

Possible research questions are:
- What is ecology?
- What is the difference between an environment and an ecosystem?
- What are some of the relationships between living things?

> **Methodology note**
>
> You can set all three questions at the same time and deal with them all together at the end. This approach may be better for faster classes. Alternatively, set each question and then elicit answers one at a time. This may be better for less able classes. In both cases, when you give feedback to the class, use an electronic projection of the encyclopedia extract and the figures.
>
> Students do not need to learn the names of all the different animals in these exercises, unless they wish to.

### D Understanding the text

1–3. See Methodology note above.

**Answers**

1. Assuming students are answering the research questions from Exercise C above.)
   - What is ecology?
     *The study of the relationship between living things and their environment.*
   - What is the difference between an environment and an ecosystem?
     *An ecosystem means all the plants and animals in an area, and their relationships. An environment is a place with a particular climate and landscape.*
   - What are some of the relationships between living things?
     *Food chains and webs.*
2. Figure 1 = A food chain.
   Figure 2 = A food web.
3. Answers depend on the students but here are some ideas:
   *Dogs eat / kill zebras.*
   *Giraffes eat leaves.*
   *Impalas, wildebeest and zebras eat grass.*

### E Understanding vocabulary in context

Set the task. Students complete the activity individually, then compare their answers in pairs. Elicit answers.

**Answers**

| 1. convert | change from one state to another |
| 2. survive | continue to live, not die |
| 3. transfer | move from one place to another |
| 4. support | help, assist, enable to exist |
| 5. destroy | damage so repair is not possible |
| 6. remove | take away |

### F Developing critical thinking

1. Set the task. Students work in pairs. Elicit answers, preferably using an electronic projection.
2. Check students understand all the vocabulary in the questions. Students discuss in pairs or small groups. Elicit ideas.

**Answers**

1. 

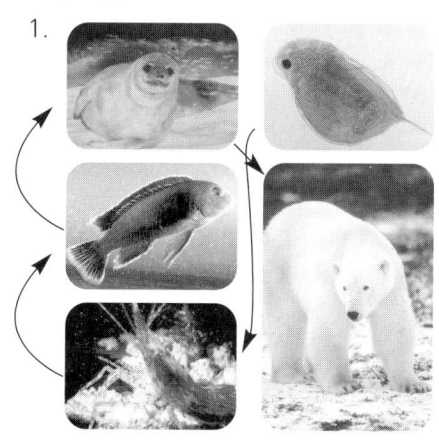

2. Answers depend on the students, but here are some ideas:
   - If fishermen catch all the fish: larger animals (seals, bears, etc.) will suffer; on the other hand, the number of prawns will rise and the amount of plankton will decline, etc.
   - If sealers kill all the seals: there will not be enough food for bears; too many fish.
   - If the ocean water becomes too warm: plankton will die and the whole chain will break down.

### Closure

Ask a few follow-up questions about the information in the highlighted sections of the text.

Ask students if they feel the research they have done in the lesson would help them with the lecture in Exercise C.

### 4.13 Learning new reading skills: Doing research with encyclopedias

**Objectives**

By the end of the lesson, students should be able to:
- practise micro-skills for dealing with encyclopedia entries.

**Introduction**

Review the information from the previous lesson about webs and chains.

### A  Reviewing vocabulary

Set the task. Students complete the activity individually, then compare their answers in pairs. Ask students to check their answers against the encyclopedia extracts in the previous lesson. When students have finished, briefly elicit answers.

**Optional activity**

Students write a sentence for each phrase. Alternatively, this could be set as a homework activity.

**Answers**

| 1. depend | on |
| 2. be involved | in |
| 3. come | from |
| 4. convert | into |
| 5. transfer | from ... to |
| 6. be part | of |
| 7. learn | from (about also possible) |
| 8. the relationship | between |
| 9. the connection | between |
| 10. the effect | of |

### B  Identifying a new skill

Focus students' attention on the Skills Check. Ask different students to read out each section, with the rest of the class following. Check students' understanding of the vocabulary and information in each entry. At the end of each section, discuss the information and ask why it is important.

Students discuss the true / false statements in pairs. Elicit answers.

**Answers**

| 1. Some useful encyclopedias are on the Internet. | T |
| 2. Research questions give you a purpose for reading. | T |
| 3. You need to read a complete entry in an encyclopedia to understand it properly. | F |
| 4. Links in an online encyclopedia are usually in red type. | F |
| 5. It is easy to lose your way in an encyclopedia. | T |
| 6. The Back button does not work with an online encyclopedia. | F |

### C  Practising a new skill

Check students understand the task. Go over the example. Remind students that they must also include the entries of any *linked* entries! Students complete the table individually, then compare their answers in pairs. Elicit answers.

**Answers**

| research questions | links |
| --- | --- |
| 1. What is a flow-through system? | energy, food chain |
| 2. What is food value? | nutrition |
| 3. What is an endangered animal or plant? | extinct, extant, ecosystem, climate, desert |
| 4. What is Gaia? | James Lovelock, environment |
| 5. What is emigration in ecology? | organism, ecosystem, climate, desert |

### D  Understanding a text

Students complete the task individually, making notes of the answers as they go along. Elicit answers, preferably using an electronic projection.

**Answers**

See the encyclopedia entries in Lesson 4.12 Real-time reading.

**Closure**
Tell students which vocabulary from the lesson they should learn.

## 4.14 Grammar for reading: Adding information with *which* / *that*

**Objectives**

By the end of the lesson, students should be able to:
- use general nouns to understand sentences in a text;
- use sentences with *which* to predict information.

**Introduction**
Ask students to study the tables in **Grammar box 21** for one minute. Meanwhile draw a blank **Table 1** – with only the correct headings inserted – on the board (or use an electronic projection). Tell students to close their books and try to elicit the three sentences from them. Use the headings of each column to give prompts and elicit answers from the students.

**A** Understanding the general noun

This exercise demonstrates the central importance of the general noun when trying to understand sentences like the ones presented here. If students can understand the general noun before *which*, it will make it easier for them to understand the extra information after *which*.

Set the task – you could set a time limit for this activity. Students complete the activity individually, then compare their answers in pairs. Elicit answers.

Highlight the verb in each part of each sentence. They are all in the present simple tense. Also highlight the fact that each general noun is preceded by *a* or *an*.

**Optional activity**

Ask students to recall either the complete sentences or sections from each one. For example, ask students to cover the last column of the table (the one with phrases with *which*). Then elicit the correct phrase for each sentence – either from the whole class, or from students working in pairs.

Make sure the correct tense is used and that all general nouns are preceded by *a/an*.

Answers
See table below.

**B** Predicting extra information after *which*

Check students understand the task and go over the example. Students complete the activity in pairs. It does not matter if they cannot complete many of the sentences; it is more important that students start trying to predict the text and at least think of some possibilities.

After a few minutes, if students are struggling, write some prompts on the board. Elicit answers.

| 1. Learning by doing is | *a theory* | which was proposed by Aristotle. |
| 2. Condensation is | *a process* | which converts water vapour into water. |
| 3. A jungle is | *an area* | which has a large number of tropical trees. |
| 4. Carbon dioxide is | *a gas* | which prevents heat energy from escaping into Space. |
| 5. A tram is | *a vehicle* | which runs along grooves in the road. |
| 6. A mammal is | *an animal* | which gives birth to live young. |
| 7. A decomposer is | *a plant* | which breaks down dead animals or plants into chemicals. |
| 8. Media studies is | *a subject* | which looks at the mass media, like television and the Internet. |
| 9. A nitrate is | *a chemical* | which helps plants to grow. |
| 10. A generator is | *a machine* | which makes electricity. |

> **Optional activities**

1. Highlight the verbs in the phrases for completion and elicit which are *active* and which are *passive*.
2. Show the sentences for completion in a jumbled order – see Model answers below – and get students to match them.

### Answers
Model answers:

| | |
|---|---|
| 1. An extinct plant is a plant which | does not exist on Earth any more. |
| 2. An endangered animal is an animal which | is close to becoming extinct. |
| 3. A food web is a number of food chains which | are linked. |
| 4. A desert is an area which | has very low rainfall. |
| 5. Short-term memory is the part of your brain | which remembers information for a few seconds. |
| 6. A prompt in a test is something which | helps a student to remember information. |
| 7. Transactional Analysis is an idea which | was developed by Eric Berne. |
| 8. *I'm OK, You're OK* is a book which | was written by Thomas Harris. |
| 9. Evaporation is a process which | converts water into water vapour. |
| 10. The Great Man-made River is a project which | is bringing water from the Sahara to cities in Libya. |

Jumbled sentence endings for optional activity:

| |
|---|
| are linked. |
| converts water into water vapour. |
| does not exist on Earth any more. |
| has very low rainfall. |
| helps a student to remember information. |
| is bringing water from the Sahara to cities in Libya. |
| is close to becoming extinct. |
| was developed by Eric Berne. |
| was written by Thomas Harris. |
| which remembers information for a few seconds. |

### C  Identifying *which* in context

Set for individual work and pairwork checking. Give feedback, ideally using an electronic projection.

### Answers
Marked up text: see box on next page.

### Closure

Revise some vocabulary. Write the following pairs of words and phrases on the board and ask students to explain the differences between them:
- extinct – endangered
- evaporation – condensation
- a tram – a train
- a jungle – a desert
- short-term memory – long-term memory
- a food web – a food chain
- a theory – an idea

## 4.15 Applying new reading skills: Producers and consumers

> **Objectives**
>
> By the end of the lesson, students should be able to:
> - use new skills to select relevant information from an encyclopedia extract;
> - demonstrate understanding of information about food pyramids and their impact on the environment.

### Introduction
Use Exercise A as the introduction.

### A  Reviewing vocabulary

Remind students about sentences with *which* (see Lesson 4.14 Grammar for reading). This activity contains more examples of sentences with *which*.

Set the task. Students complete the activity individually, then compare their answers in pairs. If students find the task difficult, provide them with the first letter of each word. Or you

| | |
|---|---|
| ecology | The study of the relationship between living things and their ⇒**environment**. We learn from ecology that livings things depend on each other to survive. This is because all living things are involved in ⇒**food chains** and ⇒**food webs**. |
| ecosystem | All the animals and plants which live in a particular area, and the relationship between them. An ecosystem supports the animals and plants but a change in the ⇒**environment** may destroy an ecosystem, e.g., the advance of a ⇒**desert** may destroy a grassland. People can change or destroy an ecosystem as well, e.g., by building towns in green areas. |
| emigration | Movement of an ⇒**organism** from one location to another, often as a result of a change in the ⇒**ecosystem**. |
| endangered | An animal or plant which is close to becoming ⇒**extinct**. |
| energy | The power which enables us to do work. All energy comes from the Sun in the first place. Some plants convert the Sun's energy into chemical energy. They are the first link in every ⇒**food chain**. |
| environment (an) | A place which has a particular ⇒**climate** and landscape. There are a number of major environments on Earth, e.g., ⇒**desert**, the ⇒**tropics**. |
| extant | An animal or plant which is still alive and ⇒**reproducing**. All species currently alive on earth are extant (opposite: ⇒**extinct**). |
| extinct | An animal or plant which is no longer living on Earth (opposite: ⇒**extant**). Species often become extinct because of changes in the ⇒**ecosystem**. |
| flow-through system | A system with an input and an output of ⇒**energy**. For example, a ⇒**food chain** is a flow-through system with some of the energy consumed by the animal at every stage. |
| food chain | This is the way in which ⇒**energy** is transferred from one living thing to another. At the top of every food chain, there is an animal which eats other animals. At the bottom of every food chain, there is a plant which can convert the Sun's ⇒**energy** into food. If we remove one part of a food chain, there will be a reaction in another part of the chain. |
| food value | The relative amount of ⇒**nutrition** which is obtained from a particular food. |
| food web | This is a connection of two or more ⇒**food chains**. It shows relationships between the animals and plants in a certain ⇒**ecosystem**. Most animals and plants are part of a food web with 10, 20 or 30 other living things. This means it is very difficult in real life to predict the effect of a change in one part of the web. |
| Gaia | This is an idea which was put forward by ⇒**James Lovelock**. It suggests that all living things are part of one mass which can change its ⇒**environment** to ensure its survival. This is not necessarily good news for human beings. Gaia might change the Earth in a way that makes it unfit for humans. |

could write the answers on the board in the wrong order so that students can do a matching activity.

Answers

| 1. food chain | the way in which energy is transferred from one living thing to another |
| --- | --- |
| 2. food value | the amount of nutrition which is obtained from a particular food |
| 3. extinct | an animal or plant which no longer exists on the Earth |
| 4. environment | the place which a group of animals and plants live in |
| 5. food web | a system which contains a number of food chains |
| 6. extant | an animal or plant which still lives on the Earth |
| 7. endangered | an animal or plant which is becoming extinct |
| 8. ecosystem | an area which has a particular climate |

### B Activating ideas

Exploit the visual (without pre-empting later activities) and elicit the names of the animals.

Students read the text about the diagram.

Set the tasks. Elicit answers, preferably using an electronic projection of the completed diagram.

Briefly discuss what would happen to this ecosystem if there was no rain for a long period of time.

Tell students they will find out more about this ecosystem later on in the lesson.

Answers

See Exercise D for a fully completed diagram.

**Methodology note**

You might wish to point out that *produce* and *consume* were used in the Speaking section of this theme for the production and consumption of oxygen and carbon dioxide.

### C Preparing to read

Students read the lecture notice. Check the meaning of *classifying*. In pairs, students discuss possible research questions and write them down. Elicit ideas.

Answers

Research questions:
What are 'producers'?
What are 'consumers'?

### D Understanding a text

1. Remind students that they should not read every piece of information. They should only select the relevant extracts and follow their links. Students complete the task individually. Elicit answers, preferably using an electronic projection.

2. Elicit the answer and write it on the board.

3. Students complete the task individually, then compare their answers. Elicit answers, preferably using an electronic projection.

Answers

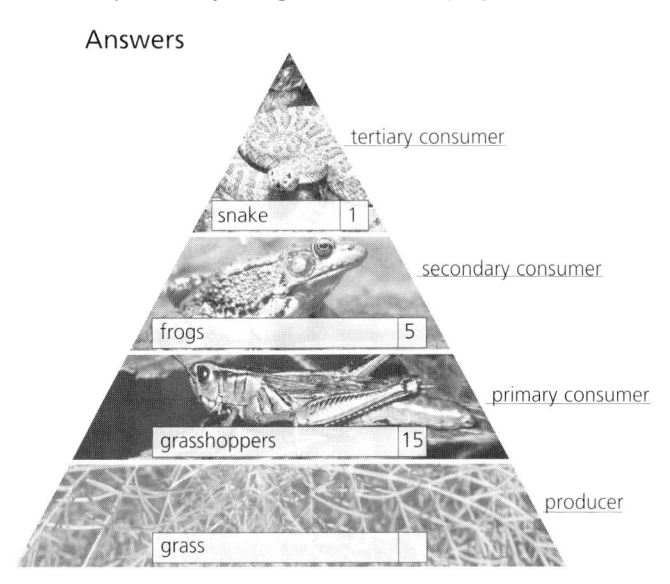

Food pyramid:
- tertiary consumer: snake — 1
- secondary consumer: frogs — 5
- primary consumer: grasshoppers — 15
- producer: grass

Figure 1: A food pyramid

200 Theme 4: Reading

> Optional activity

Ask some True / False questions about the information students have researched.

| | |
|---|---|
| Producers eat consumers. | F (false – other way round) |
| Consumers sometimes eat consumers. | T |
| All energy on earth comes from the Sun. | T (actually not 100 per cent but nearly!) |
| Consumers convert solar energy into food. | F (producers convert) |
| Ninety per cent of the energy in an animal is transferred to the next level. | F (10 per cent) |
| There are three levels of consumer. | T |
| There are more creatures at the bottom of a food pyramid than at the top. | T |
| Producers use photosynthesis. | T |
| Photosynthesis converts sugar into oxygen and carbon dioxide. | F (solar energy into sugar, oxygen and carbon dioxide) |
| Giraffes are herbivores. | T |
| Carnivores cannot get energy from plants. | T |

### E Remembering key words

Go over the example. Elicit sentences for the remaining words and write them on the board. Do not allow students to write anything down at this point. When all the sentences have been elicited, erase them from the board.

Ask students to write down the sentences.

#### Answers

Some possible answers are:

*A consumer* is an animal which eats a producer or another animal.
*A producer* is an animal which produces energy from sunlight.
*A carnivore* is an animal which eats other animals.
*A herbivore* is an animal which eats plants.
*An omnivore* is an animal which eats animals or plants.
*A food pyramid* is a diagram which shows the energy needed to keep a particular animal alive.
*Photosynthesis* is a process which converts solar energy into sugar, oxygen and carbon dioxide.

### F Developing critical thinking

Students discuss in pairs. Elicit ideas – see Answers below.
To summarize: we should at least start reducing our consumption of meat, fish and dairy products.

#### Answers

Some possible answers are:

- The UN says eating less meat reduces global warming.
- The Vegetarian Society says eating less meat and dairy:
  – reduces environmental impact, greenhouse gases;
  – conserves water, preserves ecosystems.
- Other points:
  – meat needs three times as many resources as a vegetarian diet;
  – very difficult to feed rising world population using existing factory farming methods.

### Closure

The debate on vegetarianism in Exercise F should lead to some interesting points being raised. These can be summarized for the Closure activity.

### Knowledge quiz: Natural cycles and processes

#### Objectives

By the end of the lesson, students will have:
- reviewed core knowledge from Theme 4 so far;
- recycled the vocabulary from Theme 4 so far.

#### Methodology note

See notes in the Introduction (page 16) for further ideas on how to do the exercises. As usual, the focus should be on the content rather than using the correct grammar.

### Introduction

Tell students they are going to do a knowledge and vocabulary quiz on Theme 4. If you like, while you are waiting for everyone in the class to arrive, students can spend a few minutes looking back over the theme.

**A** Desertification

Put students into groups. Give help to each group, then get all groups to present either A1 and A2, or A3 and A4, to each other.

If the students find it difficult to draw the second diagram, start them off with *more crops*.

### Answers

Desertification

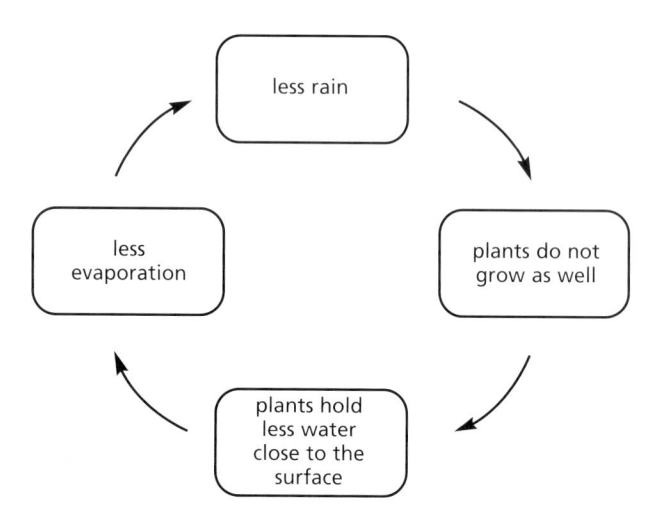

```
     less rain
    ↗        ↘
less         plants do not
evaporation  grow as well
    ↖        ↙
    plants hold
    less water
    close to the
    surface
```

Greening

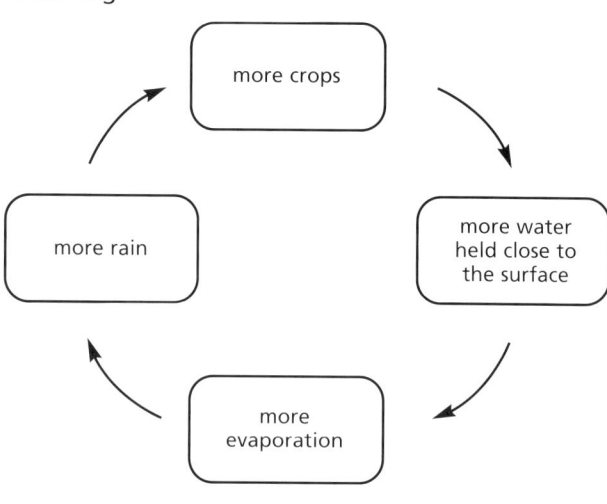

```
     more crops
    ↗         ↘
more rain    more water
             held close to
             the surface
    ↖         ↙
     more
     evaporation
```

**B** Greening projects

Set the task for pairwork. Elicit answers, preferably using an electronic projection of the completed table.

Divide the students into small groups, getting each group to describe one of the three projects. Monitor and assist each group, then get the groups to give talks to each other.

|  |  | Great Man-made River | Gobi Desert Tree | UAE Greening |
|---|---|---|---|---|
| a. | area of tree planting | 18 k² |  | ✓ |  |
| b. | evaporation of surface water p.a. | 3,200 mm |  | ✓ |  |
| c. | extra farmland produced | 1.5 k² | ✓ |  |  |
| d. | length of pipelines | 3,500 k | ✓ |  |  |
| e. | number of city parks | 39 |  |  | ✓ |
| f. | speed of desertification p.a. | 1,000 k² |  | ✓ |  |
| g. | temperature fall | 2°C |  |  | ✓ |
| h. | volume of water per day | 6.5 m. m³ | ✓ |  |  |

### C States of water

1. Set for individual work and pairwork checking. Give feedback, building up the diagram on the board.
2. Divide the students into small groups as before.

Answers

( sublimation )

( melting )   ( evaporating )

( freezing )      ( condensation )

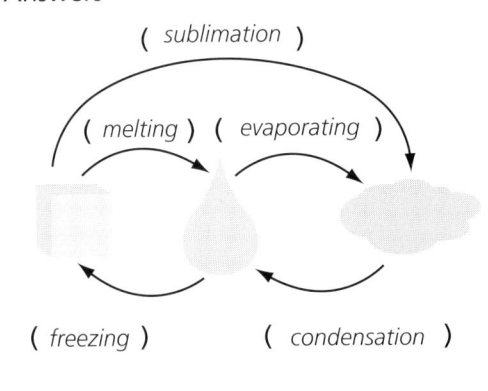

**solid    liquid       gas**

Figure 1: *Changing states of water*

### D Food chains

With a more able class, set the task for individual work. Then put the students into small groups and get each student to give a short talk to the other students in their group.

With a less able class, put the students into small groups from the beginning and then get the groups to give talks to each other.

Answers

Answers depend on students.

## Closure

Tell students to learn the information or vocabulary for any of the answers they got wrong in class.

# Writing: Energy and the oceans

## 4.16 Vocabulary for writing: Processes in nature

### Objectives

By the end of the lesson, students should be able to:
- demonstrate understanding of some of the target vocabulary from the theme;
- produce written sentences and short descriptions using target vocabulary from the theme.

### Introduction

As students are coming in the classroom, write the following words on the board, with the vowels missing. Get students to copy the words from the board and ask them to put in the correct vowels.

1. drought
2. atmosphere
3. condensation
4. photosynthesis
5. release
6. substance
7. survive
8. tropical
9. environment
10. chemical

Write the title of the section on the board, *Energy and the oceans*, and elicit the meaning of the word *cycle* (a series of events which form a process ending in the same state as it began, and repeating itself endlessly). Elicit some examples of natural cycles:
- the water cycle
- the oxygen cycle
- the carbon cycle
- the changing of the seasons

### A Building vocabulary

1. Check that students understand the task and go over the example. Remind students that the dictionary extracts contain:
   - the part of speech
   - a definition
   - an example sentence written in italics and including a tilde ( ~ ) to represent where the target word should go
   - in addition, students' dictionaries will probably also give the pronunciation

   Students work individually, then compare their answers in pairs. Elicit answers. For less able groups, you may wish to write the first letter of each word/phrase on the board to help students.

2. Check students understand the task. Point out that they should write different sentences from the ones already given. Students complete the activity individually. Monitor and assist as necessary.

### Extra activity

Students' books closed. Say one of the words/phrases from the exercise. Students must give you the definition, beginning with *It means …* This can also be done in pairs – one student with the book open, the other with the book closed.

### Answers

See table below.

| a. greenhouse | (n) building made almost completely of glass and used to grow plants<br>*In cold countries, people sometimes grow vegetables in a ~ .* |
|---|---|
| b. evaporate | (v) change from a liquid into a gas<br>*At sea level, water ~s at 100°C.* |
| c. effect | (n) result of one thing acting on another<br>*Exercise and a healthy diet have a positive ~ on university grades.* |
| d. soil | organic matter on the earth's surface; plants grow in it<br>*Different plants need different kinds of ~ to grow well.* |
| e. bacteria | (n pl) very simple living organisms<br>*Scientists often grow ~ in dishes in the laboratory.* |
| f. compound | (n) combination of two or more things, esp. chemicals<br>*Water is a ~ of hydrogen and oxygen: $H_2O$.* |
| g. dissolve | (v) combine a solid with a liquid so that the solid disappears<br>*Salt and sugar both ~ easily in water* |
| h. radiation | (n) energy in the form of waves or particles which travel out from a body<br>*X-rays, light and radio waves are all types of ~.* |

## Answers
Answers depend on students.

> **Methodology note**
>
> Students will need a dictionary for this exercise. It is up to you whether you insist on monolingual English dictionaries, but at this level, it is certainly preferable. Students should get a good English-English dictionary as soon as they can.

### B  Using new vocabulary

Elicit one or two ideas about each of the pictures. Go through the first text as a model. Show how students need to add their own words – and even their own ideas – to complete the text.

Set the remaining pictures for individual work. Point out that students can use any of the words from the vocabulary list. Allow the use of dictionaries. Monitor and assist as necessary.

### Answers
Model answers (there are also other ways to express ideas for each process):

1. *A small amount of organic material is put in a dish called a Petri dish. In the dish, there is a jelly which contains nutrients. The dish is left for a period of time. Bacteria begin to grow. When there is a large amount of bacteria, scientists analyze it to find out about the organic material.*
2. *A seed falls to the ground. The seed takes nutrients and water from the soil. The seed germinates and pushes leaves to the surface. The leaves open in the sunlight and the plants grow.*
3. *Some medicine is designed to dissolve in water. The medicine is manufactured in the form of a tablet. When the tablet is dropped into a glass of water, it fizzes and dissolves. The medicine is released into the water. When the patient drinks the water, the medicine is absorbed into the body.*
4. *Solar radiation comes into a greenhouse through the glass roof and walls. It heats the air, plants and soil. The special glass traps some of the heat. The air in the greenhouse is heated so that tropical plants can grow in a temperate climate.*

## Closure

1. Ask students to exchange the descriptions they wrote in Exercise B. They should read them silently for interest and then compare/comment on them orally in pairs. **Note**: Do not ask students to read aloud.
2. Review some of the spellings from the lesson. Ask volunteers to write words on the board with either a correct or incorrect spelling. The class must say whether the spelling is right or wrong in each case.

## 4.17 Real-time writing: The energy cycle

### Objectives

By the end of the lesson, students will have:
- gained knowledge of the Earth's energy cycle;
- corrected the register of a written text using formal language;
- been exposed to a Description essay type;
- interpreted labelled diagrams describing a process.

### Introduction
Exploit the photos. Find out how much students know about the way in which the Sun's energy affects the Earth, and about global warming. (Supply the term *climate change* if students need help.)

> **Methodology note**
>
> In English there are often pairs of verbs – one of which is a single, Latinate word and the other a two- or three-part word of Germanic origin – whose meanings are similar. Typically, the main difference between the two is that the Latinate verb is higher register – that is, more 'formal'.

Theme 4: Writing  205

### A  Previewing vocabulary

Elicit some examples of two- or three-part verbs. With a more able group, ask students which is more formal: *enter* or *go in*; *turn round* or *revolve*; *come down* or *descend*, etc.

Set the task for individual work and pairwork checking. Give feedback using an electronic projection.

### Answers

| 1. | get | 5 | insulate |
|---|---|---|---|
| 2. | get to | 7 | prevent |
| 3. | send back (light) | 6 | escape |
| 4. | take in | 1 | obtain |
| 5. | keep in | 3 | reflect |
| 6. | get out | 8 | remove |
| 7. | stop | 4 | absorb |
| 8. | take out | 2 | reach |
| 9. | let out | 10 | return |
| 10. | go back | 9 | release |

### B  Gathering information

1. Go through the list of options with the class. Give students time to read the assignment silently and mark one of the options. They can then compare their ideas in pairs or small groups. Elicit the correct answer.
2. Tell students to cover the text on page 129 of the Course Book. Elicit one or two ideas, then put students into pairs or small groups to discuss. Encourage them to use the verbs from Exercise A. Do not ask students to write down their ideas at this stage.

Give feedback to the class as a whole. Elicit ideas from volunteers.

### Answers

1. The assignment asks for a Description essay.
2. Answers depend on students. Below are some suggestions.

Figure 1: The energy cycle
*Energy comes from the Sun. It is called solar radiation. Some of the Sun's energy does not reach the Earth. During the day, clouds create shading. They reflect solar radiation back into space. Some of the radiation that reaches the Earth is reflected back too, by snow, ice and water. Some is absorbed by buildings. During the night, some energy is released into the atmosphere.*

Figure 2: Global warming
*Solar radiation reaches the Earth. Some is reflected, and some is absorbed. Then it is released. However, water vapour and carbon dioxide in the atmosphere create insulation, so the energy cannot escape. It is trapped near the Earth's surface.*

### Methodology note

The second task in this exercise requires students to replace informal language with appropriate academic English, including passive verb structures and technical vocabulary. Choosing the correct register, both in writing and in speaking, is very important. Make sure that students understand this, and that good writing is not only a question of syntactic accuracy.

### C  Noticing the discourse structure

1. Set the questions for pairwork discussion. Give feedback orally.
2. Remind students of the issue of register – formal and informal language – in Exercise A. Go through the example with the class. Point out the use of technical vocabulary (*obtain*) and of the passive verb form (*is obtained*) – these are both important features of academic writing. Make sure that all the students understand the task. Do a further example with the class if you wish.

Set the task for individual work. Monitor and assist as necessary.

Elicit answers, ideally using an electronic projection of the text.

### Answers

Model answer (target sentences in *italics*):

### The energy cycle

### 1. Introduction

[1] ~~We get nearly all* of our energy from the Sun's radiation.~~ *Nearly all of our energy is obtained from the Sun's radiation.* *It comes in*

the form of heat energy. ² ~~The Earth sends back some of this energy into space.~~ *Some of this energy is reflected back into space by the Earth.*

## 2. Absorption and reflection
When heat energy reaches the Earth's surface, some of it is absorbed by the land.

³ ~~Buildings also take in a lot of energy.~~ *A lot of energy is also absorbed by buildings.* This is why cities are often much hotter than the countryside in summer. ⁴ ~~At night, the land and buildings let this heat out again.~~ *At night, this heat is released by the land and buildings.*

⁵ ~~Bodies of water, such as seas and lakes, send back some of the heat.~~ *Some of the heat is reflected by bodies of water, such as seas and lakes.* Snow is also a good reflector of heat energy (Fig. 1).

## 3. Clouds
Some types of cloud are like white sunshades. They reflect heat energy from the Sun back into space. ⁶ ~~These clouds stop the energy from getting to the surface.~~ *The energy is prevented from reaching the surface by these clouds.* For this reason it is usually cooler on an overcast day. At the same time, other types of cloud act like an overcoat. ⁷ ~~These clouds trap the hot air near the surface of the planet.~~ *The planet is insulated by these clouds.* (Fig. 1). It is cooler if there is no cloud cover overnight, because there is no 'overcoat', and so more of the trapped heat can escape.

## 4. The greenhouse effect
Insulating clouds allow energy through to the Earth but do not allow it to escape again, so the insulating clouds operate like the glass in a greenhouse (Fig. 2). ⁸ ~~Most scientists believe that gases in the air, such as carbon dioxide, cause the greenhouse effect.~~ *Most scientists believe that the greenhouse effect is caused mainly by gases in the air, such as carbon dioxide* (see Hansen et al., 2007). However, some scientists think that the amount of water vapour in clouds is the most important cause (Latham et al., 2008).

## 5. Global warming
The greenhouse effect makes clouds thinner, so more heat gets through to the Earth. ⁹ ~~The effect also removes some of the water vapour.~~ *Water vapour is also removed by the effect.* As the atmosphere becomes drier, less heat is reflected back into space. If this happens, the surface temperature rises. The result is global warming.

*A tiny amount of energy comes from chemosynthesis under the oceans.

### Methodology note
When working on Exercise D2, stress to students that it is not important for them to remember the text word for word; only that they include the important ideas and that the language they use in their writing is academic, i.e., it uses passive verb forms and technical language.

### D  Writing the essay

1. Give students time to reread the first section of the text silently. Then ask pairs of students to decide what the main point is. Emphasize that they should use their own words – they do not need to repeat a sentence from the text. Elicit the answer and write it on the board.

If you wish, do the same for the second section as a further example. Then set the task for individual work and pairwork checking. Students, in pairs, will need to negotiate with each other until they agree on the main point. When eliciting answers, again get students to agree before they can write down the main idea for each section.

2. Elicit the first section using the notes you wrote on the board for Exercise D1. Put the answer on the board, preferably using an electronic projection. If you wish, do the same for the second section as a further example.

Set the task for individual work. Remind students to refer to the diagrams in the Course Book and to the notes for Exercise D1 on the board. Monitor and assist as necessary. Make a note of common errors. As feedback, students can read each other's work and decide whether the language used is appropriately academic.

### Answers
Answers depend on the students, but below are some suggestions:

Section 1: Almost all of our energy is from the Sun.
Section 2: Some energy is absorbed and released at night; some is reflected.
Section 3: Clouds reflect some heat; they also trap some heat.
Section 4: Carbon dioxide and water vapour cause the greenhouse effect.

Section 5: The greenhouse effect causes global warming.

### E  Critical thinking

Elicit one or two ideas, then set the task for small-group discussion. Give feedback orally.

**Answers**

Answers depend on the students, but some possibilities are:
- reduce $CO_2$ emissions from industry;
- reduce $CO_2$ emissions from traffic on the roads, seas and in the air;
- increase the area of plants and trees, which absorb $CO_2$, on the Earth's surface;
- develop ways to clean the atmosphere of $CO_2$.

**Closure**

1. Give feedback on the writing errors you noted while monitoring in Exercise D2.
2. Hold a brief class discussion on the measures that are being taken in the students' own country(ies) to deal with global warming.

## 4.18 Learning new writing skills: The Description essay

**Objectives**

By the end of the lesson, students should be able to:
- identify and plan four different discourse structures for academic writing;
- use notes and labels on diagrams to write paragraphs describing processes.

**Introduction**

Use Exercise A as the introduction.

### A  Reviewing vocabulary

1. Elicit the first match as an example. Set the task. Students work individually, then compare their answers in pairs. Elicit answers and display them on the board using an electronic projection.
2. Highlight the fact that there is not a noun for all of the verbs. Allow dictionaries if you wish. With less able students, you could tell them that there are two verbs that have no noun form.

Elicit answers onto the board.

**Note**: Students may suggest the verb-noun pair *allow-allowance*. Point out that, although *allowance* is a noun, it has a different meaning from the verb (*allowance* means a sum of money given either by a company to employees to cover personal costs during work, OR by parents to children each week/month to buy small items for themselves).

**Answers**

1.
| | | |
|---|---|---|
| absorb | – | reflect |
| allow | – | prevent |
| condense | – | evaporate |
| gain | – | lose |
| reach | – | return |
| release | – | store |

2.

| verb | noun |
|---|---|
| absorb | absorption |
| reflect | reflection |
| allow | – |
| prevent | prevention |
| condense | condensation |
| evaporate | evaporation |
| gain | gain |
| lose | loss |
| reach | – |
| return | return |
| release | release |
| store | store / storage |

### B  Identifying a key skill (1)

1. Give students time to read Skills Check 1. They should then cover it and discuss the question in pairs or in small groups. Elicit answers orally. Refer students back to the Skills Check to confirm their ideas.
2. Set the task for pairwork discussion without referring students back to Lesson 4.17 Real-time writing. Elicit ideas. Students can then confirm their ideas by looking back at the lesson.

Answers

1. See Skills Check 1.
2. There are four points in the essay in Lesson 4.17: *absorption and reflection*, *clouds*, *the greenhouse effect* and *global warming*. Section 1 is only an introduction.

## C Practising a key skill (1)

1. Set the task for discussion in pairs. Elicit answers and display them using an electronic projection.
2. Elicit one or two ideas. With a more able group, you may wish to deal with only the first essay, and then set the task; otherwise, elicit ideas for each of the essays before setting the task.

Set the task for individual work or pairwork, depending on the students' ability. Emphasize the fact that students must only write a list of points in each case – they do not need to write paragraphs. Allow students to refer to previous themes from the course as they work, in order to check the format of the different essay types. Monitor and assist as necessary. Encourage students to not only think about the different sections of the essays, but also what ideas should go into each section.

Answers

1.

| Describe the water cycle. | Description |
| --- | --- |
| Conduct a survey to find out how teenagers in your country spend their free time. | research report |
| How can we prevent global warming? | Argument |
| Should teachers set homework? | For and against |

2.

Answers depend on the students, but here are some suggestions:

*Description:* The water cycle

Evaporation – from seas, rivers

Cloud formation – condensation, clouds get thicker and thicker

Rainfall – water falls as rain, runs back to river and into sea. Cycle starts again.

*Research report:* Teenagers and free time

Introduction – teenagers have a lot of free time; a lot of different options

Method – how data was gathered; the survey form; number of people

Findings – raw data; bar/pie charts showing %; description of charts

Conclusions

*Argument:* Preventing global warming

Global warming – it can be stopped

Defining global warming

Preventative method 1: reducing $CO_2$ emissions in heavy industry

Preventative method 2: reducing $CO_2$ emissions in the transport sector

Preventative method 3: cleaning the atmosphere

Preventative method 4: planting trees

Summary

*For and against:* Should teachers set homework?

The tradition of homework – essays; learning by heart; students don't like it

Why homework is a good thing – revision; more study time; independent learning

Why homework is a bad thing – teachers have to mark it; takes up free time

Recommendation: the ideal situation – a little homework every day

## D Identifying a key skill (2)

Give students time to read Skills Check 2.

Students then cover the Skills Check. Elicit the answers to the questions.

Answers

1. You should write notes on diagrams to help you explain them. Point out that these notes are to help students while writing the essay, and should not be included on the diagram in the final version of the essay.
2. The notes should be expanded into full sentences in the essay.

**E** Practising a key skill (2)

Make sure students understand the task. Highlight the use of formal vocabulary and passive structures for academic writing. Elicit ideas for the first diagram. If you wish, write the paragraph on the board as an example.

Set the task for individual work. Monitor and assist as necessary. Make a note of common errors. When they are ready, students can read each other's work silently and then comment on it.

### Answers

Answers depend on the students, but these are possible models:

1. Plants and animals contain nitrogen. When they die, they decay. The nitrogen in their bodies is fixed by bacteria in the soil.
2. Soil contains nitrogen in the form of nitrates ($NO_2$). Denitrifying bacteria in the soil break down the nitrates into nitrogen and oxygen. Some of the nitrogen is released into the atmosphere.
3. Nitrates are contained in soil. They are absorbed by plants. If a plant is eaten by an animal, some of the nitrogen is absorbed by the animal.

### Closure

1. Go over any common errors you noted while monitoring in Exercise E.
2. Review the spelling of the verbs and nouns from Exercise A.

---

## 4.19 Grammar for writing: Compound sentences

### Objectives

By the end of the lesson, students should be able to:
- identify event and result clauses in compound sentences;
- use *when*, *as* and *if* to join sentences.

### Introduction

Write the title of the lesson, *Compound sentences*, on the board. Elicit the meaning of *compound* (joined together).

### Grammar box 22

Go through the tables in Grammar box 22 with the students. Elicit the differences in the written form of the sentences when *as*, *when* and *if* are in the middle (there is no comma).

**Note**: In the sentences in Table 1, the comma is optional, but it does make the sentence easier to read. However, when the result clause comes first, as in Table 2, there is definitely no comma.

Put students into pairs or small groups to discuss the question below the tables. Students should think about the relationship in time between event and result, as well as the meanings of *as*, *when* and *if*. Give feedback orally.

**Note**: During feedback time, point out that the word *as* also has the meaning of *because*. This is a different usage. Clarify any possible confusion.

### Answers

*as* = the event and the result happen together over a period of time
*when* = the result happens at the time of the event
*if* = the event may not happen

**A** Using *as*, *when* and *if*

Go through the example with the class. Set the exercise for individual work and pairwork checking. Give feedback, preferably using an electronic projection.

### Answers

1. A fire can only start *if* there is enough fuel, heat and oxygen.
2. *As* you travel east, the local clock time gets later and later.
3. Usually, *when* you start a new college course, you buy a set text.
4. *If* the energy in sugar is not used, it is stored as fat.
5. It's interesting that *as* computers get more powerful, they also get smaller.
6. Artists often make a lot of money *when* they become famous.

**B** Writing about events and results

1. Go through the example with the class. Set the exercise for individual work and pairwork checking. Give feedback, preferably using an electronic projection.
2. Go through the example with the class. Remind students that for all the sentences,

the order can be Event–Result or Result–Event. Elicit the alternative order for the example: *The temperature of the air falls when the Sun sets.*

Set the task for individual work and pairwork checking. Students can decide which order they prefer, but they must be careful with the use of commas. Monitor and assist as necessary. Students may have particular difficulty with pronoun replacement, e.g., *water / it* in Sentence c.

Give feedback, preferably using an electronic projection.

### Answers

1. a. The Sun sets. _E_ The temperature of the air falls. _R_
   b. Animals do not have a place to live. _R_ Forests are cut down. _E_
   c. Water gets hot. _E_ It evaporates. _R_
   d. More and more food is needed. _R_ The population of a country increases. _E_
   e. A product is very common. _E_ It is usually cheap. _R_

2. a. When the sun sets, the temperature of the air falls. / The temperature of the air falls when the Sun sets.
   b. If forests are cut down, animals do not have a place to live. / Animals do not have a place to live if forests are cut down.
   c. When water gets hot, it evaporates. / Water evaporates when it gets hot.
   d. As the population of a country increases, more and more food is needed. / More and more food is needed as the population of a country increases.
   e. If a product is very common, it is usually cheap. / A product is usually cheap if it is very common.

### C  Order of event and result

Go through the example. Point out that students must decide whether they must supply the Event or the Result, and think of a possible second part for the sentence. They should be careful with the use of commas.

Set the task for individual work. Monitor and assist. When they are ready, students can compare ideas. Give feedback using an electronic projection.

### Answers

Answers depend on the students, but see the table below for some suggestions:

| 1. Islands are sometimes formed when volcanoes … | *erupt under the ocean.* |
| 2. As the Earth turns, the Moon's gravity … | *creates the ocean tides.* |
| 3. Oil floats if … | *it is mixed with water.* |
| 4. When children eat a balanced diet, … | *their behaviour improves.* |
| 5. In football, the referee stops the game if … | *a player is injured.* |
| 6. Most parents allow their children to make more decisions as … | *they get older.* |
| 7. People remember more information if … | *they are given prompts.* |
| 8. The air temperature falls as … | *you go higher in the atmosphere.* |

### Closure

Say the first half of some of the sentences from Grammar box 22, or from Exercises A and B. Students must try to remember the second part.

### 4.20 Applying new writing skills: The ocean current cycle

#### Objectives

By the end of the lesson, students should be able to:
- use illustrations to make notes for writing a text;
- use target vocabulary, language and discourse structure from the theme to produce an essay;
- describe a natural cycle (the ocean current cycle).

**Introduction**

Review the pairs of opposites from Lesson 4.18 Learning new writing skills, Exercise A: *absorb – reflect*; *allow – prevent*; *condense – evaporate*; *gain – lose*; *reach – return*; *release – store*.

#### A  Previewing vocabulary

1. Set the exercise for individual work and pairwork checking. Allow the use of dictionaries, and monitor and assist as necessary.

   Put feedback on the board, using an electronic projection. Keep these words up so that students can refer to them in the writing stage of the lesson (Exercises C, D and E).

2. Elicit one or two ideas, then set the task for pairwork or small group work. Put feedback on the board, using an electronic projection. Make sure you elicit all the words shown in Answers below, as students will need these in their writing later on.

**Answers**

1.

| a. sink (v)    | rise    |
|----------------|---------|
| b. dense (adj) | light   |
| c. shallow (adj)| deep   |
| d. warm (v)    | cool    |
| e. eastern (adj)| western|

2. *move, flow, pass, go, travel, turn, sink, rise*

#### Methodology note

If possible, use a copy of the diagram for reference during the rest of this lesson.

#### B  Thinking and organizing

Remind students if necessary about the TOWER method of writing (see writing sections from earlier themes and also the Introduction to this book, page 11). This exercise focuses on the thinking and organizing stages of the process.

Exploit the visual of the ocean currents. Students read the notes. Check students understand the meaning of the abbreviations:

- v = very
- W. Eu. = Western Europe
- N. At. = North Atlantic
- = oxygen
- S.E. Asia = South East Asia

Ask some questions to check understanding of the information:

- *Why is the Gulf Stream warm?*
- *Why is it very salty?*
- *What is the climate like in Western Europe?*
- *Why does the current sink in the North Atlantic?*
- *Why is the North Atlantic a good fishing area?*
- *In which direction does the North Atlantic Deep Water current flow?*
- *Why is it not warmed by the sun?*
- *Where does the Cold Eastern Current flow?*
- *Where does the Warm Western Current rise?*
- *Why does it rise?*
- *Where does the Warm Western Current flow?*

Now set the four discussion questions for pairwork or small group work. Elicit answers orally. Give feedback.

**Answers**

1. This is a Description essay.
2. The red colour shows a warm current. Blue shows a cold current. The arrows show the direction of the flow.
3. Water temperature warms or cools the continents it passes near.
4. The essay will have five sections with the following headings:
   - Introduction
   - The Gulf Stream
   - The North Atlantic Deep Water
   - The Cold Eastern Current
   - The Warm Western Current

### C Writing a description

Students read through the instructions. Refer students back to the relevant pages for each language point, if necessary.

It would be a good idea for students to write their essay on a piece of paper rather than in a notebook. In this way you can collect work at the end of the lesson for marking. This is especially useful if you have a large class, as you will not have time to mark everyone's work during the lesson. Remind students to write their essay using the five section headings from Exercise B.

Elicit some sentences for the first section, *Introduction*, and write them on the board. Students copy and then complete the essay on their own. Monitor and assist where necessary. Make a note of common errors.

**Answers**

See Exercise E.

### D Editing

Remind students how to mark each other's work (see earlier themes and the Introduction). Monitor and give help where necessary. Continue to make notes of common errors. Give feedback on errors before students start writing their final drafts.

### E Rewriting

As usual, this can be done in class or set for homework. At some point the model answer can be copied and distributed for comparison, but students may have different versions that are also correct. If you are not able to monitor all the work in class, collect the essays in for marking.

**More able classes**: They could research extra information about the ocean current system and add it to their writing.

**Less able classes**: Give out copies of the model answer before students do their final writing task. Allow them to study it for a few minutes and highlight some of the features for them. Remove the model answer, then ask students to write their final essay. You could also provide students with prompts to help them with this.

**Answers**

Model answer:

1. **Introduction**

   Water in the seas and oceans is constantly moving. There is an ocean current cycle which carries water around the globe.

2. **The Gulf Stream**

   The cycle starts in the Atlantic, near the Equator. Water in this area is warmed by the sun and moves north. The water is very salty because there is a lot of evaporation from the surface. This current of warm salty water is called the Gulf Stream. The mild climate of Western Europe is caused by the Gulf Stream.

3. **The North Atlantic Deep Water**

   As the water moves away from the Equator, it cools. Cold water is denser than warm water, which means it is heavier. The cold water sinks to the bottom of the ocean. This cold water carries oxygen to the deepest parts of the ocean, so it is a good area for fish. The cold current, called the North Atlantic Deep Water, flows back towards the Equator. It passes right over the Equator, but it is not warmed by the sun because it is so deep.

4. **The Cold Eastern Current**

   When the cold current reaches Antarctica, it turns and flows to the east, under the southern tip of Africa. From there, it travels right around the world. Most of the water is carried near the coast of Antarctica but some of it flows up the eastern coast of Africa.

5. **The Warm Western Current**

   As the water approaches the Equator it is heated and it rises. It turns slowly to the west. It carries warm water to the Pacific Ocean and South East Asia. This is one of the causes of hot weather in these areas. Finally, it flows back to the South Atlantic. The process starts all over again.

**Closure**

1. If you have not already done so, give out copies of the model answer for students to compare with their own version.
2. Discuss the following questions with the class:
   - *Which ocean currents affect the weather in the students' country(ies)?*
   - *If global warming increases the temperatures on Earth, how will ocean currents change?* (Evaporation will make them more salty – as a result, animal life in the seas will change; coastal weather will change.)

## Portfolio: The rock cycle

### Objectives

By the end of the lesson(s), students should have:
- revised target vocabulary from the theme;
- used integrated skills to practise language and revise knowledge from the theme;
- practised questions to check information;
- used integrated skills to talk and write about the rock cycle;
- learnt some common core knowledge about the rock cycle.

**Introduction**

Write the following words on the board. Ask students to put them in order, and then explain the connection between them.

| mountain   rock   stone   pebble   hill   sand   dust |

Answers

They could all be made of the same material. From largest to smallest they are:

1. mountain
2. hill
3. rock
4. stone
5. pebble
6. sand
7. dust

### A Activating ideas

This is a test for how much students already know about this subject. With a more able class, put students into groups to work out the answers. With a less able class, do the activities with the whole class together.

Students may be surprised that the first picture shows the seabed. Explain that the layers were produced at the bottom of the sea, then the seabed was pushed up.

Answers

1.

| photo 1 | photo 2 | photo 3 |
|---------|---------|---------|
| layers  | volcano | earthquake |
| seabed  | eruption | split |
|         | liquid rock | plates |

2.
a. The sediment on the seabed.
b. Pressure from under the surface.
c. Plates moving apart – you may need to explain the idea of continental plates, if students have not studied this in their own language.

3.
They are all rocks in different states.

### B Gathering and recording information

Remind students about the key skill in the Reading section of this theme – only following useful links and ignoring others.

Set up the three groups. Give each group plenty of time to research their topic, helping them if necessary. Check that groups are not reading irrelevant entries. After some time, ensure that each group has made a diagram.

Point out that each student in each group must be able to talk about the research and draw the diagram for the next activity.

### C Sharing information

Divide the students into groups of three, with each new group having one student from Group 1, one from Group 2 and one from Group 3.

Get students to close their books and work only from their notes. As before, go around the class and assist as necessary.

Give feedback, using an electronic projection of a diagram of the complete rock cycle on the board.

Answers

Students should produce something like this:

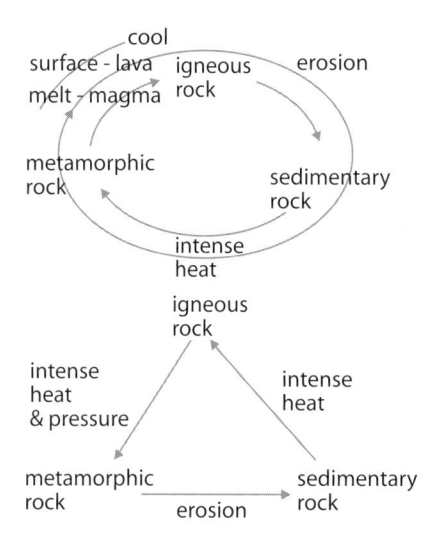

```
         cool
surface - lava    igneous      erosion
melt - magma      rock
                  ⟶
metamorphic              sedimentary
rock                     rock
         ⟵
         intense
         heat
         igneous
         rock
                  ↑
intense           intense
heat              heat
& pressure
    ↓
metamorphic              sedimentary
rock        erosion  ⟶   rock
```

### D  Writing about the rock cycle

Set for individual work in class; students can then complete this at home.

## Closure

Give the class a deadline for completion of the writing task.

# Theme 5

## Customs: origins and effects

- Cultural diversity
- Wedding customs
- The price of happiness
- Cultural change

# Listening: Cultural diversity

### 5.1 Vocabulary for listening: Canada – a multicultural country

**Objectives**

By the end of the lesson, students should be able to:
- demonstrate understanding of key target vocabulary for the Listening section, both in isolation and in context;
- relate spoken vocabulary to its written form;
- demonstrate understanding of information about multiculturalism in Canada.

**Introduction**

Write the title of the lesson on the board: *Canada – a multicultural country*.

Focus on the word *multicultural*. Ask questions:
- *How many words can you see in this long word?* (two)
- *What are they?* (*multi*, *cultural*)
- *What does* multi *mean?* ('many' – it's actually a prefix)
- *What part of speech is the whole word?* (an adjective)
- *How do you know?* (because it ends with ~al and comes between the article and the noun)
- *So what do you think the word means?* (people from different cultures, countries, etc., living together in one country)

Find out how much students already know about Canada. The answers can be quite broad:
- Location: North America
- Capital and key cities: Ottawa (c), Montreal, Toronto, Quebec, Vancouver, etc.
- Languages: English and French
- Size: very large
- Population: not large
- Industries: farming, mining, forestry, etc.

### A Activating knowledge

Set the task. Give students some language to use for the activity and write the phrases on the board:

*They might be from …*

*They are probably from …*
*I think they all live in …*

Students may guess from the title of the lesson that the people are all from Canada. That is fine; the main idea is to introduce the topic of immigration and the fact that some countries have many immigrants, while others have very few.

**Answers**

1. Answers depend on the students, but the actual answer is:
   *China, India, Iran, and Columbia in South America.*
2. They all live in Canada now but they keep their own cultures, to some extent.

### B Building knowledge

Set the task and give students time to read through the questions and answers in the table. They may not understand some of the words in the questions, but these will become clear as they complete the task.

Play 5.1. Students complete the activity individually, then compare their answers in pairs. Elicit answers.

Focus on the difference in meaning between the following:
- *Emigrate* = go to a new country to live – *My friend has emigrated to Australia.*
- *Immigrate* = to come into a new country – *My family immigrated here about 20 years ago.*

Ask students to focus on Figure 1 and ask a few questions about it:
- *What does the figure show?* (immigration figures to Canada in 2007)
- *What are the top three home countries?* (China, India, the Philippines)
- *What are some of the other countries?* (Korea, France, Columbia)
- *Is your country there? Do you know anyone who has emigrated to Canada?*

Ask students if they find any of the information surprising.

Answers

| Why is Canada a *multicultural* nation? | 3 | Because they want to get a job. |
| Why did *colonists* go to Canada from France in the 16th and 17th centuries? | 4 | China, India and the Philippines. |
| Why do many people *emigrate* to Canada now? | 1 | Because of hundreds of years of immigration. |
| Where do most of the *immigrants* come from? | 2 | Because they wanted to own the land. |
| How does the Canadian government help with *integration*? | 6 | They are part of Canadian culture. |
| What do Canadian people say about *ethnic* groups in Canada? | 5 | They provide money for services. |

Transcript

5.1

Presenter: 5.1. Theme 5: Customs: origins and effects
Lesson 5.1. Vocabulary for listening: Canada – a multicultural country

Exercise B. Listen to a text about Canada. Match the questions and answers.

Lecturer: This week, as you know, we will be looking at multicultural countries.

Now Canada is often described as a multicultural nation. This means that Canadians are not from one cultural background. In fact Canada has more immigrants than any other country in the world, including Australia. Canada today has a large diversity of ethnic groups. This diversity is a result of hundreds of years of immigration.

In the 16th and 17th centuries, people went to Canada from France and Britain as colonists. In other words, they wanted to own the land. They took large parts of the country from the Native Canadians, the indigenous people of the area.

Nowadays, about er ... 230,000 people go to live in Canada every year ... but they go in peace. Why do so many people emigrate to this country? Well, most go there for economic reasons. Canada has a large labour shortage so it is often easier to get a job in Canada than in the immigrants' home countries.

OK. Before 1967, most people were from Europe, especially Germany and Britain. Today, most immigrants are from China, India and the Philippines. The majority population of Canada is still white but the minorities in the country are now a very important part of the Canadian labour force.

In 1971, the government introduced a policy of multiculturalism. It recognized the diversity of cultural backgrounds in Canada. At the same time, it encouraged all Canadians to contribute equally to Canadian society. The government helps immigrants to integrate into society by, er, providing money for services, such as English language tuition for first generation immigrants.

People in Canada say 'Ethnic groups do not destroy Canadian culture. They are Canadian culture.'

C  Understanding new vocabulary in context

1. Ask students to work in pairs to try and complete the sentences. Remind students to change the form of the words if necessary. It does not matter if students cannot work out many of the answers. Check students have at least read to the final sentence before you play the CD.

2. Play 5.2 so that students can check their answers. As you elicit each answer, ask for the stressed syllable in each word. Ask students to mark the stressed syllable in the vocabulary list:

di'versity
in'digenous
ma'jority
mi'norities
multi'cultural
'cultural
con'tribute

Play the recording of the sentences again, if you wish, and ask students to listen in particular for the stressed syllable in each target word.

## Transcript and Answers

🔊 5.2

| Presenter: | 5.2. Exercise C2. Listen to the sentences and check your answers. |
|---|---|
| Lecturer: | a. Canada today has a large diversity of ethnic groups.<br>b. The colonists took large parts of the country from the Native Canadians, the indigenous people of the area.<br>c. The majority population of Canada is still white.<br>d. But the minorities in the country are now a very important part of the Canadian labour force.<br>e. In 1971, the government introduced a policy to create a multicultural country.<br>f. It recognized the diversity of cultural backgrounds in Canada.<br>g. At the same time, it encouraged all Canadians to contribute equally to Canadian society. |

### Closure

Choose one of the following:
- Replay the CD of the lecture in Exercise B, with students following the transcript.
- Do one or two word-building exercises based on the vocabulary from the lesson – for example, verbs and nouns:

| verbs | nouns |
|---|---|
| immigrate | immigration / immigrant |
| diversify | diversity |
| integrate | integration |

- Ask students to make new sentences using some of the words from the lesson. This can be done orally or in writing.
- Have a class discussion on the following questions:
*Is the students' country of study / home country multicultural?*
*Which countries are multicultural?*
*What problems do immigrants face?*

## 5.2 Real-time listening: Anthropology

### Objectives

By the end of the lesson, students should be able to:
- use existing skills in order to complete notes on a lecture about anthropology;
- demonstrate understanding of knowledge about the branches and history of anthropology;
- recognize target vocabulary in context.

### Introduction

Write the following statements about anthropology on the board and ask students to discuss them in pairs:

*Anthropology ...*
- *is about ancient history.*
- *is not very useful.*
- *is an easy subject.*
- *combines well with languages, psychology, religion.*
- *includes history, politics, gender studies, geography.*
- *helps us understand human behaviour.*
- *makes you more open-minded.*
- *teaches note-taking, observation, interviewing, critical analysis, writing skills.*

Students may have preconceived ideas about anthropology and may think it is a so-called 'soft' subject. Hopefully, after this section they will regard the subject in a different light.

### A  Activating ideas

Set the task. Reassure students it does not matter if they do not know the answers at this stage, and that it is fine for them to guess or leave answers out.

Students discuss the questions in pairs or small groups.

After a few minutes, elicit ideas, but do not confirm or correct just yet. For the connection between all the visuals (question 9), students will have to wait until later in the lesson.

#### Answers

Do not give the answers at this point. See Closure.

### B Understanding an introduction

Focus students' attention on the notice for the Hadford University Open Day. Elicit from the class what happens at an Open Day, and its purpose:

Students who are thinking of applying to the university can:
- visit, look at facilities, lecture rooms, etc.;
- find out about prices, accommodation, number of contact hours, etc.;
- listen to talks from different departments to see if they are really interested in the subject;
- meet lecturers and ask questions;
- meet students and ask questions.

The purpose is to help students decide which university course is best for them.

1. Elicit ideas.
2. Set the task and check students understand what to do. Play DVD 5.A. Students compare their answers in pairs. Elicit answers. Check understanding of the word *branches*. You can compare this with the *branches of a tree*; use a sketch to show how a tree has many branches, but they all belong to the same tree.

#### Answers

1. Answers depend on the students but, in most cases, the department will tell you the curriculum of the course – the different areas which you will study each year. They will probably also tell you about the pattern of work – assignments, exams, dissertation. They may also tell you about career prospects if you pass the course.
2. Branches
   Important people
   Old and new views

### Transcript

5.3 DVD 5.A

**Presenter:** Lesson 5.2. Real-time listening: Anthropology

**Lecturer:** Welcome to the Department of Anthropology. I'm delighted that you are thinking of studying Anthropology. I hope, after today, that you will decide that Anthropology is the course for you.

Some people think that anthropology is all about the past. But, in fact, it is extremely important in the present. Many conflicts are caused by problems between cultures, and many problems are caused by ignorance. If we understand other cultures, it is much easier to accept them and even to admire them. In some countries, there are many different cultures. We have multicultural countries. We need to integrate people to avoid problems, but in order to integrate, we need to understand and respect.

So, let me tell you what I'm going to do in the next 20 minutes or so. First, I want to explain exactly what anthropologists study. There are several branches of anthropology and I will briefly mention each one. Then I'm going to tell you a little bit about the history of anthropology. I'll give you the names of some important people from the discipline. Finally, I'm going to compare the old view of anthropologists with the more modern view. We'll see how attitudes have changed. We'll also see why this change is so important in the present day.

### C Understanding a talk

Give students time to study all the information in the notes. Make sure students realize there are three sections to the notes. These match the sections of the talk from Exercise B above:
- Branches of anthropology
- Important people (and timeline)
- Old and new views
- Ask some questions to check understanding, for example:
- *How many branches of anthropology are there?*
- *What are they?*
- *Who are some of the important people?*
- *What did they do?*

Play DVD 5.B. Pause, if necessary, to give students time to complete their notes – but avoid replaying sections at this point.

Students compare their answers in pairs. Use an electronic projection of the completed notes. Students refer to the notes to check and correct their answers. Ask students which pieces of information from the lecture they found the most difficult. Replay the relevant sections so that students can try to understand why they had problems.

Finally – either now or at the end of the lesson – play the complete lecture one more time with students following the transcript.

Check understanding of a few words and phrases. Some will be new, or have new meanings in this context, and some will be revision. Examples include:

*discipline*
*attitudes*
*evidence*
*in terms of*
*conduct interviews*
*human sacrifice*

Theme 5: Listening 221

*ignorance*
*beliefs*
*apes*
*admire*

*exotic*
*normal / abnormal*
*ethnocentric*
*civilized*

```
                          Anthropology
          ┌──────────┬──────────┴──────────┬──────────┐
       cultural   linguistic         archaeological  biological
          ↓          ↓                    ↓              ↓
   particular     development of    customs and habits   differences between
   cultures       language          from ancient         humans and apes
                                    cultures
   C5th BCE       Herodotus         talked to people     e.g., Minoans: women
                                    from other cultures  more important than men
                                                         Scythians: human sacrifice

   C14th CE       Marco Polo        Italy to India and China
                  Ibn Khaldun       Tunis to Middle East and Africa
   1492           Columbus          sailed to the Americas
   C15th and 16th CE  Spanish, French  met different cultures   e.g., Aztecs: human sacrifice
                  and British to                                Iriquois: women more
                  America                                       important than men
```

| old view | new view |
|---|---|
| My culture is normal, yours is abnormal; you are uncivilized and I must civilize you. | Your culture is different from mine, but both cultures are normal; cultural diversity is important. |

## Transcript

5.4 DVD 5.B

**Lecturer:** Let's look at the branches of anthropology. In the first year here, you study the discipline in general, but in your second year, you specialize. Firstly, there is cultural anthropology. In this branch, we look at particular cultures and try to understand their attitudes and beliefs. Secondly, we have linguistic anthropology. This branch looks at the way that language has developed from prehistoric times. Thirdly, archaeological anthropology. Here we look at the evidence of customs and habits from ancient cultures. Finally, there is biological anthropology, which considers the differences between human beings and our closest animal relatives, the apes. So that's cultural, linguistic, archaeological and biological. Which branch are you most interested in? Well, you don't have to decide now!

Now, let's hear a little bit about the history of the discipline. In fact, it is a very old subject. The name comes from Greek ... *anthropos* in Ancient Greek means 'a human being', and *ology* is, of course, the study of something. The first important person is Herodotus, who studied human beings in terms of culture in the 5th century before the Common Era. He was mainly a historian – in fact, he is sometimes called The Father of History, but he is also, in some ways, the father of anthropology, although he did not use that term. He wrote the history of different countries including his own. He wrote about kings and battles, like all historians through the ages. But Herodotus also studied the people themselves. He didn't stay at home and simply write down the stories which he had heard. He actually visited foreign countries and conducted interviews with people from the culture. That is very important. It is still a major way in which anthropologists do their research. He described customs and habits that were very different from those of his own culture, Ancient Greece.

For example, he wrote about the Minoan culture, where the women were more important than the men. He also described the Scythians, who practised human sacrifice in their culture. Remember these examples. We'll come back to them later.

Quite a long break then before the next important people in anthropology. In the 14th century CE, there were two famous travellers. Firstly, there was Marco Polo from Italy who visited India and China. Secondly, Ibn Khaldun who travelled from Tunisia, throughout the Middle East and Africa. They brought back amazing stories of other cultures, like Herodotus had done.

Now, some people believed the stories of exotic cultures, and some didn't. In fact, by the Middle Ages, some people called Herodotus the Father of Lies, not the Father of History. But in the 15th and 16th centuries people from Europe started to believe once again that other cultures existed with very different customs. Why did this happen?

The 15th and 16th centuries were the age of exploration. It began with Christopher Columbus. In 1492, he sailed from Spain to the Americas, which was a new world for people from Europe. In the next 200 years, Spanish, French and British colonists sailed to the Americas. These travellers found cultures that were very different from their own. For example, they encountered the Aztecs in Central America who sacrificed humans, in the same way that the Scythians did in Herodotus's books. They met the Iroquois in North America who believed that women were more important than men – just like the Minoans in the writings of Herodotus.

Oh, sorry. I see we are running out of time. I must just mention the last point – and the most important point – about anthropology. The old view and the modern view.

For most of history, up to the 20th century, anthropologists took an ethnocentric view. This means that they looked at other cultures from the standpoint of their own culture. They said, in effect, 'My culture is normal. If your culture is different from mine, your culture is abnormal.' In many cases, they went much further. They said, 'We are civilized. You are uncivilized.' In some cases, they even said, 'I must force you to be civilized.' So that is the old view. But, for most people and all anthropologists, this ethnocentric view has changed now. Anthropologists today say, 'Your culture is different from mine, but both cultures are normal.' And they go much further. They say, 'Cultural diversity is important – in other words, we need different cultures in the world.' In fact, the General Conference of UNESCO said in 2001, '… cultural diversity is as necessary for humankind as biodiversity is for nature.'

Actually, if we go back to the beginning, this was the view of Herodotus, 2,500 years ago. He believed that we should be proud of the achievements of our own culture, but we should also be proud of the achievements of other cultures. But, even today, some people do not accept the view of Herodotus, or the view of modern anthropologists. They believe that only their own culture is acceptable and other beliefs and attitudes must be changed, by violence if necessary. There are many examples. For instance, minorities in some regions are forbidden from religious worship that is different from the local culture. They are not allowed to celebrate the holidays of their culture.

OK. I'm right out of time. To sum up. anthropology is a very wide subject which has been studied for centuries, but it is still very relevant today. Anthropologists can explain cultural diversity and help to stop it becoming the cause of cultural conflict and terrorism. Thank you … and I hope to see you all here at the beginning of the next term.

### D  Reconstructing a talk from notes

The aim here is not so much to provide speaking practice but to further check understanding of the lecture. Tell students **not** to start with *The lecturer said / told us,* in order to avoid getting into complex reported speech sentences.

The activity can be done in several ways, either in pairs or small groups:

- Students can take turns to give information about different sections of the lecture.
- Students can ask each other questions about the information, e.g., *Why was Herodotus important? What happened when Europeans 'discovered' America?* etc.
- You can show the slides from the DVD and ask students to explain the information.

Monitor and give feedback. If necessary, replay any sections of the DVD students had difficulty understanding, or refer students to the relevant section of the transcript instead.

Answers
Answers depend on students.

### Closure

1. Refer students back to the questions in Exercise A. Do students want to change their answers to any of the questions? Elicit answers and give feedback.

2. Refer students back to the statements about anthropology in the introduction. Have students changed their mind about any of the statements?

3. Ask students which information in the lecture was …
   … *new?*
   … *surprising?*
   … *interesting?*
   … *useful?*

Answers (for Exercise A)
1. 5th century BCE.
2. 14th century BCE.
3. Tunisia.
4. Killing something as part of a ceremony.
5. Spain.
6. The Americas.
7. The people who lived in North America before the colonists arrived.
8. A problem between people, possibly even a war.
9. They are all connected with anthropology – the study of human culture.

## 5.3 Learning new listening skills: Choosing the best form for notes

### Objectives

By the end of the lesson, students should be able to:
- recognize common endings for adjectives;
- select the best form of notes for spoken information.

**Introduction**

Play Stupid Teacher. Tell the students about the information in the previous lesson's lecture (use the model notes as guidance) but make lots of mistakes – silly ones, ideally. Students correct the mistakes you make. For example:
- *The lecture was about anthropology, which is the study of anthros.*
- *There are three main branches.*
- *The branches are cultural, linguistic and architectural.*
- *Herodotus is called the mother of anthropology.*
- *He lived in the 15th century BCE.*
- *He studied other cultures, including the Minorities.*
- *The Minoans believed that animals were more important than people.*
- *Marco Polo travelled to the Moon.*
- *Ibn Khaldun went to the Americas.*
- *Columbus discovered America – nobody lived there before 1492.*
- *In the 15th and 16th centuries, people went to the Americas because they wanted to marry the native Americans.*
- *Anthropologists used to think that their own culture was abnormal.*
- *Nowadays, anthropologists think that cultural diversity is impossible.*

## A Reviewing vocabulary

1–2. Refer students to Skills Check 1. When students have finished reading, point out there are 13 common endings for adjectives! Check understanding of the meanings of some of the adjectives. Now set the task. Students complete the activity individually, then compare their answers in pairs. Students may need to discuss the meaning of some of the adjectives at this point if they cannot remember them, but discourage them from looking back at the transcript or notes from the previous lesson. Do not elicit answers at this stage.

3. Play 5.5 so that students can check their answers. Replay the CD if necessary. Do not elicit every answer, but help students with any they are still not sure about. Check the meanings of any words students may have forgotten, or allow them a minute or two to look back at the previous lesson. Alternatively, you can allow students to use their dictionaries.

4. Students work in pairs to identify the stressed syllable in each adjective for a minute or two. Then play the CD one more time for them to check their answers. Once again, do not elicit every answer; instead, focus on the problematic words only.

### Transcript

5.5

Presenter: 5.5. Exercise A3. Listen and check your answers.

Voice:
a. linguist-ic
b. biolog-ical
c. cultur-al
d. amaz-ing
e. exot-ic
f. centr-al
g. ethnocentr-ic
h. civiliz-ed
i. norm-al
j. accept-able
k. religi-ous
l. relev-ant

## B Identifying a new skill

1. Give students a moment to look back at the previous lesson. Elicit ideas.
2. Focus students' attention on Skills Check 2. When students have finished reading, ask them to complete this sentence:

   *You need different kinds of notes for … (different kinds of information).*

In pairs, students match the diagrams to the note form and type of information. Elicit answers.

## Answers

1. There are three sections with different kinds of notes.
2.
   a. spidergram
   b. flow chart
   c. table
   d. timeline
   e. tree diagram

### C  Practising the new skill

Set the task. Tell students they will hear a short introduction to four lectures. They must identify the topic of each one. Then they must listen for key words, for example *compare*, which will tell them what kind of notes to make. Students do NOT need to make the actual notes, only to identify what *type* of notes is needed.

Play the introduction to each extract from ◉ 5.6, then pause. Students discuss in pairs what kind of information they heard and what notes should be written. Once the fourth introduction has been played and discussed, elicit answers.

In this task, students should write the notes in the format discussed in Exercise C1. Play ◉ 5.7. Pause after each extract. Students compare their notes in pairs. You can elicit answers, and give feedback using an electronic projection, either after each extract or until all four extracts have been played. Discuss any differences between the students' notes and the model answers (see Answers below), and whether these differences are acceptable or not.

## Answers

1.

### Lecture 1
Topic: Short-term memory
Note form: Timeline

### Lecture 2
Topic: Keeping friends
Note form: Tree diagram

### Lecture 3
Topic: Two selves
Note form: Table

### Lecture 4
Topic: Desertification
Note form: Flow chart

2.

### Lecture 1

Short-term memory

| | |
|---|---|
| 1880s | Jacobs – average = 6 or 7 things |
| 1959 | Peterson and Peterson – meaningless shapes – 3 secs; 18 secs = nothing |
| 1964 | Conrad – memory = sound |
| 1970 | Shulman – memory = meaning |

### Lecture 2

See tree diagram below.

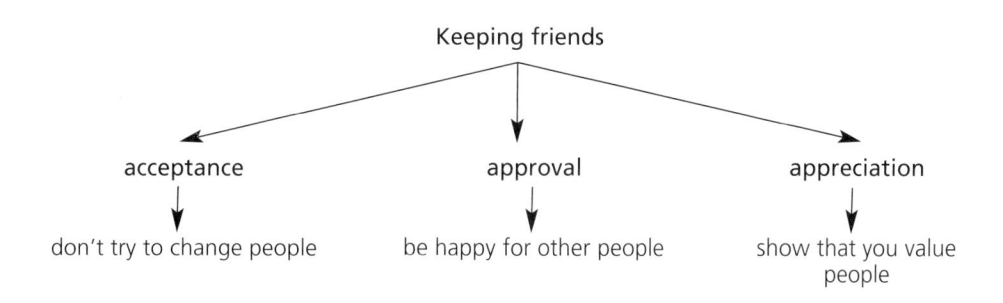

```
                    Keeping friends
          ┌──────────────┼──────────────┐
      acceptance      approval      appreciation
          ↓              ↓               ↓
  don't try to      be happy for    show that you value
  change people    other people        people
```

## Lecture 3

| Self 1 | Self 2 |
|---|---|
| confident | doubtful |
| how other people see us | how we see ourselves |
| everything doesn't have to be perfect | everything or nothing |
| optimistic | pessimistic |

## Lecture 4

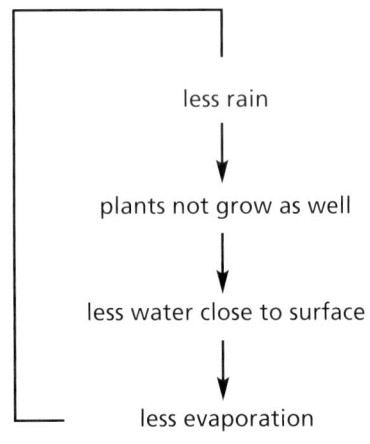

less rain
↓
plants not grow as well
↓
less water close to surface
↓
less evaporation
↑ (loops back to less rain)

## Transcripts

### 5.6

Presenter: 5.6. Exercise C1. Listen to the introduction to four lectures. What is each lecture about? Choose the best form of notes.

One.

Lecturer 1: OK. In today's session, we are going to look at the history of research into short-term memory.

Presenter: Two.

Lecturer 2: So we talked last time about making friends. This time, I'm going to consider the problem of keeping friends. I'm going to describe the three main barriers to keeping friends, and give you some examples.

Presenter: Three.

Lecturer 3: Right. We have heard about the idea of two selves. Now let's compare Self 1 and Self 2. Let's look at each point in turn.

Presenter: Four.

Lecturer 4: We talked last week about the great deserts of the world. Today, we're going to look at the process of desertification. How does a fertile area become a desert?

### 5.7

Presenter: 5.7. Exercise C2. Listen to each introduction again and the first part of the lecture. Make notes in the best form.

One.

Lecturer 1: OK. In today's session, we are going to look at the history of research into short-term memory.

The first real research was conducted over 130 years ago in the 1880s. A man called Joseph Jacobs gave people sets of numbers to remember. The sets got longer and longer. Jacobs found the average is around six or seven.

There's a long break then until 1959. In that year, Peterson and Peterson published a study that looked at the length of short-term memory if there was no rehearsal. They found that people can remember meaningless shapes without rehearsal for about three seconds. But after 18 seconds, nearly everything is forgotten.

OK. Where have we got to? 1959. Right … In 1964, someone called Conrad said that we encode sensory information as sound. But only six years later, in 1970, another researcher called Shulman found that some information is encoded for meaning, not sound.

Presenter: Two.

Lecturer 2: So we talked last time about making friends. This time, I'm going to consider the problem of keeping friends. I'm going to describe the three main barriers to keeping friends, and give you some examples.

Firstly, we have acceptance. Some people want to change other people. They cannot accept them the way they are. But most people don't want to change, or can't change, so that is the first barrier to friendship.

Secondly, there is approval. Some people find it easier to criticize than to find the good things in a person. Sometimes we find it difficult to be happy for another person's success, even a close friend. People want to be approved of, so constant lack of approval is the second barrier to friendship.

Finally, appreciation. We have heard that you must accept a person for what they are. We have also heard that you must approve of your friends, their behaviour, their attitudes or their achievements. But you must go further if you want to keep friends. You must show that you accept and approve. Show that you value them, show that you appreciate them.

Presenter: Three.

Lecturer 3: Right. We have heard about the idea of two selves. Now let's compare Self 1 and Self 2. Let's look at each point in turn.
Self 1 is confident. Self 2 is doubtful.
Self 1 is how other people see us but Self 2 is how we see ourselves.
Self 1 looks at work and life and says, 'Everything doesn't have to be perfect.' But for Self 2 it is everything or nothing.
Self 1 is optimistic – the future will be better than the present. Self 2 is pessimistic. The future will be worse than the present.

Presenter: Four.

Lecturer 4: We talked last week about the great deserts of the world. Today, we're going to look at the process of desertification. How does a fertile area become a desert?

Desertification starts with slightly less rain one year than the year before. This means that the plants do not grow quite as well. So less rain, fewer plants. This in turn means that the leaves of the plants hold less water close to the surface. So fewer plants leads to less water close to the surface. Less surface water means there is less evaporation into the air … which means there is less rain the next year. So we go back to the beginning and go through the vicious circle again.

## Closure
Allow students to read the transcripts for Exercise C and play the CDs once more.

### 5.4 Grammar for listening: Understanding information after relative pronouns

### Objectives

By the end of the lesson, students should be able to:

- discriminate between question words and relative pronouns;
- demonstrate understanding of spoken information following relative pronouns;
- predict information following a relative pronoun.

## Introduction
Replay the DVDs of the lecture from Lesson 5.2 Real-time listening, or allow students a few minutes to reread the transcript. (Several of this lesson's example grammar sentences come from that lecture, so this will provide a context for the activities.) If you are worried about time, just play a short extract from the lecture.

### Methodology note
Put the table in Grammar box 23 on the board using an electronic projection so that you can refer to it during the lesson. If possible, put the words in the 'extra information' column on one line. This will make it easier for students to read. (We have had to put the words on two lines in the Course Book due to lack of space.)

### Grammar box 23
Give students time to study the table. Tell students the words *who*, *which*, *where* are really joining words. Elicit the two short sentences for each long sentence, and write them on the board:

Example 1:
*The first person is Herodotus.*
***He*** *studied human beings in the 5th century* BCE.

Example 2:
*The travellers found cultures.*
***They*** *were very different from their own.*

Example 3:
*Herodotus described the Minoan culture.*
***The women*** *were more important than the men.*

Point out that sometimes the relative pronoun replaces the subject of the second sentence (Examples 1 and 2). Sometimes there is a new subject for the extra information (Example 3).

Erase each of the second sentences from the examples on the board. Ask students to close their books or to cover the table. Elicit each complete sentence with the relative clause. Play 5.8 to check students are producing the sentences correctly.

Note: In theory, all the *wh-* question words can also be relative pronouns. However, according to corpus findings, *which / that*, *who* and *where* are by far the ones most commonly used as relative pronouns.

### Transcript
5.8

Presenter: 5.8. Lesson 5.4. Grammar for listening: Understanding information after relative pronouns. Grammar box 23. Listen. How does the speaker say the relative pronouns?

Voice: The first person is Herodotus, who studied human beings in the 5th century BCE.
The travellers found cultures which were very different from their own.
Herodotus described the Minoan culture where the women were more important than the men.

## A  Question word or relative pronoun?

Tell students that when they hear *who*, *which* or *where*, they must decide if it is a question or a relative pronoun. This activity will help them identify between the two.

Set the task and go over the example. Play 5.9. Students complete the activity individually, then compare their answers in pairs. Elicit answers. Replay any of the extracts students had difficulty with.

### Answers
1.
1. a  2. b  3. b  4. b  5. a  6. b  7. b
8. b  9. b  10. a  11. b  12. b

2.
Point out that relative pronouns have the same sound as question words but:
- There is an intonation fall before a question word – there is no fall, perhaps even a slight rise, before a relative pronoun.
- There is a pause before starting a question.
- Question words have a high pitch. Relative pronouns have a middle pitch.

### Transcript
**5.9**

Presenter: 5.9. Exercise A1. Listen to some extracts from lectures. They each contain *which*, *who* or *where*. Tick in the correct column in each case.

Voices:
1. We are going to talk about a great anthropologist, Margaret Mead. Who was she and what did she do for anthropology?
2. Herodotus didn't simply write down the stories which he had heard.
3. He described the Scythians who practised human sacrifice.
4. First, I'm going to talk about Marco Polo who came from Italy.
5. Then I'll look at Ibn Khaldun. Where did he come from?
6. Columbus sailed to the Americas, which was a new world for people from Europe.
7. They met the Iroquois who believed that women were more important than men.
8. The Sahara occupies most of the northern third of the continent of Africa, which, of course, is a huge continent.
9. There are some rock paintings in the Sahara which show fish.
10. The ancient people of the Sahara left the area. Where did they go?
11. The theory of self-management comes from a fascinating book which was published in 1974.
12. Miller wrote an article which described research into short-term memory.

## B  Understanding extra information

Remind students that relative pronouns introduce extra information. In this activity they will practise listening for the extra information after a relative pronoun. Students have heard the sentences before (in Exercise A), so that will help them with this activity.

Check students understand the task. Give students time to read the phrases in the first column. Play 5.10 as far as the first example and check understanding once more. If necessary, do the second sentence with the class as another example. Play the rest of the sentences. Students complete the table individually, in note form, then compare their answers in pairs. Elicit answers and show students the transcript if necessary.

### Answers

| 1. … stories which | he had heard. |
|---|---|
| 2. … the Scythians who | practised human sacrifice. |
| 3. … Marco Polo who | came from Italy. |
| 4. … the Americas which | was a new world for people from Europe. |
| 5. … the Iroquois who | believed that women were more important than men. |
| 6. … Africa which | is a huge continent. |

### Transcript
**5.10**

Presenter: 5.10. Exercise B. Listen again to some of the sentences from Exercise A with relative pronouns. What is the extra information in each case?

Voices:
1. Herodotus didn't simply write down the stories which he had heard.
2. He described the Scythians who practised human sacrifice.
3. First, I'm going to talk about Marco Polo who came from Italy.
4. Columbus sailed to the Americas, which was a new world for people from Europe.
5. They met the Iroquois who believed that women were more important than men.
6. The Sahara occupies most of the northern third of the continent of Africa, which, of course, is a huge continent.

### C Predicting the information after a relative pronoun

1. Students should already know by now the importance of the sub-skill of predicting information when listening to a text. Relative pronouns are another way of doing this. Check students understand the task and give them time to read all the sentence completions. Play 5.11. Students complete the activity individually, then compare their answers in pairs. Elicit answers.

2. Play 5.12 for students to check their answers.

### Transcripts and Answers

**5.11**

Presenter: 5.11. Exercise C1. Listen to the first part of some sentences. What sort of information do you expect to come next? Think, then find and number a sentence completion.

Voices:
1. The researchers did experiments which …
2. Mead was an anthropologist who …
3. Ueno did a survey in Florida where …
4. Urgent items are things which …
5. When we are young, friends are people who …
6. There are many barriers which …
7. Self 2 is the part of a person which …
8. Deserts are areas which …

**5.12**

Presenter: 5.12. Exercise C2. Listen and check your answers.

Voices:
1. The researchers did experiments which proved that the theory was correct.
2. Mead was an anthropologist who studied adolescents in Samoa.
3. Ueno did a survey in Florida where he was studying.
4. Urgent items are things which must be done now.
5. When we are young, friends are people who make us laugh.
6. There are many barriers which get in the way of friendship.
7. Self 2 is the part of a person which is doubtful.
8. Deserts are areas which have little or no rain.

### Closure

Go over the main points of the lesson by asking questions about the grammar. For example:

- *Which words are relative pronouns?* (*which, who, where*)
- *What do relative pronouns do?* (give extra information)
- *What should we do when we hear* which, who, where? (decide if it is a question or a relative pronoun)
- *How do we know if it is a question?* (there's a pause, and a high pitch)
- *If it's a relative pronoun, what should we do?* (predict the extra information)

## 5.5 Applying new listening skills: Franz Boas

### Objectives

By the end of the lesson, students should have:
- produced the correct type of notes to match the information given;
- developed knowledge for the fundamental principles of anthropology.

### Introduction

1. Write the following words on the board as the students are arriving. Say the stressed syllable of some words from the lecture in Lesson 5.1 Vocabulary for listening. Then ask students to identify the complete word in each case.
   Note: Only say the stressed syllable in each case.

   anthro'pology      ethno'centric
   'attitude          'evidence
   be'lief            'integrate
   'civilized         m'inority
   'colonist          multi'cultural
   'discipline
   di'versity

2. Remind students about relative pronouns. Give the beginning of some of the sentences from the previous lesson and ask students to complete them logically, e.g.,
   - *Herodotus didn't simply write down stories which …*
   - *He described the Scythians who …*
   - *First, I'm going to talk about Marco Polo who …*
   - *Columbus sailed to the Americas where …*
   - *They met the Iroquois who …*
   - *The Sahara occupies most of the northern third of Africa which …*
   - *In the Sahara, there are some rock paintings which …*
   - *The theory of self-management comes from a fascinating book which …*
   - *Miller wrote an article where …*

### A Activating ideas

Set the task, giving the example of *learn the language*. You can discuss if the question means 'understand about another culture' as an anthropologist, or as an individual. You can either leave the class to think of their own ideas completely, or you can write the following list on the board for students to discuss:
- *marry someone from the culture (or have a boy/girlfriend)*
- *live in the culture*
- *visit the culture on holiday or field trip*
- *learn the language*
- *migrate to the country*
- *do research about the culture*
- *make online friends from the culture*
- *collect data*

Elicit some ideas but do not confirm or correct at this stage.

### Answers
Answers depend on students.

### B Understanding an introduction

Exploit the visuals and set the task, making sure students understand about leaving enough space in between each section for further notes to be added later.

Play DVD 5.C. Students complete their notes individually then compare them in pairs. Elicit answers, preferably using an electronic projection. Make sure students have the correct notes at this point or they could go off on a tangent during the rest of the listening task.

Ask one or two questions and encourage students to predict the type of information that is coming up in the main part of the lecture, e.g.,
- *Who was Franz Boas?* (an anthropologist)
- *What information will you hear in the 'Life' section of the lecture?* (when he was born, when he died, education, where he worked, etc.)
- *From the photographs, when do you think he lived?* (late 19th and early 20th century)
- *Again from the photos, what work do you think he did?* (perhaps studied immigrants, language, etc.; perhaps studied Native Americans, customs, etc.)
- *What about the last section – what were the old ideas about anthropology? What were Boas's new ideas?* (Students may have no ideas, and that is fine! But they might suggest, for example, that old anthropologists compared other cultures with Western culture.)

### Answers
*Franz Boas*
*Life*
*Examples of work*
*Old view* vs *Boas's new view*

### Transcript

5.13 DVD 5.C

| | |
|---|---|
| Presenter: | 5.13. Lesson 5.5. Applying new listening skills: Franz Boas |
| Lecturer: | Today, we're talking about the life and work of one of the greatest anthropologists of all time. His name is Franz Boas. We have heard in previous lectures about Herodotus who is The Father of Anthropology for some people. Well, Boas is the father of modern anthropology. Quite simply, he changed the way people thought about other cultures. I'm going to start by talking briefly about his life, then I'm going to give one example each of the work which he did in three different fields of anthropology. Finally, I'm going to compare older views with his new ideas. |

> **Methodology note**
>
> Students may find some of Boas's ideas difficult to understand. Point out that this is not surprising! People have been arguing about them since he proposed them, and, indeed, some anthropologists today say that they cannot be correct – all cultures cannot be equally developed and civilized, for example, and there should be some universals of behaviour.

**C** Following a lecture

Remind students about the different ways to organize notes, and if necessary refer students back to Lesson 5.3 Learning new listening skills. However, avoid telling students which type of notes to use for each section. A key skill is for students to work this out for themselves.

You can deal with the lecture in different ways:

- **Less able classes**: Play one section from [DVD] 5.D. Elicit the kind of information given. Ask one or two questions about the information. Play the DVD again; this time, students should take notes. Elicit answers, using an electronic projection. Complete the next section in the same way.
- **Average classes**: Play one section at a time. Students complete only the notes for that section. Elicit answers, using an electronic projection. Replay the section. Ask one or two questions to check understanding.
- **More able classes**: Play the lecture all the way through, possibly with a short pause after each section in order to give students enough time to write their notes.

Once you give feedback to the class, you can then play the DVD once more, with students following the transcript if you wish. Alternatively, you can wait to do this until after Exercise D.

Answers
Model notes:

Life
| | |
|---|---|
| 1858 | b. Germany |
| | studied geog., phy. at uni |
| 1881 | grad from Heidelberg; PhD from Kiel |
| 1883 | exp. to Canada – fieldwork with Inuit; became int. in anth. |
| 1885 | emi. to US; became ed. of Science |
| 1885–96 | more fieldwork with Nat. Am. |
| 1892 | presented findings at World's Fair, Chi. |
| 1899 | prof. anth. Col. Uni, NYC |
| 1942 | d. |

Examples of work

| biol. | ling. | cult. |
|---|---|---|
| – 18,000 imm. body shapes, etc.<br>– changes in one or two generations | – Nat. Am. lang. not properly developed = not civil.<br>– Boas = not prod. but perception | – 1883–86 with Inuit<br>– collected data on everything<br>– most anth. stayed at home and made theories |

Old view *vs* Boas's new view

| old view | Boas |
|---|---|
| – civilization = evolution<br>– all cultures – same stages<br>– people are uncivilized / savages – can or must be civilized | – 'Civilization is not something absolute', West civ. NOT the standard<br>– all cultures have customs which seem strange<br>– learn to accept cultures and live without conflict |

# Transcript

Lecturer: Nowadays, there are many multicultural cities around the world. In these cities, people are trying to integrate. Why do they face problems? Anthropologists have some of the answers. Today, we're talking about the life and work of one of the greatest anthropologists of all time. His name is Franz Boas. We have heard in previous lectures about Herodotus who is the father of anthropology for some people. Well, Boas is the father of modern anthropology. Quite simply, he changed the way people thought about other cultures. I'm going to start by talking briefly about his life, then I'm going to give one example each of the work which he did in three different fields of anthropology. Finally, I'm going to compare older views with his new ideas.

Franz Boas was born in 1858 in Germany. As a young man, he was interested in geography and physics, which he studied at various universities in Germany. He graduated from the University of Heidelberg in 1881 and got his PhD from Kiel University in the same year.

In 1883, Boas joined a geography expedition which travelled to Canada. He did fieldwork amongst the Inuit people, who were called Eskimos at that time. He became interested in anthropology.

Two years later, Boas emigrated to the United States where he became editor of a journal called *Science*.

Between 1885 and 1896, he did more fieldwork in North America. He studied Native American cultures. In 1892, he presented some of his findings at the World's Fair in Chicago. The aim of the exhibition was to teach the majority population of the country about the indigenous people of their land. In 1899, he became Professor of Anthropology at Columbia University in New York City.

Boas taught many students during his long career and wrote nearly 20 books on anthropology, including one which was called *Race, language and culture*. Boas died in 1942.

Boas did work in three of the main fields of anthropology. I'm going to give you one example of each.

Firstly, he did research into biological anthropology. This is usually concerned with physical differences between human beings and apes. The physical changes in this case have happened over hundreds of thousands of years. But Boas looked at biological changes which happened over very short periods. For example, he studied nearly 18,000 immigrants to the United States. He found that migrants from a particular country or region had typical heights, body shapes, head sizes. But even in one or two generations, the children of immigrants developed body shapes and sizes which were much closer to those of the majority population. The important point here is … environment is part of human biology as well as inheritance from parents and grandparents.

Secondly, Boas worked in linguistic anthropology. Let me give you an example of his work in this area. A well-known linguist of the day argued that Native American language was not properly developed, because the same person sometimes pronounced the same word in different ways. The thing is – the linguist was saying that Native Americans were not civilized. After a great deal of study, Boas concluded that the problem was not with the production of sounds by the Native American. The production was perfectly consistent. The problem was the perception by an American. It was the way which the person heard the words. He went on to point out that culture can make us perceive things in a particular way. Remember that. It is a very important point. Boas said that culture affects the way which we perceive things.

Thirdly, Boas did research in cultural anthropology. He believed very strongly in fieldwork. He said that you had to go out and live with the people, learn their language, experience their culture. For example, between 1883 and 1886, he spent many months with the Inuit. He tried to find out about every aspect of their culture. He collected data on family life, discipline of children, marriage, birth and death customs, food and so on. What I want you to understand is this: fieldwork and research were not normal at the time. Many anthropologists stayed at home and made theories about other cultures.

What did Boas contribute to anthropology? Well, he changed it forever. Let's look at the old view and then see the new view after Boas.

In the old view, civilization was a question of evolution. Most people in the West accepted this view at the beginning of the 20th century. All cultures started off in an uncivilized state and gradually developed. On the way, all cultures passed through the same stages of development. That was the old view. The important point is … in this view, it was acceptable to try to civilize people to a Western way of life.

Boas did not agree with this. He said 'Civilization is not something absolute.' In other words, Western civilization is not the standard for civilization, and we cannot apply the norms of Western civilization to other cultures. All cultures have customs which seem strange to other cultures. We must learn to accept other cultures and live together, without conflict. However, some of Boas's ideas are contentious today – I mean, they are not accepted by everyone. What do you think? We'll have a tutorial on Boas later this month. Do some research before then.
OK. Next week, we are going to look at one of the very few customs which is present in all cultures. What is that custom? Marriage, of course.

### D  Checking understanding of facts

Set the task, making sure students refer only to their notes and not to the transcript. Students complete the activity individually, then compare their answers in pairs. Elicit answers and check the meanings of new vocabulary as you do so.

Answers
1. Boas was born *in Germany in 1858*.
2. At university, he studied *geography and physics*.
3. In 1885, he *emigrated to the US*.
4. During his life, he did fieldwork with *the Inuit and with Native Americans*.
5. He did work in three areas of anthropology – *biological, linguistic and cultural*.
6. In biological anthropology, he studied *nearly 18,000 immigrants and looked at changes to their body shape*.
7. In 1899, he became *Professor of Anthropology at Columbia University*.
8. He died *in 1942*.

### E  Checking understanding of ideas

Set the task. Students discuss each point in pairs or small groups. If students are not sure of the answers, play again the relevant section of the DVD from Exercise C, or refer students to the transcript.

Elicit answers and go over the meaning of any new vocabulary once again.

Answers
1. All cultures pass through the same stages of development.
2. Anthropologists should collect data. ✓
3. Culture can affect perception. ✓
4. We must accept other cultures. ✓
5. We should try to civilize people from other cultures.
6. Western civilization is the standard for other cultures.

### F  Transferring information to the real world

Students discuss the questions in pairs or small groups. Elicit ideas.

Answers
Answers depend on students.

**Closure**
Choose one of the following:

- Use the discussion in Exercise F for Closure.
- Replay the DVDs of the lecture if you have not already done so, with or without students following the transcript.
- Focus on some of the key vocabulary from the lesson.

---

**Methodology note**

Some anthropologists say that if you take Boas's view – that we must not judge other cultures – to the logical conclusion, then we cannot say that, for example, human sacrifice is wrong.

You can add this point to the discussion and see what students make of it.

---

Theme 5: Listening  233

# Speaking: Wedding customs

### 5.6 Vocabulary for speaking: Love, marriage and evil spirits

**Objectives**

By the end of the lesson, students should be able to:
- demonstrate understanding of meanings of target vocabulary from the Speaking section;
- pronounce target vocabulary, both in isolation and in context;
- use knowledge about wedding customs in order to complete tasks.

**Introduction**

Choose one of the following, or you can do both if you wish:

1. If appropriate to do with your class, write the following questions on the board for students to discuss in pairs:
   - *Are you married?*
   - *(yes) How long have you been married?*
   - *(no) Do you think you will get married one day?*

2. Exploit the visuals and elicit/teach the following vocabulary:
   *heart*
   *vein*
   *bride*
   *groom*
   *priest*
   *wedding*
   *evil spirit*

### A  Activating ideas

Set the task for pairwork and make sure students cover the vocabulary list on the right. Set a time limit of two minutes for students to write a list of ten (or more) words. They should not worry too much about the words' spelling. After the two minutes are up, ask the pair of students with the longest list to read out their words. Help with students' pronunciation where necessary. The rest of the class listen and tick off any words which are on their own lists. Now elicit from the rest of the class any additional words, again helping with students' pronunciation as necessary.

Finally, students look at the list of words on the right-hand side in the Course Book. They can correct any spelling mistakes in their lists, and check to see if there are any words they did not think of.

Do not spend too much time on either meaning or pronunciation at this point, as further help is given with these in the following activities.

**Answers**

Answers depend on students. Accept any reasonable answers, as long as students can justify why a word is on their list.

### B  Understanding new vocabulary in context

Divide the class into pairs, or groups of three, and set the task. Tell them it does not matter if they cannot solve some of the clues. Also tell students to guess the pronunciation of new words, if necessary. Do not elicit answers at this stage and stop the activity after a few minutes.

Now play DVD 5.E. Students listen and check their answers. This activity is not so much about confirming the correct answers, as giving students the correct pronunciation of the target vocabulary. Once students have listened to the pronunciation of the target vocabulary in context on the DVD, you can then use flashcards – or point to the words on the board – in order to practise the correct pronunciation.

Play the DVD again, pausing after some of the phrases or sentences for students to repeat.

### Optional activity

Play the DVD again, with students following the transcript. Focus on some of the phrases used in the dialogue for taking turns and confirming correct answers. You can highlight the forms and practise them with the class, if you wish.

**Answers**
a. Bride and groom
b. Gold and silver
c. The heart
d. A priest
e. Marriage
f. Evil spirits
g. The reception
h. Honeymoon

## Transcript

🔊 5.15  [DVD]  5.E

| | |
|---|---|
| **Presenter:** | Lesson 5.6. Vocabulary for speaking: Love, marriage and evil spirits |
| **Student A:** | OK, let's look at the first clue. 'What are the words for the important couple at a wedding?' I think that's easy. |
| **Student B:** | Yes. Bride and groom? |
| **Student A:** | Yes. So you read out the next clue. |
| **Student B:** | OK. 'What words in English do the symbols Au and Ag represent? People often give presents at weddings which are made of these metals.' |
| **Student A:** | Another easy one. That's gold and silver. So the next one is c. 'Where did people use to believe love came from? In fact, it sends blood round the body.' What is *use to*? |
| **Student B:** | It means 'in the past'. |
| **Student A:** | Ah. OK. So, that's obviously heart. OK – d. 'Who is the person in charge of a wedding ceremony in some cases?' Umm … I think that's priest. |
| **Student B:** | Yes, that's right. Priest. So whose turn is it to read out the next clue? |
| **Student A:** | Mine. 'The wedding is the event, but what do we call the legal union of two people?' |
| **Student B:** | I guess that's marriage. I never really knew the difference before. So *marriage* is the noun, and the verb is *marry*, but the ceremony is *wedding*. |
| **Student A:** | Anyway, it's your turn to read out letter f. |
| **Student B:** | OK. 'Which mythical creatures did people use to believe were present at weddings?' What are mythical creatures? |
| **Student A:** | Mmm … I think it means 'not real', like in a children's story. [PAUSE] Have you found the answer? |
| **Student B:** | Maybe. Is it evil spirits? |
| **Student A:** | Yes, I think so. And I think the answer for g, the party after a wedding, is reception. |
| **Student B:** | Yes, I agree. And what about the last one? Is it honeymoon? |
| **Student A:** | That's right. I know that word. *Month* comes from *moon*. |
| **Student B:** | Great. That's it. Finished. |

### Pronunciation check

This can be dealt with after Exercise B or it can be left until the end of the lesson.

Remind students that in English we can have different sounds for the same letters, and vice versa.

Set the task. Students work in pairs. Encourage them to pronounce each pair of words aloud in order to complete the task. Before you elicit answers, play 🔊 **5.17** and 🔊 **5.18** so that students can check their ideas.

Practise pronunciation of some of the pairs of words.

## Answers

| believe | priest | same sound |
|---|---|---|
| blood | groom | different sounds |
| creature | heart | different sounds |
| ceremony | represent | different sounds |
| couple | union | different sounds |
| marriage | origin | same sound |
| married | evil | different sounds |
| symbol | silver | same sound |

### Optional activity

Ask students to mark the stressed syllable on the multi-syllable words in the list.

## Answers

be'lieve
'creature
'ceremony
repre'sent
'couple
'marriage
'married
'symbol
'union
'origin
'evil
'silver

## Transcripts

🔊 5.17

| | |
|---|---|
| **Presenter:** | 5.17. Pronunciation Check. Is the underlined sound the same or different in each pair of words? |
| **Voice:** | believe, priest; blood, groom; creature, heart; ceremony, represent |

🔊 5.18

| | |
|---|---|
| **Presenter:** | 5.18. Pronunciation Check. What about these pairs? |
| **Voice:** | couple, union; marriage, origin; married, evil; symbol, silver |

### Methodology notes

1. As presented in the Course Book, Exercise C follows a fairly traditional approach. If you prefer, or if you have a very able class, you can get them to do the question and answer practice first. The CD can then be used for students simply to check if their questions were correct.

2. The verb *arrange* (question f) has a special meaning in this context. It refers to the custom, in many cultures, where the parents of the bride and groom choose their child's partner. This is referred to as an *arranged marriage*. There is more opportunity to discuss this custom in the Reading section of this theme, which includes a text about it.

### C  Using new vocabulary

1. This activity:

- revises question and answer forms in the present simple;
- practises pronunciation of the target vocabulary in sentence context;
- activates background knowledge about the topic of the section.

Ask students to study the question prompts individually and think about how to complete each question. Only allow a minute or two for this, in order to discourage students from writing out the full questions at this point. If you wish, ask students to tell you what they think each question is, but do not confirm or correct ideas just yet.

Play 5.16. Pause after each question for students to repeat.

2. Set the task for pairwork. Monitor while students are working. Give feedback. If you have a multicultural class, you can spend a reasonable amount of time eliciting the information students learnt about weddings in different countries. In a monocultural environment, you can elicit the answers and check that everyone agrees with them, before moving on to Closure.

The questions can be written for consolidation either later in the lesson or as a homework activity, with or without answers.

### Transcript

5.16

**Presenter:** 5.16. Exercise C1. Listen and repeat the questions.

**Voices:**
a. What does the bride usually wear during the ceremony?
b. Does the groom wear any special clothes?
c. Is there a reception after the wedding?
d. Do the couple go on a special holiday?
e. Where do people (usually) get married?
f. Do the families of the bride and groom arrange the marriage?
g. Does anyone still believe in evil spirits at weddings?

### Closure

If you have not already done so, you can complete one or more of the following:

- Further discussion concerning weddings in the students' culture(s).
- Marking stress on the multi-syllable words from the lesson.
- Further drilling, or practice of the target vocabulary using flashcards.
- Ask students to write the questions from Exercise C.

### 5.7 Real-time speaking: Wedding customs in Britain

### Objectives

By the end of the lesson, students should be able to:

- use existing skills to talk about the origins of wedding customs;
- pronounce target vocabulary in context.

**Introduction**
Write the words below (from Lesson 5.6 Vocabulary for speaking) on the board. Ask students what they have in common. They might say weddings, but they also have the same pronunciation pattern – two syllables, stress on the first.
*creature*
*couple*
*marriage*
*silver*
*special*
*symbol*
*married*

Write the three-syllable words below (again from Lesson 5.6) on the board and ask students to put them into groups, according to the stressed syllable.
*honeymoon*
*important*
*mythical*
*origin*
*reception*
*represent*
*union*

Answers

| O o o | o O o | o o O |
|---|---|---|
| union | reception | represent |
| mythical | important | |
| honeymoon | | |
| origin | | |

**A  Activating ideas**
When students have read the information about the tutorial, ask one or two questions to check understanding:
- What's the word that means …
  - 'all cultures'? (universal)
  - 'are different' or 'change'? (vary)
  - 'the beginning of something'? (origins)
- What do all cultures have? (a form of marriage)
- What is different in each culture? (the marriage customs)

Remind students – or elicit from them – the difference in meaning between the words *marriage* and *wedding* (see previous lesson).

Exploit the visual of the rings. Elicit the fact that rings are a wedding custom in many countries. Ask students if they have this custom in their country(ies). If so, do they know the origins?

Now set the task, asking students to write a list of more customs. If students are all from the same culture, they can make a list of the wedding customs in pairs or in small groups. If students are from different cultures, they can try to make a list of similarities and/or differences in wedding customs from their cultures.

Monitor and give help with vocabulary if necessary.

After a few minutes, elicit ideas. Ask students if they know the *origins* of any of the customs.

Answers
Answers depend on students.

**B  Understanding a model**
Set the task. You may want to pre-teach the word *vein* and write it on the board. Play DVD 5.F. Students complete the notes individually, then compare their answers in pairs. Elicit answers using an electronic projection. Check and practise the pronunciation of some of the vocabulary and phrases:
*veins*
*symbol of union*
*couple*
*exchange*
*blood*
*heart*

Ask questions to further check understanding:
- *What is the ring a symbol of?* (the couple's union or joining together)
- *Where do people wear the rings?* (on the third finger of the left hand)
- *Why do they wear it there?* (people thought there was a special vein there)
- *Why was the vein special?* (because it carried blood to the heart)

Answers

| the custom: | exchange of rings |
|---|---|
| now: | symbol of union = couple are joined together<br>ring on 3rd fing. L. hand |
| origins: | vein in 3rd fing.<br>blood to heart = 'centre of love' |

Theme 5: Speaking  237

## Transcript

🔊 5.19  DVD  5.F

| Presenter: | Lesson 5.7. Real-time speaking: Wedding customs in Britain |
|---|---|
| Student A: | Right. I'm going to talk about my culture, which is the British culture. There are several important wedding customs in my culture. Firstly, the bride and groom exchange rings. |
| Student B: | Exchange? |
| Student A: | Yes, it means the bride gives the groom a ring and the groom gives the bride a ring. |
| Student B: | I see. |
| Student A: | OK. Where was I? Oh, yes. The ring is a symbol of union. |
| Student B: | I'm sorry. I don't understand. |
| Student A: | What I mean is, the ring shows that the couple are joined together. |
| Student B: | OK. |
| Student A: | In British culture, a wedding ring is always worn on the third finger of the left hand. Apparently, people used to think that there was a special vein in that finger. |
| Student B: | I don't get your point. |
| Student A: | OK. I'll explain a bit more. Veins carry the blood to the heart. People used to believe that the heart was the centre of love. OK. So, that's the rings. Secondly, ... |

### Methodology notes

1. Students may already be familiar with the expression *used to* for describing a habitual past action. If they are not familiar with it, it is enough that they simply understand it as a past expression for now. Students should also be told not to confuse it with the verb *use* as in *I use my laptop when I'm on the train*.
   Do not spend too long on this grammar point as it is fully explained and practised in the following grammar lesson.

2. *What I mean is* ... is a very strange phrase because the two verbs *mean* and *is* are next to each other. It's an example of a pseudo-cleft sentence. However, it is not necessary to go into lengthy grammar explanations here; teach it as a very strange but very useful phrase!

### C Studying a model

1. This activity helps students to 'notice' the target language for the section. Set the task. Students work in pairs to find the three types of expressions. You can ask them to underline or circle the expressions, if you wish. Elicit answers. Briefly check understanding of the sentences with *used to* and explain this is a verb phrase for something that happened in the past, but which does not happen now. (See Methodology note above.)

2. It is important for students to notice pauses when listening to a text. They need to learn that they should wait for suitable pauses before they can interrupt a speaker.

   It is also important to use polite intonation when asking for an explanation, and also for giving explanations.

   Play 🔊 5.20. Discuss the points where there were suitable pauses for someone to interrupt. There should be pauses, for example, after introductory phrases – such as *apparently ...*, *what I mean is ...*, etc.

   Play the CD again. Pause after a few of the phrases or sentences, and ask students to repeat and copy the intonation. Also check students' pronunciation of the phrase *used to* /ˈjuːstə/.

3. Students practise the extracts in pairs. Monitor and give feedback.

### Answers

1.
Asking for help
*I'm sorry. I don't understand.*
*I don't get your point.*

Explaining
*What I mean is, the ring shows that the couple are joined together.*
*OK. I'll explain a bit more. Veins carry the blood to the heart. People used to believe that the heart was the centre of love.*

Talking about the past
*Apparently, people used to think that there was a special vein in that finger.*

## Transcript

🔊 5.20

| Presenter: | 5.20. Exercise C2. Listen to the extracts. Notice the pauses and the intonation. |
|---|---|
| | Extract 1. |
| Student A: | ... The ring is a symbol of union. |
| Student B: | I'm sorry. I don't understand. |
| Student A: | What I mean is, the ring shows that the couple are joined together. |
| Student B: | OK. |
| Presenter: | Extract 2. |
| Student A: | Apparently, people used to think that there was a special vein in that finger. |

Student B: I don't get your point.
Student A: OK. I'll explain a bit more. Veins carry the blood to the heart. People used to believe that the heart was the centre of love.

### D  Producing a model

1. Set the task. Students can use a dictionary if necessary, or you can go around the class and help with comprehension. Make sure students make notes (refer them back to Exercise B for an example).

2. Make sure students' books are closed. Remind students of key language to use and the pronunciation points you want them to focus on. Make a list on the board for them to refer to:
   - pauses
   - polite intonation
   - *I'm sorry, I don't understand …*
   - *OK, I'll explain …*
   - *used to + do*

Monitor while students complete the task. Give feedback.

### Answers
Answers depend on students.

### Closure
Choose one of the following:
- Give feedback on the activity in Exercise D, if you have not already done so.
- Discuss the customs described in Exercise D and ask if they are similar to any in the students' own country(ies).
- Practise the pronunciation of some of the words or phrases from the lesson. You can write them on the board in random order. Give each word or phrase a number. Say the numbers either in order or randomly; students then say the corresponding word.

## Everyday English: Suggesting and responding to suggestions

### Objectives
By the end of the lesson, students should be able to:
- use the forms for some common ways of suggesting and responding, with accuracy of form and pronunciation;
- take part in conversations using suggestions and responses.

### Introduction
1. Write the title of the lesson on the board, *Suggesting and responding to suggestions*. Elicit an example of a suggestion and write it on the board. Elicit a response and add that to the board too. Tell students they will learn some more ways of making suggestions and responses during this lesson.

   Elicit the following infinitive and noun forms:
   *suggest – suggestion*
   *respond – response*
   Practise the pronunciation of the four words.

2. Focus students' attention on the photographs. Ask them to cover the rest of the page. In pairs, students discuss what the photos have in common.

### Methodology note
In some countries, it is customary to give cash rather than presents. In the UK, it is not always appropriate to give cash. However, gift tokens are more acceptable.

It is worth pointing out that the custom of giving practical wedding presents began a long time ago as a way to help a young couple, probably without much money, to set up a home.

Toasters are very popular wedding presents in the UK. However, students from many countries, including southern Europe, may not be familiar with them.

### A  Activating ideas

Divide the class into pairs or groups of three to discuss the questions. Monitor. Elicit some of the students' ideas. Ask some follow-up questions such as:

*Why isn't it a good idea to give a kitten (or other pet) for a wedding present?*

*Why do some people give practical presents such as toasters?*

*Do people spend too much money on wedding presents?*

**Answers**
Answers depend on students.

> **Methodology note**
>
> It is very common in some Western cultures for couples to send all the wedding guests a 'wedding list'. This is a list of presents they would like. Many department stores now provide a wedding list service. The advantage of this is that the couple only receives presents they actually want, and they do not receive duplicate presents. There is a well-known British joke about couples receiving several toasters and not much else! However, some people are against wedding lists as they often make people spend more money than they want to.
>
> The conversation in this exercise mentions a wedding list, and you might like to raise some of these points with your students.

### B  Studying a model (1)

1. Focus students' attention on the two questions. Check students' pronunciation of the word *suggest*. Play 5.21. Students discuss the questions in pairs. Elicit answers.

2. Set the task. Play 5.22. Students complete the activity individually, then compare their answers in pairs. Replay the CD if necessary. Elicit answers. Drill the sentences and questions, and check students are using suitable intonation patterns.

Ask students to look at the answers again, and mark them *S* for suggestion, *R* for response.

Highlight the forms for the suggestions on the board:

- *Why don't we + do …?*
- *Let's + do …*
- *We could + do …*
- *We'd better + do ('d = had)*

Highlight these forms for responses:

- *That's (not) very exciting / a good idea.*
- *I don't think we should + do*

Leave room to add more exponents after Exercise C.

If you wish, elicit different ways of completing the phrases on the board and use them as the basis for further repetition or drilling work.

> **Grammar note**
>
> Here are some usage notes on two of the phrases for suggestions listed above:
>
> 1. *We could + do …* has a more tentative feel to it, depending on the intonation used.
>
> 2. *We'd better + do* is a subjunctive form. The shortened form *'d* represents *had*; students, of course, may think it represents *would*. However, avoid going into grammatical explanations and simply teach it as a phrase. We tend to use *we'd better* as a result of another piece of information. For example:
>
>    - *It's starting to rain. We'd better go home.*
>    - A: *When's our presentation?*
>      B: *Friday morning. We'd better start work on it this afternoon.*
>
> We would not use it for a new idea or suggestion, for example:
>
> ~~We'd better~~ *go to the cinema this evening.*
>
> In this situation, we would say:
>
> *Let's go to the cinema this evening. / Shall we go to the cinema this evening?*

**Answers**

1.
a. A toaster, a cookery book, gift tokens, money.
b. They decide to check whether there is a wedding list.

2.
a. *Have you got any ideas* for a present?
b. *Why don't we* buy them a toaster? (S)
c. *That's not* very exciting! (R)
d. *Well, you suggest* something then.
e. *Let's get them* a cookery book. (S)

f. *We could just give them* money or gift tokens. (S)

g. *Perhaps we'd better ask them* if they've made a list. (S)

h. *I'll* text them now. (R)

## Transcripts

🔊 5.21

| Presenter: | 5.21. **Everyday English: Suggesting and responding to suggestions. Exercise B1. Listen to a conversation about wedding presents.** |
|---|---|
| Voice A: | Have you got any ideas for a present for John and Mary? |
| Voice B: | Mmm. Why don't we buy them a toaster? |
| Voice A: | A toaster! That's not very exciting. |
| Voice B: | Well, you suggest something then. |
| Voice A: | OK. Let's get them a cookery book. |
| Voice B: | I think they've already got lots of those. |
| Voice A: | We could just give them money … or gift tokens. |
| Voice B: | I don't think we should give them money. |
| Voice A: | OK. Perhaps we'd better ask them if they've made a list. |
| Voice B: | That's a good idea. I'll text them now. |

🔊 5.22

| Presenter: | 5.22. **Exercise B2. Listen again and complete the sentences.** |
|---|---|

[REPEAT OF SCRIPT FROM 🔊 5.21]

### Methodology note

It would be worth spending a few minutes in class discussing which phrases are more formal or informal, and which phrases are stronger than others. For example, *You should do …* is quite a strong suggestion and should therefore be used with care, and with good intonation, in order not to sound rude.

*It would be better if …* is usually a more tentative form where the speaker wishes to be polite. Perhaps the speaker feels the listener may not like the suggestion. It is more formal than some of the other phrases from the lesson. It is a second conditional sentence but, again, you need not go into too much grammatical explanation at this point; simply teach it as a phrase.

*I'd rather do …* is another example of a conditional sentence. It is a polite, more formal way of disagreeing. You may also wish to teach the more formal, but very common, response *I'd rather not* as a polite way of disagreeing.

**C** Studying a model (2)
If you prefer, you can switch around Exercises C1 and C2.

1. Set the underlining task. Elicit answers and add the phrases to the list on the board (see Exercise B). Organize them according to the verb forms that follow:
   - *Shall we + do …?*
   - *You should + do …*
   - *What / How about + ~ing?*
   - *It would be better if you / we + did …*

   Elicit possible ways to complete each phrase and drill the sentences. Obviously the final suggestion form, *It would be better if …*, will be the most challenging for the students due to its length and getting the forms correct. For this reason, make sure you allow enough time for students to practise it (see also Methodology note above).

   Now move on to the responses for the suggestions. Ask students to find the responses in the conversations. Elicit and add them to the board:
   - *OK*
   - *Fine with me*
   - *I'd rather + do …* ('d = would)
   - *I've already done (that)*
   - *Yes, I'll do (that)*

   Elicit what the 'd stands for in *I'd rather*. Once again, avoid a grammatical explanation and teach it as a phrase.

2. Replay the conversations on 🔊 5.23, pausing after each line for students to listen and repeat. Make sure students are using appropriate intonation patterns. Students then practise in pairs. Monitor and give feedback, especially on using polite intonation.

3. Set the task. Elicit some possible sentences for a conversation for one of the situations listed in the Course Book, and write them on the board. Students practise the example conversation from the board and then continue with the other situations. Monitor and give feedback.

### Answers

1.
A: <u>Shall we</u> go away this weekend?
B: OK. Where to?
A: Well, <u>what about</u> going to London?
B: <u>I'd rather</u> go somewhere cheaper.
A: OK, <u>how about</u> Brighton, then?
B: Fine with me.
A: I'll look up some hotels on the web.

2.
A: What's wrong?
B: I really can't do this assignment.
A: Well, maybe <u>you should</u> take a break.
B: I've already tried that. It didn't work.
A: Perhaps <u>it would be better if you</u> talked to your tutor.
B: Yes, I'll do that.

### Transcript

🔊 5.23

Presenter: 5.23. Exercise C2. Listen, then practise the conversations in pairs.

Conversation 1.

Voice A: Shall we go away this weekend?
Voice B: OK. Where to?
Voice A: Well, what about going to London?
Voice B: I'd rather go somewhere cheaper.
Voice A: OK, how about Brighton, then?
Voice B: Fine with me.
Voice A: I'll look up some hotels on the web.

Presenter Conversation 2.

Voice A: What's wrong?
Voice B: I really can't do this assignment.
Voice A: Well, maybe you should take a break.
Voice B: I've already tried that. It didn't work.
Voice A: Perhaps it would be better if you talked to your tutor.
Voice B: Yes, I'll do that.

### Closure

Choose one of the following:

1. Give further situations for students to practise conversations on, for example:
   - You have been invited to a relative's 80th birthday party. You don't know what to buy as a present.
   - You have been offered a job in China. You need to learn the language and the culture as quickly as possible.
   - You have been invited to the wedding of someone from a very important family. You don't know what to wear.
   - A student in your tutor group is unhappy. He/she says it's because he/she hasn't got any friends.
   - Your company is losing money. You don't know what to do to make a profit.

2. Students write down one or two of their conversations, either in class or for homework.

## 5.8 Learning new speaking skills: Checking and explaining

### Objectives

By the end of the lesson, students should be able to:
- pronounce words with consonant clusters;
- use phrases for checking, explaining and asking to wait, at appropriate points in a conversation.

### Introduction

Use flashcards of vocabulary from this section for pronunciation practice.

### A  Reviewing vocabulary

1. Set the task. Students complete the activity individually, then compare their answers in pairs. Elicit the missing letter in each row. For the second part of the task (pronunciation of the words), students should select 'new' or more difficult words to attempt the pronunciation. Students can do this in pairs.

2. Play 🔊 5.24 for students to check their ideas. If you wish, get individual students to read aloud each column of words – rather than each row – so they can get used to the range of clusters.

Now focus on the Pronunciation Check.

### Transcript

🔊 5.24

Presenter: 5.24. Lesson 5.8. Learning new speaking skills: Checking and explaining. Exercise A2. Listen and check.

Voice:
a. priest, groom, tradition, bride, friend
b. place, club, blue, flow, glass
c. steal, spirit, snow, small, straight
d. custom, respiration, instead, transpiration, disturb
e. sublimation, conclusion, supply, reflect, ugly
f. agree, improve, petrol, hydrogen, distract

> **Methodology note**
>
> If you prefer, you could do the Pronunciation Check before Exercise A.

### Pronunciation check

Students study the information. Ask:
*What is a consonant cluster?* (two – or more – consonants together without a vowel sound in the middle)

Practise pronunciation, firstly with each consonant cluster in isolation, then in words. Make sure students do not put a vowel sound between the two consonants in each cluster. Play 5.26, if you wish.

Point out that all the words in Exercise A have consonant clusters. Ask:

*Which words in Exercise A have clusters of three consonants?* (tran**sp**iration, **str**aight, con**cl**usion, di**str**act, i**mpr**ove)

You may also need to point out that we are talking about consonant sounds rather than spelling, so the letters *ght* in *straight*, or *pp* in *supply*, do not count as consonant clusters.

### Transcript

5.26

| Presenter: | 5.26. Pronunciation Check. |
|---|---|
| Voice: | bride, groom, tradition; place, club, blue; steal, spirit, straight |

### B  Identifying a key skill

1. Remind students about the tutorial extracts they listened to in Lesson 5.7 Real-time speaking. Ask them if they can remember any of the phrases for checking understanding and explaining.

   If you wish, you could replay the DVD again as a reminder, and also to give a context for this activity.

   Students read the Skills Check. Check students understand the verb *interrupt*. Discuss when it is fine to interrupt someone in a conversation or a discussion, e.g.,
   - at a natural pause;
   - when they have finished speaking;
   - at the end of a phrase or sentence.

   Point out that they will usually know when speakers are coming to the end of a phrase or sentence because of a falling intonation pattern.

   Ask students to look at the example phrases from the *Explaining* section in the Skills Check box. Write the phrases on the board and highlight the verbs. They are not strange new tenses but a different way of joining sentences. Students should not worry about the grammar of the sentences here; they should only learn them as phrases. (See the Methodology note for Exercise C in Lesson 5.7.) Play 5.27, if you wish.

2. Set the task. Students complete the activity individually, then compare their answers in pairs. Elicit answers.

3. Ask students to close their books or cover the exercise. Play 5.25. Pause after each phrase so that students can repeat the phrases. Make sure they are stressing the correct words and are using polite intonation patterns.

### Optional activity

Refer students back to the tutorial extracts in Lesson 5.7 Real-time speaking. Ask them to practise them again, but this time they should substitute different phrases from the Skills Check and Exercise B. Monitor and give feedback.

### Answers

| a. | Could I answer questions at the end? | A |
| b. | I don't get your point. | C |
| c. | My point is … | E |
| d. | It's still not clear to me. | C |
| e. | I'll explain that in a minute. | A |
| f. | I'll explain a bit more. | E |
| g. | That doesn't make sense to me. | C |
| h. | What I meant was … | E |

### Transcripts

5.25

| Presenter: | 5.25. Exercise B3. Listen and repeat some of the phrases. Copy the intonation patterns. |
|---|---|
| Presenter: | Checking |
| Voices: | I don't get your point.<br>It's still not clear to me.<br>That doesn't make sense to me. |
| Presenter: | Explaining |
| Voices: | My point is …<br>I'll explain a bit more.<br>What I meant was … |

Theme 5: Speaking  243

Presenter: Asking to wait

Voices: Could I answer questions at the end?
I'll explain that in a minute.

🌐 5.27

Presenter: 5.27. Skills Check.

Presenter: Checking

Voices: Sorry, I don't understand.
I'm not sure what you mean.

Presenter: Explaining

Voices: No, what I mean is …
What I'm trying to say is …

Presenter: Asking to wait

Voices: Can I deal with that in a little while?
I'm just coming to that.

### C  Practising a new skill

Set the task. You will probably need to demonstrate it first. Give students time to read the statements on pages 169 and 171 of the Course Book. They should be familiar with the topics, which come from the book's earlier themes. Make sure students are given enough time to practise saying the statements and explanations before starting to work in pairs. You can set this up by moving students into groups (1 and 2) so they can help each other practise. Or, students can remain in pairs and simply 'mumble' the sentences to themselves, or say the sentences 'in their heads'.

During this phase, monitor and give help where necessary.

Remind students to use the phrases from the Skills Check and Exercise B wherever possible. Also remind them to try and wait for pauses.

You can set the task in two ways:

1. Set two statements at a time (one for each student) for each pair to work on. Then monitor and give feedback.
2. Ask students to work through all of the statements until you run out of time.

### Closure

Give feedback on Exercise C, if you have not already done so.

If you think it is appropriate for your class, ask some of the more successful pairs to repeat their conversations for the class.

## 5.9 Grammar for speaking: *Used to …*

### Objectives

By the end of the lesson, students should be able to:
- talk about past customs, beliefs and habits with *used to / didn't use to*;
- produce correct sentences, negative and question forms for *used to*.

### Introduction

Write two sentences on the board:
*I went to Greece on holiday.*
*I used to go to Greece on holiday.*
Ask students to explain the difference. Do not confirm or correct answers at this stage.

### Methodology notes

1. The phrase *never used to* is often heard instead of *didn't use to*. For example: *I never used to eat cheese but I do now.*

   Grammarians state that the morpheme *d* should not be used with the negative of *used to*. However, you will often see, for example, *I didn't **used** to like her very much.*

   When speaking, it is almost irrelevant as the *d* is not pronounced due to the elision with *to*.

2. In this lesson we have deliberately avoided referring to the pattern *be + used to + doing* (as in: *He isn't used to doing much exercise*). We feel this would be too confusing for the students at this point.

### Grammar box 24

Refer students back to Lesson 5.7 Real-time speaking and remind them about the topic, the origins of wedding customs. Ask students to look back and find example sentences with *used to*. This will contextualize the grammar of this lesson for them. The sentences with *used to* in Lesson 5.7 were:
*People **used to** think there was a special vein in that finger.*
*People **used to** believe the heart was the centre of love.*
*The best man **used to** help the best man steal the bride.*

*People **used to** believe that evil spirits wanted to steal the bride.*

Ask students to study the tables. Play 5.28, if you wish.

Write the following sentence on the board:
*Peter used to have very long hair.*

Ask 'concept questions' to check understanding:
*When did Peter have very long hair?* (in the past, when he was young, etc.)

*Does Peter have long hair now?* (no, he doesn't)
You could add something along the lines of *Now that Peter is a very successful businessman, he can no longer have long hair.*

Write the following sentences on the board. Ask students to tell you what's wrong with each one:
*We used to living in a big house in the country.*
*Susan used to cycle to work last year.*
*That shop wasn't used to open on Sundays.*

## Transcript

🎧 5.28

**Presenter:** 5.28. Lesson 5.9. Grammar for speaking: *Used to* ... Grammar box 24.

**Voices:** The best man used to help the groom.
I used to live in the capital.
People didn't use to believe that the Earth was round.
She didn't use to like this kind of music.
Did people use to believe in evil spirits?
Did you use to work for the National Bank?

### A  Talking about the past

1. In pairs, students read the phonemic scripts and try to work out the three pronunciations. Elicit answers.

   Set the task. Play the sentences on 5.29. Elicit answers.

2. Play 5.30. Pause after each sentence so that students can repeat.

> **Optional activities**
>
> 1. Replay the CD from Exercise A1 and pause after each sentence so that students can repeat.
>
> 2. Write prompts on the board based on the sentences from the transcripts for Exercises A1 and A2. In pairs, students make the full sentences with *used to*. Finally, students can write some of the sentences for consolidation.

Example prompts:
*People / caves*
*People / not / cars*
*We / school*
*She / not / glasses*
*Where / live?*
*Young children / factories*
*What job / do?*

## Transcripts

🎧 5.29

**Presenter:** 5.29. Exercise A1. Listen to some sentences with *used to / didn't use to*. What is the correct pronunciation?

**Voices:** People used to live in caves.
People didn't use to have cars.
We used to walk to school.
She didn't use to wear glasses.
Where did you use to live?

🎧 5.30

**Presenter:** 5.30. Exercise A2. Listen and repeat some sentences with *used to*. Use the correct pronunciation.

**Voices:** 1. Young children used to work in factories.
2. He used to like playing tennis.
3. She used to be very short.
4. I used to have a cat.
5. They used to be married.
6. I didn't use to like classical music.
7. What job did you use to do?

### B  Talking about past beliefs, customs, habits and situations

Check understanding of the word *belief*. Elicit that it is the noun form of the verb *believe*. Ask students to read the list of beliefs. Check understanding of the words *dragons*. Write up this example sentence: *People used to believe that the Earth was at the centre of the Solar System.* Point out that it is really two sentences joined together:

1. *People used to believe something.*

2. *The Earth was at the centre of the Solar System.*

Explain that every sentence must:
- begin with *People used to believe that ...*;
- have two past tense verbs.

In pairs, students take turns to make the full sentence for each answer. Elicit answers.

Finally, students can write some of the sentences for consolidation (or set this as a homework task).

Theme 5: Speaking  245

### Answers
Many sentences are possible, including:
1. People used to believe in dragons. / People didn't use to know that dragons were mythical.
2. People used to light the streets with gas. / People didn't use to have electricity.
3. People used to carry goods in sailing ships. / People didn't use to have ships with engines.
4. People used to use stone tools. / People didn't use to have metal tools.
5. People used to travel by stagecoach. / People didn't use to have cars, buses or trains.

### C Talking about past customs, habits, situations, appearance

1. Set the task and go over examples. Elicit ideas for topics students could talk about and write a list on the board. For example:
   *computers*
   *mobile phones*
   *large families*
   *university education*
   *big cities*
   *bicycle*
   *car*
   *holidays*
   *a sport*
   *food*

   Monitor while students produce sentences in pairs. Give feedback. Elicit some of the students' sentences.
2. Repeat the procedure for Exercise C1.

### Answers
Answers depend on students.

### Closure
Ask students to write down some of their sentences from Exercise C.

## 5.10 Applying new speaking skills: Wedding customs around the world

### Objectives
By the end of the lesson, students should be able to:
- use a piece of research about wedding customs as a basis for a presentation;
- use explaining skills and deal with questions for a presentation about wedding customs in a different culture;
- pronounce target vocabulary from the Speaking section with accuracy in an extended turn.

### Introduction
Say the stressed syllable of some words from this section. Make sure you say the stressed syllable exactly as it appears in the complete word. Ask students to tell you the complete word, e.g.,

| | |
|---|---|
| lieve | believe |
| range | arrange |
| cer | ceremony |
| coup | couple |
| spi | spirit |
| e | evil |
| hon | honeymoon |
| or | origin |
| marr | marriage / marry / married |
| cep | reception |
| sent | represent |

### A Previewing vocabulary

1. Set the task and go over the example. Students work in pairs. Do not elicit answers.
2. Play ⊙ 5.31 once so that students can check their answers. Play the CD again, pausing after each sentence or question for repetition. If necessary, refer students back to Lesson 5.8 Learning new speaking skills on page 148 of the Course Book.

### Transcript and Answers
⊙ 5.31

Presenter: 5.31. Lesson 5.10. Applying new speaking skills: Wedding customs around the world. Exercise A2. Listen. How many did you get?

|  | Checking |
|---|---|
| Voices: | I don't get your point.<br>It's still not clear to me.<br>That doesn't make sense to me.<br>I'm not sure what you mean. |
| Presenter: | Explaining |
| Voices: | I'll explain a bit more.<br>What I mean is …<br>What I meant was …<br>What I'm trying to say is … |
| Presenter: | Asking to wait |
| Voices: | Could I answer questions at the end?<br>I'll explain that in a minute.<br>Can I deal with that in a little while?<br>I'm just coming to that. |

### Methodology note

As usual, you can adapt the activity in Exercise B to suit the dynamics of your class. Here are some alternative suggestions:

- Students can work in smaller groups of three or four. In this case, not all the research texts would be used.

- Students work in groups of three, with only three of the six texts allocated. Students complete the task. Monitor and give feedback. Then allocate the three remaining texts so that students can have a second attempt at the activity.

- In large classes – where you cannot physically move the students into groups – you could ask students to work in pairs. Allocate two texts to each pair. When students have worked on the first two texts, and after giving feedback, you could then ask them to work on two different texts.

- Here is a variation on a wall dictation which prevents students from simply reading aloud sentences from the texts. Instead of allowing students to look at the texts at the back of the book, you can enlarge each text and stick it on the wall in different parts of the classroom. Students have to take turns to go to the wall text, read it, come back to their group and explain it. The other students in the group then make notes of the information. This should generate a great deal of spoken language.

### B Researching information

1. Focus students' attention on the assignment on the right-hand side of the page. Check they understand the task.

2. Set the task carefully and divide the class into groups (see Methodology note above). Make sure each group understands they should only read **one** text. Make sure they also realize that they should only explain the extra information if they are asked – point out that asking for explanations and giving them are two of the main points of this section. In their groups, students should make notes of the information – they will not be able to simply read aloud in the next phase of the activity. Students should practise presenting the information. Students can help each other with pronunciation and so on. Monitor to check students have understood the task. Give help where necessary.

### C Using a key skill

1. Set the task and go through each point in the exercise, eliciting examples and drilling where appropriate.

2. Re-divide the class into groups of six, with one student from each of the original groups. Students take turns to give their information. Make sure they are not reading the texts aloud. Monitor and give feedback.

If you feel your students need further practice, ask three students from each group (Students 1, 2 and 3) to move around to the next group clockwise. In this way you are shuffling the groups in order to provide some variety. Now ask students to repeat the activity, keeping in mind the points from your feedback.

### Closure

Use your feedback for Exercise C as Closure. If you have not already done so, you can ask students to repeat the activity in their groups. You do not have to ask all six students in each group to give their information again – you can just ask, for example, Students 1 and 2 to repeat the information, while the other students check the information and ask questions.

# Reading: The price of happiness

## 5.11 Vocabulary for reading: Doing research

### Objectives

By the end of the lesson, students should be able to:
- demonstrate understanding of new vocabulary from the Reading section;
- recognize the spelling of new vocabulary;
- demonstrate understanding of information about the critical evaluation of research articles.

**Note**: This lesson is a little different from others in that it is an introduction to the *skill* rather than the *topic* of the Reading section. Therefore the focus is on bias in articles.

### Introduction

Write the title of the article on the board, *How to do research*.

Discuss with the class when they have had to do research for an assignment and elicit some of the methods they used.

You could suggest that using file cards is a good way of organizing and making notes:

- Write the reference at the top (book / article title, author, chapter / page, etc.).
- Make notes.
- Put quotes in quote marks so you do not simply copy by mistake.
- Always make a note of other references / authors quoted in an article.

The file cards can be laid out on a desk in order to help students organize their writing. They can be shuffled or reordered easily, and they are great for revision.

### A  Understanding vocabulary in context

1. Set the task. Students complete the activity individually, then compare their answers in pairs. Elicit answers, giving further help with the meaning of words if necessary.
2. Point out that students have to compare each statement with the writer's view in the article. If necessary, point out that each statement is slightly wrong. Students discuss in pairs. Elicit answers.

### Answers

1. Correct form of word in *italics*:

When you write assignments, you have to do research, which means reading *widely* / wide, using a variety of source / *sources*, including, nowadays, the Internet. But it does not mean just checking out Wikipedia and quote / *quoting* it word for word.

When students did all their research in the library, it was easy to find *authoritative* / author sources, because they could see the difference between a *popular* / popularity magazine and an academic *journal* / journals. On the web, you need to check who the writer is, who he/she is writing for, and whether the article just provides an overview or *detailed* / detail research.

You need to *validate* / valid all 'facts' on the web because many writers of web articles are bias / *biased* in favour of or against their topic. For example, people are often ethnocentric and think their own culture is always right. Sometimes they *state* / are stating their bias. They say clearly 'In my *opinion* / opinions ...' Sometimes, though, they are not so direct, but they use extremely / *extreme* words, particularly adjectives, like *stupid* and *disgusting*, or *brilliant* and *delicious*. Sometimes, they only *imply* / implies things – in other words, you have to work out the opinion of the writer from the kind of *evidence* / evidences they give.

So you must *critically* / critical evaluate any information you read on a website. Keep thinking: *What does the writer think about this point?* Or perhaps, more importantly: *What does the writer want* **me** *to think?* If the writer gives evidence in *support* / supporting of a particular point of views / *view*, you may need to find evidence *against* in another article.

2.
Possible corrections:

1. Information on the Internet is *sometimes* wrong.
2. Writers on the web are *sometimes* biased.
3. It is *sometimes* easy to recognize bias.
4. You *always* need to check several sources.

**B** Using new vocabulary

Set the task. Students can work in pairs or in groups of three. Monitor while students are discussing the questions and give help where necessary. Question 9 may seem to be out of place but leads on to question 10. The two questions together practise key target vocabulary. You may need to revise the meaning of *arranged marriage* – avoid too much discussion as this issue is dealt with in more detail in the following Reading lessons.

Elicit answers.

Answers

Some answers depend on the students, but here are some ideas:

1. By reading different types of material: books, articles, journals, newspapers, magazines, the Internet.
2. It will have quotation marks and the reference will be stated (if it is a quote from an authoritative source).
3. Depends on students' knowledge but in the UK: *Hello*, *OK*.
4. Depends on students' knowledge but *Nature*, *The Lancet*.
5. Yes, because it will include research and references.
6. By checking references and by finding multiple sources with the same information.
7. Depend on students' knowledge but in the UK: *The Daily Mail*, *The Daily Telegraph*, etc., have a right-wing bias. *The Guardian* and *The Mirror* have a left-wing bias.
8. Depends on students but they may already know *terrible*, *fantastic*, *great*.
9. Depends on students.
10. Depends on students.

**Closure**

Choose one of the following vocabulary activities:
1. Write the following verbs on the board and elicit the noun forms:
   - *quote (quotation)*
   - *validate (validation / validity)*
   - *state (statement)*
   - *imply (implication)*
   - *criticize (criticism)*
   - *support (support)*
2. Write the following nouns on the board and elicit the adjectives:
   - *author (authoritative)*
   - *width (wide)*
   - *popularity (popular)*
   - *detail (detailed)*
   - *validity (valid)*
   - *extremity (extreme)*
   - *criticism (critical)*
   - *bias (biased)*
3. Work on collocation; write the verbs below on the board and elicit possible collocations based on the topic of the lesson. The words in brackets are one possible answer; there may be several others.
   - *read (widely)*
   - *do (research)*
   - *quote (an author)*
   - *validate (facts)*
   - *state (an opinion)*
   - *give (evidence)*
   - *support (a point of view)*

### 5.12 Real-time reading: The cost of marriage

**Objectives**

By the end of the lesson, students should be able to:
- use co-text and topic sentences to predict information in a text;
- use existing skills to deal with a journalistic type text.

**Introduction**

With Course Books closed, ask students to guess the average cost of a wedding in the USA. Write any figures they suggest on the board, for example:
*$5,000*
*$100,000*
*$2,000*

Now ask students to look at the graph for Exercise A in their books. Which student(s) guessed correctly? (The answer is just over $30,000.)

You can tell students that in the UK the average cost is similar, about £20,000.

**Methodology note**

It is not clear from the sources for the graph if the figures have been rebased so they show the equivalents of today's money (in other words, taking inflation into consideration). Some students may raise this point.

### A  Activating ideas

Ask students to focus on the graph. Ask questions:

- *What's the title of the graph?* (Average wedding budget for 1990–2012)
- *What was the average cost of a wedding in 1990?* ($15,000)
- *What about 2012?* ($30,000)
- *So what can we say about the cost of US weddings from 1990 to 2012?* (the cost has doubled)

1–2. Students discuss the questions in pairs. If necessary, revise vocabulary from the Speaking section, for example:
*the wedding dress*
*the ring(s) or other jewellery*
*the reception*
*the honeymoon*

You can write some supplementary questions on the board, such as:

- *Who pays for the wedding in your country?*
- *Does fashion or social pressure make people spend more money on weddings?*

Monitor while students are discussing the questions, then elicit ideas. Some students may raise the topic of a 'bride price'; that is fine but do not let the discussion go on for too long or you will pre-empt the reading activity.

#### Answers

1. Answers depend on the students, but here are some ideas:
- Clever marketing by hotels, restaurants, wedding dress shops, etc., make people want more for their weddings; they also exploit the romance and emotion of the event.
- Social pressure also creates competition among family and friends – who can have the 'best' wedding.
- For a full white wedding there is a long list of essentials, all very expensive:
  – dresses for bride and bridesmaids
  – suit for the groom
  – rings, jewellery
  – invitations
  – gifts for the bridesmaids
  – reception, food and drink, waiters, hire of restaurant, etc.
  – wedding cars
  – flowers
  – wedding cake
  – honeymoon
  – hen and stag parties
  – hire of church or register office
  – cost of marriage licence

2. Answers depend on students.

### B  Preparing to read

1. Make sure students understand they should not read the whole text at this point. If students have little or no idea of what the text is going to be about, you can write the following ideas on the board for students to discuss in pairs:

   a. Many people do not get married because it is too expensive.
   b. Governments have the answer to expensive weddings.
   c. The history of marriage.
   d. Marriage is expensive but there are ways to make it cheaper.
   e. The cost of marriage around the world.

   Elicit ideas but do not confirm or correct at this point.

2. Remind students that reading the topic sentences only is an effective way of summarizing and predicting a text. Set a time limit for the activity so that students do not have time to read the whole text. Alternatively, reproduce the topic sentences on a handout, or show them using an electronic projection, and ask students to cover the text. Do not elicit answers at this point.

#### Answers
1. Answers depend on students – do not give an answer at this point.
2. See Exercise C.

### C  Understanding the text

1. Set the task. Elicit answers to Exercise B, including the ideas written on the board for Exercise B1 above.
2. Set the task, reminding students about this skill, which was practised in the Reading section in Theme 3. Students complete the activity individually, then compare their answers in pairs. Elicit answers, using an electronic projection of the text.

#### Answers
(for Exercise B)
1.
*Marriage is expensive but there are ways to make it cheaper.*
This is probably the best overall answer, but the text mentions some other points too.

250 Theme 5: Reading

2.

| a | the attempts of governments to deal with the problem | 5 |
|---|---|---|
| b | mass weddings | 6 |
| c | the cost of weddings in different countries | 2 |
| d | hiring wedding clothes | 7 |
| e | the introduction to the article | 1 |
| f | quotes from young people about the cost of weddings | 3 |
| g | marrying a foreign bride – reasons for this and perhaps problems | 4 |

(for Exercise C)
2.
Possible facts:
– details of costs (amount plus what it goes on)
– information about personal loans
– fact that some governments have made marriages between nationals and foreigners illegal
– number of people helped in the UAE
– information about wedding dresses

Possible opinions quoted in the text:
– quotes from Huda – a waste of money; sister regrets it
– quote from Nabilah
– quote from Ali Salem

Note that there are also opinions implied by the writer of the article; this is the point of the next lesson but if students raise it at this stage, deal with it briefly.

### D Understanding the main point of a text

Set the task. Students read the two paragraphs individually then discuss the answer in pairs. Elicit the answer and discuss why it is correct. Check understanding of the words *deter* and *unlikely*.

Answer
Paragraph 1 is the best way to complete the activity. (It cannot be Paragraph 2 because in the main article the author does not say that fewer people are getting married.)

### E Developing critical thinking

The questions can be discussed in pairs or students can work individually to make notes for the answers. Elicit answers for questions 1 and 2 and ideas for question 3.

Answers
Possible answers for problems / solutions in the text – other solutions depend on the students:

| problems | solutions |
|---|---|
| weddings cost too much so people go into debt | – marry foreign brides<br>– get help from the government<br>– hire clothes<br>– have mass-weddings |

### F Understanding vocabulary in context

Students work in pairs to find at least ten words or expressions connected with money in the text and write them down. (Or, they could underline or circle the words/expressions in the text.) Ask one student from a pair to read out their list. Write the words on the board. Check understanding of any new words. Elicit the part of speech for each word. Ask the rest of the class if they have any different words and add them to the board.

Answers
afford (*v*)
cost (*n* and *v*)
debt (*n*)
economy (*n*)
expense (*n*)
expensive (*adj*)
hire (*v*)
(personal) loan (*n*)
money (*n*)
pay – paid, pay off (*v*)
price (*n*)
rising (*adj*)
spend (*v*)
sum (*n*)
waste of money (noun phrase)

Theme 5: Reading 251

**Closure**
Write some phrases, connected with money, on the board for students to complete. For example:
- *I can't afford …*
- *The economy of my country …*
- *Last week I spent …*
- *It's a waste of money to …*
- *How much does it cost to hire …?*
- *I need a loan for / to …*
- *Supermarket prices are …*
- *Huge debts are a problem for …*

### 5.13 Learning new reading skills: Writer's point of view or bias

#### Objectives

By the end of the lesson, students should be able to:
- recognize the writer's stance in a journalistic text;
- distinguish between neutral and 'marked' or stance adjectives.

**Introduction**
Choose one of the following:
- Ask students to reread the text from Lesson 5.12 Real-time reading on page 153 of the Course Book.
- Ask students to summarize the main points from the text in Lesson 5.12.
- Revise some of the *wedding* or *money* vocabulary from the text in Lesson 5.12.

#### Methodology notes

1. Exercise A1: The word *and* is deceptively simple. In fact, it has several functions in English and it is therefore quite complicated. For example, it can join clauses, link nouns in a subject or object/complement, and link adjectives in a subject or object/complement.
2. Exercise A2: In sentence a), *huge reception* is the complement, and the phrase *for all the friends and relatives* post-modifies it.

### A Reviewing sentence structure
Remind students that they looked at this issue in the Reading section of Theme 3, in Lesson 3.14 Grammar for reading on page 91 of the Course Book.

1. Set the task and encourage students to think of possible answers before they read the words in the box. Elicit answers.
2. Students read the questions. Tell students that understanding the purpose of the word *and* is an important reading strategy. Ask students to focus on the first sentence from the exercise:

   *There is often a huge reception for all the friends and relatives.*

   Ask students what the function of *and* is in this sentence. Elicit that it is part of the complement. (See Methodology note above.)

   Ask students to focus on sentence c):

   *It was a traditional wedding and it lasted three days.*

   Ask students what the function of *and* is in this sentence. Elicit that it is a 'new sentence' (or, strictly speaking, a clause).

   Students work through the remaining sentences. Elicit answers.

**Answers**
1.
a. There is often a huge reception for all the friends and *relatives*.
b. The expense is too high for many brides, grooms and *their families*.
c. It was a traditional wedding and *it lasted three days*.
d. It was beautiful and *it made us very happy*.
e. I could spend the money on my child and *my house*.
f. … if men marry out of their religion and *their culture*.
g. … ceremonies with hundreds and brides and *grooms*.
h. These dresses have hundreds of hand-sewn beads and *crystals*.
i. A wedding dress is only worn once and *then it is put away*.

2.
a. part of complement
b. part of complement
c. new sentence / clause
d. part of complement
e. part of object
f. part of object

g. part of complement
h. part of object
i. new sentence / clause

**B** Identifying a new skill (1)

1. Focus on the title of the Skills Check, *Recognizing the writer's point of view*. Check understanding; the title could be paraphrased as *Understanding the opinion of the writer*. Check/teach the meaning of *bias*. Point out that particularly when using magazine and newspaper articles for research, it is very important to decide if the article is biased or neutral.

Students read the information. Check understanding of each point and the verbs *imply* and *evaluate*.

2. Check students understand the task and go over the example. Students work individually, circling or underlining the evidence for each opinion or bias in the text. Ask students if the writer offers any evidence in support of the opinion/bias. Then students compare their answers in pairs. Elicit answers and give feedback.

Answers

| Possible opinion | The writer says: | Evidence / support |
|---|---|---|
| a. Weddings are too expensive in many countries. | *The expense is simply too high for many grooms and their families.* | 80 per cent of personal loans; opinions of people who regret spending so much |
| b. Men should only marry nationals. | *But surely that (marrying foreigners) is not really a solution?* | No evidence but the writer supports the point: 'If men marry out of their religion and their culture, there may not be enough nationals for local women to marry in the future.' |
| c. Governments should not make marriage with foreigners illegal. | *taken extreme decisions* | none |
| d. Governments should help couples to get married. | *the more sensible option; these schemes seem to be very successful.* | UAE helped 44,000 couples with this scheme |
| e. People should not spend £10,000 on a wedding. | *That is still a great deal of money.* | none |
| f. The bridal gown should be hired. | *they should hire the bridal gown; hire the dress ... at a fraction of the cost.* | none |

**C** Identifying a new skill (2)

1. Set the task. Students discuss in pairs. Elicit answers.

2. Set the task and go over the examples. Students work in pairs. Elicit ideas. Ask students to make sentences using an adjective + noun from the activity, for example:

- *The bride and groom didn't want an expensive wedding so they had a **tiny** reception.*
- *I can't do this task. It's **impossible**.*
- *I like him but he's a bit **loud**.*

**Answers**

1.

| a. | tiny | large | huge | party |
|---|---|---|---|---|
| b. | childish | hard | impossible | task |
| c. | shy | quiet | loud | person |
| d. | boring | long | lengthy | book |
| e. | crowded | busy | lively | place |

2. Answers may vary, depending on students.

**Closure**
You could spend a few minutes eliciting or teaching some pairs of neutral and 'bias' adjectives. For example:

big – enormous
good / nice – wonderful, fantastic, etc.
bad – terrible
angry – furious
afraid – terrified
interesting – fascinating
sad – miserable
tired – exhausted
cold – freezing
hot – boiling
old – ancient

## 5.14 Grammar for reading: Conditionals

**Objectives**

By the end of the lesson, students should be able to:
- identify a range of conditional sentences and their function in a reading text;
- use conditional sentences to predict information in a text.

**Note**: As the focus is on reading in this lesson, students are not asked to produce conditional sentences either in speech or writing. You can however, if you wish, provide written practice of the structures from this lesson. See also Workbook activities for further consolidation.

**Introduction**
You could spend a few minutes revising first conditional sentences. For example, put the following clauses on the board for students to complete:
- *If I don't finish my assignment on time, …*
- *If you arrive late for a lecture, …*
- *If the bus is on time, …*
- *I'll stay in tonight if …*
- *Your tutor will help you if …*

**Grammar box 25**
Ask students to focus on the example sentences in the table. Read out the example sentences yourself or ask two or three students to do so.

Use the questions under the table to focus on meaning. Elicit answers.

It is important that students begin to understand that the choice of using the first or the second conditional depends on the view of the speaker/writer:
- If the writer/speaker's view is that the action is likely or possible, use the first conditional.
- If the writer/speaker's view is that the action is unlikely, imaginary, hypothetical or improbable, use the second conditional.

Use an electronic projection to show the table – focus on forms as follows:
- the two halves of the sentences – check understanding of 'action' and 'result';
- there is an SVO/C pattern for both clauses;
- the verb tenses used in the 'action' clauses for each type of conditional;
- the verb tenses used in the 'result' clauses for each type of conditional;
- we use past tenses for the second conditional, but the meaning is present or future.

For students who have a subjunctive in their language, or who are familiar with the term *subjunctive*, you can point out that the second conditional is the English form of this.

The forms of conditionals can be summarized in a table as follows:

| conditional | | action | result |
|---|---|---|---|
| zero | If When | present simple | present simple |
| first | If When | present simple | will + infinitive *may* + infinitive |
| second | If | past simple | *would* + infinitive *might* + infinitive |

254 Theme 5: Reading

Now ask students to close their books. Do one of the following:
- Ask students to work in pairs to rebuild the complete table in the Course Book from memory (perhaps write a few prompts on the board to assist them).
- Ask students to write the full sentences from prompts.
- Write the action clauses on the board and ask students to copy and complete them with the result clause.

### A  Recognizing conditional sentences in context

Set the task. Students complete the activity individually. Elicit answers, using an electronic projection. Ask questions about each sentence, such as:
- *What is the action clause?*
- *What is the result clause?*
- *What is the tense in each clause?*
- *So what type of conditional is it?*

**Answers**
Conditional sentences in order:

| If they don't have the money, | they often go into debt to pay for the wedding. | zero |
| If I had the money now, | I would spend it on my child and my house. | second |
| When I get married, | I won't spend a lot of money. | first |
| If men marry out of their religion and their culture, | there may not be enough nationals for the local women to marry in the future. | first |
| Nationals may get loans or gifts | if they marry a local girl. | first |
| If I got married by myself, | I would need over £30,000. | second |
| If I go for this kind of wedding, | I'll only spend around £10,000. | first |

Conditional sentences reordered by type and clause:

| conditional | action | result |
|---|---|---|
| zero | If people don't have the money, | they often go into debt to pay for the wedding. |
| first | If men marry out of their religion and their culture, | there may not be enough nationals for the local women to marry in the future. |
|  | If I go for this kind of wedding, | I'll only spend around £10,000. |
|  | Nationals may get loans or gifts | if they marry a local girl. |
|  | When I get married, | I won't spend a lot of money. |
|  | If I had the money now, | I would spend it on my child and my house. |
| second | If I got married by myself, | I would need over £30,000. |

### B  Recognizing the form of conditional sentences

Set the task. Students complete the activity individually, then compare their answers in pairs. Elicit answers. Once again, ask the same questions for selected sentences as suggested in Exercise A above.

**Answers**
Corrections to words in *italics*:

| | |
|---|---|
| 1. If you cool metal, | it *contracts*. |
| 2. If you ~~will~~ heat water to 100°C, | it boils. |
| 3. If an animal eats plants and other animals, | it *is* called an 'omnivore'. |
| 4. If the climate changes too quickly in an area, | some of the plants and animals may ~~to~~ die. |
| 5. If students get more than 70 per cent on average in all the assignments, | they *will* get a first. |
| 6. People react badly | if managers ~~will~~ treat them like children. |
| 7. You may *remember* more | if you highlight key words in your notes. |
| 8. I *would* move to a better flat | if I had more money. |
| 9. Weddings would be a lot cheaper | if people *did* not invite so many guests to the reception. |
| 10. The problem *will get* worse | if the government *does not* take action. |

**C** Predicting the result clause in conditional sentences

1. Set the task. Students complete the activity individually, then compare their answers in pairs. Elicit answers, preferably using an electronic projection.
2. Elicit the use of *if* / *when* with no change of meaning – it is only possible with zero conditional sentences. Elicit also the sentence where it can be used – with certain first conditional sentences – but it changes the action from possible to definite.

**Answers**
1–2.

Answers depend on the students, but here are some possible endings:

| | | |
|---|---|---|
| a. If / When you heat metal, | it expands. | no change with *when* |
| b. If / When you drop ice into water, | it floats. | no change with *when* |
| c. If you don't do this assignment, | the tutor will be angry. | |
| d. If you revise information regularly, | you won't forget it. | |
| e. If you don't revise at all, | you will do badly in the exam. | |
| f. If / When I move closer to the university, | I will be able to walk. | with *when* = you are definitely going to move |
| g. If I had more time, | I would do more research. | |
| h. If I owned a car, | I would drive to the university. | |
| i. If life expectancy continues to rise, | we will have a big problem with large numbers of retired people. | |

| j. If / When a person has an autocratic management style, | he/she behaves like a dictator. | no change with *when* |
|---|---|---|
| k. If governments were more democratic, | people would have better lives. | |
| l. If one part of a food web is removed, | there is an effect on another part. | no change with *when* |
| m. If I was in charge of the country, | I would create more parks. | |

**Closure**
Give students the result clauses of some of the sentences in Exercise C and ask them to supply a possible action clause in each case.

## 5.15 Applying new reading skills: Child brides

### Objectives

By the end of the lesson, students should be able to:
- use new reading sub-skills, vocabulary and grammar from the theme in order to make notes on a text;
- demonstrate understanding of a journalistic type text about cultural and social issues.

**Introduction**
Find out how much students know about child brides.
Discuss with the class what the minimum legal age for marriage is in their country and/or selected other countries. Ask: *What's the best age to get married? Is it the same for a man or a woman?*

### A  Activating ideas
Students' books closed. Ask students:
*Is the average age of marriage increasing or decreasing in …*
- *your country?*
- *the USA?*

Elicit ideas.
Now ask students to study the graph in Exercise A. Ask questions to check understanding:
- *What happened to the average age of marriage from 1890 to 1930?* (it fell steadily)
- *What happened in about 1940–55?* (there was a sharp drop)
- *Why was that?* (possibly because of World War II)
- *What has happened since about 1970?* (there has been a sharp increase in the average age)

Now set the task. Students discuss in pairs or small groups. Elicit ideas but do not confirm or correct at this stage.

**Answers**
Answers depend on students.

### B  Preparing to read
Check students understand the information in the assignment. Elicit the meaning of the word *bias* and refer them back to the text in Lesson 5.12 Real-time reading if necessary.

Set the task; students discuss in pairs. Elicit the answer and reasons why the article on page 157 of the Course Book is suitable.

**Answers**
The article is suitable for the assignment because it is about an arranged marriage. From the topic sentences it is also clear that the girl was underage. Therefore, the article will also be about legal as well as social issues such as poverty.

### C  Understanding a text
1. Elicit headings for the notes:
   - location
   - events
   - wider social and legal issues

   Students may want to add further headings, for example:
   - bias
   - data
   - sources

   Students make notes individually, then compare their answers in pairs. Show the model notes (see Answers below) on the board, using an electronic projection. Students compare their notes with the model ones. Discuss any differences.

2. Try to keep the students on task, discussing *the writer's* opinions. Do not discuss with the class their reaction to the text at this point.

This is covered in Exercise E below.

### Answers
1. Model notes:

| location | northeastern India |
|---|---|
| events | – parents arranged marriage<br>– girl refused |
| wider social and legal issues | – marriage of underage girls<br>– education of girls<br>– Child Marriage Prohibition Act |
| bias | arranged marriage = not a problem but Rekha too young |
| data | 22.6 per cent of marriages = illegal |
| sources | *The Lancet* |

2.
The writer …
a. agrees with Rekha's action:
 - 'the bravery of this young girl'
 - 'right to refuse'
 - 'did not weaken' – did not go back on a good decision
 - 'clearly' = it is clear to the writer that she is a national symbol
b. does not object to arranged marriages:
 - 'not a problem in itself' / 'perfectly normal'
c. thinks the parents' actions were wrong
 - 'and *even* stopped giving her food' = extreme action
 - thinks her actions were that of a national symbol
d. thinks girls' education is a good thing but won't happen
 - 'If more girls were educated, would more girls say no to illegal marriages? The answer is probably yes' = correct but unlikely – uses second conditional

**D** Understanding new words in context

1. Students discuss each phrase in pairs. Elicit answers.
2. Students complete the activity individually, then compare their answers in pairs. Elicit answers.

### Answers
1.
a. child labour – children working at a very young age, often as almost slaves

b. prospective husband – husband-to-be; the person a woman is going to marry
c. against the law – illegal, not allowed
d. underage children – not at the minimum legal age to do something, e.g., work, get married

2.
a. ordinary     *extraordinary*
b. legal     *illegal*
c. literacy     *illiteracy*
d. acceptance     *refusal*
e. causes     *consequences*
f. allow     *forbid*

**E** Developing critical thinking

The activity can be done in several ways, e.g., as a pairwork, group or whole-class discussion, or answers can be written. Alternatively, divide the class into groups, and allocate one of the four topics only to each group. At the end of the discussion, the groups report their opinions back to the rest of the class so that all groups can listen to opinions on all four topics.

Before you set the task, elicit some phrases which students could use and write them on the board:
*Governments must / should(n't) …*
*In my opinion …*
*It should be illegal to …*
*There are too many …*
*I (strongly) believe that …*

### Answers
Answers depend on students.

**Closure**
Choose one of the following:
1. Summarize the points made in the discussion in Exercise E.
2. Recap on new vocabulary from the lesson.
3. Ask students to find and underline conditional sentences in the text. They are:
   • *If she (Rekha) married the man, she would become a housewife and mother.*
   • *If more girls were educated, would more girls say no to illegal marriages?*

### Knowledge quiz: What? Who? When? Which? How? Where? Why?

**Objectives**

By the end of the lesson, students will have:
- reviewed core knowledge from Theme 5 so far;
- recycled the vocabulary from Theme 5 so far.

**Methodology note**

See notes in the Introduction, page 16, for further ideas on how to do the quiz. As usual, the focus should be on the content rather than using the correct grammar.

### Introduction

Tell students they are going to do a knowledge and vocabulary quiz on Theme 5. If you like, while you are waiting for everyone in the class to arrive, students can spend a few minutes looking back over the theme.

### Question 1

Divide the class into groups of three or four. Make sure the final column is covered (if you prefer, photocopy the quiz with the final column left blank for students to make notes).

Students discuss the questions and make notes of their ideas.

Do not elicit answers at this point.

### Question 2

Students match the questions and answers in their groups, or you could reorganize the students into pairs.

Finally, elicit answers – preferably using an electronic projection of the text.

### Question 3

Tell students to cover the final column, or hand out another version of the quiz with only the answers. Elicit questions round the class, or put into groups to complete the activity.

### Closure

Tell students to learn the information or vocabulary for any of the answers they got wrong in class.

### Answers

| | | | |
|---|---|---|---|
| 1. What does a *multicultural* country have? | 9 | 1492 |
| 2. Why did *colonists* go to countries in the past? | 18 | 18 |
| 3. Where do *immigrants* in a country come from? | 12 | a holiday immediately after a wedding |
| 4. What is *anthropology*? | 6 | Franz Boas |
| 5. Why do people sometimes call Herodotus the *father of anthropology*? | 20 | Au and Ag |
| 6. Who is sometimes called the *father of modern anthropology*? | 3 | another country |
| 7. Which places did Marco Polo visit? | 16 | Hawaii |
| 8. Which places did Ibn Khaldun visit? | 5 | he actually visited other cultures and learnt about their customs |
| 9. When did Columbus first sail to the Americas? | 13 | many, including dragons, fairies and evil spirits |
| 10. Which *indigenous* people did Boas study? | 8 | many, including the Middle East and Africa |
| 11. What do wedding rings *symbolize*? | 7 | many, including India and China |
| 12. What is a *honeymoon*? | 17 | money paid by the bride's family to the groom's family |
| 13. What *mythical creatures* did people use to believe in? | 1 | people from many different cultures |
| 14. What do brides wear *veils* for? | 10 | several, including the Inuit and Native Americans |
| 15. How did people use to light their house before electricity? | 19 | the ability to read and write |
| 16. Where do the local people give visitors *leis* to welcome them? | 4 | the study of humans in cultures |
| 17. What is a *dowry*? | 11 | the union of two people |
| 18. What age can girls *legally* marry at in India? | 14 | to hide the face |
| 19. What is *literacy*? | 2 | to take the land for themselves |
| 20. What are the chemical *symbols* for gold and silver? | 15 | with candles or gas |

# Writing: Cultural change

## 5.16 Vocabulary for writing: Defining culture

### Objectives

By the end of the lesson, students should be able to:
- demonstrate understanding of, and spell, target vocabulary from the Writing section;
- demonstrate understanding of aspects of a culture.

**Introduction**

Write the headline from the article on the board:

*How can we define 'culture'?*

Ask students to discuss the headline in pairs or groups of three. After two or three minutes, elicit ideas but do not confirm or correct any of them.

### A  Understanding vocabulary in context

1. Ask students to read the introduction to the article. Revise the meanings of the words *areas*, *disciplines*, *theorists*.

   Set the task. Divide the class into pairs. Tell students to work on half of the words each, exchanging information as they go along. For example, Student A works on words beginning with a–m (*access*, *aspect*, *beliefs*, etc.) and Student B works on words beginning with n–w (*ownership*, *restrict*, etc.).

   Students should also find the part of speech for each word.

   If you like, you can ask students to draw up a table for the words – as given in Answers below. Elicit answers, making sure students give the meaning of each word in the context of the article only. Words that also have other meanings from the ones given here include *access*, *aspect*, *ruler* and *value*.

   Students do not need to learn all the forms of the words – tell them which ones you think are the most useful for them.

   Ask students to paraphrase the following questions from the text:
   - *To what extent is religion central to everyday life?* (e.g., *How important is religion in everyday life?*)
   - *Is it (technology) a driving force for change?* (e.g., *How important is technology in changing a culture?*)

2. Set the task. You can do it as an exercise with students writing one or two sentence answers for each question. Or, students can write answers to form part of an essay on cultural aspects in their country.

   Elicit one or two answers as examples. Students complete the activity individually. Monitor, making a note of common errors. Students exchange written work and comment on each other's work from the point of view of:
   - content
   - readability – including organization, spelling, grammar, etc.

   Give feedback on the common errors you noted while monitoring.

### Optional activities

Choose one of the following:

1. With students' books closed, read out some of the questions. Students tell you which aspect they belong to. For example:
   T: *To what extent is religion central to everyday life?*
   Ss: *Beliefs.*
   T: *Who is powerful in the family?*
   Ss: *Social organization.*
   T: *Can people access the Internet?*
   Ss: *Technology.*

2. Students cover the text. Students try to recall the aspects and some of their related questions. If you wish, encourage students to think of further possible questions for each aspect.

Answers
1.

| word | meaning in this context | related forms |
|---|---|---|
| access (v) | find information | access (n)<br>accessible (adj)<br>accessibility (adv) |
| aspects (n) | one part of a situation or idea | – |
| beliefs (n) | the thought that something is true | believe (v)<br>believer (n)<br>believable (adj)<br>believability (adv) |
| domestic (adj) | used at home | domesticate (v)<br>domesticated (adj)<br>domesticity (n) |
| economy (n) | a country's money system | economic (adj)<br>(un)economical (adj)<br>economically (adv)<br>economics (n)<br>economist (n)<br>economize (v) |
| impact (n) | effect | impact (on) (v)<br>impacted (adj) |
| literate (adj) | able to read and write | illiterate (adj)<br>literal (adj)<br>literary (adj)<br>literarily (adv)<br>literature (n)<br>literacy (n) |
| monitored (v) (past participle) | to watch and check a situation | monitor (n) |
| ownership (n) | when something belongs to you | (dis)own (v)<br>owner (n) |
| restrict (v) | to control or limit a number of things | restriction (n)<br>restricted (adj)<br>restrictive (adj) |
| rulers (n) | a leader of a country | rule (v)<br>ruling (n and adj) |
| rural (adj) | connected with the countryside | – |
| social (adj) | connected with society / meeting with other people | *society (n)<br>socialize (v)<br>sociable (adj)<br>socialization (n)<br>sociology (n) |
| values (n) | your principles about what is right and wrong | value (v)<br>valuer (n) |
| worship (v) | to show love for a god, especially by praying | worship (n) |

*There are many derivatives of the word *social*, including *socialist*, *socioeconomic*, etc. We have limited the examples to just a few but students may well suggest others.

2.
Answers depend on students.

### B  Producing correct forms

Set the task. Students complete the activity individually. When most of the students have finished writing, ask them to uncover the vocabulary list in their books and correct their own work.

## Closure

Say aloud the words below or write them on the board.
- music
- architecture
- natural resources (water, oil, coal, etc.)
- healthcare
- sport
- food
- customs, festivals, traditions
- climate
- science
- nature (wildlife, plants, environment, etc.)
- fashion, clothes

Ask:
*Which aspect are they connected with?*
*Are they relevant to a definition of culture? Why (not)?*

Summarize by telling students that many aspects overlap. For example, healthcare can involve government, technology, beliefs and values.

Defining culture is not easy and there are many aspects to consider.

### 5.17 Real-time writing: Technology and cultural change – Africa

### Objectives

By the end of the lesson, students should:
- know more about the effect of technology on culture;
- demonstrate understanding of the organization of a Discussion essay;
- have produced sentences to complete an essay.

## Introduction

With students' books closed, write the question from the assignment on the board:
*To what extent have technological advances caused cultural change in the world recently?*
Check that students understand that *technological advances* = computers, the Internet, mobile phones, satellite TV, etc.
Ask students to discuss the question in pairs or small groups with reference to:
- the students' own culture(s)
- other countries / cultures – for example, Egypt and the Middle East, Europe, China, Africa, India, etc.

After a few minutes, elicit some of their ideas. Students should be aware of changes – including dramatic changes in some countries – brought about by the widespread access to social networking sites, Internet blogs, etc., and mobile phones.

### A  Previewing vocabulary

This activity could be done at the very end of the lesson if you prefer to go straight into the writing activity.

Remind students that we often use long noun phrases as subjects in academic English. Set the task and go over the example. If students find it difficult, do one or two more sentences as further examples. Students work individually, then compare their answers in pairs. Elicit answers. Summarize on the board as follows, eliciting the spelling of the nouns as you go along:

| own | ownership |
| use | usage (point out spelling – *e* changes to *a*) |
| access | access (spelling – double *c*, double *s*) |
| grow | growth (consonant cluster) |
| affect | effect + on (*affect* = verb, *effect* = noun – native speakers often confuse the two as well!) |
| monitor | monitoring |
| introduce | introduction |
| arrive | arrival |

### Optional activity

Students can suggest ways to complete each sentence:
*Mobile phone ownership has increased rapidly during the past few years.*
*Mobile phone usage is banned on planes.*

**Answers**
1. Mobile phone *ownership* ...
2. Mobile phone *usage* ...
3. Internet *access* ...
4. The *growth* of usage ...
5. The *effect* of phones *on* social organization ...
6. The *monitoring of elections by UN officials* ...
7. The *introduction of the technology* ...
8. The *arrival of the Internet* ...

### B  Gathering information

Exploit the photograph focusing on the contrast between the 'old' world (traditional buildings, etc.) and the new world (mobile phone). Use the photo to elicit the meaning of *rural Africa*. Contrast it with *urban Africa*.

Focus students' attention on the assignment. Give a little more information about Veblen. For example:

- Norwegian-American economist and sociologist
- against 'conspicuous consumption' = showing everybody how much money you have
- best-known book: *The Theory of the Leisure Class*

Discuss the meaning of the statement *technology is the driving force in cultural change*.

Discuss with the class how they would go about doing research for this assignment, and which technology and countries they would probably write about.

1. Remind students of the meaning of the word *thesis*, if necessary. (You could refer students back to theses they have written about in previous themes.) Elicit the answer. Ask students for their opinions about the thesis – do they agree or disagree with it? (They may change their minds if they wish later in the lesson.)
2. Set the task. Spend a minute or two checking students understand the notes and the abbreviations in them. Students complete the activity individually, then compare their answers in pairs. Elicit answers.
3. Set the task. You can paraphrase it by saying students might find some of the information surprising or different from their culture. They may find more than three pieces of information. Elicit ideas.

**Answers**
1. Veblen's thesis is *'Technology is the driving force in cultural change'*.
2. 
   a. mobile phone
   b. rural Africa
   c. Society, government and economics.
3. 
   – high percentage of population for mobiles
   – low percentage for Internet access
   – high growth rate for both phones and Internet access

### C  Noticing discourse structure

Students read the essay and then discuss how to complete the activity in pairs. Elicit answers, preferably using an electronic projection of the model essay in order to highlight relevant information.

**Answers**

| Para 1 | introduction |
| --- | --- |
| Para 2 | effect on beliefs and values |
| Para 3 | effect on social organization |
| Para 4 | effect on government |
| Para 5 | effect on the economy |
| Para 6 | conclusion |

### D  Writing the essay

1. Do the first answer with the class as an example. Students complete the activity individually. If they find it difficult, you can provide prompts for each phrase for completion. Elicit answers and write them on the board, correcting any grammar mistakes as you do so.
2. Refer students to the list of possible endings. Students complete the table individually. Ask students to compare their answers in pairs. Elicit some comparisons. Point out that it is fine if students have different responses from the model answers, as long as their responses are logical.
3. Discuss with the class what points should be in the conclusion:
   - beliefs and values
   - cultural change – government and the economy
   - future changes

If you think your class may find the task of producing the full sentences difficult, then do one of the following:
- Provide prompts for the sentences.
- Allow students to read the model answer for two minutes (use an electronic projection). Then remove it. Students write down the conclusion.
- Students' pens down. Elicit sentences from the class and build the conclusion up on the board. Then erase sections of the sentences. Students copy and complete.

Answers
1. Answers depend on students.
2.

| ... have also used mobile phones for the monitoring of elections in rural areas. | 4 |
| ... I will reach a conclusion. | 1 |
| ... in Kwa Zulu in South Africa, women can use SMS messaging to report domestic violence. | 3 |
| ... is due to greater efficiency in communications for small businesses. | 5 |
| ... there is no evidence that mobile phones have changed beliefs or values in this part of the world. | 2 |

3. Model answer:
They have not had any effect on beliefs and values, but they have contributed significantly to cultural change in terms of government and the economy. In the future, they may also make an important contribution in terms of social organization, if projects like the Kwa Zulu one succeed.

**Closure**
Focus on one of the features of the text, for example:
- phrases such as *is due to ... / is related to ...*
- vocabulary – find words from Exercise A, e.g., *affect*, *usage*, etc.
- present perfect tense (This was dealt with in Lesson 3.19 Grammar for writing, so this is useful revision.)

## 5.18 Learning new writing skills: The Discussion essay

### Objectives

By the end of the lesson, students should:
- have demonstrated understanding of the discourse structure for a Discussion essay;
- have practised identifying the thesis for an essay title;
- have produced points for and against theses for various essay titles.

**Introduction**
Exploit the visual of a bicycle mobile phone charger. Ask students if they see any significance between the mobile phone and the bicycle. Try to elicit the significance, i.e., in parts of rural Africa (and elsewhere), there is no access to current electricity so it must be made from some other way. There is a clear mismatch here between the very advanced technology of the mobile phone and the 19th-century technology of electricity supply. Mismatches like this happen nowadays when new technology sweeps around the world.

**A** Reviewing vocabulary
1. Set the task. Students work individually, then compare their answers in pairs. If they get stuck, you can refer them back to the model answer in the previous lesson. Elicit answers.
2. Set the task, explaining that students should find the *kind* of information, rather than the exact words. After a few minutes, elicit ideas.

Answers
1–2.

| phrase | will be followed by ... |
|---|---|
| a. As a *result*, ... | a result or consequence |
| b. As can be *seen* in Table 1, ... | some information from an accompanying graph or chart |
| c. As *stated* above, ... | repetition, probably in different words, of a previous point |
| d. In *this* essay, ... | a summary of what is to come – if this is in the introduction – or what the writer has said – if it is in the conclusion |
| e. It has been *estimated* that ... | a piece of data – percentage, amount, etc., which has come from research |
| f. It is *clear* that ... | a statement which the writer agrees with – even if it is not true! |
| g. Research has *shown* that ... | a statement which the writer agrees with – even if there is not, in fact, good research, or any at all; tell students to look for specific references if a writer uses this early in a paragraph; if they do not find specifics, it may not in fact be research-driven |
| h. There is some *evidence* that ... | a statement which the writer agrees with or, perhaps, only partly agrees with |

**B** Identifying a key skill

Go through the information in the Skills Check. Refer students back to the model answer from the previous lesson to show students examples of each point.

1. Ask the question, pause to give everyone a chance to think. Elicit the answer.
2. Elicit answers, showing them on the board to make sure everyone is clear:

*Sections*
1. Introduction
2. Aspects of the issue
   a. e.g., beliefs (new paragraph)
   b. e.g., values (new paragraph)
   c. e.g., social organization, etc. (new paragraph)
3. Conclusion

Emphasize that although there are three **sections**, there may be more **paragraphs** (because students will probably need to make a new paragraph for each aspect stated in the middle section of the essay).

3. Set the task. Students discuss in pairs. Elicit answers. Summarize the activity by reminding students that a Discussion essay needs points for and against each aspect.

Answers
1. Technical change causes cultural change.
2. Three sections but there may be more paragraphs.
   a. Two or possibly three: government and economics, and possibly social organization (there may be an effect on this in the future).
   b. Beliefs and values.

**C** Practising the new skill

Set the three questions together. Do one of the theses with the class as an example. Ask students to look at the remaining theses, then check understanding of each one. Elicit one or two ideas for a point for or against. (Students will have to use their own knowledge and common sense to come up with each point.) Then students continue to think of more points in pairs. Ask students to make notes for each point.

Elicit answers and make a list of points for and against each thesis on the board.

Answers

| thesis | possible points for | possible points against |
|---|---|---|
| a. Grammar tests show the language ability of second-language learners. | – grammar an important part of language learning<br>– 'easy' to test grammar | – other important skills: listening, speaking, reading, writing and vocabulary<br>– tests can be demotivating<br>– tests do not show usage in the real world |
| b. Decision-making inside families is a cultural issue. | – different people inside families are important in different cultures | – there is a transfer of decision-making from parents to child in all cultures |
| c. The location of a business decides whether it will be a success in the market. | – people must know that you exist so very important | – marketers say that price, promotion and product are equally important |
| d. People are responsible for global warming. | – carbon emissions have risen in recent years, e.g., cars, air travel, power stations | – there are natural cycles of warming and cooling |
| e. Developed countries 'show the future' to less developed countries. | – developed countries have better living standards – for housing, sanitation, etc. | – developed countries have bad aspects like poverty, people not cared for in extended family |

**Closure**
Select one of the theses from Exercise C and spend a few minutes discussing it further.

## 5.19 Grammar for writing: Long subject noun phrases; *also*

### Objectives

By the end of the lesson, students should be able to:
• produce guided sentences with long subject noun phrases;
• produce sentences with correct word order using *also*.

**Introduction**
Students' books closed. Dictate the following words:
*rise*
*social*
*aspect*
*effect*
*growth*
*access*
*organization*
*ownership*

Ask students to look at Grammar box 26 and check the spelling of the words.

**Grammar box 26**
Give students time to read all the information. Check understanding. Ask students to cover the table and study the example short sentences underneath it. Ask students to recall and write the long sentences from the table. When they have finished writing, students can uncover the table and check their own work.

### Methodology note

If students find Exercise A difficult, write the first few words of each sentence on the board. Students copy and complete. Alternatively, with students' pens down, elicit each sentence and write it on the board. Then erase either the entire sentences or some of the words in each sentence. Students copy and complete.

### A  Making long subject noun phrases

Set the task and go over the example. You could, if you wish, ask students to find the verb in each sentence and elicit the noun (or revise Exercise A in Lesson 5.17 Real-time writing on page 160 of the Course Book):

| 1. arrive | arrival |
| 2. use | usage |
| 3. develop | development |
| 4. release | release |
| 5. raise | rise |
| 6. relocate | relocation |
| 7. store | storage |
| 8. change | change |

Students complete the activity individually, then compare their answers in pairs.
Monitor while students are writing down the sentences and give help where necessary. Use an electronic projection so that students can correct their own work. Give feedback on any problems you noted while monitoring in the writing phase. Highlight the parts of some of the sentences: the beginnings and endings of the three noun phrases, the verb and the object.

Answers

| 1. The mobile phone arrived in rural Africa. It has had a significant impact. ||||
| The arrival | of the mobile phone | in rural Africa | | has had a significant impact. |
| 2. The Internet is used for social networking. This is changing behaviour. ||||
| The usage | of the Internet | for social networking | | is changing behaviour. |
| 3. The company has developed new products. These products should help the company to make higher profits. ||||
| The development | of new products | by the company | | should help it to make higher profits. |
| 4. Carbon is released from the oceans. This carbon contributes to $CO_2$ in the atmosphere. ||||
| The release | of carbon | from the oceans | | contributes to $CO_2$ in the atmosphere. |
| 5. Greenhouse gases raise the global temperature. This may cause sea levels to go up. ||||
| The rise | in global temperature | from greenhouse gases | | may cause sea levels to go up. |
| 6. The company was relocated to the south coast. This was responsible for the increase in sales. ||||
| The relocation | of the company | to the south coast | | was responsible for the increase in sales. |
| 7. Information is stored in short-term memory for a few seconds. This is necessary for a person to be able to use it. ||||
| The storage | of information | in short-term memory | for a few seconds | is necessary for a person to be able to use it. |
| 8. There are small changes in the tilt of the Earth. They change the climate significantly. ||||
| Small changes | in the tilt | of the Earth | at regular intervals | change the climate significantly. |

**Grammar box 27**
Give students time to study the table.
Elicit answers to the questions under the table. Point out that the word *also* follows the same rules as frequency verbs such as *always*, *never*, etc., although of course *sometimes* is more flexible.

**B** Using *also* in sentences

Set the task. Students complete the activity individually. If you wish, ask students to rewrite the whole sentence with *also* in the correct place in each case.

Use an electronic projection for students to correct their own work.

Answers
1. The arrival of the mobile phone in rural Africa <u>has *also* had</u> a significant impact.
2. The usage of the Internet for social networking <u>is *also* changing</u> behaviour.
3. The development of new products by the company <u>should *also* help</u> it to make higher profits.
4. The release of carbon from the oceans <u>*also* contributes</u> to $CO_2$ in the atmosphere.
5. The rise in global temperature from greenhouse gases <u>may *also* cause</u> sea levels to go up.
6. The relocation of the company to the south coast <u>was *also*</u> responsible for the increase in sales.
7. The storage of information for a short time <u>is *also*</u> necessary for a person to be able to use it.
8. Small changes in the tilt of the Earth at regular intervals <u>*also* change</u> the climate significantly.

**Closure**
Show the final sentences from Exercise B with all the prepositions missing from the subject noun phrase. Ask students to tell you the missing items.
1. The arrival *of* the mobile phone *in* rural Africa has also had a significant impact.
2. The usage *of* the Internet *for* social networking is also changing behaviour.
3. The development *of* new products *by* the company should also help it to make higher profits.
4. The release *of* carbon *from* the oceans also contributes to $CO_2$ in the atmosphere.
5. The rise *in* global temperature *from* greenhouse gases may also cause sea levels to go up.
6. The relocation *of* the company *to* the south coast was also responsible for the increase in sales.
7. The storage *of* information *for* a short time is also necessary for a person to be able to use it.
8. Small changes *in* the tilt *of* the Earth *at* regular intervals also change the climate significantly.

**5.20 Applying new writing skills: The Internet and cultural change**

**Objectives**

By the end of the lesson, students should be able to:
• organize research notes and ideas about the impact of the Internet in their culture, in preparation for the writing task;
• use target vocabulary, language and discourse structure from the Writing section in order to produce a Discussion essay about cultural change.

**Introduction**
Use Exercise A as the introduction.

**A** Reviewing vocabulary and grammar

Set the task. Students complete the activity individually, then compare their answers in pairs. Monitor. Use an electronic projection to show the correct sentences so that students can correct their own work.

Go over any common errors you noted while monitoring. Point out that these are all sentences which students can use in the writing activities later in the lesson.

Answers
1. I am going to consider the impact *of* the mobile phone in Africa in the *last* ten years.
2. I *will* look at several aspects of a culture.
3. I will consider *whether* the mobile phone *has changed* each aspect.
4. There *is no evidence* that the mobile phone *has changed* beliefs and values.
5. Therefore, the effect *on* social organization *has been* small.
6. Some *current* projects *may also have* an effect in the future.

268  Theme 5: Writing

> **Methodology note**
>
> The assignment can be modified if you wish. For example, you could ask students to write about a different technology, e.g., television. The time reference may be different, for example, the impact of television in the second half of the 20th century.
>
> Another alternative is to specify a different culture rather than students writing about their own, if you feel your students are able and willing to do the research.

**B** Thinking and organizing

When students have studied the assignment, you can point out it is similar to the one in Exercise B in Lesson 5.17 Real-time writing (on page 160 of the Course Book). The main differences are that in Lesson 5.17 the essay was about rural Africa and the mobile phone – this one is about students' own country and the Internet. However, the similarities between them mean that students can use many of the features of the previous essay in the new one.

1. Divide the class into pairs or small groups to brainstorm ideas before they start making notes. Even if you do not have a mono-cultural class, the activity will be useful for gathering information. Elicit ideas from the class. This will be useful for any students who struggled to think of a range of ideas.
2. Monitor while students make notes individually. Give help where necessary. Students then compare their notes in pairs or small groups.

Answers

Answers depend on students.

**C** Writing

Read through the five points and make sure students understand what they are expected to include *before* they start writing.

**D** Editing and rewriting

The final version of the report can be written in class or set up for homework. If done in class, monitor and make a note of common errors.

**Closure**

Give feedback on any common problems you noted while monitoring the students during the writing activities.

**Portfolio: Developing cultures**

> **Objectives**
>
> By the end of the lesson(s), students will:
> - have worked independently to produce presentations in speech and/or in writing about the aspects of a culture of their choice;
> - have used vocabulary, grammar, sub-skills and knowledge from the theme in integrated skills activities.

> **Methodology note**
>
> In this lesson, research, note-taking and other preparation may have to be set as assignments. The presentations can then be given at a later date in class.

**Introduction**

Tell students that in this lesson they will practise working independently. This differs from previous Portfolio lessons as this lesson has no input texts for listening or reading. Students will have to do all the research themselves.

**A** Activating ideas

Exploit the visuals and establish the name of each culture and its geographic location. Remind students to think about the different aspects for each culture, referring them back to Lesson 5.16 Vocabulary for writing (on page 159 of the Course Book) if necessary. After a few minutes' discussion, elicit ideas.

Theme 5: Writing 269

### Answers

1. Answers depend on students.
2. Answers depend on the students, but here are some suggestions:

Similarities
- the three cultures are all from remote areas
- small populations
- traditional way of life
- poverty
- unvaried diet

Differences
- climate – warm and wet, cold, hot and dry
- geographical location – southeast Asia, north Atlantic, East Africa
- landscape – mountains, ice sheets, high plains

> **Methodology note**
>
> Students can work individually on different cultures. If, however, some students have chosen the same cultures as others, they can, if they wish, work in a pair or a group on the same culture.

### B Gathering and recording information

When students have finished reading the assignment, check understanding and clarify some of the points. Students can choose any culture they wish to research, or they can choose one of the cultures shown in the photographs in Course Book. Spend a couple of minutes eliciting other possible ideas for different cultures, for example:

- Scottish islanders
- inner cities in various parts of the world
- immigrant groups in the UK, Canada, US, Germany, Australia, etc.
- Amazon Indians
- Afghanistan
- Egypt

Elicit possible headings for the students' notes.

Elicit phrases to type into a search engine in order to find relevant articles. This will usually be the name of the culture plus the cultural aspect, e.g., *Igorot beliefs*, *Inuit government*, etc.

Set a deadline or a time limit for the research to be completed. (The research may have to be done as a home assignment.) If the research is done in class, then monitor and give help where necessary.

### C Preparing a presentation

1. Divide the class in pairs or groups. You can choose how you select the pairs, i.e., students working on the same or different cultures. Set the task. Students show each other their notes and explain what they have discovered so far. Students make suggestions to improve each other's notes and make comments about interesting or unusual facts.

   Remind students about the work they did in Lesson 5.8 Learning new speaking skills on *checking and explaining* (see page 148 of the Course Book) and point out that this is a good opportunity to practise those phrases.

2. This activity will partly depend on whether students are working individually or in pairs, or groups, for the presentations. However, at this point, students should practise saying sentences for the talk, and prepare slides and/or visuals if possible. Monitor and give help where necessary. If they are working in pairs or groups, students should decide who is going to say what, and the order of each speaker.

### D Listening to a presentation

Check students understand the task and the questions. Monitor while students are giving their presentations, and check the 'listening' students are making notes to answer the questions.

When the presentations are finished, you can:
- give feedback on the presentations;
- discuss answers to the questions – this can be done as a whole-class activity or students can discuss in small groups.

### Answers

Answers depend on students.

> **Methodology note**
>
> Once again, this is a very flexible exercise. Choose one of the following procedures:
>
> - You can allow individual students to choose one of the writing activities.
> - You could select one activity yourself for the whole class to work on.
> - Elicit ideas for how to approach each activity, then take a vote on which activity the class wants to work on.
> - You could allocate different activities to individuals or groups according to their level of ability (for example, the poster activity may be easier for students whose writing ability is less fluent).
> - As usual, the activity can be done in class or set for homework.

### E  Writing

Remind students to follow the usual procedure for writing activities. They have already researched most of the information, so now they should:

- organize their notes;
- write a first draft;
- edit it;
- rewrite a final version.

During the editing stage, students can show their work to other students for feedback.

Answers

Answers depend on students.

**Closure**

Give feedback on oral or written presentations, if you have not already done so.
Discuss further some of the points raised in the lesson, or you could ask students to discuss the following with regard to the cultures researched:

- *Are there any inequalities in the culture you researched?*
- *What is the role of women? Has new technology changed their lives in any way?*
- *What is the role of the elderly? How about children? When do they become 'adults'?*
- *Has new technology affected the style of government in any way?*
- *Have beliefs changed in recent times?*
- *Is the culture getting richer or poorer? Is it in danger of being destroyed?*

## A

| | | |
|---|---|---|
| a complete picture | 1.11 | |
| a couple of | 3.6 | |
| a fifth (n) | 2.16, 3.16 | |
| a great deal of | 1.11 | |
| a little while | 2.6 | |
| a third (n) | 2.16, 3.16 | |
| abnormal (adj) | 5.1 | |
| absolute (adj) | 5.1 | |
| absolutely (adv) | 3.6 | |
| absorb (v) | 4.6 | |
| absorption (n) | 4.6 | |
| acceptance (n) | 2.1 | |
| access (n) | 5.16 | |
| accident (n) | 2.6 | |
| acquaintance (n) | 2.1 | |
| acronym (n) | 3.11 | |
| admire (v) | 5.1 | |
| adolescent (n) | 2.1 | |
| affair (n) [= event] | 5.11 | |
| affect (v) | 5.16 | |
| afford (v) | 5.11 | |
| agree (v) [with] | 3.6 | |
| agreement (n) | 2.6 | |
| allow (v) | 2.1 | |
| almost all | 2.16, 3.16 | |
| aloud (adj) | 1.6 | |
| alternative (n) | 3.1 | |
| alternatively (adv) | 3.1 | |
| amount (n) | 4.16 | |
| analysis (n) | 2.16, 3.16 | |
| anger (n) | 2.6 | |
| announce (v) | 4.1 | |
| annoying (adj) | 1.6 | |
| anthropology (n) | 5.1 | |
| ape (n) | 5.1 | |
| apologize [for] | 2.6 | |
| apology | 2.6 | |
| appendix (n) | 2.16, 3.16 | |
| appreciation (n) | 2.1 | |
| approach (n) [= method] | 3.11 | |
| approval (n) | 2.1 | |
| approve (v) [of] | 2.1 | |
| approximately (adv) | 2.16, 3.16 | |
| argument (n) [= point of view] | 1.16 | |
| arise (v) | 2.11 | |
| arrange (v) | 2.6, 5.6 | |
| arranged marriage | 5.11 | |
| as a result | 5.16 | |
| as stated above | 5.16 | |
| aspect (n) | 5.1, 5.16 | |
| associated (adj) | 1.1 | |
| association (n) | 1.1 | |
| astonishing (adj) | 4.1 | |
| at the same time | 3.11 | |
| atmosphere (n) | 4.6 | |
| attention span | 1.11 | |
| attitude (n) | 5.1 | |
| attract (v) | 4.1 | |
| aural (adj) | 1.6 | |
| autobiographical (adj) | 1.1 | |
| autocrat (n) | 3.11 | |
| available (adj) | 2.1 | |
| avoid (v) | 2.6 | |

## B

| | | |
|---|---|---|
| bacteria (n pl) | 4.6, 4.16 | |
| bar chart (n) | 2.16, 3.16 | |
| barrier (n) | 2.1 | |
| behind (adj) [= late] | 3.1 | |
| belief (n) | 5.1, 5.16 | |
| believe in | 5.6 | |
| best man | 5.6 | |
| bias (n) | 5.11 | |
| blame (v) | 2.6 | |
| blood (n) | 5.6 | |
| body [of water] | 4.16 | |
| bones (n pl) [= remains (n pl)] | 4.1 | |
| bored (adj) | 1.11 | |
| boredom (n) | 1.11 | |
| bow (n) | 2.6 | |
| break down (v) | 4.16 | |
| bridal (v) | 5.11 | |
| bride (n) | 5.6 | |
| bride price | 5.11 | |
| bursary (n) | 3.6 | |
| by accident | 2.6 | |
| by heart | 1.1 | |
| by itself | 2.6 | |

## C

| | | |
|---|---|---|
| candle (n) | 5.6 | |
| caption (n) | 2.11 | |
| carbon (C) | 4.6 | |
| carbon dioxide ($CO_2$) | 4.6, 4.16 | |
| carnivore (n) | 4.11 | |
| carry on (v) | 2.6 | |
| category (n) | 2.16, 3.16 | |
| ceremony (n) | 5.6 | |
| change my mind | 3.6 | |

| | |
|---|---|
| chemical energy | 4.11 |
| child bride | 5.11 |
| child labour | 5.11 |
| choice (n) | 2.16, 3.16 |
| chores (n pl) | 3.1 |
| civilized (adj) | 5.1 |
| clearly (adv) | 1.6, 5.11 |
| close friend | 2.1 |
| clue (n) | 4.1 |
| collect (v) [= bring from a place] | 1.6 |
| colonist (n) | 5.1 |
| colour-coding (n) | 1.6 |
| combustion (n) | 4.6 |
| come up with (v) | 3.11 |
| communicate (v) | 2.1 |
| communicative (adj) | 2.1 |
| comparison (n) | 2.16, 3.16 |
| complex (adj) | 2.1 |
| complicated (adj) | 1.16 |
| component (n) | 1.1 |
| compound (n) | 4.16 |
| concentrate (v) | 3.6 |
| concentrate on (v) | 1.11 |
| concept (n) | 1.6 |
| condensation (n) | 4.6 |
| condense (v) | 4.16 |
| consequences (n pl) | 5.11 |
| consider (v) | 1.6 |
| considerate (adj) | 2.1 |
| consistent (adj) | 5.1 |
| consult (v) | 2.16, 3.16 |
| consume (v) | 4.6 |
| consumer (n) [animal] | 4.11 |
| consumption (n) | 4.6 |
| contribute (v) | 5.1 |
| contribution (n) | 2.11 |
| convert (v) | 2.16, 3.16, 4.6, 4.11, |
| corridor (n) | 1.6 |
| couple (n) | 5.6 |
| cover (v) [= occupy] | 4.1 |
| creature (n) | 5.6 |
| critical (adj) | 2.1 |
| critically (adv) | 5.11 |
| criticize (v) | 2.1 |
| cross (n) | 3.11 |
| cross out (v) | 3.1 |
| crown (n) | 5.6 |

| | |
|---|---|
| cubic (adj) | 4.1 |
| current (adj) [= at the moment] | 3.1, 5.16 |
| **D** deal with | 5.6 |
| decay (v) | 4.16 |
| decide (v) | 3.11 |
| decision (n) | 2.16, 3.16 |
| decision-making (n) | 2.16, 3.16 |
| decompose (v) | 4.6 |
| decomposition (n) | 4.6 |
| decrease (v) | 1.11 |
| define (v) | 3.11 |
| democrat (n) | 3.11 |
| demonstrate (v) [= prove a point] | 1.16 |
| desert [climate] | 4.11 |
| desertification (n) | 4.1 |
| destroy (v) | 4.11 |
| determined (adj) [= fixed] | 2.6 |
| developed (adj) | 5.1 |
| difficulties appear | 2.11 |
| discipline (n) | 5.1 |
| discomfort (adj) | 1.11 |
| disorganized (adj) | 3.1 |
| display (results) (v) | 2.16, 3.16 |
| dissolve (v) | 4.16 |
| distract (v) | 3.6 |
| disturb (n) | 2.16, 3.6, 3.16 |
| diversity (n) | 5.1 |
| do the right thing | 3.11 |
| do what you are told | 2.11 |
| domestic (adj) | 5.16 |
| doubtful (adj) | 3.1 |
| dowry (n) | 5.11 |
| draw (v) [= pull] | 2.1 |
| drill (v) [teaching] | 1.16 |
| driving force | 5.16 |
| drought (n) | 4.1 |
| due to | 5.16 |
| **E** ecology (n) | 4.11 |
| economy (n) [= saving] | 5.11 |
| economy (n) | 5.16 |
| ecosystem (n) | 4.11 |
| edit (v) | 5.11 |
| effect (n) | 4.16, 5.16 |
| efficiency (n) | 1.6, 5.16 |
| efficient (adj) | 1.11 |
| emigrate (v) | 5.1 |
| emphasis (n) | 2.6 |

| | |
|---|---|
| emphasize (v) | 2.6 |
| encode (v) | 1.1 |
| encounter (n and v) | 5.1 |
| endangered (adj) | 4.11 |
| enormous (adj) | 4.1 |
| enough (adv) | 3.1 |
| ensure (v) | 1.16 |
| environment (n) | 4.11 |
| equal (v) | 3.1 |
| equally (adv) | 5.1 |
| equation (n) | 3.1 |
| Equator | 4.11 |
| escape (v) | 4.16 |
| estimate | 5.16 |
| et al. | 1.16 |
| ethnocentric (adj) | 5.1 |
| evaluate (v) | 3.11 |
| evaporate (v) | 4.1, 4.16 |
| evaporation (n) | 4.1, 4.6 |
| everything or nothing | 3.1 |
| evidence (n) | 4.1, 5.1, 5.11, 5.16 |
| evil spirit | 5.6 |
| evolution (n) | 5.1 |
| exactly | 2.16, 3.16 |
| exchange (v) | 5.6 |
| excuse (n) | 2.6 |
| exhibition (n) | 5.1 |
| exist (v) | 4.6 |
| exotic (adj) | 5.1 |
| expand (v) | 4.1 |
| expense/s (n) | 5.11 |
| extant (adj) | 4.11 |
| extinct (adj) | 4.11 |
| extreme (adj) | 4.1 |
| extreme (n) | 5.11 |
| extremely (adv) | 5.16 |
| **F** face (v) | 3.1 |
| face to face | 2.6 |
| fairy (n) | 5.6 |
| family member | 1.16 |
| fault (n) | 2.6 |
| feel good about | 2.11 |
| fertile (adj) | 4.1 |
| fieldwork (n) | 5.1 |
| fire alarm | 1.6 |
| fixed (adj) [= attached] | 1.11 |
| food chain | 4.11 |

| | |
|---|---|
| food pyramid | 4.11 |
| food web | 4.11 |
| forbid (v) | 5.11 |
| foreigner (n) | 5.11 |
| forever (adv) | 1.11 |
| forget (v) | 1.1 |
| forgive (v) | 2.6 |
| forgiveness (n) | 2.6 |
| forgotten (v, pp) | 1.16 |
| formal (adj) | 2.6 |
| formality (n) | 2.6 |
| found (v) | 2.11 |
| fraction | 2.16, 3.16 |
| freezing | 4.6 |
| frequency (n) | 1.1 |
| frighten (v) | 5.6 |
| **G** gain (v) | 4.16 |
| gap fill | 1.16 |
| generate (v) | 3.11 |
| generation (n) [= group of people] | 5.1 |
| germinate (v) | 4.16 |
| get on with (v) [= continue] | 3.6 |
| gift (n) | 5.11 |
| give out | 4.6 |
| give up (v) | 2.1 |
| global warming (n) | 4.16 |
| go away (v) | 2.6 |
| go back to [= date from] | 5.6 |
| go over (v) [= repeat] | 1.16 |
| gold (n) | 5.6 |
| government (n) | 5.16 |
| gradually (adv) | 1.11 |
| green (v) | 4.1 |
| greenhouse (n) | 4.16 |
| groom (n) | 5.6 |
| grow (v) | 4.1 |
| grow up (v) | 2.11 |
| growth (n) | 5.16 |
| **H** habitat (n) | 4.11 |
| hearing (n) [= sense] | 1.1 |
| heart (n) | 5.6 |
| heat (v) | 4.16 |
| heat energy | 4.11 |
| herbivore (n) | 4.11 |
| herself (pron) | 2.16, 3.16 |
| highlight (v) | 1.6 |
| himself (pron) | 2.16, 3.16 |
| hire (v) | 3.11, 5.11 |

| | | |
|---|---|---|
| hold (v) [= keep] | 4.1 | |
| honestly (adv) | 2.1 | |
| honeymoon (n) | 5.6 | |
| hopeless (adj) | 3.1 | |
| huge (adj) | 4.1 | |
| hunger (n) | 1.11 | |
| husband (n) | 2.11 | |
| hydrogen | 4.6 | |

**I**

| | |
|---|---|
| I suppose so | 3.6 |
| identify (v) | 3.11 |
| ignorance (n) | 5.1 |
| ignore (v) | 2.6 |
| illegal (adj) | 5.11 |
| illiteracy (n) | 5.11 |
| illustrate (v) | 2.16, 3.16 |
| imagine (v) | 3.11 |
| immigrant (n) | 5.1 |
| impact (n) | 5.16 |
| imply (v) | 5.11 |
| impossible (adj) | 3.1 |
| improve (v) | 1.6 |
| improvement (n) | 1.6 |
| in halls | 1.6 |
| in reality | 3.11 |
| in the first place | 4.11 |
| incentive (n) | 5.11 |
| increase (v) | 1.11 |
| independent (adj) | 2.1 |
| indigenous (adj) | 5.1 |
| inferior (adj) | 2.11 |
| influence (v) | 5.16 |
| informal (adj) | 2.6 |
| inheritance (n) | 5.1 |
| initial (adj) | 1.11 |
| instead (adv) | 3.6 |
| instinct (n) | 3.11 |
| institute (n) | 1.6 |
| insulate (v) | 4.16 |
| integrate (v) | 5.1 |
| intend (v) | 3.1 |
| internal/external factor | 1.11 |
| interrupt (v) | 3.6 |
| interruption (n) | 3.6 |
| interval (n) | 1.11 |

**J**

| | |
|---|---|
| jelly (n) | 4.16 |
| jewellery (n) | 5.11 |
| join (v) | 5.6 |
| journal (n) | 5.11 |

| | |
|---|---|
| just over/under | 2.16, 3.16 |

**K**

| | |
|---|---|
| kinaesthetic (adj) | 1.6 |
| know your way around | 1.6 |

**L**

| | |
|---|---|
| lateness (n) | 2.6 |
| learner (n) | 1.6 |
| learned information | 1.16 |
| let out (v) | 4.16 |
| light (v) | 5.6 |
| limited (adj) | 5.16 |
| live on (v) [= continue] | 4.1 |
| live your own life | 2.1 |
| loan (n) | 5.11 |
| logical (adj) | 3.11 |
| long-term (adj) | 1.1 |
| look after (v) | 2.11 |
| loss (n) | 1.11 |

**M**

| | |
|---|---|
| majority (n) | 5.1 |
| make an effort | 2.6 |
| make an excuse | 2.6 |
| make friends | 2.1 |
| management (v) | 3.11 |
| management style | 3.11 |
| marriage (n) | 5.6 |
| matter (n) [= substance] | 4.6 |
| me, too | 3.6 |
| meaning (n) | 5.1 |
| melting | 4.6 |
| member (n) [of family] | 2.16, 3.16 |
| memorable (adj) | 1.1 |
| memorize (v) | 1.1 |
| memory (n) | 1.1 |
| migrant (n) | 5.1 |
| mind (v) | 3.6 |
| minority (n) | 5.1 |
| miss (v) [= not attend] | 3.1 |
| misspell (v) | 1.16 |
| mnemonic (n) | 1.1 |
| mode (n) | 1.6 |
| model (n) [= idea] | 1.1 |
| monitor (v) | 5.16 |
| more/less than | 2.16, 3.16 |
| multicultural (adj) | 5.1 |
| multiple choice | 1.16 |
| mythical (adj) | 5.6 |

**N**

| | |
|---|---|
| name (v) | 1.16 |
| national (n) [= person] | 5.11 |
| natural process | 1.11 |

Word list 275

| | | |
|---|---|---|
| negative (*adj*) [= attitude] | 2.1 | |
| neighbourhood (*n*) | 2.1 | |
| neither do I | 3.6 | |
| nitrate (*n*) | 4.16 | |
| nitrogen (*n*) | 4.16 | |
| noisy (*adj*) | 1.6 | |
| nor me | 3.6 | |
| normal (*adj*) | 5.1 | |
| note (*v*) | 1.11 | |

## O

| | |
|---|---|
| oasis (*n*) | 4.1 |
| obey (*v*) | 2.11 |
| obtain (*v*) | 4.16 |
| obvious (*adj*) | 3.11 |
| omnivore (*n*) | 4.11 |
| on campus | 1.6 |
| opinion (*n*) | 5.11 |
| opportunity (*n*) | 1.16 |
| organism (*n*) | 4.11 |
| organized (*adj*) | 3.1 |
| origin (*n*) | 5.6 |
| ourselves (*pron*) | 3.1 |
| overall (*adv*) | 1.11 |
| overcast (*adj*) | 4.16 |
| overdue (*adj*) | 3.1 |
| overnight (*n*) [= quickly] | 4.1 |
| ownership (*n*) | 5.16 |
| oxygen (O) | 4.6 |

## P

| | |
|---|---|
| parent (*n*) | 2.11 |
| participant (*n*) | 2.16, 3.16 |
| participatory (*adj*) | 3.11 |
| pay attention to | 1.1 |
| pay off | 5.11 |
| per cent (*adv*) | 2.16, 3.16 |
| perceive (*v*) | 5.1 |
| percentage (*n*) | 2.16, 3.16 |
| perception (*n*) | 5.1 |
| perfect (*adj*) | 3.11 |
| perform (*v*) | 1.1 |
| photosynthesis (*n*) | 4.6, 4.11 |
| photosynthesize (*v*) | 4.6 |
| physical factor | 1.11 |
| plant (*v*) | 4.1 |
| point (*n*) [= meaning] | 5.6 |
| polar [climate] | 4.11 |
| popular (*adj*) | 5.11 |
| population (*n*) | 5.1 |
| portal (*n*) | 3.6 |
| positive (*adj*) [= attitude] | 2.1 |

| | |
|---|---|
| possibility (*n*) | 3.11 |
| possible (*adj*) | 3.6 |
| practise [= medicine] | 2.11 |
| preference (*n*) | 1.6 |
| preferred (*adj*) | 1.6 |
| prevent (*v*) | 2.16, 3.16 |
| previous (*adj*) | 3.1 |
| priest (*n*) | 5.6 |
| prioritize (*v*) | 3.1 |
| process (*n*) | 4.6, 4.11 |
| produce (*n*) | 4.6 |
| producer [plant] | 4.11 |
| production (*n*) | 4.6 |
| promise (*n*) | 2.6 |
| promise (*v*) | 2.1 |
| prompt (*n* and *v*) | 1.16 |
| prompted (*adj*) | 1.16 |
| properly (*adv*) | 5.1 |
| propose (*v*) [= suggest] | 1.1 |
| prospective (*adj*) | 5.11 |
| prospectus (*n*) | 2.16, 3.16 |
| proud of | 5.1 |
| psychiatric | 2.11 |
| psychiatry (*n*) | 2.11 |
| psychoanalysis (*n*) | 2.11 |
| psychoanalyst (*n*) | 2.11 |
| public transport | 3.11 |
| push out (*v*) | 1.1 |
| put off (*v*) [= delay] | 3.6 |
| put out [= e.g., a candle] | 5.6 |
| put things right | 2.6 |

## Q

| | |
|---|---|
| quotation (*n*) | 3.6 |
| quote (*n*) | 5.11 |

## R

| | |
|---|---|
| radiation (*n*) | 4.16 |
| raise (*v*) | 4.1 |
| range (*v*) | 4.1 |
| rating (*n*) | 3.1 |
| raw (*adj*) | 2.16, 3.16 |
| ready and willing | 2.1 |
| rebel (*n* and *v*) | 2.11 |
| recall (*n*) | 1.16 |
| recall (*v*) | 1.1 |
| reception (*n*) | 5.6 |
| recognize (*v*) | 1.1 |
| recommendation (*n*) | 1.6 |
| references (*n pl*) | 5.11 |
| reflect (*v*) [= show] | 2.11 |
| reflect (*v*) | 4.16 |

| | |
|---|---|
| reflector (n) | 4.16 |
| refuse (v) | 3.1 |
| rehearsal (n) | 1.1 |
| rehearse (v) | 1.1 |
| related to (adj) | 1.1 |
| release (n and v) | 4.6 |
| release (v) | 4.16 |
| reliable (adj) | 2.1 |
| remain (v) | 1.11 |
| remember (v) | 1.1 |
| remind (v) | 1.1 |
| renew (v) | 3.6 |
| rent (n) | 1.6 |
| repetition (n) | 1.1 |
| represent (v) | 5.6 |
| reserve (v) | 3.6 |
| respiration (n) | 4.6 |
| respond (v) | 2.11, 2.16, 3.16 |
| response (n) | 2.11 |
| rest (n) [= relaxation] | 3.1 |
| restrict (v) | 5.16 |
| retain (v) | 3.11 |
| retrieval (n) | 1.16 |
| retrieve (v) | 1.1 |
| reverse (v) | 4.1 |
| reward (n) | 3.6 |
| ring (n) | 5.6 |
| rote learning (n) | 1.1 |
| roughly (adv) | 2.16, 3.16 |
| ruler [= person in charge] | 5.16 |
| rural (adj) | 5.16 |

**S**

| | |
|---|---|
| sample (n) | 2.16, 3.16 |
| saying (n) | 3.11 |
| screen (v) | 3.6 |
| see (v) [= have a view on] | 2.1 |
| see the point of (doing) something | 2.11 |
| seed (n) | 4.16 |
| self (n) | 3.1 |
| sense (n) [hearing, etc.] | 1.1 |
| sensible (adj) | 5.11 |
| sensory (adj) | 1.1 |
| share (v) | 5.11 |
| short-term (adj) | 1.1 |
| sight (n) [= sense] | 1.1 |
| significantly (adv) | 5.16 |
| silver (n) | 5.6 |
| simply (adv) | 2.1 |
| sincere (adj) | 2.6 |

| | |
|---|---|
| sincerity (n) | 2.6 |
| slightly (v) | 4.1 |
| so (adv) [= very] | 2.1 |
| so do I | 3.6 |
| social network site | 2.1, 3.6 |
| social organization | 5.16 |
| soil (n) | 4.16 |
| solar energy | 4.11 |
| solve (v) | 3.1 |
| source (n) | 5.11 |
| special (adj) | 5.6 |
| specialist (n) | 5.11 |
| speech group | 2.6 |
| standpoint (n) | 5.1 |
| state (n) [= form] | 4.6 |
| state (n) | 5.11 |
| steal (v) | 3.6, 5.6 |
| steeply (adv) | 1.11 |
| step (n) [= small movement] | 4.1 |
| stick to (v) [= keep] | 3.11 |
| still (adv) [= up to now] | 3.6 |
| stimulus (n) | 2.11 |
| storage (n) | 1.16 |
| store (v) | 4.16 |
| stranger (n) | 2.6 |
| stress (n) | 3.1 |
| stressed (adj) | 3.1 |
| sublimation (n) | 4.6 |
| substance (n) | 4.6 |
| sum up (v) | 1.6 |
| summarize | 3.11 |
| supply (v) | 1.16 |
| support (n) | 5.11 |
| support (v) [a theory] | 1.16 |
| support (v) | 2.1 |
| supportive (adj) | 2.1 |
| surface (n) | 4.16 |
| survive (v) | 4.11 |
| switch (v) | 2.11 |
| symbol (n) | 5.6 |
| symbolize (v) | 5.6 |
| synonym (n) | 1.16 |

**T**

| | |
|---|---|
| take (v) [= get/catch] | 3.11 |
| take in | 4.6 |
| take over (v) | 2.11 |
| task (n) | 3.1 |
| technological (adj) | 5.16 |
| technology (n) | 5.16 |

| | |
|---|---|
| temperate [climate] | 4.11 |
| term (n) [= special word] | 1.16 |
| test item | 1.16 |
| the economy | 5.16 |
| the exact reason | 1.11 |
| the human brain | 1.11 |
| theory (n) | 1.6 |
| thesis (n) | 1.16 |
| thief (n) | 3.6 |
| thieves (n) | 3.6 |
| think of (v) [= opinion] | 1.6 |
| thinker (n) | 2.1 |
| thirst (n) | 1.11 |
| through history | 2.1 |
| tilt (n and v) | 4.1 |
| time management | 3.1 |
| tiny (adj) | 4.1 |
| tiredness (n) | 1.11 |
| To Do list | 3.1 |
| to what extent | 5.16 |
| together | 5.6 |
| tool (n) | 5.11 |
| trace (n) [= evidence] | 4.1 |
| transaction (n) | 2.11 |
| transfer (v) | 4.11 |
| transpiration (n) | 4.6 |
| trap (v) | 4.16 |
| tropical [climate] | 4.11 |
| true/false question | 1.16 |
| two thirds | 2.16, 3.16 |

## U
| | |
|---|---|
| ugly (adj) | 3.1 |
| uncivilized (adj) | 5.1 |
| underground (adj) | 4.1 |
| underline (v) | 1.6 |
| (un)expected (adj) | 2.11 |
| union (n) | 5.6 |
| universal (adj) | 5.6 |
| untidy (adj) | 1.6 |
| upset (v) | 2.6 |
| urgent (adj) | 3.1 |
| usage (n) | 1.16, 5.16 |
| used to | 5.6 |
| useful (adj) | 3.1 |

## V
| | |
|---|---|
| validate (v) | 5.11 |
| value (v) | 2.11 |
| values (n pl) | 5.16 |
| variety (n) | 1.1 |
| vary (v) | 1.11 |
| veil (n) | 5.6 |
| versus (prep) | 3.1 |
| view (n) | 5.11 |
| visual (adj) | 1.6 |
| visualize (v) | 1.6 |

## W
| | |
|---|---|
| waste (n and v) | 3.6 |
| waste (n) | 5.11 |
| waste (v) [of time] | 3.1 |
| weaken (v) | 5.11 |
| wealth (n) | 5.6 |
| wear (v) | 5.6 |
| wedding (n) | 5.6 |
| wife (n) | 2.11 |
| with reference to | 5.16 |
| without (prep) | 1.16 |
| without thinking | 3.11 |
| work flow | 3.1 |
| work through (v) | 3.11 |
| worker (n) | 3.11 |
| workmate (n) | 2.11 |
| worship | 5.16 |

## Y
| | |
|---|---|
| yet (adv) | 3.6 |

SUSSEX CENTRE FOR LANGUAGE STUDIES
UNIVERSITY OF SUSSEX
FALMER, BRIGHTON
BN1 9SH
UNITED KINGDOM